Introduction
to Catholic Theological Ethics

Introduction to Catholic Theological Ethics

Foundations and Applications

TODD A. SALZMAN AND MICHAEL G. LAWLER

ORBIS BOOKS

Maryknoll, New York 10545

ORBIS BOOKS
Maryknoll, New York 10545

Fathers and Brothers
MARYKNOLL™

Founded in 1970, Orbis Books endeavors to publish works that enlighten the mind, nourish the spirit, and challenge the conscience. The publishing arm of the Maryknoll Fathers and Brothers, Orbis seeks to explore the global dimensions of the Christian faith and mission, to invite dialogue with diverse cultures and religious traditions, and to serve the cause of reconciliation and peace. The books published reflect the views of their authors and do not represent the official position of the Maryknoll Society. To learn more about Maryknoll and Orbis Books, please visit our website at www.maryknollsociety.org.

Manufactured in the United States of America.
Manuscript editing and typesetting by Joan Weber Laflamme.

Library of Congress Cataloging-in-Publication Data

Names: Salzman, Todd A., author. | Lawler, Michael G., author.
Title: Introduction to Catholic theological ethics : foundations and applications / Todd A. Salzman and Michael G. Lawler.
Description: Maryknoll, NY : Orbis Books, [2019] | Includes bibliographical references and index. |
Identifiers: LCCN 2018045722 (print) | LCCN 2018051513 (ebook) | ISBN 9781608337859 (e-book) | ISBN 9781626983243 (print) | ISBN 9781608337859 (ebook)
Subjects: LCSH: Christian ethics—Catholic authors.
Classification: LCC BJ1249 (ebook) | LCC BJ1249 .S3284 2019 (print) | DDC 241/.042—dc23
LC record available at https://lccn.loc.gov/2018045722

When the music changes,
so does the dance.
—OLD HAUSA PROVERB

With gratitude to
Charles Curran, Joe Selling, and Norbert Rigali
who taught us new theological music
for a changed ethical dance.

Contents

Part II

CHRISTIAN FORMATION OF CONSCIENCE AND
CONTEMPORARY ETHICAL ISSUES

Conclusion

POSSIBLE FUTURE DIRECTIONS
FOR CHRISTIAN ETHICS

Abbreviations

Address	*Address of John Paul II to the Participants in the Internation Congress on "Life Sustaining Treatments and Vegetative State: Scientific Advances and Ethical Dilemma"* (March 20, 2004)
AL	*Amoris Laetitia (The Joy of Love),* Francis I (2016)
AAS	*Acta Apostolicae Sedis: Commentarium Officiale* (Rome: Typis Polyglottis Vaticanis)
ANH	artificial nutrition and hydration
ARTs	artificial reproductive technologies
CCC	*Catechism of the Catholic Church*
CDF	Congregation for the Doctrine of the Faith
CRP	*Considerations regarding Proposals to Give Legal Recognition to Unions between Homosexual Persons,* CDF
DH	*Dignitatis Humanae (Declaration on Religious Freedom),* Vatican Council II (1965)
DS	*Enchiridion Symbolorum Definitionum et Declarationum de Rebus Fidei et Morum,* ed. H. Denzinger and A. Schoenmetzer (Fribourg: Herder, 1965)
DV	*Dei Verbum (Dogmatic Constitution on Divine Revelation),* Vatican Council II (1965)
ENDA	Employment and Non-Discrimination Act
EV	*Evangelium Vitae (The Gospel of Life),* John Paul II
FC	*Familiaris Consortio (Exhortation on the Role of the Christian Family),* John Paul II (1982)

GS	*Gaudium et Spes (Pastoral Constitution on the Church in the Modern World)*, Vatican Council II (1965)
HV	*Humanae Vitae (On Human Life)*, Paul VI (1968)
Inst.	*Donum Vitae (Instruction on Respect for Human Life in Its Origin and on the Dignity of Procreation: Replies to Certain Questions of the Day*, CDF (1987)
LS	*Laudato Si, On Care for Our Common Home)*, Francis I, (2015)
LGBT	lesbian, gay, bisexual, and transgender
LG	*Lumen Gentium (Dogmatic Constitution on the Church)*, Vatican Council II (1964)
MD	*Mulieris Dignitatem*, John Paul II (1988)
NE	Aristotle, *Nicomachean Ethics,* trans. David Ross (Oxford: Oxford University Press, 2009)
NFP	natural family planning
OS	*Ordinatio Sacerdotalis (Priestly Ordination)*, John Paul II (1994)
OT	*Optatum Totius (Decree on Priestly Formation)*, Vatican Council II (1965)
PH	*Persona Humana (Declaration on Certain Questions concerning Sexual Ethics)*, CDF
PL	*Patrologiae Cursus Completus: Series Latina*, ed. J. P. Migne
PVS	permanent vegetative state
SRS	*Sollicitudo Rei Socialis (The Social Concern of the Church)*, John Paul II (1988)
ST	*Summa Theologiae Sancti Thomae de Aquino*
USCCB	United States Conference of Catholic Bishops
VS	*Veritatis Splendor (The Splendor of Truth)*, John Paul II (1993)

Note: All official church documents are available in English on the Vatican website.

Introduction

Every semester at the beginning of our Christian ethics courses, which enroll students of diverse national, cultural, religious, and ethnic backgrounds, we show three slides. The slides differ depending on whether we are teaching biomedical or sexual ethics. In biomedical ethics the three slides are children in a Nazi concentration camp who have been used for human experimentation; Paul Farmer treating patients in a hospital facility in Haiti; and Terri Schiavo, a patient in a permanent vegetative state, shown hooked up to artificial nutrition and hydration (ANH) in a hospital bed.[1] After describing the ethical issues surrounding each slide, we ask the students, all things being equal, whether the act indicated in the slide is right or wrong. Are the Nazi experiments on children right or wrong? Is Paul Farmer's medical treatment serving the poor in Haiti right or wrong? Is removing Terri Schiavo from ANH, which led to her death, right or wrong? With the first two slides there is always unanimous agreement: It is wrong what the Nazis did; it is right what Paul Farmer is doing. The third question always has a mixture of responses, some saying it was right to remove Terri Schiavo from ANH, others saying it was wrong.

In sexual ethics we also put up three slides: ISIS throwing a gay man from a building to his death; a heterosexual couple getting married in a church; and a gay couple getting married on a beach. After describing the ethical issues surrounding each slide, we ask the students, all things being equal, whether the act indicated in the slide is right or wrong. Is ISIS throwing an innocent gay man from a building because he is gay right or wrong? Is a heterosexual couple getting married in a church right or wrong? Is a gay couple getting married on a beach right or wrong? Again, with the first two slides, there is always unanimous agreement: What ISIS did is wrong; getting married in church is right for the heterosexual couple. Unlike the third response in the biomedical ethics course, however, the response to the third slide in the sexual ethics course has begun to receive

---

[1] Terri Schiavo died in 2005, fourteen days after her feeding tube was removed. She had been on ANH for fifteen years.

xiii

more agreement—especially since the national legalization of same-sex marriage in 2015—that the gay couple marrying on the beach is right.

What is the point of this exercise and what can we learn from it that guides us in writing this book? First, the exercise demonstrates that, though there are diverse social, cultural, religious, and ethnic backgrounds among our students, there is universal consensus on what is right or wrong on some ethical issues. This consensus among people of diverse backgrounds challenges claims that relativism is the dominant ethical stance in the United States, Canada, and Europe. Relativism is a metaethical theory that claims that there are no universal ethical truths and that the ethical terms *good* and *right* are defined either culturally or individually. Our students, who reflect the ethnic, religious, and cultural diversity of the wider culture, do not espouse relativism but recognize some ethical universals, such as respect for innocent human life and human dignity. They recognize what is commonly called metaethical objectivism. They also have differences in analyzing and evaluating ethical issues, as is indicated by their varied responses to the third slides. A first goal of this book is to account for both their universal agreement and their particular differences in ethics.

A second and related goal is to discover how different people can agree that there are universal truths, like what is good or right facilitates human dignity and what is bad or wrong frustrates human dignity, and yet disagree on the definition of human dignity and on the formulation and justification of norms that facilitate and do not frustrate it. All our students agree that some acts can never be justified, such as throwing an innocent human being from a building to his death simply because of his sexual orientation. They disagree, however, on the rightness or wrongness of other acts, such as removing ANH from a person in a permanent vegetative state. What accounts for these disagreements are often unarticulated foundational commitments about the nature of reality and relationships, and cultural, contextual, political, religious, and ethical beliefs that yield different ethical perspectives. These commitments and beliefs contribute both to shaping definitions of human dignity and formulating and justifying norms for what facilitates and does not frustrate human dignity. It is at the level of foundational commitments and beliefs and the discernment of their anthropological and normative implications that interesting and important ethical discussions occur.

A third goal of the exercise is to uncover how historical and cultural contexts affect ethical analysis and evaluation. Before the legalization of same-sex marriage, some students said that same-sex marriage was wrong; after its legalization, very few students say that it is wrong. So few, in fact, that we have considered finding a different, more ethically debated issue to put on the third slide to make our point. However, the reality is that the general consensus that same-sex marriage is right highlights an important, foundational point: ethics must be in constant dialogue with historical context and "the signs of the times."

Over fifty years ago the Second Vatican Council's *Pastoral Constitution on the Church in the Modern World, Gaudium et Spes*, wisely instructed the Catholic Church, pope, bishops, priests, lay people, and all people of goodwill to discern "the signs of the times" and to interpret them in light of the gospel. Although the content of this scrutiny has changed and evolved in the last fifty years depending on culture and context, the sage advice remains an ongoing invitation and challenge. Some of the tools *Gaudium et Spes* suggests to guide us in this discernment process are "the experience of past ages, the progress of the sciences, and the treasures hidden in the various forms of human culture, by all of which the nature of man . . . is more clearly revealed and new roads to truth are opened" (no. 44). These three sources of ethical knowledge, experience, science, and human culture, combined with the gospel and Christian tradition, are often called the Wesleyan Quadrilateral and are more commonly classified as scripture, tradition, science and secular disciplines of knowledge,[2] and human experience, which always includes culture.

The Second Vatican Council called for the renewal of Catholic theological ethics, and we use the Wesleyan Quadrilateral to respond to this call and to propose a Catholic ethical method for the twenty-first century. We employ the Quadrilateral for four reasons. First, it includes the sources of ethical knowledge we judge essential for doing Christian ethics, sources highlighted in various ways throughout Christian tradition, especially in *Gaudium et Spes* and other documents of the Second Vatican Council.

Second, these four sources are essential to any *Christian* discernment of what is right or wrong, good or bad, though particular perspectives, as we shall see, select, interpret, prioritize, and integrate the sources in different ways.

Third, there is a growing appreciation for, and specific reference to, these sources in Christian ethical literature from divergent normative perspectives, though there remains the need for dialogue to investigate how the sources are to be selected, interpreted, prioritized, and integrated.[3]

---

[2] We understand by the term *secular discipline* any discipline distinct from, and not dependent upon, revelation. See Margaret Farley, *Just Love: A Framework for Christian Sexual Ethics* (New York: Continuum, 2006), 188–89.

[3] Lisa Sowle Cahill, *Between the Sexes: Foundations for a Christian Ethics of Sexuality* (Minneapolis: Fortress Press, 1985), 4–7; Charles E. Curran, *The Catholic Moral Tradition Today: A Synthesis* (Washington, DC: Georgetown University Press, 1999), 47–55; Farley, *Just Love*, 182–96; Todd A. Salzman, *What Are They Saying about Roman Catholic Ethical Method?* (New York: Paulist Press, 2003).

This dialogue will clarify the various sources and their use and account for pluralist perspectives. Depending on their selection, interpretation, prioritization, and integration of the sources of moral knowledge, people may well reach different conclusions on ethical issues. Some will conclude that removing Terri Schiavo from ANH was wrong; some will conclude it was right. Some will conclude same-sex marriage is wrong; some will conclude it is right.

Fourth, use of these four sources combined informs Christian ethics and aids in the formation of a well-formed conscience. The sources are ethical methodological components to facilitate a perspectivist, ongoing, evolving understanding of human dignity and of the norms that facilitate its attainment. *Gaudium et Spes* provides revolutionary methodological insights that serve as a "manifesto" for Christian ethics to aid all people of good will in the search for truth.[4]

Christian ethics is grounded in faith in a God of love, hope, peace, and justice from whom we can discern meaning in life and find inspiration to realize peace and justice through love guided by hope. The four Christian sources of ethical knowledge—scripture, tradition, science/reason, and experience—can guide us in our analysis, evaluation, and response to complex ethical issues that confront us on a daily basis and can invite a comprehensive and comprehensible response.

The fourth goal of our introductory exercise is to introduce the importance of conscience and its formation. The search for truth about an ethical issue, the deliberation about what to do about it, and the coming to a practical judgment and decision that this is what I *must* ethically do in this concrete situation is the process of coming to a decision of conscience. We often speak of the voice of conscience, but conscience is not a voice; conscience is *me* coming to a judgment and decision that this is what *I* must do to act ethically in this situation. That judgment and decision emerge from the perspective and values to which I am committed and the decision that this is what I must do is evidence of the values to which I am committed. The authority and inviolability of individual conscience has been a longstanding teaching in the Christian ethical tradition and is, indeed, fundamental to it. That teaching became even stronger and more theologically based in the Catholic tradition through the careful and sustained work of the fathers of the Second Vatican Council in the 1960s, particularly in their document *Gaudium et Spes*, which speaks of conscience three times.

---

[4] See Joseph A. Selling, "*Gaudium et spes*: A Manifesto for Contemporary Moral Theology," in *Vatican II and Its Legacy*, ed. Mathijs Lamberigts and Leo Kenis (Leuven: Peters Press, 2002), 145–62.

First, *Gaudium et Spes* teaches, conscience is "the most secret core and sanctuary of man . . . [where] he is alone with God whose voice echoes in his depth. In a wonderful manner conscience reveals that law which is fulfilled by love of God and neighbor" (no. 16). Second, it continues, among the things necessary for "leading a life truly human" is the right to action "in accord with the upright norm of one's own conscience" (no. 26). Third, the gospel of Christ, it adds, "has a sacred reverence for the dignity of conscience and its freedom of choice" (no. 41). *Dignitatis Humanae,* the council's *Declaration on Religious Freedom,* went further and prescribed the authority and inviolability of conscience. "In all his activity a man is bound to follow his conscience faithfully, in order that he may come to God, for whom he was created. It follows that he is not to be forced to act in a manner contrary to his conscience. Nor, on the other hand, is he to be restrained from acting in accordance with his conscience, especially in matters religious" (no. 3). In the 1960s these were unheard-of words in Catholic magisterial circles and liberating words in educated Catholic lay circles, but the incontestable reality is that they express a teaching that is longstanding in the Christian moral tradition, is fundamental to it, and is seeing a resurgence in Pope Francis's papacy. The authority and inviolability of a well-informed conscience is firmly established in the Catholic tradition, though conscience is not infallible and needs ongoing formation through reading the signs of the times, discernment, and dialogue.

Audience

Not only does investigating the signs of the times and how we interpret and respond to them in light of the gospel provide insight into the ongoing methodological, anthropological, and normative developments of Christian ethics that guide our responses to the ethical issues indicated in the slides, but it also provides insight into our targeted audience for this textbook, undergraduate students and an educated lay public interested in Christian ethics. The social sciences, through surveys and sociological analysis, tell us a great deal about the current signs of the times of undergraduate students and indicate a road map for navigating those signs. For our purposes there are two important sets of data that highlight the need for this book: the growth of the "nones," and the values, ideas, and beliefs of Generation Z, who are the demographic group following the Millennials. First, a distinguishing demographic factor that has changed radically since the 1970s is the development and expansion of so-called nones. The term *none* designates religiously unaffiliated Americans, and the number of nones has grown exponentially over the years. In the 1970s and 1980s, less than 10 percent of US adults described themselves as having no religious affiliation; currently, 23 percent describe themselves as agnostics, atheists, or "nothing in particular."[5] Of those unaffiliated, the highest percentage is made up of Millennials: 34 percent of older Millennials (born 1981–89) classify themselves as nones; 36 percent of younger Millennials (born 1990–96) classify themselves as nones.[6] Some frequently cited reasons for Millennials choosing to be unaffiliated is that they find institutional religion intolerant, rigid, especially with regard to sexual and LGBT issues, and too politically outspoken and motivated.

We are currently in a transitional generational stage from Millennials to Generation Z (or Gen Z), born between 1997 and 2005. With this transition comes shared and evolving ethical perspectives, beliefs, and concerns as compared to Millennials. Sociological data on Gen Z provides insight into these perspectives, beliefs, concerns, and how this textbook can build on those perspectives and beliefs and address those concerns. First, like Millennials, Gen Zers are committed to social justice, equity, and equality. Second, and fundamentally, they are "strongly motivated by relationships."[7] Third, they are solution oriented, meaning they have the capacity to recognize complex ethical issues like homelessness and the motivation to seek solutions to them. Fourth, unlike Millennials, participation in religion is increasing rather than decreasing. Questioned about their spirituality, 31 percent of Gen Zers indicated they are spiritual but not religious and 47 percent indicate they are religious. As young adults, 41 percent attend weekly religious services as compared to 18 percent of Millennials who were in the same age group.[8] This is a large shift in religious beliefs and may have long-term implications, curbing the increase of "nones" in the United States.

We draw from this sociological data the following points that aid us in discerning how to develop this text to reach and affect our audience most effectively. First, commitment to social justice and the common good, as well as exposing individual acts and social structures that threaten the common good are central to our book. We attempt to expose and confront acts and structures that require systemic responses to effect change and to create a more just society, especially for the most marginalized of society.

---

[5] Gregory A. Smith and Alan Cooperman, "The Factors Driving Growth of Religious 'nones' in the US," Pew Research Center, September 14, 2016.

[6] Michael Lipka, "Millennials Are Increasingly Driving Growth of 'Nones,'" Pew Research Center, May 12, 2015.

[7] Joan Hope, ed., "Get Your Campus Ready for Generation Z," *Dean and Provost* 17, no. 8 (April 2016): 1, 6–7.

[8] Ibid., 7.

Part of this systemic response will require transforming structures that prevent, for example, more women and minorities being in leadership roles, an ethical concern of Gen Zers.

Second, we view Gen Zers' focus on the importance of persons and relationships rather than on the acts they do as foundational for virtue ethics, which emphasizes personal relationship and virtues that motivate persons and are expressed in acts that affect relationships. Our ethical method, which we develop in Chapter 2, explains a virtuous perspective and how that perspective enables us to perceive and respond virtuously to our relationships with God, self, neighbor, and the environment.

Third, this text attempts to provide Christian ethical tools for "solution-oriented" students. We often tell our students that the facts, data, and information they study in class will pass away, but the most important aspect of a Christian ethics class in particular, and a liberal arts education in general, is to teach students to become critical-analytical thinkers so that they have the tools to seek solutions to complex ethical issues. In our Christian ethics classes the tools we provide are grounded in the Christian tradition and help to shape a perspective—guided by the four sources of ethical knowledge and a virtuous perspective grounded in the Christian tradition—to live an ethical life and create a just society. There will be differences in perspective in what constitutes an ethical life and a just society, just as there are initial differences in response to our third slides, but the tools we present allow for charitable dialogue about those differences that may facilitate a search for common ground in the solutions to complex ethical issues.

Fourth, whereas Millennials have moved away from religion in their search for solutions to complex ethical issues, Gen Zers are returning to religion. This return is where the sociological data and Christian sources of ethical knowledge that shape perspectives intersect. A guiding principle of this textbook is the epistemological principle of perspectivism. This perspective means that the truth we know is always partial and fashioned by how we look at reality, and how we look at reality is shaped historically, culturally, biologically, relationally, contextually, religiously, and spiritually. Gen Zers' more positive outlook on, and participation in, religious institutions reflects an openness to Christian perspectives that many Millennials view with suspicion.

Structure of the Book

The exercise described at the beginning of this Introduction and the important points we deduce from it in light of our intended audience aided in structuring this book, which is divided into three parts. Part I (Chapters 1–5) explores and develops a comprehensive Christian ethical theory, drawing from the four sources of ethical knowledge to inform a virtuous ethical perspective, to define and defend a definition of human dignity, and to formulate and justify norms that facilitate and do not frustrate human dignity. Part II (Chapters 6–13) investigates the Christian formation of conscience and applies our theory to contemporary ethical issues. The Conclusion looks at possible future directions for Christian ethics, especially given the concerns raised in Chapter 7 on ecology and climate change and how they might affect the way we do Christian ethics in the future.

Finally, in line with the current emphasis in institutions of higher learning on learning outcomes and assessment, we begin each chapter with bullet points describing the learning outcomes for the chapter, and we end the chapter with specific questions to facilitate discussion around those outcomes. We also provide short bibliographies for further reading.

PART I

Exploring and Developing a Comprehensive Christian Ethical Theory

1

Metaethics

Relativism and Perspectivism

Learning Objectives

- Define *metaethics* and explain why it is foundational to ethics.
- Explain perspectivism as a metaethical theory.
- Distinguish between perspectivism and relativism.
- Use the example of the Employment Non-Discrimination Act (ENDA) legislation to explain how two people can adhere to a perspectivist metaethic and yet come to different conclusions on the definition of *human dignity* and the norms (and laws) that facilitate its attainment.

While many people understand ethics to be primarily about what is good or right, the most fundamental question of ethics is whether the terms *good* and *right* have any meaning. That is, do ethical terms have meaning for which we can ethically evaluate reality or human experience, or do they merely express sentiments, feelings, or emotions that contain no criteria for determining their truth or falsity? Until this question is answered we cannot proceed to the next question in ethics on normative assertions that define ethical terms (*the good,* for example, is defined as that which facilitates human dignity) and formulate and justify norms for attaining the good. In this chapter we present four metaethical theories that respond to the following question: Do ethical terms *(good, right, wrong, bad)* have meaning, that is, can these terms be defined? In this book we propose perspectivism as a metaethical theory that accounts for plural definitions of the good as human dignity but is thoroughly distinct from relativism.

3

Metaethical Theories

The classification of ethics that attempts to answer the question of whether there is ethical truth, or whether the terms *good* or *right* and their opposites have meaning, is known as *metaethics*. *Meta* comes from the Greek meaning "to go beyond," "higher," or "transcend." The area of ethics classified as metaethics attempts to define the very foundation or basis of ethics. It asks the most basic questions: Do ethical terms have meaning? Can such meaning be justified? If the answers to these questions are in the negative, then our book concludes right here. If ethical terms, that is, cannot be defined and do not have meaning, then ethics is a meaningless discipline. If the answer to these questions is in the positive, then we must proceed to define these terms and justify those definitions. There are various metaethical theories that respond to this issue. The specific definition of ethical terms and the formulation and justification of norms belong to the realm of normative ethics. We discuss this level of ethical discourse in Chapter 3.

Nihilism

The first metaethical theory is *nihilism*, which comes from the Latin *nihil*, meaning "nothing." Friedrich Nietzsche offers some of the most developed insights on the theory of moral nihilism, which is defined as "the doctrine that there are no moral facts, no moral truths, and no moral knowledge."[1] According to moral nihilism, therefore, murder, rape, and torture cannot be wrong because they are meaningless moral terms. Obviously, such a position is counterintuitive to anyone with a moral conscience; nihilism goes against basic moral knowledge and understanding. Consequently, ethicists do not often defend moral nihilism. According to this metaethical theory ethical terms (*good, right, wrong, bad,* and so on) do not have any meaning, and therefore ethics is a meaningless discipline.

Emotivism

A second type of metaethical theory similar to moral nihilism is *emotivism*, which asserts that ethical terms are defined by individual emotions and desires. For emotivism, there is no objective truth because emotions are relative to each individual.[2] To say abortion is wrong, for example, is equivalent to saying, "Abortion, yuck!" There is no way to know whether

---

[1] Gilbert Harmann, *The Nature of Morality: An Introduction to Ethics* (New York: Oxford University Press, 1977), 11.

[2] For a discussion of emotivism, see Charles L. Stevenson, *Ethics and Language* (New Haven, CT: Yale University Press, 1944).

this assertion is true or false. Ethics expresses emotions, emotivists argue, and since emotions are neither right nor wrong, we cannot, and indeed need not, verify their truth or falsity. While some ethicists have defended nihilism and emotivism, we do not espouse these metaethical theories in this book.

Relativism

A more prevalent and widely defended metaethical theory is *relativism*. Throughout their pontificates popes John Paul II and Benedict XVI consistently raised concerns over relativism, which they understand to deny the existence of an objective moral order or a universal moral truth, thus fundamentally threatening the human search for truth in general and moral truth in particular. In his homily at the opening of the 2005 papal conclave Cardinal Joseph Ratzinger (later Pope Benedict XVI) spoke of the "dictatorship of relativism," which "does not recognize anything as definitive and whose ultimate standard consists solely of one's own ego and desires."[3] Concern about relativism is undoubtedly warranted in the twenty-first century. In 2002 Barna Research Group conducted two national surveys, one among adults and one among teenagers, which asked participants if they believed that there are unchanging moral absolutes or that moral truth is relative to contextual circumstances. In the adult group, 64 percent responded that truth is always relative to the person and situation; in the teenage group, 83 percent responded that truth is always relative to the person and situation and a mere 6 percent responded that moral truth is absolute.[4] These statistics verify Allan Bloom's famous claim made fifteen years earlier that "there is one thing a professor can be absolutely sure of: almost every student entering the university believes, or says he believes, that truth is relative."[5]

As our class exercises with slides mentioned in the Introduction indicate, however, even though the vast majority of teenagers may claim that truth is relative to the person and situation, our ethnically, culturally, and religiously diverse students do agree that some actions are always right and some are always wrong. The tension between the Barna surveys and

---

[3] Joseph Ratzinger, "Cappella Papale Mass 'Pro Eligendo Romano Pontifice,' Homily of His Eminence Card. Joseph Ratzinger of the College of Cardinals," Vatican Basilica, April 18, 2005. This and all official church documents cited in this book are available on the Vatican website.

[4] Barna Research, "Americans Are Most Likely to Base Truth on Feelings" (February 12, 2002).

[5] Allan Bloom, *The Closing of the American Mind* (New York: Simon and Schuster, 1987), 25.

Bloom's claim and our nonscientific surveys may indicate more of a difference in how relativism is defined in relation to an alternative metaethical
theory, such as perspectivism, which we will discuss below. After all, if
relativism was as prevalent as is claimed, we would expect some variability on responses to the first two slides in our biomedical and sexual ethics
courses. We find it inconceivable that those surveyed in the Barna study
would defend Nazi human experimentation or throwing innocent men from
tall buildings just because of their sexual orientation. Universal agreement
on these ethical issues implies objective truth and indicates that we need
to define relativism, which recognizes no universal truth, and distinguish
it from objectivism or perspectivism, which recognizes universal truth. We
agree, therefore, with popes John Paul and Benedict, that relativism is a
concern in the twenty-first century. We do not yet, however, specify why
and in what way it is a concern.

Relativism is, of course, not a new doctrine in the world; it has been
around a long time. So much so that philosophical ethicist Alasdair
MacIntyre is moved to judge that relativism "is one of those doctrines that
have by now been refuted a number of times too often. Nothing is perhaps a surer sign that a doctrine embodies some not-to-be-neglected truth
than that in the course of the history of philosophy it should have been
refuted again and again." He goes on to make the defensible assertion that
"genuinely refutable doctrines need to be refuted once."[6] Though there is
evidence of relativism in earlier, pre-Socratic philosophers, it is usually
traced back to the fifth century BCE sophist Protagoras of Abdera, called
by Plato "the wisest man alive,"[7] and his famous dictum that "man is the
measure of all things." We have little direct knowledge of Protagoras since
there remain only fragments of his writing, but we have indirect knowledge
from Plato and Aristotle, both of whom are anti-relativists.

Plato argues in his *Theaetetus* that the doctrine of relativism is incoher-
ent and self-refuting. His argument can be summarized in the following
syllogism: Protagoras believes his doctrine of relativism is true *for him* and
false *for others*; but most people believe that man is not the measure of
all things and this belief, according to Protagoras, must be true for them;
therefore, in proportion to the number of people who believe it to be false,
Protagoras's doctrine of relativism must be false.[8] The Barna statistics we
cited above might mathematically disprove that syllogism, and we shall
return to that suggestion later, but this subjective relativism is close to

---

[6] Alasdair MacIntyre, "Relativism, Power, and Philosophy," *Proceedings and Addresses
of the American Philosophical Association* 59 (1985): 22.
[7] John M. Cooper and D. S. Hutchinson, eds., *Protagoras*, in *Plato: Complete Works*
(Cambridge: Hackett Publishing, 1997), 746–90.
[8] See Plato *Theaetetus,* 171a-c, in Cooper and Hutchinson, *Plato,* 157–234.

Aristotle's interpretation of Protagoras in his *Metaphysics*. There he assigns a relativist position to Protagoras, arguing that he is "compelled to say that everything is *relative to opinion* and sensation, so that nothing has occurred and nothing will be unless someone has first formed an opinion about it."[9] Aristotle's major problem with Protagorean relativism is that it contradicts what he considers to be the most certain of all basic principles, namely, the principle of non-contradiction. If man is the measure of all things, then man can assign different properties or values to the same thing, saying it is black or white, sweet or sour, true or false, and therefore the same thing must both be and not be.[10] We do not find either Plato's or Aristotle's argument against relativism convincing, for both drop Protagoras's relativizing phrase from their arguments. Protagoras does not argue that a thing, for instance, is both sweet and sour, but that it is sweet for man A and sour for man B, which means that it is not both sweet and sour at the same time and in the same place. And so we must look further.

Relativism takes many forms. There is *alethic* relativism (relativism about truth), *ethical* relativism (relativism about goodness and morality), and *aesthetic* relativism (relativism about beauty). In this book we are concerned only with alethic and ethical relativism. It is now time to define *relativism*, and it can be easily defined negatively and not-so-easily defined positively. Negatively, relativism is defined in contrast to certain other philosophical positions: it denies universalism, the position that there can and ought to be universal agreement on matters of truth and goodness; it denies objectivism, the position that truth and goodness are independent of both individual and communal human judgment; it denies absolutism, the position that truth and goodness are timeless and immutable; and it denies monism, the position that there is only one correct judgment about truth and goodness. Positively, relativism claims that the presence or absence of properties such as truth and goodness and the ascription of predicates such as "is true" and "is ethical" depend not only on the object to which the ascription is being made but also on the human social, cultural, and historical factors from which they are being made.[11] All of which brings us back to Protagoras: "Man is the measure of all things."

Perspectivism

A fourth metaethical theory is *perspectivism*. When popes John Paul and Benedict express their concern over the controlling prevalence of relativism

---

[9] Aristotle, *Metaphysics*, Book I 1001b5, in *The Works of Aristotle*, vol. 8, ed. W. D. Ross (Oxford: Clarendon, 1908), emphasis added.

[10] Ibid., 1006a.

[11] See Maria Baghramian, *Relativism* (London: Routledge, 2004), 2–3.

in the contemporary world, they fail to note the difference between *relativ-ism*, which rejects all universal, objective, and absolute ethical truth, and *perspectivism*, which acknowledges universal, objective, and absolute ethical truth but insists that humans can attain that truth only partially but adequately and reliably. Whatever truth they attain is not absolute and the only possible correct truth but a truth that is always in need of further clarification and development. They also fail to distinguish between the pluralism created by relativism and the ethical pluralism produced by various partial truths, which the International Theological Commission's document "Theology Today"[12] advances as an essential criterion of Catholic theology. Neither ethical nor theological pluralism is to be uncritically equated with the relativism just described.

Pope John Paul II writes of the influence of perspective in his encyclical *Veritatis Splendor (The Splendor of Truth),* where he notes: "In order to be able to grasp the object of an act which specifies that act morally, it is therefore necessary to place oneself *in the perspective of the acting person*" (no. 78). We explain perspective by the visual analogy of a man in a multistory building. He looks out a first-story window and sees what that window allows him to see; he then looks out a tenth-story window and a twentieth-story window and sees what those windows allow him to see. What he sees outside the three windows, though different and clearly partial to the extent that our viewer can see only what each window allows him to see, puts into adequate, reliable but partial focus what truly lies outside each window. When he looks out a first-story window, he sees what truly lies outside the window; when he looks out a twentieth-story window, he sees what truly lies outside the window. Perspective is also what accounts for the different moral judgments in the third slide we discussed in the Introduction, the woman in the permanent vegetative state. Seeing from different perspectives accounts for different moral judgments on the rightness or wrongness of removing Terri Schiavo from artificial nutrition and hydration.

Canadian theologian Bernard Lonergan developed a theory of perspectivism with respect to human knowledge and truth. It applies to our present question in that different definitions of human dignity and of ethical norms that derive from those definitions derive from different perspectives. Just as his perspectives from three different windows lead the man to different, partial, but adequately and reliably true views of what truly lies outside his building, so also the approach to questions about human dignity from two different intellectual perspectives will lead

---

[12] International Theological Commission, "Theology Today: Perspectives, Principles and Criteria" (November 29, 2011).

us to two different, partial, but possibly true answers to questions about human dignity and the principles, norms, and judgments that facilitate or frustrate its attainment. The lenses we use to look at human dignity determine what we can see and judge about it and the ethical implications of what we can see and judge. This perspectival, different-lenses approach confronts every charge of relativism and shows they are not sustainable. Writing on the nature of historical knowledge, Lonergan puts the foregoing in stark philosophical language: "Where relativism has lost hope about the attainment of truth, perspectivism stresses the complexity of what the historian is writing about and, as well, the specific difference of historical from mathematical, scientific and philosophic knowledge."[13] In plain language, looking through the different lenses of mathematical, scientific, philosophical, and theological theories will lead to different conclusions about human dignity and the implications of those conclusions for ethical decision and action. Relativism, we repeat, concludes to the falsity of a judgment; perspectivism concludes to its partial, but adequate and reliable, truth.

Two non-ethical analogies will help to explain the perspectivist model. In 2015, "the dress" phenomenon flooded social media. In a widely circulated photograph, a dress appears as either black and blue or white and gold, depending on the viewer. The phenomenon demonstrates differences in individual perceptions of color that is a research interest of neuroscientists and vision scientists. While we do not want to do an in-depth analysis here about what the neuroscience research demonstrates, when we explore the impact of science in general and neuroscience specifically on how different people look at reality differently and make moral judgments based on those differences, the dress phenomenon demonstrates an important epistemological point about how human beings know. When the brain is confronted with "profound uncertainty," such as the uncertainty of color in this case, it fills in gaps of knowledge by making assumptions based on past experiences of sensory perception, lighting, and color.[14] On these bases individuals judge that the dress is either black and blue or white and gold. It is incorrect to say that one judgment is right and the other judgment is wrong since, for an individual person, sensory perception, lighting, color, and historical experience are what inform that judgment and ground the partial truth of that judgment for that individual. What all can agree on is that it is a picture of a colored dress. Perspectivism accounts for both universal agreement and particular differences.

---

[13] Bernard J. F. Lonergan, *Method in Theology* (New York: Herder, 1970), 217.

[14] Pascal Wallisch, "Two Years Later, We Finally Know Why People Saw 'The Dress' Differently," *Slate* (April 12, 2017).

Similarly, the color-blind test that one must take to procure a driver's license presents a pattern of dots and a number portrayed within the pattern. Depending on a person's physiological eye structure and the operational functioning of the eyes' rods and cones combined with lighting, a person may or may not see the number depending on whether he or she is color blind to the combination of colors displayed. Again, all viewers have the same pattern before them, but they see differently and respond differently depending on how their rods and cones function and whether they are color blind to any of the colored dots in the pattern.

Both examples demonstrate parallels, analogically, with perspectivism. People can have the same object or ethical situation before them, the dress or Terri Schiavo, and come to different conclusions about the nature of the object or ethical situation depending on physiological perspectival differences or ethical perspectival differences, respectively. However, they can also agree on universals, which set parameters for what falls within or without perspectivism. This is a dress, not a car; Nazi experiments on human beings are always wrong; same-sex marriage may be right or wrong, depending on one's perspective.

Lonergan offers three factors that account for differences in perspectival human knowledge, including ethical knowledge. First, human knowers are finite, the information available to them at any given time is incomplete, and they cannot attend to or master all the data available to them. Second, knowers are selective, given their different historical and cultural socializations, personal experiences, and ranges of data offered to them. Third, knowers are individually different, and we can expect them to have different interpretations of the data available to them. The theologian-knower trained in the philosophy of Plato and Augustine will attend to different data, achieve different understanding, and make different judgments from the theologian-knower trained in the philosophy of Aristotle and Aquinas. Augustine, Aquinas, and their various followers produce different theologies, which are partial but adequate and reliable explanations of a very complex theological reality. They are like our viewer at first-story and twentieth-story windows, who gets a partial but adequate and reliable view of what truly lies outside the windows. Out of normal experience, we would easily predict that, if both our viewer at the windows and the theological ethicist ascended to higher levels, they would each get a different, but still partial but adequate and reliable, view again.

Every human judgment of truth, including every judgment of ethical truth, is a limited judgment based on limited data and understanding. "So far from resting on knowledge of the universe, [a judgment] is to the effect that, no matter what the rest of the universe may prove to be, at least this is so,"[15] and an ethical judgment of a well-informed conscience is to the effect that, no matter what the rest of the universe may prove to be, at least *this action* is to be done and *that action* is to be avoided. It is precisely the necessarily limited nature of human understandings and judgments that leads to perspectivism, not as to a source of falsity but as to a source of partial but adequate and reliable truth. We offer here an analogy between ethical knowledge and the systematic theological knowledge of God, whom "no one has ever [visually] seen" (John 1:18).

Restating earlier Greek theologians, Augustine expresses the basic Christian approach to truth about God in a famous declaration, "Si comprehendis non est Deus" (if you understand, what you understand is not God).[16] Aquinas expresses the same truth in his mature doctrine: "Now we cannot know what God is but only what God is not; we must, therefore, consider the ways in which God does not exist rather than the ways in which God does exist."[17] Revelation, German theologian Karl Rahner writes in the same vein, "does not mean that the mystery [of God] is overcome by gnosis [or knowledge] bestowed by God. . . . On the contrary, it is the history of the deepening perception of God *as* mystery."[18] What humans know of God and of God's words and ways is always a third- or fourth-story vision of God through human lenses, never what God absolutely is, or does, or says. There is always *more* to be grasped about God and God's words, always another interpretation to be offered of them, which is precisely why religious believers and their theologians must eschew mutual condemnations and embrace the way of dialogue in charity marked out by popes John Paul II and Francis I. This dialogue, which is to be carefully distinguished from debate in which the various participants *defend* their versions of Christian truth, is a mutual seeking after truth, John Paul says in *Ut Unum Sint*, "in a manner proper to the dignity of the human person," in which participants *explain* "to one another the truth they have discovered, or think they have discovered, in order thus to assist one another in the quest for truth" (no. 18). Francis agrees, advising in *Amoris Lactitia (AL)* that those in a dialogue "keep an open mind. Don't get bogged down in your own limited ideas and opinions but be prepared to change or expand

---

[15] Bernard J. F. Lonergan, *Insight: A Study of Human Understanding* (London: Longmans, 1957), 344, emphasis added. See also Lonergan, *Method in Theology*, 217–19.

[16] Augustine, *Sermo* 52, 16, *PL* 38, 360; and International Theological Commission, "Theology Today," no. 97. For a detailed analysis, see William Hill, *Knowing the Unknown God* (New York: Philosophical Library, 1971).

[17] Thomas Aquinas, *Summa Theologiae Sancti Thomae de Aquino* I, 3, Preface.

[18] Karl Rahner, "The Hiddenness of God," *Theological Investigations* 16 (London: Darton, Longman, Todd, 1979), 238.

them." He sees no problem in two different partial truths for, he judges, "the combination of two different ways of thinking can lead to a synthesis that enriches both" (no. 139).

The God whom Christians believe in is always *Deus absconditus*—a partially revealed and understood but still ultimately hidden God. Human intelligence is simply not up to plumbing the depth of the mystery that is the wholly other God.[19] Since, however, humans are created in the image of the mystery-God, there is a mysteriousness also in human nature, its connection to the mystery-God, that humans will never fully grasp, though they may come to an ever-deepening knowledge and understanding of it in and through theological reflection and meditation. Human nature is a mystery, and no single definition of it can comprehensively capture either its full truth or the full truth of the dignity flowing from it. There can be and are, however, partial, adequate, and reliable objective truths, and per-spectivism accounts for their plurality. Perspectivism offers a theory of knowledge that presents human persons as human experience and praxis shows them truly to be, that selects those dimensions of the human person deemed most important for defining human dignity, that interprets and pri-oritizes those dimensions if and when they conflict, and that formulates and justifies norms that facilitate and do not frustrate the attainment of human dignity. To put this in other words, the only way for humans to achieve universal knowledge is via perspectives that are particular.[20] This focus on different particular perspectives leads to different, partial, adequate, and reliable definitions of human dignity and the formulation of different objective norms that facilitate or frustrate its attainment.

In summary, there is broad metaethical agreement within Catholic theological ethics. First, it accepts metaethical objectivism; there *are* objective, universal definitions of human dignity, even if they are as yet only partially, but adequately and reliably, grasped. Second, it defines the ethical terms *good* and *right* in relation to an objective definition of human dignity. Third, given different perspectives, different Catholic theological ethicists can and sometimes do disagree on both the definition of universal human dignity and the formulation and justification of objective norms that facilitate or frustrate its attainment. Fourth, perspectivism, which recog-nizes the inherent limitations of human knowledge, helps to account for the

[19] See Rudolph Otto, *The Idea of the Holy: An Inquiry into the Non-Rational Factor in the Ideas of the Divine and Its Relation to the Rational* (London: Oxford University Press, 1923).

[20] Bryan Massingale, "Beyond Revisionism: A Younger Moralist Looks at Charles E. Curran," in *A Call to Fidelity: On the Moral Theology of Charles E. Curran*, ed. James J. Walter, Timothy O'Connell, and Thomas A. Shannon (Washington, DC: Georgetown University Press, 2002), 258.

different definitions of human dignity and the different formulations and justifications of objective norms that facilitate or frustrate its attainment. Fifth, the variability that arises from perspectivism is an essential part of an objectivism that recognizes universals; the good is *objectively* defined as human dignity. Different objective definitions of human dignity and of the ethical norms flowing from it are not indications of relativism that denies universals but the unavoidable outcome of viewing ethical questions from different perspectives and through different cultural, historical, philosophical, and theological lenses.

Ethical Implications: Employment Non-Discrimination Legislation against LGBT People

The metaethical foundation of all Catholic ethics, we submit, is natural law understood as nature-as-reason,[21] and moral norms and judgments are deduced from natural law-as-reason under the influence of various perspectives related to culture, history, and the various intellectual disciplines. Though Catholic ethical norms are, and are magisterially acknowledged to be, related to historical and cultural perspectives, they are not to be understood as objectively untrue as in relativism but as partially, adequately, and reliably objectively true as in what we have explained as perspectivism. Now, through a consideration of the ethics of the Employment Non-discrimination Act (ENDA) for lesbian, gay, bisexual, and transgender (LGBT)[22] people, we explore the moral (and legal) implications, where official Catholic teaching and many Catholic ethicists specifically, and people of good will in general, have diametrically opposed perspectives on the definition of human dignity and the norms (and laws) that facilitate attaining human dignity.

Employment Non-Discrimination Act and Plural Perspectives

In 2016, Georgia and North Carolina were embroiled in controversy over ENDA-type legislation and claims to religious liberty. In a nutshell, the debate is whether LGBT people have a right, on the basis of sexual

---

[21] For detail, see Jean Porter, *Nature as Reason: A Thomistic Theory of the Natural Law* (Grand Rapids, MI: Eerdmans, 2005).

[22] While LGBT is a commonly used acronym, some current thinking is that it is too restrictive. Thus, LGBTQ (where Q stands for queer or questioning) is becoming increasingly common, or LGBTQI (where I stands for intersex). And, for those who find those terms also too limiting, the acronym GSD (gender and sexual diversities) is finding favor. Because the terminology is still very fluid, in this book we use LGBT, acknowledging that it may well be replaced by a better term in the future.

orientation and gender identity, to nondiscrimination in employment, housing, education, or federally funded programs, or if people who have moral objections to homosexuality or transgender people have a right, on the basis of religious liberty, to deny employment or housing to them. Currently, there is not a federal ENDA law to protect against discrimination on the basis of sexual orientation and gender identity, and sixteen states do not have any ENDA-type legislation to protect against such discrimination. Recently, the governor of Georgia vetoed legislation to discriminate against the LGBT community; the governor of North Carolina supported similar legislation. A 2016 survey reveals overwhelming support for nondiscrimination laws among the general (71%) and Catholic (73%) populations.[23] Although many states have already passed ENDA-type laws, there is ongoing resistance to those laws from Catholic bishops who believe they are a violation of religious freedom and, implicit in that belief, a violation of human dignity.

In April 2015, an urgent communication was sent out by the Nebraska Catholic Conference regarding a proposed state legislative bill prohibiting all discrimination on the basis of sexual orientation and gender identity. Among other things the conference warned the bill "would require employers, including Catholic schools, to engage in employment practices that would *affirm sexual behavior contrary to Church teaching.*"[24] These statements are drawn from the USCCB's *Backgrounder,*[25] which argues against ENDA legislation.

In the *Backgrounder* there is a brief nod to the Catholic teaching that "all people . . . possess an innate human dignity that must be acknowledged and respected by other persons and by the law," but this is quickly qualified by fear-mongering language that claims ENDA-type legislation promotes immoral sexual behavior and threatens religious liberty.[26] At the heart of Catholic teaching on ENDA legislation are two anthropological claims about human dignity. The first claim regards immoral sexual behavior and is grounded in the Catholic sexual teaching that only heterosexual marital reproductive-type sexual acts facilitate human dignity; all heterosexual non-reproductive-type sexual acts, even among married couples, and all homosexual acts, always and absolutely frustrate human dignity. The second claim regards religious liberty and is grounded in the Catholic teaching

---

[23] Betsy Cooper et al., "Beyond Same-sex Marriage: Attitudes on LGBT Nondiscrimination Laws and Religious Exemptions from the 2015 American Values Atlas," *Public Religion Research Institute* (February 18, 2016).

[24] Nebraska Catholic Conference, "LB 586 Information" (February 27, 2015).

[25] USCCB, "Questions and Answers about the Employment Non-Discrimination Act," *Backgrounder* (2013).

[26] Ibid.

that religious liberty is a basic human right and must be prioritized over another person's rights, such as the right to housing or employment. The fundamental question surrounding religious freedom and ENDA is how to balance one's moral and civil right to religious freedom with the moral and civil rights of homosexual or transgender people to nondiscrimination when the two rights conflict. The claims for religious freedom in both the USCCB and Nebraska Catholic Conference statements have evolved from seeking to protect the practice of the Catholic institution while seeking to protect also its practice in a pluralist society with plural definitions of human dignity. The bishops seek to move beyond a religious exemption from a *just* law to advocate for the prevention or repeal of nondiscrimination laws they regard as *unjust*. How did we get to this point?

USCCB on Religious Freedom and ENDA: A Critical Analysis

In April 2012, the USCCB issued a statement on religious freedom that states that freedoms in the United States are "threatened" and that "religious liberty is under attack."[27] There are two issues in the text that have a bearing on the USCCB's stance against ENDA legislation: the common good, and just and unjust laws. We consider each in turn and conclude that, based on a perspectivist definition of human dignity, ENDA legislation is a civil rights imperative that the Catholic Church is obligated to support in a pluralist society.

The Common Good

The USCCB statement on religious liberty proclaims: "What is at stake is whether America will continue to have a free, creative, and robust civil society—or whether the state alone will determine who gets to contribute to the common good, and how they get to do it."[28] This claim, of course, requires that we define the common good, the role of the church in relation to the common good, and whether and how ENDA legislation threatens the common good. The Second Vatican Council in *Gaudium et Spes (GS)* describes the common good as "the sum of those conditions of social life which allow social groups and their individual members relatively thorough and ready access to their own fulfillment" (no. 26). What facilitates this social and personal fulfillment or human dignity is good, moral, and to be supported; what frustrates it is evil, immoral, and to be opposed. The

---

[27] USCCB, "Our First, Most Cherished Liberty: Statement on Religious Liberty" (2012), available on the USCCB website.

[28] Ibid.

sociological surveys reveal a pluralism within the church with respect to sexual norms, and this pluralism has implications for defining and then realizing human dignity and the common good.[29]

How, then, are we to realize human dignity and the common good in the public realm, given pluralism within and without the church? On the one hand, the USCCB emphasizes that every person's human rights must be protected; on the other hand, this "should be done without sacrificing the bedrock of society that is marriage and the family and without violating the religious liberty of persons and institutions."[30] ENDA legislation presents a conflict of values between protecting human rights and protecting religious freedom, marriage, and family as these are defined by the bishops. David Hollenbach and Tom Shannon raise this question: "When and how is civil legislation an appropriate means for the promotion of the moral norms taught by the Church's Magisterium?"[31] They respond by arguing correctly that there needs to be a reevaluation of both the church's role in defining and realizing the common good and how this definition and realization should affect the church's involvement in the political realm.

Just and Unjust Law

With its opposition to ENDA legislation the USCCB has shifted its religious liberty claims from exemptions from a just law on the basis of conscience to prevention or repeal of an unjust law. They explain in their statement on religious liberty: "Conscientious objection permits some relief to those who object to a just law for reasons of conscience. . . . An unjust law is 'no law at all.' It cannot be obeyed, and therefore one does not seek relief from it, but rather its repeal."[32] ENDA legislation, the bishops maintain, is an unjust law and should be blocked or repealed. The justification for their claim is a particular definition of human dignity that includes a moral bias against people with a homosexual orientation and distorted notions of gender, religious liberty, and conscience. We consider each in turn.

First, the USCCB's *Backgrounder* focuses on ENDA's definition of sexual orientation and problems that definition poses. ENDA fails, the bishops argue, to distinguish between "sexual inclination" and "sexual conduct," and since that distinction has not been made, "courts have construed

[29] See, for example, Robert P. Jones and Daniel Cox, "Catholic Attitudes on Gay and Lesbian Issues," *Public Religion Research Institute* (March 2011).
[30] USCCB, "Marriage: Love and Life in the Divine Plan" (November 17, 2009).
[31] David Hollenbach, SJ, and Thomas Shannon, "A Balancing Act: Catholic Teaching on the Church's Rights—and the Rights of All," *America* (March 5, 2012).
[32] *Statement.*

a term such as 'homosexuality' to protect both same-sex attraction and same-sex conduct." Catholic teaching distinguishes between homosexual acts, which frustrate human dignity absolutely and are judged to be intrinsically immoral, and homosexual inclination, judged to be "objectively disordered" but not immoral.[33] Since ENDA makes no distinction between sexual inclination and sexual conduct, and it *might* happen that homosexuals will engage in homosexual acts (though many are celibate), it is just and moral to discriminate against them, according to the *Backgrounder* on ENDA, since the church "teaches that all sexual acts outside of the marriage of one man and one woman are morally wrong and do not serve the good of the person or society." On this basis all employers, religious and nonreligious alike, can exercise their religious freedom by claiming an exemption from an already approved law or by preventing or repealing proposed ENDA legislation.

There are several possible responses to the USCCB's argument. First, its *Backgrounder* assumes and asserts the Catholic teaching that all sexual acts outside of heterosexual marriage and all sexual acts within marriage not open to procreation are morally evil and frustrate human dignity. A religious exemption from ENDA is based in part on the concern that the failure to distinguish between sexual orientation and act would force employers to promote immoral sexual activity. If this is really the USCCB's argument, it should also argue that there should be a religious exemption to discriminate against both married heterosexuals who *might* use artificial contraceptives or have oral or anal sex and unmarried heterosexuals who also *might* engage in these acts, since these acts frustrate human dignity as well. Heterosexuals *might* engage in immoral sexual acts that would "not serve the good of the person or society" any more than would homosexual acts. The USCCB has not made this logical argument, which would indicate that its objection is not to immoral sexual acts but simply to homosexual orientation. By rejecting ENDA legislation, the USCCB is violating the common good, the protection of individual human dignity, on the basis of a generalization that homosexuals *might* engage in immoral sexual activity and promoting unjust discrimination against even celibate homosexuals performing no homosexual acts.

There is a more fundamental response to the USCCB's concern with homosexual activity, one that challenges the very claim that homosexual activity is intrinsically immoral and destructive of human dignity. The church has consistently taught that homosexual acts are intrinsically immoral, but that teaching and its theological bases are now seriously challenged, and many surveys show that the majority of contemporary Catholics do not

---

[33] *Catechism of the Catholic Church (CCC)*, no. 2358.

accept that teaching.[34] The fact that the majority of Catholic faithful do not accept Catholic teaching on the immorality of homosexual acts is not an argument for their morality, which is not determined by majority consensus. The burden of proof, however, is on the church to make a compelling argument that convinces both Catholic and non-Catholic citizens that the teaching is true. Hollenbach and Shannon advise, and we agree, that "the church should not ask the State to do what it has not been able to convince its own members to do."[35] The burden of proof is on the church to demonstrate that homosexual acts are destructive of human dignity and cannot serve "the good of the person or society," and so far it has not offered a compelling argument. An unproven assertion should not be advanced as the basis for an abuse of religious freedom aimed at preventing or repealing ENDA legislation and imposing the church's morally questionable doctrine on the broader society.

Second, the bishops argue in the *Backgrounder* that ENDA uses law to support a misperception of gender as "nothing more than a social construct or psychosocial reality that can be chosen at variance from one's biological sex." According to Catholic views on gender, humans are born with not only female or male genitalia but also female or male gender designed to serve the complementarity of the spouses in a sexual relationship between a man and a woman in a monogamous marriage. Reducing gender to a social construct or psychological reality would allow for a continuum between the physical sex of a person and the perceived psychological and/or social perception of gender that would, in turn, allow for gender transformation that violates the gender identity assigned by God.

The distinction between biological sex (male/female) and socially conditioned gender (masculine/feminine) is frequently absent in magisterial discussions of gender.[36] One also finds gender stereotypes in magisterial documents where femaleness is defined primarily in terms of motherhood, receptivity, and nurturing, and maleness is defined primarily in terms of

---

[34] Surveys show that only 32 percent of Catholics believe that homosexual acts are wrong and only 13 percent believe that contraceptive acts are wrong. See Michael J. O'Loughlin, "Poll Finds Many US Catholics Breaking with Church Over Contraception, Abortion, and LGBT Rights," *America* (September 28, 2016); and Pew Research Center, "Where the Public Stands on Religious Liberty vs. Nondiscrimination" (September 28, 2016).

[35] Hollenbach and Shannon, "A Balancing Act."

[36] Susan A. Ross, "The Bridegroom and the Bride: The Theological Anthropology of John Paul II and Its Relation to the Bible and Homosexuality," in *Sexual Diversity and Catholicism: Toward the Development of Moral Theology*, ed. Patricia Beattie Jung with Joseph A. Coray (Collegeville, MN: Liturgical Press, 2001), 56n5.

fatherhood, initiation, and activity.[37] The claim of ontologically gendered psychological traits does not recognize the culturally conditioned nature of gender and does not adequately reflect the complexity of the human person and of his or her relationships. Within individuals and relationships, psycho-affective, social, and spiritual traits are not "natural" to one gender but may be found in either gender.[38] The "masculinity" and "femininity" of the non-biological elements are conditioned and defined by culture and are not ontological components of male and female human nature.[39] The church's view of gender as a biological given is a reductionist definition of human dignity and ignores the complexity of the human person, gender, and identity.

The bishops in the *Backgrounder* also assert that ENDA's definition of gender identity "would adversely affect the privacy and associational rights of others." Without proof, they assert that it would, for instance, *"prevent a Catholic school from reprimanding a transgender male coach who insists on using the girls' shower and restroom facilities."*[40] This is an example of what transgender activist CN Lester calls "the production of ignorance," the spreading of homophobic fear with no supportive basis in reality.[41] We have two responses to these assertions. First, if empirically reliable evidence as a source of moral knowledge is a basis for defining human dignity and for helping to make a compelling argument, and we believe it is, then there is no reliable evidence of trans male coaches or teachers who insist on using female facilities of any kind. There is, however, abundant evidence of workplace discrimination based on sexual orientation and gender identity throughout the nation.[42] Second, federal law and many state laws include the categories of gender and sexual orientation as bases for hate crimes, increasing the penalties for such crimes.[43] The multiplicity of lawsuits charging discrimination in housing and employment on the

---

[37] See Pope John Paul II, *Familiaris Consortio (FC)* (1982), no. 23; "Letter to Women" (June 29, 1995), no. 9; *Mulieris Dignitatem (MD)* (1988); and "Women: Teachers of Peace" (January 1, 1995).

[38] Cristina Traina, "Papal Ideals, Marital Realities: One View from the Ground," in Jung with Corey, *Sexual Diversity and Catholicism*, 280–82.

[39] Elaine L. Graham, *Making the Difference: Gender, Personhood, and Theology* (Minneapolis: Fortress, 1996), 55, 148, 223.

[40] Nebraska Catholic Conference, "LB 586 Information."

[41] CN Lester, *Trans Like Me: Conversations for All of Us* (New York: Seal Press, 2017), 1–18.

[42] See Brad Sears and Christy Mallory, "Documented Evidence of Employment Discrimination & Its Effects on LGBT People," *The Williams Institute* (July 2011).

[43] Ibid. The Matthew Shepard and James Byrd Jr. Hate Crimes Prevention Act expands a federal hate-crimes law to include crimes committed against people based on gender identity or sexual orientation.

basis of sexual orientation and sexual identity, of hate crimes rooted in the same, and legislation that recognizes these crimes, disproves claims that, since proponents of ENDA legislation cannot produce empirical evidence of "widespread" employment discrimination based on sexual orientation and gender identity, it is not a moral or legal concern.

Third, the USCCB also cites religious liberty to argue for exemption, prevention, or repeal of ENDA legislation. Law Professor Douglas Laycock notes that "reliance on a distinction between just laws that violate the tenets of a particular faith, for which the solution is an exemption, and unjust laws for which the only solution is repeal" is the most problematic aspect of the bishops' statement on religious liberty.[44] Seeking an exemption, prevention, or repeal under the auspices of religious liberty is to confuse the argument about the moral issues and the argument about religious liberty.[45]

The USCCB statement cites Pope Benedict in its defense of religious liberty. "Many of you have pointed out that concerted efforts have been made to deny the right of conscientious objection on the part of Catholic individuals and institutions with regard to *cooperation in intrinsically evil practices.*" Among those intrinsically evil practices are homosexual acts and contraception. However, Hollenbach and Shannon note that "Catholic moral tradition has long stressed that civil law should be founded on moral values but need not seek to abolish all immoral activities in society."[46] The bishops are free to assert that government and secular agencies should exclude homosexuals from employment and from becoming foster or adoptive parents. That, however, is a moral argument seeking to regulate life in the public society.[47] Should such a moral argument be codified in legislation? It is one thing to claim an exemption for a religious institution from a just law based on conscientious objection to the moral contents of the law; it is quite another to seek repeal or prevention of a law based on that objection. The bishops have not made this distinction in their resistance to ENDA legislation, and seek to make Catholic moral doctrines on sexuality nationally legal imperatives. They claim that ENDA laws are "unjust laws" because they promote immoral sexual conduct. They note that it is essential to understand the distinction between conscientious objection and an unjust law. Conscientious objection applies to a just law and seeks a religious exemption from that law. The bishops' statement asserts: "An unjust law is 'no law at all;' it cannot be obeyed, and therefore one does not seek relief from it, but rather its repeal." Laycock notes that

---

[44] Douglas Laycock, in William Galston, "The Bishops & Religious Liberty," *Commonweal* (May 30, 2012).

[45] Ibid.

[46] Hollenbach and Shannon, "A Balancing Act."

[47] Laycock, in Galston, "The Bishops & Religious Liberty."

"the difference between exemption and repeal is the difference between seeking religious liberty for Catholic institutions and seeking to impose Catholic moral teaching on the nation."[48]

In their statement on religious liberty, borrowing a phrase from Martin Luther King, Jr., the bishops want to be the "conscience of the state." They seek to extend Catholic moral teaching beyond a religious exemption from a just law to the prevention or repeal, on the basis of that teaching, of what they view as an unjust law. Although the Catholic Church teaches that same-sex relationships, abortion, and contraception are morally wrong, a majority of Americans consider them basic human rights. As William Galston notes, "The bishops make no effort to understand why their antagonists think that justice requires what the Catholic hierarchy thinks it forbids."[49] The bishops have every right to teach a moral position grounded in their definition of human dignity and to seek to protect religious institutions from participating in what they perceive as immoral activity, but they do not have a right to seek to impose their moral teachings legislatively in a pluralistic society where there are plural definitions of human dignity. To do so is akin to proselytizing and can be a violation of a well-informed conscience, which we discuss in detail in Chapter 6.

Fourth already in the thirteenth century, Thomas Aquinas established the authority and inviolability of conscience.[50] Seven hundred years after Aquinas, *Gaudium et Spes* issued a clarion cry with respect to conscience. "Conscience is the most secret core and sanctuary of man. There he is alone with God whose voice echoes in his depth. In a wonderful manner conscience reveals that law which is fulfilled by love of God and neighbor" (no. 16). *Dignitatis Humanae (DH)* went further to assert the inviolability of conscience. "In all his activity a man is bound to follow his conscience faithfully, in order that he may come to God for whom he was created. It follows that he is not to be forced to act contrary to his conscience. Nor, on the other hand, is he to be restrained from acting in accordance with his conscience, especially in matters religious" (no. 3).[51]

Several points are evident from the statements in *Gaudium et Spes* and *Dignitatis Humanae* on the nature and inviolability of conscience, which

---

[48] Ibid.

[49] William Galston, in Galston, "The Bishops & Religious Liberty."

[50] Thomas Aquinas, *In IV Sent.*, dist. 38, q. 2, art. 4. "Anyone upon whom the ecclesiastical authorities, in ignorance of the true facts, impose a demand that offends against his clear conscience should perish in excommunication rather than violate his conscience."

[51] The lack of gender-inclusive language in many earlier magisterial documents, and most literature of the time, reflects the fact that they were written before the current sensitivy to inclusive language. The reader is asked to read quotations from these documents in the inclusive manner in which they were (it is to be hoped) intended, even when the language appears exclusive to modern eyes.

is an essential dimension of human dignity. First, conscience is sacred; it is a gift from God (*GS,* no. 16). Second, it is an intrinsic faculty of the human person (*GS,* no. 16). Third, following one's conscience on moral and religious matters facilitates human dignity; violating one's conscience on moral and religious matters frustrates human dignity (*GS,* no. 16; *DH,* no. 3). Fourth, no one is ever to be forced to act against her or his conscience; such force is a fundamental violation of conscience and of human dignity (*DH,* no. 3). Fifth, the authority granted to conscience presumes that one's conscience is well-informed (*GS,* no. 16). Though there is consensus on many aspects of the nature of conscience and its inviolability in *Gaudium et Spes* and *Dignitatis Humanae,* debate continues over the nature of conscience and its inviolability in relation to religious freedom and civil legislation.

While the freedom, authority, and inviolability of personal conscience are all affirmed in Catholic tradition, in the public realm all of them must be assessed against the competing rights and responsibilities of others, in particular, the responsibility to promote the common good in a pluralistic society. In their statement the bishops seem to be unaware of any competing rights and responsibilities and present their religious freedom as an absolute. In the final part of the statement, the authors issue an invitation to fellow bishops to "be bold, clear, and insistent in warning against threats to the rights of our people. Let us attempt to be the 'conscience of the state.'" As Cathleen Kaveny points out, and as we have seen, however, "Vatican II's *Declaration on Religious Freedom* recognizes that there are 'due limits' on the exercise of religious freedom, including the need to promote a 'just public order,' and preserve the 'equality of the citizens before the law.'"[52] This equality of citizens before the law in a democratic, pluralistic society, in which one person's or institution's exercise of conscience and religious liberty can come up against another person's or institution's exercise of conscience and religious liberty raises serious questions of conscience.

Douglas NeJaime and Reva Siegel refer to these conscience questions as "conscience wars" manifested in "complicity-based conscience claims." These are "faith claims about how to live in community with others who do not share the claimant's beliefs, and whose lawful conduct the person of faith believes to be sinful."[53] It is one thing to follow one's conscience on religious and moral matters; it is quite another *to force* one's conscience on religious and moral matters legislatively onto others who disagree about them. Such enforcing may be a violation of conscience for, and can cause

---

[52] Cathleen Kaveny, in Galston, "The Bishops & Religious Liberty." See also Cathleen Kaveny, *A Culture of Engagement: Law, Religion, and Morality* (Washington, DC: Georgetown University Press, 2016).

[53] Douglas NeJaime and Reva B. Siegel, "Conscience Wars: Complicity-Based Conscience Claims in Religion and Politics," *Yale Law Journal* 124, no. 7 (2015): 2519.

extensive material and dignitary harm to, others. Perspectivism supports plural definitions of human dignity and invites constructive dialogue when these definitions, and the norms or laws that follow from them, come into conflict.

The bishops have taken it upon themselves to become the "conscience of the state" in sexual matters, seeking to impose one understanding of Catholic sexual ethics on the broader society and moving beyond a mere exemption from a just law to advocating for prevention or repeal of what they perceive as an unjust law based on their judgment that the law violates their moral code. What is most striking about the bishops' strategy in claims to religious liberty is the absolute nature of those claims, the use of their freedom of conscience to justify those claims, and the total ignoring of the equal claims to freedom of conscience of others who disagree with them. The bishops' statement asserts: "If we are not free in our conscience and our practice of religion, all other freedoms are fragile. If citizens are not free in their own consciences, how can they be free in relation to others, or to the state?" The problem here, however, is clear: when my conscience conflicts with the consciences of others and I seek to impose my conscience-claims legislatively, the consciences of others will be violated. Kaveny notes that the bishops provide no indication that such claims "must be assessed in a framework of competing rights and duties [and, we add, consciences], particularly the duty to promote [human dignity and] the common good."[54]

Rights claims and conscience claims must always take into consideration relational responsibilities. Complicity-based conscience claims attempt to impose one person's or one institution's conscience on another person's or institution's conscience under the umbrella of religious freedom and the maintenance of the moral integrity of individuals or institutions to avoid complicity in sin. It is one thing to make such a claim on undisputed moral issues such as segregation, where there is virtually unanimous social and moral agreement that they are fundamental violations of human dignity and the common good. It is quite another to make the claim on disputed sexual ethical issues where the majority of the people in the society, including Catholics with well-informed consciences, disagree with the Catholic Church's definition of human dignity and its sexual teachings.

The bishops have every right to advocate for their moral position and to protect religious institutions from participating in what they perceive as immoral activity, but they do not have the right to impose their moral teachings legislatively in a pluralistic society. That, we conclude, would be the very worst kind of proselytism. One final comment on the USCCB's

---

[54] Kaveny, in Galston, "The Bishops & Religious Liberty."

statement; the bishops should be ashamed of themselves for citing Martin Luther King, Jr., the genuine and undisputed "conscience of the state" for civil rights, to trample on the equal civil rights of homosexual, bisexual, and transgender citizens.

Conclusion

In the example we have just explored on ENDA legislation, the USCCB's perspective on it, and the perspective of those who disagree with it, we conclude that both perspectives recognize that the good is defined as human dignity and that this definition includes claims about sexuality and religious liberty. The USCCB defines sexual human dignity narrowly as heterosexual; only heterosexual marital reproductive-type sexual acts facilitate human dignity. Since ENDA legislation can allow for homosexual acts, this legislation can promote a violation of sexual human dignity. Human dignity also requires religious liberty as a basic human right. Any law that does not allow individuals to exercise their right to adhere to their moral beliefs, such as an ENDA law requiring them to employ or provide housing to a homosexual or transgender person, is a violation of religious liberty and frustrates their human dignity. Other theorists define sexual human dignity as allowing for just and loving sexual acts between two people—heterosexual, homosexual, or bisexual—and argue that such acts can facilitate human dignity. Human dignity also recognizes the authority and inviolability of conscience and, although religious liberty is part of this authority and inviolability, it cannot justify moral or legal discrimination against another person on the basis of sexual orientation or gender identity. Justice and equal treatment of persons are higher values than merely avoiding what the *Catechism of the Catholic Church* calls "every sign of unjust discrimination in their regard" (no. 2858) defended by claims to religious liberty. Both the USCCB and those who disagree with it represent perspectivist metaethical theories. They propose different definitions of human dignity and different norms and laws that facilitate and do not frustrate its attainment. Just as the third slide in our sexual ethics course indicates greater ethical acceptance of same-sex marriage because of the historical and cultural development of the definition of sexual human dignity and norms that facilitate its attainment, our brief investigation of ENDA legislation and the plural definitions of human dignity that defend or critique that legislation demonstrates the impact of historical and cultural developments on the issues of sexual orientation, gender identity, and religious liberty.

Questions for Reflection

- Why is metaethics the most foundational question of ethics?
- What are the differences between perspectivism and relativism?
- How does perspectivism account for pluralism in ethics on the definition of human dignity and norms that facilitate attaining human dignity?
- What social, cultural, historical, and/or religious factors account for the different definitions of human dignity in discussion of ENDA legislation? What are the anthropological, normative, and legal implications of these definitions? Which definition, if any, do you defend? Why do you defend it?

Suggested Readings

Baghramian, Maria. *Relativism.* London: Routledge, 2004.

International Theological Commission. "Theology Today: Perspectives, Principles and Criteria" (November 29, 2011).

Salzman, Todd A., and Michael G. Lawler. "Natural Law and Perspectivism: A Case for Plural Definitions of Objective Morality." *Irish Theological Quarterly* 82, no. 1 (2017): 3–18.

———. "Nondiscrimination Laws Merit Church Support." *National Catholic Reporter* 52, no. 14 (April 22–May 5, 2016): 1, 18–19.

2

Virtue Ethics

Learning Objectives

- Explain a virtue.
- Understand virtue theory.
- Understand virtue ethics.
- Understand Christian virtue ethics.
- Distinguish between theological virtues and cardinal virtues.
- Understand the interrelationship between virtues and acts.

In Chapter 1 we defended metaethical perspectivism, which posits that the good can be defined and that it is defined as human dignity. What facilitates human dignity is good or right; what frustrates human dignity is bad or wrong. Perspectivism also recognizes plural definitions of human dignity and plural formulations and justifications of norms that seek to attain human dignity. In this chapter we build on this metaethical foundation by exploring and explaining how virtue ethics in general and Christian virtue ethics specifically shape perspectives on the definition of human dignity and the norms and acts that facilitate and do not frustrate its attainment.

In contemporary ethics there are three approaches to determining the ethics of an action. There is the *utilitarian approach*, that is, the ethical action is the one that maximizes utility. There is the *deontological approach,* which emphasizes rules and duties. There is the "new" *virtue-ethical approach,* which gives precedence not to the acts of agents but to their personal characters formed in their ethical communities and learned through the imitation of respected role models in those communities. We share with Philippa Foot and Alasdair MacIntyre the judgment that neither utilitarianism nor deontology offers an adequately comprehensive ethical theory, indeed that, because of them, "we have—very largely if not entirely—lost our comprehension, both theoretical and practical, of morality."[1] We join with them and many other modern theological ethicists who advance virtue ethics as a normative ethics more promising to the ethical life than utilitarianism or deontology.[2] In what follows we give an account of virtue ethics. That requires, first, a virtue *theory* and then, based on that theory, a virtue *ethics*.

Virtue Theory

Since the notion of virtue is central to this chapter, we need to be clear from the outset what we mean by the term *virtue*. We need a virtue theory. We may begin, as one may frequently begin in the Western tradition, with Aristotle. He defines virtue as "a state of character concerned with choice, lying in a mean."[3] Thomas Aquinas follows Aristotle's tradition but rephrases his definition. A virtue, Aquinas argues, is a "habit or a disposition" "ordered to an act."[4] Virtues are involved in "both the intellectual and rational part of the self and the affective or desiring part of the self."[5] As character state or habit, virtue explains not only why a person acts this way on a particular occasion but also why the person can be relied on to act this way always or, given human frailty, at least most of the time. Immediately, then, we can isolate three dimensions of a virtue: it is a character state, habit, or disposition; it involves a judgment of truth and choice of action; and it lies in a mean between excess and defect. "Each of the virtues involves getting things right, for each involves *phronesis*, or practical wisdom, which is the ability to reason correctly about practical matters."[6] The more common English translation of Aristotle's *phronesis* is "prudence," without which no right action, and therefore no virtue, is possible.

---

[1] Alasdair MacIntyre, *After Virtue* (Notre Dame, IN: Univesity of Notre Dame Press, 1984), 2. See also Philippa Foot, "Moral Beliefs," in *Proceedings of the Aristotelian Society* 59 (1958–59): 83–104.

[2] In addition to Foot and MacIntyre, whom most judge to be the preeminent modern virtue theorists, other important theorists in the field of virtue ethics will be introduced as the chapter unfolds.

[3] Aristotle, *Nicomachean Ethics,* trans. David Ross (Oxford: Oxford University Press, 2009), II, 6, 1106b, 36 (hereinafter, *NE*). See Rosalind Hursthouse, *On Virtue Ethics* (Oxford: Oxford University Press, 1999), 11.

[4] Thomas Aquinas, *Summa Theologiae Sancti Thomae de Aquino* I–II, 49, 1 (hereinafter, *ST*); ibid., 49, 3.

[5] Joseph J. Kotva, Jr., *The Christian Case for Virtue Ethics* (Washington, DC: Georgetown University Press, 1996), 23.

[6] Hursthouse, *On Virtue Ethics*, 12.

Common to all theories of virtue is the conviction that virtues are not only preconditions for human flourishing but also constituents of that flourishing. "A virtue is a character trait that human beings, given their physical and psychological nature, need to flourish (or to do and fare well)."[7] The person who has the virtues of benevolence and justice will be a benevolent and just person who will act benevolently and justly. This direction was mapped out by Aristotle, who names the ultimate human good *eudaimonia* (happiness or fulfillment);[8] it was Christianized by Aquinas, who names the ultimate Christian good union with God achieved through the virtue of charity or self-sacrificing love.[9] Given their different ends, happiness in the case of Aristotelian virtue ethics and union with God in Christian virtue ethics, we would expect the two ethics to be different, and at the end of this chapter we will show that they are different.

A central element of Aristotle's definition of virtue is that it is the result of deliberation and choice. Deliberation is of possible choices and actions, and choice is of one action in preference to others. Choice involves reason and *phronesis* (prudent) practical judgment. The choice of one action in preference to others is made of the mean that is appropriate and proportionate for this person, on this occasion, for this right reason. We must carefully note, however, that the mean that is virtuous action is not an arithmetic mean but a mean relative to the individual and the circumstances in which an individual finds himself or herself. The arithmetic mean between ten and two pounds of food is six pounds, but six pounds would be "too little for Milo" (a famous wrestler of Aristotle's day) and too much for "the beginner in athletic exercises." The mean to be chosen is "not in the object but relatively to us."[10] Importantly, deliberation is about means, never about ends; ends are given and not to be deliberated. We deliberate only about what lies in our power to do or not to do;[11] actions we are forced to do are not freely chosen and therefore cannot be either virtuous or vicious, ethical or unethical. It is because we are rational that we can know, first, that action is called for and, second, that we can choose this virtuous action or this vicious action. To understand virtue fully a theory of rationality is required. To that we now turn.

---

[7] Rosalind Hursthouse, "Applying Virtue Ethics," in *Virtues and Reason: Philippa Foot and Moral Theory*, ed. Rosalind Hursthouse, Gavin Lawrence, and Warren Quinn, 57–75 (Oxford: Clarendon, 1995), 68. See also Hursthouse, *On Virtue Ethics*, 13; Brad Hooker, "Does Moral Virtue Constitute a Benefit to the Agent?" in *How Should One Live? Essays on the Virtues*, ed. Roger Crisp (Oxford: Clarendon, 1998), 141–55.

[8] *NE* I, 4, 1095a, 17–20.

[9] *ST* I, 23, 6.

[10] Ibid. II, 6, 1106b, 3–8.

[11] Ibid. III, 3, 1112a, 31.

Knowledge

That virtue includes a reasonable, deliberative, and decisive dimension means that some epistemological theory is required for its full understanding. To act rightly is not only to act rightly in choice and action, it is also to know rightly and to feel rightly. To understand rightly the process of human knowing, we espouse the epistemology established by Bernard Lonergan in his magisterial *Insight*[12] because we believe that epistemology fully elucidates the process of both coming to know and coming to virtue. "All human beings," Aristotle teaches, "desire to know by nature."[13] Lonergan agrees, arguing that human knowing begins in wonder and question, in the "pure desire to know."[14] There is no human knowledge, no genuine answer, without a prior question. Human knowing is not simply taking a look at reality. It is endlessly discursive; that is, it cycles and recycles through various levels of cognitive activity until knowledge and truth are reached in the judgment, deliberated on, and a decisive choice is made for action according to the known truth. It begins with attention and cycles on through perception, imagination (sometimes as memory), insight, conceptualization, deliberation, and culminates in the judgment of truth.[15] It is in this judgment of truth and only in this judgment that genuine human truth is achieved. This judgment may be followed by decision and action, and it is only at the moment of decision and action that ethics enters in.

Perception is critical in the process of coming to know. Perception, Lonergan argues, is the active patterning of an object by a rational subject, a dialectical interaction between a personal subject seeking knowledge and an object in the external world. An object does not simply impress itself upon rational subjects, as it impresses itself upon non-rational animals, nor do rational subjects simply construct or project it. Rather, an object is shaped for knowledge by a person's attention, interests, goals, emotions, and in general the character lens through which the person views the object.[16] The world individuals encounter and attend to is not a world that is "out, there, now, real"[17] without any action on their part but a world shaped by their interpretations called perceptions. Perception is an exercise of practical reason leading to choice; what we "see" is a function of who we are. This claim will later have implications for virtue ethics.

---

[12] Bernard J. F. Lonergan, *Insight: A Study of Human Understanding* (London: Longmans, 1957).

[13] Aristotle, *Metaphysics*, ed. Joseph Sachs (Santa Fe: Green Lion Press, 1999), 980a20.

[14] Lonergan, *Insight*, 74, 372–75.

[15] Ibid., 273–74.

[16] Ibid., 190.

[17] Ibid., 251; see also Bernard J. Lonergan, *Method in Theology* (New York: Herder, 1972), 263.

William James puts the cognitive psychology nicely: "My experience is what I agree to attend to. Only those items which I notice shape my mind—without selective interest experience is an utter chaos."[18] Character states explain not only why a person acts this way on this particular occasion but also why the person acts this way always. Character is an enduring psychological state that affects how a person perceives, judges, acts, and ultimately lives. As philosopher Norwood Russell Hanson notes, "There is more to seeing than meets the eyeball."[19] In other words, for humans unbiased observation is a myth. What, we may ask, does perception have to do with virtue? Aristotle writes that "we become just by first performing just acts."[20] We pose two questions to that assertion. First, how do we know which actions are just and therefore to be performed? Second, what motivation might we have for performing those actions? The first question is easily answered. We learn what are just acts or acts of any other virtue from respected others—parents, teachers, mentors, saints—whom we hold as virtuous and ethical. We judge an action ethical if it is one that a virtuous person would do in the circumstances, and it is by imitation of the virtuous person that we learn which actions are right, ethical, and virtuous. We need to be careful, however, how we understand the word *learn*.

Words and explanations will never make anyone virtuous; virtues are states or habits learned only by repeated and habitual performance. It is by habituation, critically questioned and re-questioned in the cycle of attention, perception, insight, judgment, decision, and action, that we come to learn and value the goodness of justice and love and of just, loving, and virtuous actions in general. The perception of ethical relevance is the product of both experience and habituation but, we repeat, there is no real morality until that ethical relevance is judged to be true in the judgment of truth and then followed by personal decision and action. Aristotle is pointing at this critical approach to learning virtues when he claims that "a morally praiseworthy act must be done in full awareness of *what* we are doing and *why* we do it. It must be an act freely chosen and not done from coercion."[21] We have already pointed out the universal Catholic position that ethics enters the process of knowing only at the stage of decision and action. There is no ethical action prior to a person's choice to do this

---

[18] William James, *The Principles of Psychology* (Cambridge, MA: Harvard University Press, 1983), 380–81.

[19] Norwood Russell Hanson, *Patterns of Discovery: An Inquiry into the Conceptual Foundations of Science* (Cambridge: Cambridge University Press, 1958), 7.

[20] *NE* II, 1103a31–1103b2.

[21] Robert J. Fitterer, *Love and Objectivity in Virtue Ethics: Aristotle, Lonergan, and Nussbaum on Emotions and Moral Insight* (Toronto: University of Toronto Press, 2008), 6.

action, nor is there any ethical praise to be earned from simply imitating another person. "We are morally obliged not only to *act* well but also to *think* well."[22] That thinking well, Aristotle and Lonergan agree, requires ethical agents to be open to ongoing inquiry and reflective grasp of their attention, understanding, judgment, and decision, for personal bias and pleasure can distort them and will need to be corrected.[23]

The second question about motivation is also easily answered. MacIntyre situates virtues within a broad category he names *practice*, a "coherent and complex form of socially established cooperative human activity through which goods internal to that form of activity are realized in the course of trying to achieve those standards of excellence which are appropriate to, and partially definitive of, that form of activity."[24] That complex definition requires instantiation for clarification. That a practice is a "socially established cooperative human activity" signals the importance of membership in, and the influence of, a community and culture on the individual learning virtue. By definition, this rules out individual relativism, in which the individual alone defines the good. It also recognizes the importance of community and culture in shaping a virtuous perspective. The form of "socially established cooperative human activity" here is the search for virtue or goodness; "goods internal to that form of activity" are the virtues and the acts they prescribe as defined in the community and culture; the desire "to achieve those standards of excellence appropriate to" being virtuous provides motivation to strive to achieve those virtuous goods. It is a central claim of virtue theory from Aristotle to MacIntyre that virtues are shaped in a community and culture by narratives and role models judged to be virtuous.

Virtues are *learned* and can only be learned within a community; they can be *sustained* only within that community; they get their *content* from that community; they get their *worth* from and in that community; and they *act back* on that community to sustain it.[25] Humans are not absolutely the self-determining persons they are frequently claimed to be. Persons who are "role-figures"[26] in their communities first exemplify what it means to be just, loving, and so on, and then by personal repetition of acts of justice and love an individual establishes those virtues as personal habits and disposi-

---

[22] Ibid.

[23] *NE* II, 1109b1–12; Lonergan, *Insight*, 225–42.

[24] MacIntyre, *After Virtue*, 187.

[25] See Lawrence Bloom, "Community and Virtue," in Crisp, *How Should One Live?*, 231–50.

[26] Daniel Statman, "Introduction to Virtue Ethics," in *Virtue Ethics: A Critical Reader*, ed. Daniel Statman (Washington, DC: Georgetown University Press, 1997), 15.

tions. As habits are stabilized, both the virtuous exemplars and the acts of virtue learned from them need to be more and more focused and "purified" by critical examination and reexamination in the process of knowing that issues in the judgment of truth, value, decision, and action. This process of critical examination and reexamination not only purifies the agent and the agent's virtues but also leads him or her nearer to the self-determination and authenticity that enable his or her full morality.[27] MacIntyre is still correct, however, when he asserts the sociologically accepted position that "separated from the *polis* [community and culture] what could have been a human being becomes instead a wild animal."[28]

As we learn from role models, we must also submit them and their characters to critical attention, perception, insight, and the judgment that each is or is not a virtuous person with virtues that are means to his or her flourishing and will be to ours *in our own way*. The child's virtue is not *his* virtue but the virtue of those who serve as role models or are in authority over the child. To become authentically virtuous the child must develop into *his* or *her* virtue and adulthood. The virtuous life, like human life itself, is essentially developmental. As each person has an original way of being human, so also each has an original way of being virtuous. Neither the original human nor the original virtuous character can be finally created by imitating past models. They can be shaped by imitating past models but finished only by an articulation of their own virtue. The dynamic of the virtuous life begins with imitation of role models but concludes with authentic ethics through personal decision and responsibility.

Emotions

We must say a brief word about emotions and their contribution to virtue. Since Kant and his categorical imperative of invariant duty, it has been philosophically fashionable to dismiss human emotions as unreliable and of no ethical value. Only rationality, especially will, Kantians say, is of importance for ethics. Modern virtue ethicists judge that to be a mistake. Martha Nussbaum, for instance, argues that emotions "involve judgments about important things, judgments in which, appraising an external object as salient for our own being, we acknowledge our own neediness and incompleteness before parts of the world that we do not

---

[27] Jennifer Herdt gives a splendid account of the historical travails of this mimetic approach to learning virtue and ultimately comes down in its favor (*Putting on Virtue: The Legacy of the Splendid Vices* [Chicago: University of Chicago Press, 2008]).

[28] Alasdair MacIntyre, *Whose Justice? Which Rationality?* (Notre Dame, IN: University of Notre Dame Press, 1988), 98.

fully control."[29] Emotions, we accept, (1) convey knowledge as value judgments of things and persons as (2) salient or critical for (3) a person's own flourishing. We accept these three claims relative to the cognitive function of emotions, but not with the language in which they are articulated. In agreement with Robert Fitterer, we make a distinction between the *apprehension* of truth and value and the *judgment* of truth and value. Given the epistemology we have elaborated above, we cannot agree with Nussbaum's description of emotion as a *judgment* of value, for we restrict the word *judgment* to the intellectual judgment of truth and value. That judgment is not merely an apprehension of an object or situation but the outcome of the cognitive process of attention, perception, understanding, and judgment that this is truly so, that this emotion—compassion or distrust, for instance—is not just a mere passing feeling but a feeling that signals something salient for my happiness and fulfillment. We are willing to describe emotion as a *prima facie judgment*, but such prima facie judgments are no more than apprehensions of *possible* truth and value that must be refined through the cognitive process before any judgment of *actual* truth or value can be made and acted upon. Only in the judgment of truth and value at the conclusion of the cognitive process can the possible truth and value that emotion initially signals be judged an actual truth and value for a person's good and flourishing.

That emotions are salient for a person's individual goodness and flourishing is central to any consideration of virtue. The value I initially apprehend in an emotion is not just a value for every human person but a value apprehended as a salient value for *my* particular good and flourishing. Emotions, Nussbaum claims, and we agree, "contain an ineliminable reference to me."[30] They are the world seen and interpreted specifically through the lens of *my* apprehension, perception, understanding, and judgment. It is a culturally universal value, let us assume, that mothers are to be loved. When *your* mother dies, then, I might feel the emotion of grief, but my grief will be nothing compared to yours. Nor will my grief at the death of your mother be as powerful as my grief when *my* mother dies. The fact that it is *my* mother who has died is not just an accidental fact of *my* life but a fact that essentially structures the entire experience for me and

---

[29] Martha C. Nussbaum, *Upheavals of Thought: The Intelligence of Emotions* (Cambridge: Cambridge University Press, 2001), 19; idem, *The Therapy of Desire: Theory and Practice in Hellenistic Ethics* (Princeton, NJ: Princeton University Press, 1994); Robert C. Roberts, *Spiritual Emotions: A Psychology of Christian Virtues* (Grand Rapids, MI: Eerdmans, 2007); and idem, *Emotions: An Essay in Aid of Moral Psychology* (Cambridge: Cambridge University Press, 2003).

[30] Nussbaum, *Upheavals of Thought*, 52.

concentrates my keen attention on it. When that attention is cognitively processed through to the judgment of truth, my emotions reveal my deepest values and goals not only to me but also to all attentive observers.

There is a specifically Christian consideration here. When asked which commandment was the first of all, Jesus replied: "You shall love the Lord your God with all your heart. . . . The second is this, you shall love your neighbor as yourself" (Mark 12:30–31). That injunction is widely known but perhaps not so well understood. It contains three separate injunctions: love God, love yourself, and love your neighbor as yourself. Since Aquinas, Jesus's saying has been interpreted in Christian teaching as grounding a wholly legitimate and virtuous self-love.[31] Self-love that locks me into myself and closes me off to those around me is certainly not virtuous, for it ignores all the real relationships I have in the real world. Self-love, however, that empowers me (1) to the understanding of myself and my right place in those real relationships and (2) inserts me justly and lovingly into them, is as virtuous as any love of neighbor and is, indeed, a necessary precondition for genuine love of neighbor.

We are in agreement here with Margaret Farley: "Love is the problem in ethics, not the solution."[32] It is the problem because it is frequently without content, and so we give it content. We begin with Thomas Aquinas's definition: To love is to will the good of another.[33] Love is an activity of the will, a willing of and a decision for the good of another human being. Love of another person is ecstatic; that is, in love I go out of myself to seek the good of another equal and unique self. That there are two equal selves in any loving relationship introduces the cardinal virtue of justice, defined as being "the constant and perpetual will to render each one his rights."[34] There is, therefore, in right love always an integration of love and justice. There is always, in Farley's apposite phrase, "just love."[35]

We summarize our position on the ethical significance of emotions in a passage borrowed from Hursthouse:

> 1. The virtues (and vices) are morally significant. 2. The virtues (and vices) are all dispositions not only to act, but to feel emotions, as

---

[31] See, for example, *ST* II–II, 25, 4.

[32] Margaret A. Farley, "An Ethic for Same-Sex Relations," in *A Challenge to Love: Gay and Lesbian Catholics in the Church*, ed. Robert Nugent, 93–106 (New York: Crossroad, 1983), 100.

[33] See *ST* I–II, 28, 1c.

[34] *ST* II–II, 58, 1.

[35] Margaret Farley, *Just Love: A Framework for Christian Sexual Ethics* (New York: Continuum, 2006).

*re*actions as well as impulses to action. . . . 3. In the person with the virtues, these emotions will be felt on the *right* occasions, towards the *right* people or objects, for the *right* reasons, where "right" means "correct."[36]

Emotions are ethically significant, sometimes as ethically significant as the virtues with which they are associated.

Virtue Ethics

We have just discussed virtue *theory*, which is concerned neutrally with the nature of virtue in general; in this section, we discuss virtue *ethics*, which is more an advocacy of virtue and virtuous action. In the post-Enlightenment period virtue was distrusted, largely because of anxiety over both the authenticity of virtues humanly acquired through imitation of role models and questions of divine and human agency.[37] In *After Virtue*, however, MacIntyre makes the "disquieting suggestion" that in the contemporary world the language of morality is in a state of disorder. "We possess indeed," he argues, "simulacra of morality; we continue to use many of the key expressions. But we have—very largely, if not entirely—lost our comprehension, both theoretical and practical, of morality."[38] Herdt comments that "contemporary revivers of virtue ethics, in contrast [to the distrust of virtue] have enthusiastically embraced the notion that habituation in virtue takes place within the context of a community and its practices."[39] Post-Kantian moral philosophers concentrated their attention on specific acts that are mandated by laws, rules, or consequences. Post-Tridentine Catholic moral theologians also concentrated their attention on acts mandated by laws and rules, and they created a taxonomy of *sins* arising from the violation of those laws and rules. Such an approach ignored questions of personal and social virtue, character, happiness, human flourishing. It ignored, Louis Janssens argued in an oft-quoted article, "the human *person* integrally and adequately considered."[40]

Janssens developed a personalism rooted, he argued, in the transformation in the Second Vatican Council's *Gaudium et Spes* from an exclusively

---

[36] Rosalind Hursthouse, "Virtue Ethics and the Emotions," in Statman, *Virtue Ethics*, 108.

[37] See Herdt, *Putting on Virtue*.

[38] MacIntyre, *After Virtue*, 2.

[39] Herdt, *Putting on Virtue*, 350.

[40] Louis Janssens, "Artificial Insemination: Ethical Considerations," *Louvain Studies* 8 (1980): 4.

physical and biological to a personalist interpretation of natural law. "The moral aspect of any procedure," the council decreed in that document, "must be determined by objective standards. These [are] *based on the nature of the human person and his acts*" (no. 51, emphasis added). At the same time, other philosophers and theologians, not all of them challenged by the Second Vatican Council, were also paying increasing attention to the human person—character, habits, dispositions, emotions, perceptions, judgments, and perhaps above all, the person's flourishing. Virtue ethics was coming, not so much to birth as to *re*birth, for it had already flourished in the Greece of Plato and Aristotle and in the Europe of Thomas Aquinas, not to mention in the Christian New Testament of the first centuries. We consider Christian virtue ethics at the end of this chapter.

Focus on the human person rather than on his or her acts led to the common assertion that virtue ethics focuses on *being* and *character*, the being of a personal subject, and that the deontological ethics of duty or utilitarian ethics of consequences focuses on the subject's *doing* or *actions*. That assertion is true enough, but it is not particularly clarifying of virtue ethics. If, indeed, it is understood to mean that virtue ethics ignores *doing*, it is untrue, for we expect the virtuous person to *do* or *act* virtuously. We expect the human being with the virtue of benevolence to *do* benevolent actions; we expect the human subject with the virtue of justice to *do* just actions; and so on for all the virtues. Contrary, therefore, to critics who suggest that virtue ethics does not offer ethical directions, it surely does offer rules. It offers prescriptive rules: do benevolently when benevolence is called for; do justly when justice is called for; and do them on the right occasions, toward the right people, and for the right reasons. It offers also a proscriptive rule: do not do what is mean, unjust, or dishonest. Ethical action is action according to some virtue, unethical action is action according to some vice. It is, in fact, as we argued earlier, the habitual doing of acts of benevolence, justice, and so on that first instills and then stabilizes the habits that are virtues and the actions they prescribe. Morality, John Mahoney asserts, "is ultimately in this view not about actions but about the acting subject."[41]

Rather than say, then, that virtue ethics focuses on being and character and deontological ethics focuses on action or doing, we prefer to say that virtue ethics gives precedence to being, character, and virtue over action and doing. Broadly speaking, deontological ethics holds that right action is basic in ethics and that virtue and the virtuous character are always derivative from right action. In virtue ethics the converse is the case; the

---

[41] John Mahoney, *The Making of Moral Theology: A Study of the Roman Catholic Tradition* (Oxford: Clarendon Press, 1984), 220.

virtuous person and his or her character are basic in ethics, and right action is derivative from virtue and the virtuous character. In virtue ethics
the ethical agent and that agent's character come first and ethical actions
come second; in virtue ethics, that is, action truly follows being.

In virtue ethics "the project of the moral life is to become a certain
kind of person,"[42] a virtuous person, one who, in Aristotle's language,
knows how to act and feel in ways appropriate to the circumstances. This
approach, John McDowell argues, means that the moral question of how
one should live is approached from the notion of the virtuous person, so
that the notion of right and ethical behavior "is grasped, as it were, from
the inside in."[43] The right action in any particular circumstance is what
a virtuous person would characteristically do in that circumstance. We
believe this approach to and articulation of virtue ethics are correct and
provide greater insight into and understanding of the nature of virtue ethics than the bald statement that virtue ethics is an ethics of being rather
than doing. The precedence of virtue over action in contemporary ethical
theory is no small shift. It is, in Thomas Kuhn's sense, a paradigm shift
and has led and will lead to a struggle of minds and ethics between those
committed to the older deontological ethics and those committed to the
renewed virtue ethics.[44]

That conclusion can be elucidated by a critical consideration of the
personal subject. A subject is a rational, attending, perceiving, understanding, judging, choosing, and acting person, and one who carries out these
rational operations not only on external objects but also on his or her internal self. Subjects operate freely and consciously; they are free agents,
the cause of their own actions in the sense that they have the power to
produce the results they choose, will, and intend to produce. Subjects "are
in essence self-determining beings, who act upon and through their nature
and environment to give their lives particular form. In a sense men control
their futures by becoming the kind of men they are through their present
choices and actions."[45] English poet John Donne wrote that "no man is an

---

[42] Paul Waddell, *Friendship and the Moral Life* (Notre Dame, IN: University of Notre
Dame Press, 1989), 136.

[43] John McDowell, "Virtue and Reason," *Monist* 62 (1979): 331.

[44] Thomas S. Kuhn, *The Structure of Scientific Revolutions* (Chicago: University of
Chicago Press, 1996).

[45] Stanley Hauerwas, *Character and the Christian Life: A Study in Theological Ethics*
(San Antonio: Trinity University, 1979), 18. For the turn to the subject in contemporary
philosophy and theology, see Michael Himes, "The Human Person in Contemporary Theology: Human Nature to Authentic Subjectivity," in *Introduction to Christian Ethics: A
Reader*, ed. Ronald Hamel and Michael Himes (New York: Paulist Press, 1989), 49–62;
Bernard J. F. Lonergan, *A Second Collection* (Louisville, KY: Westminster Press, 1974);
idem, *The Subject* (Milwaukee: Marquette University Press, 1968).

island";[46] no human subject/agent is a completely isolated person. We are essentially social subjects; we live and learn in a specific community and culture. From our community and culture we initially learn all sorts of meanings, including (for our purpose here) meanings of what, in general, constitutes the good and, specifically, what is the right thing to do on this occasion, toward this person, and for this right reason. In short, we learn rules and reasons for ethical or virtuous behavior. When we are children, we follow those rules to be good in the sense that we do what adults want us to do, to be praised by others, or simply, unthinkingly, and legalistically to follow the rules we have learned.[47] We can say two things about the child's "ethical" actions.

First, children act, not out of any genuine desire or intention to do good because it is the right thing to do on this occasion, toward this right person, for this right reason, but because of children's selfish desire for praise or fear of punishment. They do the right things for the wrong reasons; they are far from acting virtuously or ethically. Second, however, those less than virtuous actions learned and habitually done in their community become the dispositions and habits leading to genuine adult virtuous actions. Their habitual repetition and the child's ongoing critical attention to them, perception, understanding, and judgment of them, and personal choice of them can ultimately lead the child to do the right thing on the right occasion, toward the right person, and for the right reasons out of a personal habit or virtue. Habitually doing the right things for the right reasons shapes the child's very being and character from one that *looks like* that of a virtuous and ethical person to one that *is truly* a virtuous and ethical person.

Michael Slote raises an objection to virtue ethics and its agent-based approach. If morality is to be judged on the basis of the inner state agents have reached, if they are agents of virtuous character, does it not follow that *every* action they do will be automatically an act of virtue? In other words, does the transition from an act-based to a character-based ethics mean that "anything goes," that any and every act of the virtuous person will be automatically deemed an act of virtue? There are, we suggest, two

---

[46] John Donne, "Devotions Upon Emergent Occasions," in *The Works of John Donne*, ed. Henry Alford (London: John Parker, 1839), III, 574–75.

[47] Lawrence Kohlberg has schematically outlined the child's moral development in his two-volume work *Essays on Human Development* (New York: Harper and Row, 1981, 1984). Along with a host of contemporary ethicists, we judge Kohlberg's scheme to be too rigid and reductive. It does, however, illustrate the point we are making here. For critiques of Kohlberg and other approaches to moral education, see Sharon Parks, *Big Questions, Worthy Dreams: Mentoring Young Adults in Their Search for Meaning, Purpose, and Faith* (San Francisco: Jossey-Bass, 2000); and Owen Flanagan, *Varieties of Moral Personality: Ethics and Psychological Realism* (Cambridge, MA: Harvard University Press, 1991).

answers to this question. The first is one that Slote himself suggests.[48] Since every agent, including every virtuous agent, is endowed with free will, each is perfectly capable of choosing a variety of actions that may or may not be virtuous. Virtuous actions, not merely virtuous character states, are important. Virtue is hard to achieve. Many, acting only in imitation of virtuous models, may have the semblance of virtue, but history shows that fewer reach authentic and consistent virtue.

There is, we suggest, a second answer to the question Slote raises: the human subject adequately considered is a historical, always-developing being. Lonergan delineates what he calls "the theoretical premises from which there follows the historicity of human thought and action." They are as follows:

> (1) That human concepts, theories, affirmations, courses of action are expressions of human understanding. . . . (2) That human understanding develops over time and, as it develops, human concepts, theories, affirmations, courses of action change. . . . (3) That such change is cumulative, and (4) that the cumulative changes in one place or time are not to be expected to coincide with those in another.[49]

From these premises flows the conclusion that the meanings, values, ethical norms, virtues, and virtuous actions of one historical era or person are not necessarily the meanings of another era or person. The world, both the world free of every human intervention, the corporeal world, and the human world fashioned by socially constructed meanings, is in a permanent state of evolution. It is essentially for this reason that anyone wishing to make an ethical judgment about an action in the present on the basis of its past meaning has, at least, two facts to keep in mind.

First, the past did not know either the entire reality and development of the human person or its individual elements hidden in human biology and psychology. "If one wishes to make an objective moral judgment today," Joseph Fuchs points out, "then one cannot take what Augustine or the philosophers of the Middle Ages knew about sexuality as the exclusive basis of a moral reflection." Second, "we never simply 'have' nature or that which is given in nature." We know nature, rather, "always as something that has already been interpreted in some way."[50] The careful attention

---

[48] Michael Slote, "Agent-Based Virtue Ethics," in *Virtue Ethics*, ed. Roger Crisp and Michael Slote, Oxford Readings in Philosophy (Oxford: Oxford University Press, 1997), 243–44.

[49] Lonergan, *Method in Theology*, 325.

[50] Joseph Fuchs, *Moral Demands and Personal Obligations* (Washington, DC: Georgetown University, 1993), 36.

to, the perception, understanding, and judgment of, and the responsible decisions and choices of rational agents about *nature* are what constitutes *natural law*,[51] never simply the pure givenness of *nature* alone. In the ethical tradition, argument is never from nature alone or reason alone, but always from nature as *interpreted by* reason. For the human person subject to historicity, ethical decision making and virtuous action are always the outcome of a process controlled by reason, never the outcome of simply looking at nature.

Lonergan was convinced that something new was happening in history in the twentieth century and that, since a living ethics and virtuous life ought to be part of what was taking place in history, humans were living in a new age that required a new ethical approach. That new approach, he prophesied correctly, would be necessarily historical and empirical. His distinction between a classicist and a historical or empirical notion of culture has itself become classical. "The classicist notion of culture was normative: at least *de iure* there was but one culture that was both universal and permanent." The empirical notion of culture is "the set of meanings and values that informs a way of life. It may remain unchanged for ages. It may be in the process of slow development or rapid resolution."[52] Classicist culture is static, historical culture is dynamic, and ethics, which is necessarily part of culture, mirrors this distinction. In its classicist mode ethics is a static, permanent achievement that anyone can learn; in its historical mode it is a dynamic, ongoing process requiring a rational, attentive, perceptive, insightful, understanding, judging, and decisive human agent.

The classicist understanding, Fuchs writes, conceives of the human person as "a series of created, static, and thus definitively ordered temporal facts." The historical understanding conceives of the person as a subject in process of "self-realization in accordance with a project that develops in God-given autonomy, that is, along a path of human reason and insight, carried out in the present with a view to the future."[53] Classicist ethics sees ethical norms coming from the past as once and for all definitive; virtue norms enunciated in the fifth or sixteenth centuries continue to apply absolutely in the twenty-first century. Historical ethics sees the ethical norms of the past not as facts for uncritical acceptance but as partial insights that provide bases for critical attention, perception, understanding, judgment, and choice in the present. What Augustine and his medieval successors

---

[51] See Aquinas, *In Duo Praecepta Caritatis*, ed. Taurinem (1954), 245; John Paul II, *Veritatis Splendor*, nos. 40, 42, 44; Martin Rhonheimer, *Ethics of Procreation and the Defense of Human Life*, ed. William F. Murphy, Jr. (Washington, DC: Catholic University of America Press, 2010), 3–7.

[52] Lonergan, *Method in Theology*, xi.

[53] Fuchs, *Moral Demands and Personal Obligations,* 39.

knew, for instance, about human sexuality cannot be the exclusive basis for a moral judgment about sexuality today. Contemporary theologians say that subjects-in-history, along with their virtues and ethics, are ineluctably eschatological. Poet Rainer Maria Rilke, perhaps, says it best: "Just keep going. No feeling is final."[54]

Christian Virtue Ethics

We have argued that virtue, virtue ethics, and the learning of both are rooted in some community and culture, and up to this point we have been developing a virtue ethics rooted broadly in human community. We have, that is, been developing a natural virtue ethics. We turn our attention now briefly to a Christian virtue ethics, one rooted in the belief that Jesus of Nazareth is the Christ and the revelation of God.[55] In the 1970s some Catholic theological ethicists were tempted to argue that Christian ethics was not distinctively different from natural ethics.[56] They meant by that claim that virtuous actions were the same in both natural and Christian ethics. We, and most Christian ethicists today, do not accept their argument. Those earlier ethicists were locked into an ethics that focused only on acts as ethical or unethical, and they meant that natural ethics and Christian ethics held many of the same actions as ethical. We grant that many of the virtues and the ethical acts they demand and enable are the same in natural and Christian ethics, but the community in which Christians learn virtues, the plethora of role models they have for the imitation and habituation of virtuous actions, the proximate and final ends to which their virtuous actions tend, the vision out of which they are done, all are entirely different in natural and Christian ethics. That, we submit, creates differences between natural and Christian ethics.

The Christian vision, which controls our subsequent discussion, shines out throughout the New Testament, but we call attention to two specific texts, one in the conclusion to the parable of the Good Samaritan, the other

---

[54] Rainer Maria Rilke, "Let Everything Happen," *The Book of Hours: Love Poems to God*, trans. Anita Barrows and Joanna Macy (New York: Riverhead, 1996), I, 59.

[55] For modern treatments of Christian virtue ethics, see Joseph J. Kotva, Jr., *The Christian Case for Virtue Ethics* (Washington, DC: Georgetown University Press, 1996); William C. Spohn, *Go and Do Likewise: Jesus and Ethics* (New York: Continuum, 1999); James F. Keenan, "Proposing Cardinal Virtues," *Theological Studies* 56 (1995); Daniel J. Harrington and James F. Keenan, *Jesus and Virtue Ethics: Building Bridges between New Testament Studies and Moral Theology* (Lanham, MD: Sheed and Ward, 2002); and *Paul and Virtue Ethics: Building Bridges between New Testament Studies and Moral Theology* (Lanham, MD: Rowman and Littlefield, 2010).

[56] See Norbert J. Rigali, "On Christian Ethics," *Chicago Studies* 10 (1971): 227–47.

in Paul's letter to the Philippians. After offering his parable of the happenings on the road from Jerusalem to Jericho, Jesus asks the lawyer who initiated the discussion, "Which of these do you think proved neighbor to the man who fell among robbers?" The lawyer answered, "The one who showed mercy on him." And Jesus said to him, "Go and do likewise" (Luke 10:36–37). That "go and do likewise" controls everything ethical that Christians are called to do; in every situation do what Jesus would do. Paul articulated this same vision in slightly different language: "Have this mind among yourselves which is yours in Christ Jesus, who though he was in the form of God did not count equality with God a thing to be grasped, but emptied himself, taking the form of a servant, being born in the likeness of men" (Phil 2:5–7). Self-sacrificing love for God and neighbor and obedience to God's known will specifically distinguish the person the Christian is called to be.

Virtue ethics, we have argued, offers an answer to the question, Who am I to become? The New Testament invites the followers of Jesus to *become* like Jesus and, because they *are* like him, to *do* like him. The controlling principle of Christian virtue ethics is the imitation of Christ: first, *be* like Jesus, and then *do* like Jesus. That principle founds a specifically Christian virtue ethics. Note that it is, as is all virtue ethics, agent centered; who Christians are called to be takes precedence over what they are called to do. The imitation of Christ is not some means external to character that makes being and doing like Christ possible; it is something that is an internal, essential constituent of the specifically Christian character. Christians act out of their "heart" (e.g., Matt 5:8, 28; 6:21; 12:34, 40; 13:15; 15:8, 18, 19; 22:37), in Jewish anthropology the zone of "intelligence, mind, wisdom, folly, intention, plan, will, affection, love, hate, sight, regard, blindness."[57] Consideration of the "heart" leads us immediately to the virtue Thomas Aquinas called "the mother and root of all virtues,"[58] namely, charity or self-sacrificing love. In the Christian vision there is no other virtue greater than charity or self-sacrificing love, for all other virtues are informed or, as Aquinas says, "quickened," by charity and receive from charity their full complement as virtues. Virtues, we already explained, are both means to and constituents of human flourishing.

Charity, the *Catechism of the Catholic Church* teaches, "is the theological virtue by which we love God above all things for his own sake, and our neighbor as ourselves for the love of God" (no. 1822). Faith, the *Catechism* teaches, "is the theological virtue by which we believe in God

---

[57] Bruce, J. Malina, *The New Testament World: Insights from Cultural Anthropology* (Louisville, KY: Westminster/John Knox, 1993), 74.

[58] *ST* I–II, 62, 4.

and believe all that he has said and revealed to us" (no. 1814). Paul insisted on the necessity of theological faith for salvation (Rom 1:16–17; 3:26–30; 5:1; Gal 3:6–9), and that theological tradition flowered on both sides of the Reformation controversies. Another difference appears here between natural and Christian ethics: the natural person practices virtue according to reason; the Christian practices virtue through reason quickened by both faith in Christ and charity. Hope, the *Catechism* teaches, "is the theological virtue by which we desire the kingdom of heaven [or God] and eternal life as our happiness, placing our trust in Christ's promises" (no. 1817). Hope, too, must issue in action. There is a critical caveat to which we must attend when we talk of virtues, even God-infused virtues, and their contribution to supernatural flourishing or happiness. All virtues, including the three theological virtues, are dispositions or habits[59] ordered to acts.[60] A virtue is a necessary prerequisite to its corresponding act, but it is not the act nor does it ineluctably lead to the act. Translation from the virtue to the act requires an agent to be rational, attentive, insightful, understanding, judging, and decisive, and again it is only at the point of judgment, decision, and action that ethics enters in. The Catholic tradition holds that the virtues of love, faith, and hope are infused by God into the new Christian at baptism, hence they are *theo*logical virtues, but for any of them to become personal acts of love, faith, or hope they must be translated by the believer into free and therefore ethical action.

Besides the three infused virtues, Christians list four cardinal virtues, cardinal because they are hinges around which all other human virtues turn. They are prudence, justice, fortitude, and temperance. Prudence, Aquinas argues, is a special virtue[61] by which "right reason is applied to action."[62] Prudence is a virtue of the practical intellect that discerns and applies universal principles to particular situations and enables agents to make practical judgments that this is the right thing to do on this occasion, toward this right person, and for this right reason. The pivotal position of prudence can be seen by a consideration, again, of the parable of the Good Samaritan. The Samaritan finds the injured man on the road; it appears that this is the right occasion and the injured man is the right person for the Samaritan to exercise compassion for the right reason. It is the task of prudence to go through the rational process to reach the judgment and decision that this is, indeed, the right occasion, the right person, and the right reason for compassion. Prudence here controls the right exercise of compassion; it similarly controls the right exercise of all other virtues. It

---

[59] *ST* III, 69, 4.
[60] *ST* I–II, 49, 3.
[61] *ST* II–II, 47, 5.
[62] *ST* II–II, 47, 2.

is because prudence controls the practical judgments that precede the exercise of all virtues that Aristotle and Aquinas hold that without it no other virtuous state or action can be achieved. Prudence is crucially important for both the natural and the Christian agent.

Aquinas defines justice as "the perpetual and constant will to render to each one his right."[63] Justice is essentially about equality,[64] from the natural point of view equality as human, from the Christian perspective that, too, but also equality as child of God. Aristotle writes that "justice is often thought to be the greatest of virtues,"[65] and Aquinas agrees. Justice, he writes, "excels the other *moral* virtues," and it excels them for two reasons: first, it is "in the more excellent part of the soul, viz. the rational appetite or will;" second, "justice is somewhat the good of another person."[66] Jesus condemns the scribes and Pharisees because, he judges, they "have neglected the weightier matters of the law, justice and mercy and faith" (Matt 23:23). The virtuous or excellent Christian, thus far in our analysis, is the one who *is* prudent and just and *does* prudent and just acts quickened by charity.

Fortitude and temperance are cardinal virtues required to clear away difficulties for the practice of other moral virtues. Fortitude, which also goes by the name of courage, the *Catechism* teaches, "is the moral virtue that ensures firmness in difficulties and constancy in the pursuit of the good" (no. 1808). It strengthens an agent to overcome obstacles that present themselves to the practice of the virtues and the ethical life. Humans easily understand physical fortitude or courage in the face of physical challenge, but Aquinas emphasizes fortitude of mind, which is required in the face of intellectual, emotional, and sometimes even physical difficulties. Every virtuous act hinges on a prior act of mental fortitude; that makes fortitude a cardinal virtue. Temperance, the *Catechism* teaches, "is the moral virtue that moderates the attraction of pleasures and provides balance in the use of created goods" (no. 1809). Temperance is about balance, the mean between excess and defect that prudence finds to indicate where, on this particular occasion, virtue lies. Temperance, quickened by charity and illuminated by prudence, clears the way for balanced virtuous acts and is a cardinal virtue.

Jesuit James Keenan offers an alternative list of cardinal virtues based on "rightly realizing the ways that we are related." "Our identity," he

---

[63] *ST* II–II, 58, 1 and 11.

[64] See Paul Ricoeur, "Love and Justice," in *Radical Pluralism and Truth: David Tracy and the Hermeneutics of Religion*, ed. Werner G. Jeanrond and Jennifer L. Rike (New York: Crossroad, 1991), 195. Ricoeur argues that from Aristotle to Rawls justice has always been about equality.

[65] *NE* V, 1, 1129b, 27.

[66] *ST* II–II, 58, 12, emphasis added.

argues, "is relational in three ways: generally, specifically, and uniquely."[67] For a reason that will become apparent, we prefer to name a different trinity: generally, particularly, and *self*ishly. In general, we are beings in relation to other beings who, as humans, are our equals and, as Christians, are equal children of God. This essential human and religious equality demands the virtue of justice as we have explained it. Specifically, we are in relation to particular persons with bonds of family or friendship. Christians, the letter to Timothy instructs, are to provide for these particular persons, and "especially for family members" (1 Tim 5:8). We are, of course, in general, Augustine specifies, to love all within our reach,[68] but we are, Aquinas further specifies, to love those nearest to us most of all.[69] Justice is about universality and impartiality; fidelity is about legitimate particularity and partiality. John Henry Newman endorses legitimate partiality when he argues that "the best preparation for loving the world at large, and loving it duly and wisely [under the guidance of prudence], is to cultivate an intimate friendship and affection toward those who are immediately about us."[70] All these relationships demand the virtue of fidelity and its cognates, loyalty and constancy.

Each of us is also in essential relationship to our self; we are in a relationship that is *self*ish and/or self-loving. Everything we said earlier about the Christian legitimacy of self-love recurs here, and this legitimate and ethical virtue of self-love demands what Keenan calls the virtue of self-care. Self-care includes self-awareness, self-knowledge, self-acceptance, and self-love. Psychological studies repeatedly indicate that one of the greatest threats to healthy human flourishing is poor self-esteem[71] and, despite Jesus's injunction to "love your neighbor *as yourself*" (Mark 12:31), the Christian tradition has not been a noted promoter of healthy self-love.[72] Self-care is the virtue that permits healthy self-love and invites reflection on my unique self as a gift of God that summons me to recognize, accept, appreciate, and use that gift in the Christian task of drawing closer in self-sacrificing love to neighbor and to God. The three virtues of justice,

---

[67] Harrington and Keenan, *Jesus and Virtue Ethics*, 122, 123.

[68] Augustine, *The City of God*, trans. Marcus Dods (New York: Modern Library, 1994), 693.

[69] *ST* II–II, 26, 6, 7, and 8.

[70] John Henry Newman, *Parochial and Plain Sermons* (San Francisco: Ignatius Press, 1987), Sermon 5, 258.

[71] See Jack Dominian, "Sexuality and Personal Relationships," in *Embracing Sexuality: Authority and Experience in the Catholic Church*, ed. Joseph Selling (Burlington, VT: Ashgate, 2001), 13.

[72] In "Proposing Cardinal Virtues," Keenan eschews self-love and self-esteem in favor of self-care (727). We have no problem with the notion of self-love as we have explained it.

fidelity, and self-care, neither of which precedes the others in importance, clear the ground for the practice of other virtues in each relationship. They are, that is, Keenan argues, cardinal virtues. They are, however, all preceded in importance by a fourth cardinal virtue, prudence, which discerns and judges which acts qualify as just, faithful, and self-caring, just as it discerns and judges which acts are just, courageous, and temperate for the traditional cardinal virtues. Whether one numbers the cardinal virtues with the Catholic tradition or with Keenan, it remains critical that they be habituated by repeated exercise in imitation of role models respected in one's community of meaning.

It is inevitable that different groups of rational human beings, and different individuals within those groups, attending, perceiving, understanding, judging, and deciding through different perspectives, will derive different interpretations of nature and ethical obligation deriving from nature, and that any given interpretation may be right or wrong. That is a fact that has been demonstrated time and again in history, including Christian history,[73] and it is also a fact taken for granted in the sociology of knowledge. Alfred Schutz, one of the founders of that discipline, presents its taken-for-granted principle: "It is the *meaning* of our experiences and not the *ontological structure* of the objects which constitutes reality."[74] "The potter, and not the pot," Alfred North Whitehead adds metaphorically, "is responsible for the shape of the pot."[75] Nature is void of meaning, a quality that does not inhere in objects but is assigned to them by social and rational beings in interpretive acts.

For all their different perspectives, however, the great ethical systems reach conclusions that are not as different as is frequently supposed. They all agree broadly on core ethical values, norms, and behaviors, as evidenced by their various, and uncommonly similar, versions of the Golden Rule. For Christians it is, "In everything do to others as you would have them do to you; for this is the law and the prophets" (Matt 7:12); for Jews, "What is hateful to you do not do to your fellowman. This is the entire Law; all the rest is commentary" (Talmud, Shabbat, 3id); for Muslims, "No one of you is a believer until he desires for his brother that which he desires for himself" (Sunnah); for Buddhists, "Hurt not others in ways that you yourself would find hurtful" (Udana-Varga 5,1); for Hindus, "This is the sum of duty. Do not unto others that which would cause you pain if

---

[73] See John T. Noonan, Jr., *A Church That Can and Cannot Change: The Development of Catholic Moral Teaching* (Notre Dame, IN: University of Notre Dame Press, 2005); Michael G. Lawler, *What Is and What Ought to Be* (New York: Continuum, 2005), 127–29.

[74] Alfred Schutz, *Collected Papers* (The Hague: Martinus Nijhoff, 1964–67), I, 230.

[75] Alfred North Whitehead, *Symbolism: Its Meaning and Effect* (New York: Capricorn Books, 1959), 8.

done to you" (Mahabharata 5, 1517). The saints in these various religious traditions, the virtuous persons to be imitated for the habituation of virtue, all endorse and exhibit a common core of behaviors. Since action follows being, it is easy to conclude to similar character states and virtues that are shaped and limited, but in no way nullified, because they derive from different perspectives.

Conclusion

We conclude this chapter by considering our slides, mentioned in the Introduction, to demonstrate how a virtuous perspective allows different responses to an ethical issue. Recall our third slide in each biomedical and sexual ethics, that is, Terri Schiavo and artificial nutrition and hydration (ANH), and a homosexual couple marrying. People can espouse perspectivism, which defines the good as human dignity and yet, guided by different virtues or even the same virtues, come to a different conclusion on the above ethical issues. For example, in the case of Terri Schiavo an individual may focus on the virtue of justice, rendering a person her due, to judge that removing Terri from ANH violated justice, since a person is due food and water. Another individual may focus on the virtue of prudence, the ability to reason correctly about ethical issues.[76] An essential aspect of Terri's diagnosis and prognosis is what science indicates about any permanent vegetative state, the prognosis was that she would never regain the capacity to relate to others, even minimally. Given her physical condition and its relational implications, it was prudent, some conclude, to disconnect her from ANH since treatment was no longer efficacious. It could not help her regain her human capabilities for relationship.

In the case of a homosexual couple marrying, two people could focus on the same virtue, chastity, a specification of the cardinal virtue temperance, and come to different conclusions on whether same-sex marriage is right or wrong. The *Catechism of the Catholic Church* defines the virtue of chastity as follows:

[Chastity means] the successful integration of sexuality within the person and thus the inner unity of man in his bodily and spiritual being. Sexuality, in which man's belonging to the bodily and biological world is expressed, becomes personal and truly human when it is integrated into the relationship of one person to another in the

---

[76] Hursthouse, *On Virtue Ethics*, 12.

complete and lifelong mutual gift of *a man and a woman*. (no. 2337, emphasis added)

One person may focus on the entire definition of chastity and conclude that homosexual marriage is a violation of chastity because it is not between a man and a woman and is, therefore, wrong. Another person may focus on the partial definition of chastity, excluding the last phrase, "of a man and a woman" because this phrase is grounded in an exclusively heterosexual anthropology and norm, and conclude that homosexual marriage fulfills the partial definition of chastity and is, therefore, right.

Both of these examples confirm perspectivism and how different virtuous perspectives shape different normative judgments about what is right and wrong. It remains to be seen whether one perspective of partial truth is more ethically credible than another perspective of partial truth. That will be taken up later. In this chapter we focused on the nature and meaning of virtues and specifically Christian virtues and how they shape perspectives. In Chapter 3 we focus on normative ethics and how a virtuous perspective justifies a specific definition of human dignity and formulates and justifies norms for its attainment.

Questions for Reflection

- What are the three theories of normative ethics available in the contemporary world? Which do you find most practical to your life?
- What is a virtue? How is virtue learned and practiced? Virtue necessarily contains a rational, deliberative, and decisive element. When does a virtue become truly yours? Please explain and discuss.
- What role does emotion play in the practice of virtue? Can emotion be discounted in a theory of virtue ethics? Please explain and discuss.
- Explain the difference between focusing on a person's acts and on a person's being and character when forming an ethical theory? What difference, if any, does it make to an ethical theory? Which focus do you find most instructive for your ethical life?
- What do you understand by the term *theological virtue* and by the term *cardinal virtue?* Do you think that the traditional Catholic theory of cardinal virtues or James Keenan's alternative theory is more instructive for your life? Please explain.

Suggested Readings

Harrington, Daniel J., and James F. Keenan. *Jesus and Virtue Ethics: Building Bridges between New Testament Studies and Moral Theology.* Lanham, MD: Sheed and Ward, 2002

———. *Paul and Virtue Ethics: Building Bridges between New Testament Studies and Moral Theology*. Lanham, MD: Rowman and Littlefield, 2010.

Kotva, Joseph J., Jr. *The Christian Case for Virtue Ethics*. Washington, DC: Georgetown University Press, 1996.

MacIntyre, Alasdair. *After Virtue.* Notre Dame, IN: University of Notre Dame Press, 1984.

Snow, Nancy E. *The Oxford Handbook of Virtue*. Oxford: Oxford University Press, 2018.

Spohn, William C. *Go and Do Likewise: Jesus and Ethics.* New York: Continuum, 1999.

Statman, Daniel, ed. *Virtue Ethics: A Critical Reader*. Washington, DC: Georgetown University Press, 1997.

3

Normative Ethics

Learning Objectives

- Define the Wesleyan Quadrilateral and its significance for Christian ethics.
- Explain scripture and its interpretation as a source of ethical knowledge.
- Explain tradition as a source of ethical knowledge.
- Explain science/reason as a source of ethical knowledge.
- Explain experience as a source of ethical knowledge.
- Understand how a virtuous perspective affects the selection, interpretation, prioritization, and integration of the sources of ethical knowledge to define human dignity and to formulate and justify norms that facilitate its attainment.

In this chapter we address two related questions. The first is the question of the sources of ethical knowledge; the second is the related question of the selection, interpretation, prioritization, and integration of these sources from a virtuous perspective. By common theological and ecumenical agreement the sources of Christian ethical knowledge are found in what is called the Wesleyan Quadrilateral, four established sources of Christian ethical knowledge, namely, scripture, tradition, reason/science, and human experience. In this chapter we employ the Quadrilateral both to respond to the Second Vatican Council's call for the renewal of Catholic theological ethics and to propose a Catholic virtuous-perspective method for the twenty-first century.

Sources for a Catholic Ethical Method

We employ the Quadrilateral for four reasons. First, it includes the sources of ethical knowledge we judge essential for doing Catholic ethics, sources highlighted in various ways throughout Christian tradition. Second, these four sources are essential to every Catholic ethical method, though particular methods select, interpret, prioritize, and integrate them in their own ways. Third, there is a growing appreciation for, and specific reference to, these sources in the Catholic ethical literature from divergent normative perspectives,[1] though there remains the need for methodological discussion about the selection, interpretation, prioritization, and integration of the sources. Our discussion here seeks to clarify the sources, their use, and their integration, and to account for pluralist Catholic ethical perspectives. Fourth, use of these four sources may encourage ecumenical methodological considerations that should inform Catholic ethics and aid in the formation of a well-formed conscience.[2]

Scripture

The Second Vatican Council's *Decree on Priestly Formation (Optatam Totius)* prescribes that the scientific exposition of moral theology should be "nourished more on the teaching of the Bible" (*OT*, no. 16), because scripture, as *Dei Verbum* states, is the "very soul of sacred theology" (*DV*, no. 24). Consequently, any Catholic ethical method must integrate scripture and demonstrate how it functions in its method. When using scripture, two things need to be kept in mind. First, when investigating the role of scripture in a particular method, it is important to recognize that contemporary readers of scripture bring their own perspectives and presuppositions to the text. A crucial part of an investigation of Catholic ethics is to bring these perspectives and presuppositions to the fore in order to comprehend a particular method more fully.[3] Second, the attempt to incorporate scripture into an ethical method is akin to coherently integrating the full mystery of the divine reality to which scripture attests. As both Augustine

---

[1] Lisa Sowle Cahill, *Between the Sexes: Foundations for a Christian Ethics of Sexuality* (Minneapolis: Fortress Press, 1985), 4–7; Charles E. Curran, *The Catholic Moral Tradition Today: A Synthesis* (Washington, DC: Georgetown University Press, 1999), 47–55; Todd A. Salzman, *What Are They Saying about Roman Catholic Ethical Method?* (New York: Paulist Press, 2003).

[2] See James Gustafson, "Charles Curran: Ecumenical Moral Theologian Par Excellence," in *A Call to Fidelity: On the Moral Theology of Charles E. Curran*, ed. James J. Walter, Timothy O'Connell, and Thomas A. Shannon (Washington, DC: Georgetown University Press, 2002), 211–34.

[3] See William C. Spohn, *Go and Do Likewise: Jesus and Ethics* (New York: Continuum, 2007); Daniel J. Harrington and James F. Keenan, *Jesus and Virtue Ethics: Building Bridges between New Testament Studies and Moral Theology* (Lanham, MD: Sheed and Ward, 2002); and idem, *Paul and Virtue Ethics: Building Bridges between New Testament Studies and Moral Theology* (Lanham, MD: Rowman and Littlefield, 2010).

and Aquinas remind us, this cannot be comprehensively and definitively done. "Si comprehendis non est Deus" (if you understand, it is not God), Augustine judges.[4] Sacred scripture, a collection of diverse books from diverse times and cultures, seeks to reveal the mystery of God, but this mystery is so incomprehensibly rich that it can never be grasped in a single citation or perspective.[5]

The fullness of revelation, Christians believe, is not contained in a scriptural book. It is contained, they believe, in a person, the person of Jesus the Christ, who even after his incarnational revelation remains a mystery. The project of developing an ethical method cannot be content to live with mystery, and as a result, there is a fundamental tension between the truths contained in scripture and how those truths are used in Christian ethics. Christian ethics will never contain the fullness of revelation, no more than does Christian scripture, though it can reflect certain parts of that revelation that, while no doubt important and foundational, do not tell the whole story. The use of scripture in Catholic ethics is similar to viewers at the fourth story, thirteenth story, and twentieth story windows of a skyscraper; each gets a different and only partial view of the total panorama that unfolds outside the building. The richness of scripture and the mystery to which it attests defy full human comprehension, though there are methodological guidelines from magisterial documents for interpreting it.

In his 1943 encyclical *Divino Afflante Spiritu (Inspired by the Holy Spirit)*, Pope Pius XII laid the foundation for the methodological integration of scripture into ethical method by endorsing the historical-critical method for its interpretation. This method was reaffirmed by the Second Vatican Council's *Dei Verbum*, which prescribes that scriptural texts are to be read in the "literary forms" of the writer's "time and culture" (no. 12). The Pontifical Biblical Commission's *The Interpretation of the Bible in the Church* continues this line, teaching that "Holy Scripture, in as much as it is 'the word of God in human language,' has been composed by human authors in all its various parts and in all the sources that lie behind them. Because of this, its proper understanding not only admits the use of [the historical-critical] method but actually requires it."[6] The commission insists that "the scientific study of the Bible requires as exact a knowledge as possible of the social conditions distinctive of the various milieus in which the traditions recorded in the Bible took shape."[7] An authentic

---

[4] Augustine, *Sermo* 52, c. 6, 16, *PL* 38, 360.

[5] See Karl Rahner, *Foundations of Christian Faith: Introduction to the Idea of Christianity* (New York: Seabury, 1978), 44–81.

[6] Pontifical Biblical Commission, "Interpretation of the Bible in the Church," *Origins* (January 6, 1994): 500 (I, A).

[7] Ibid., 506 (I, D, 1).

Catholic approach to reading biblical texts could not be clearer: it is to be done using a historical-critical methodology.

Of particular relevance to this book is the commission's application of its principles for biblical exegesis to Catholic theological ethics. Though the Bible is God's word to the church, this does not mean that God has given the historical conditioning of the message a value which is absolute. It is open both to interpretation and being brought up to date.

> It is not suffient, therefore, that the Old Testament should indicate a certain moral position (e.g., the practice of slavery or divorce; or that of extermination in the case of war) for this position to continue to have validity. One has to undertake a process of discernment. This will review the issue in the light of the progress in moral understanding and sensitivity that has occurred over the years.[8]

It is for these same reasons that Joseph Fuchs can assert correctly that what Augustine, Aquinas, and the Council of Trent said about ethical behavior cannot exclusively control what theological ethicists say today.[9] One must understand, judge, and apply scripture according to the signs of the times in dialogue with the other sources of moral knowledge, all in a particular historical-cultural context.

Discovering what scripture says about ethics, therefore, is never as straightforward as simply reading a text. The reader must "get behind" the text to understand how the church and its theologians interpret scripture and apply it to contemporary ethical issues. The Second Vatican Council issued instruction on how the scriptures of both Testaments are to be read:

> Those who search out the intentions of the sacred writers must, among other things have regard for "literary forms." For truth is proposed and expressed in a variety of ways, depending on whether a text is history of one kind or another, or whether its form is that of prophecy, poetry, or some other type of speech. The interpreter must investigate what meaning the sacred writer *intended to express and actually expressed* in particular circumstances as he used contemporary literary forms in accordance with the situation of his own time and culture. (*DV*, no. 12, emphasis added)

---

[8] Ibid., 519 (III, D, 3).
[9] Joseph Fuchs, *Moral Demands and Personal Obligations* (Washington, DC: Georgetown University Press, 1993), 36.

It is never enough simply to read a scriptural text to find out what it says about Christian ethics. Its original socio-historical context must first be clarified, and then the text can be translated, interpreted, and applied in a contemporary context.[10]

Tradition

The second source of ethical knowledge is tradition, and it is intrinsically related to scripture. Scripture and tradition, indeed, are but one source of divine revelation, because the New Testament is itself the tradition of the earliest Christian communities. Scripture was written in a particular time and place for a particular people and may be said to be secondary revelation as the early Christian community's written interpretations of the primary revelation, God's self-communication in the person of Jesus the Christ. The word *tradition* is used with two meanings. It can mean both the handing on of the church's continuing interpretation of the primary revelation in Jesus and the theological content that is handed on. That content is believed in faith by Catholics and the word *faith* is also used with two meanings. It can mean both the act of faith, actually believing the content of tradition, as well as the content that is believed. There are fundamental truths contained in tradition, Trinity and incarnation, for example, and Catholics believe them, but our *understanding* of even these believed truths develops in light of contemporary advances in history, culture, reason, knowledge, and experience. This evolution takes place not only in dogmatic truths but also in ethical truths and praxis, which also evolve and develop in light of advances in ethical questions and challenges. Under the guidance of the Holy Spirit, tradition interprets and applies the primary revelation in Jesus and the secondary revelation in scripture in ever new and contextually appropriate ways.

Since the impact of tradition on theological ethics is extensive and warrants far greater treatment than we can provide here, we narrow our investigation of that impact to what Sandra Schneiders presents as three meanings of tradition: foundational gift, content, and mode.[11] *Foundational gift* is the unfolding experience of the church in history under the guidance of "the Holy Spirit who is the presence of the risen Jesus making the church the Body of Christ."[12] All Catholic ethical methods accept tradition

---

[10] Daniel J. Harrington and James F. Keenan do this in *Jesus and Virtue Ethics* and *Paul and Virtue Ethics*.

[11] Sandra Schneiders, *The Revelatory Text: Interpreting the New Testament as Sacred Scripture* (San Francisco: Harper, 1991; Collegeville: Liturgical Press, 1999), 72.

[12] Ibid.

as foundational gift, but they can fundamentally disagree over who in the church is *gifted* to discern and interpret that gift and the criteria for determining that *giftedness*, often referred to as charism.[13] In his 1906 encyclical *Vehementer Nos*, Pope Pius X established the Catholic approach prior to the Second Vatican Council in the 1960s. The church, he taught, "is essentially an unequal society, that is, a society comprising two categories of persons, the Pastors and the flock, those who occupy a rank in the different degrees of the hierarchy and the multitude of the faithful." This pyramidal structure of the church, he went on to teach, means that only clerics of the various ranks are gifted to interpret and teach both tradition and faith and "the one duty of the multitude is to allow themselves to be led and, like a docile flock, to follow the Pastors" (no. 8). This pyramidal structure predominated in the Catholic Church from the eleventh century until the Second Vatican Council.

Richard McCormick notes, however, that even in the documents of the council there are unresolved theological tensions,[14] which are evident in different passages within the same document describing who are the gifted for discerning ethical truth. *Lumen Gentium,* for instance, follows the lead of Pius X in one section, teaching the following: "Bishops who teach in communion with the Roman Pontiff are to be revered by all as witnesses of divine and Catholic truth; the faithful, for their part, are obliged to submit to their Bishops' decision, made in the name of Christ, in matters of faith and morals, and to adhere to it with a ready and respectful allegiance of mind" (*LG,* no. 25). In this passage those who are gifted to teach are bishops in communion with the pope; the faithful are gifted to accept and obey episcopal teaching.

Lumen Gentium, however, in another section teaches that the entire people of God, bishops and laity alike, are gifted to discern both dogmatic and moral truth. "The whole body of the faithful who have an anointing that comes from the holy one . . . cannot err in matters of belief. This characteristic is shown in the supernatural appreciation of the faith *(sensus fidei)* of the *whole* people, when, 'from the Bishops to the last of the faithful' they manifest a universal consent in matters of faith and morals" (no. 12, emphasis added). This gifting of the "whole people" is further affirmed in *Gaudium et Spes* and other council documents on the nature and authority of conscience. "*Sensus Fidei* in the Life of the Church," a 2014

---

[13] See Todd A. Salzman and Michael G. Lawler, "Theologians and the Magisterium: A Proposal for a Complementarity of Charisms through Dialogue," *Horizons* 36 (2009): 7–31.

[14] Richard A. McCormick, *The Critical Calling: Reflections on Moral Dilemmas since Vatican II* (Washington, DC: Georgetown University Press, 1999), 103.

document from the International Theological Commission, an arm of the Congregation for the Doctrine of the Faith (CDF), teaches that *sensus fidei* is "a sort of spiritual instinct that enables the believer to judge spontaneously whether a particular teaching or practice is or is not in conformity with the Gospel and with apostolic faith" (no. 49). That instinct enables all believers both "to recognize and endorse authentic Christian doctrine and practice and to reject what is false," and "to fulfill their prophetic calling" (no. 2). The document repeats *Lumen Gentium*'s teaching that through this spiritual instinct "the holy People of God shares in Christ's prophetic office," and that "the body of the faithful as a whole, anointed as they are by the Holy One (cf. Jn 2:20, 27), cannot err in matters of belief."

Discerning who are gifted in the church has implications for Schneider's second meaning of tradition, namely, *content*. Content is "the sum total of appropriated and transmitted Christian experience, out of which Christians throughout history select the material for renewed syntheses of faith."[15] The content of tradition is drawn from scripture, church fathers, councils, encyclicals and official teachings of the magisterium, the ongoing theological reflection within the church in dialogue with culture, science, experience, and *sensus fidei*, "the instinctive capacity of the whole church to recognize the infallibility of the Spirit's truth."[16] The content from these sources must be critically selected, understood, and interpreted for its ongoing truth and usefulness for the present moral life of the church, using the same historical-critical method that is used for understanding and interpreting scripture. If found not useful for advancing Catholic ethical life, traditional content may be renewed, as was the traditional content related to the denial of the right to religious freedom, or it may be discarded, as was the traditional content related to slavery.

Judging who is gifted in the people of God, who has the authority to discern, interpret, and transmit the content of ethical truth, and the type of content that is transmitted, are all intrinsically linked to Schneider's third meaning of tradition, *mode*. Mode is the way "that content is made available to successive generations of believers, the way in which the traditioning of the faith is carried on throughout history."[17] Mode is congruous with tradition, the infrastructure and process for handing on lived faith. The point is frequently made that how one understands the role of the teaching authority within the church is intimately linked with one's ecclesiology, or

---

[15] Schneiders, *The Revelatory Text*, 72.

[16] John E. Thiel, *Senses of Tradition: Continuity and Development in the Catholic Faith* (Oxford: Oxford University Press, 2000), 47.

[17] Schneiders, *The Revelatory Text*, 72.

how one understands the nature of church.[18] One's ecclesiology is central
to how one understands tradition as mode and the role and function of the
magisterium in relation to the rest of the people of God, theologians and
faithful.

Since the Second Vatican Council, Catholic theologians have generally
adhered to one of two fundamentally different ecclesiological models.
The model that predominated in the second millennium is a hierarchical
model, according to which the content of revelation and tradition flows
downward from the magisterium to the faithful. The role and function of
theologians in this model is to make clear to the faithful the teaching of
the magisterium, but not to question or challenge that teaching.[19] Experience and *sensus fidei* are both sources of ethical knowledge, but it is for
the magisterium to determine how those sources are to be selected, interpreted, prioritized, and integrated into its teaching. In cases where there
is a disparity between the faith of the people of God and the teaching of
the magisterium, as is now the case with norms prohibiting contraception,
divorce and remarriage without annulment, and homosexual activity, the
magisterium gives the definitive interpretation of the meaning of human experience for human dignity and the formulation and justification of norms
that facilitate or frustrate its attainment. If we think of this hierarchical
model as a pyramid, the magisterium is at the pinnacle of the pyramid and
is the hermeneutical key for discerning, understanding, and interpreting all
sources of ethical knowledge.

The Second Vatican Council introduced a renewed model of church
and, by implication, a renewed model of ethical epistemology, namely, a
people of God or communion model.[20] In this model, ethical knowledge
is discerned, understood, and interpreted through the people of God in its
totality—magisterium, theologians, and faithful alike. There is a trialogue
among these three groups guided by the Holy Spirit, with scripture, tradition, science, and human experience at the center of the trialogue. It is
this ongoing trialogue, always conducted in mutual charity, that moves

---

[18] See, for example, McCormick, *The Critical Calling*, 19–21, 34–45, 54–55, 163–69;
and "Some Early Reactions to *Veritatis Splendor*," in *John Paul II and Moral Theology:
Readings in Moral Theology No. 10*, ed. Charles E. Curran and Richard A. McCormick
(New York: Paulist Press, 1998), 28–30.

[19] This model is clearly reflected in Pius XII's *Humani Generis* (see, for example,
Enchiridion Symbolorum Definitionum et Declarationum de Rebus Fidei et Morum (DS),
nos. 2313–14) and more recently in the CDF's *Donum Veritatis*.

[20] For the explanation of church as communion, see Gustave Martelet, *Les idées mai-
tresses de Vatican II* (Paris: Desclée, 1966); J.M.R. Tillard, *Church of Churches: The
Ecclesiology of Church as Communion* (Collegeville, MN: Liturgical Press, 1992); Michael G. Lawler and Thomas J. Shanahan, *Church: A Spirited Communion* (Collegeville,
MN: Liturgical Press, 1995).

the pilgrim church forward in history toward a fuller knowledge, under-standing, and judgment of the truth of God's self-communication to God's human creatures. The magisterium maintains authority in this model, and there is a presumption of the truth of its teaching, but its authority is quali-fied by its role as learner as well as teacher. The faithful in general and theologians in particular can facilitate, contribute to, and sometimes even challenge non-infallible magisterial teachings in this learning-teaching process. Yves Congar, the great Catholic ecclesiologist of the twentieth century, points out that obedience to church authority is required when the church is conceived on the pyramidal, hierarchical model and that dialogue and consensus are required when it is conceived on the people of God in communion model. He adds the historical note that "it is certain that this second conception was the one that prevailed effectively during the first thousand years of Christianity, whereas the other one dominated in the West between the eleventh-century reformation and Vatican II."[21]

Science/Reason

Both soft and hard sciences aid in reflecting on, analyzing, and evaluating all forms of human experience and are essential sources of ethical knowl-edge for a well-formed conscience. Pope John Paul II states in *Familiaris Consortio* that "the Church values sociological and statistical research when it proves helpful in understanding the historical context in which pastoral action has to be developed and when it leads to a better under-standing of the truth" (*FC,* no. 5) and laments the fact that theologians have not fully utilized the sciences in exploring theological questions.[22] He also highlights the need for intense dialogue between science and theology.[23] Theology and science must enter into a "common interactive relationship" whereby, while maintaining its own integrity, each discipline is "open to the discoveries and insights of the other." Physicist Ian Barbour proposes a fourfold typology of the relationship between theology and science: conflict, independence, dialogue, and integration.[24] Particularly germane to theological ethics are dialogue and integration.

The *dialogue* typology explores parallels in method, content, and boundary questions in science and theology. It seeks out similarities and

---

[21] Yves Congar, "Reception as an Ecclesiological Reality," in *Election and Consensus in the Church,* ed. Giuseppe Alberigo and Anton Weiler, *Concilium* 77 (1962), 62.

[22] John Paul II, "The Relationship of Science and Theology: A Letter to Jesuit Father George Coyne," *Origins* 18/23 (November 17, 1988): 375–78.

[23] Ibid.

[24] Ian G. Barbour, *Nature, Human Nature, and God* (Minneapolis: Fortress Press, 2002), 1–2.

dissimilarities between the methods of each discipline that may serve and complement the method of the other. Boundary questions delimit the capabilities of each discipline and stipulate how far each may go in explanation of reality. The *integration* typology encompasses a systematic synthesis of science and religion. For natural theology the natural world is the point of departure and the goal is to deepen theological understanding by integrating theological insights from that world. For theology of nature a particular theological tradition is the point of departure and the goal is to integrate the two into a single system.[25] Barbour's dialogue and integration typologies parallel John Paul II's proposal for a "community of interchange" between theology and science to expand the partial perspectives of each to "form a new unified vision." An important caveat must be heeded, however: theology should not seek to become science and science should not seek to become theology in terms of either method or content. "Unity always presupposes the diversity and the integrity of its elements."[26] Neither science nor theology should become less itself but, rather, more itself in a dynamic interchange. Each discipline retains its own autonomy and language and yet draws knowledge and insight from the other.[27]

The unity between theology and science that John Paul II calls for has common threads with Ted Peters's hypothetical consonance model. Peters posits that consonance "indicates that we are looking for those areas where there is a correspondence between what can be said scientifically about the natural world and what is said theologically about God's creation.[28] Consonance may be either strong or weak. Strong consonance means virtual accord between theology and science. This type of consonance can be misleading, Peters suggests, because the insights of theology and science are often thoroughly dissonant. Weak consonance identifies "common domains of question-asking" and proposes hypothetical answers to these common questions. For theologians, weak consonance invites a shift away from claims to absolute truth and calls for willingness to subject theological assertions to investigation, confirmation or disconfirmation.[29]

Gavin D'Costa places John Paul II's stance on the interrelationship between science and theology "squarely within" Peters's hypothetical

---

[25] Ibid., 1–2. See also Robert John Russell and Kirk Wegter-McNelly, "Science and Theology: Mutual Interaction," in *Bridging Science and Religion*, ed. Ted Peters and Gaymon Bennett (Minneapolis: Fortress Press, 2003), 19–34.

[26] John Paul II, "The Relationship of Science and Theology," 377.

[27] Ibid. See also Michael J. Buckley, "Religion and Science: Paul Davies and John Paul II," *Theological Studies* 51 (1990): 310–24.

[28] Ted Peters, *Science, Theology, and Ethics* (Burlington, VT: Ashgate, 2003), 19.

[29] Ted Peters, "Science and Theology: Toward Consonance," in *Science and Theology: The New Consonance*, ed. Ted Peters (Boulder, CO: Westview Press, 1998), 18.

consonance, where it corresponds more closely with strong than with weak consonance.[30] D'Costa disagrees with the inferences for theology and theological method that Peters draws from strong consonance. For Peters, progress in human knowledge and understanding requires a new theological method in which inviolable theological truth claims are considered actually hypothetical and subject to ongoing illumination through the contribution of the sciences and theology in dialogue. Truth claims should never be determined by ecclesial fiat. For D'Costa, "Theology, on a Roman Catholic model, can make no 'progress' without reference to scripture, tradition, and ecclesial authority. In practice, 'progress' may sometimes be hampered by authority and sometimes be wisely guided by it.[31]

We argue that D'Costa's defense of strong consonance and critique of Peters is correct in one sense and incorrect in another. He is correct to the extent that, in the ongoing discernment of truth, theology must certainly utilize scripture and tradition, but it must, we argue, also utilize science and human experience in dialogue with ecclesial authority. Peters would certainly accept the revelatory aspects of theology and its contribution to consonance both methodologically and in terms of content, including its need to dialogue with ecclesial authority. What he is rejecting is another model of the relationship between science and theology, namely, *ecclesiastical authoritarianism*. This authoritarianism, which perceives science as a threat, is evident throughout history but especially in the post-Enlightenment period. Peters does not reject theological method per se. What he rejects is ecclesiastical authority "sailing past the port" of science in the same way that D'Costa would reject theology "sailing past the port" of scripture, tradition, and ecclesial authority. In light of the historical record of ecclesiastical suspicion of the contributions of science, especially if those contributions challenge the truth claims of magisterial ethical teaching, D'Costa's view of ecclesiastical authority as a wise guide on the incorporation of science into theology might be overly optimistic. On occasion, the Galileo case, for instance, church authority has been more a flight from critical realism into an uncritical realism.

On moral issues such as artificial nutrition and hydration and the permanent vegetative state patient,[32] population control and contraception,[33]

---

[30] Gavin D'Costa, *Theology in the Public Square: Church, Academy, and Nation* (Oxford: Blackwell Publishing, 2005), 209.

[31] Ibid., 211.

[32] See Kevin O'Rourke, OP: "Reflections on the Papal Allocution Concerning Care for Persistent Vegetative State Patients," *Christian Bioethics* 12 (2006): 92.

[33] See Todd A. Salzman and Michael G. Lawler, "Experience and Moral Theology: Reflections on *Humanae vitae* Forty Years Later," *INTAMS Review* 14 (2008): 160–62.

homosexuality and same-sex parenting,[34] and sexual anthropology, as we shall see, ecclesial authority has not always served as a wise-guide in incorporating the insights of science. The "dialogue in charity" that Pope John Paul II proposed in *Ut Unum Sint* (nos. 17, 36–39) has often been lacking when it comes to openness to exploring "inviolable truths."[35] Historically, ecclesial suspicion of the sciences and their understanding of reality as a threat gives credence to Peters's option for weak consonance. Despite Peters and D'Costa's disagreements on whether strong or weak consonance is the preferred model for the theology-science dialogue, the epistemological method for determining confirmation or disconfirmation affirmed by John Paul II, Peters, and many other theologians and scientists is *critical realism.*

Critical realism builds a bridge between science and theology in the process of discerning the meaning of reality and its implications for human flourishing. Critical realism is to be distinguished from uncritical realism. Uncritical realism "invokes the correspondence theory of truth to presume a literal correspondence between one's mental picture and the object to which this picture refers."[36] Critical realism, John Haught suggests, "maintains that our understanding, both scientific and religious, may be oriented toward a real world, whether the natural world or God, but that precisely because both the natural world and God are too colossal for the human mind to encompass, our thoughts in both science and religion are also always open to correction."[37] By definition, critical realism realizes that human understanding is perspectivist, partial, revisable, but adequate. This insight is what the theologian-scientist Bernard Lonergan labeled a historically conscious worldview, distinguishing it from a classicist worldview.

A classicist worldview asserts that natural reality is static, necessary, fixed, and universal. The anthropology formulated and the norms taught in this worldview are timeless, universal, and immutable, and the acts either prescribed or proscribed by those norms are always so prescribed or proscribed without exceptions. Historical consciousness fundamentally challenges this view of reality. In a historically conscious worldview, reality is dynamic, evolving, changing, and particular. The anthropol-

---

[34] Cf. CDF, "Considerations regarding Proposals to Give Legal Recognition to Unions between Homosexual Persons," no. 7; and Paige Averett, B. Nalavany, and S. Ryan, "Does Sexual Orientation Matter? A Matched Comparison of Adoption Samples," *Adoption Quarterly* 12 (2009): 129–51.

[35] Compare, for example, the attitude toward dialogue in Pope John Paul's *Ut Unum Sint* and the CDF's *Donum Veritatis*. See Salzman and Lawler, "Theologians and the Magisterium," 7–31.

[36] Peters, *Science, Theology, and Ethics*, 24.

[37] John F. Haught, *Science and Religion: From Conflict to Conversation* (New York: Paulist Press, 1995), 20.

ogy formulated and the norms taught in this worldview are contingent, particular, and changeable, and the acts prescribed or proscribed by those norms are ethically evaluated in terms of evolving human knowledge, understanding, and circumstances. A historically conscious worldview is dependent upon critical realism; a classicist worldview is dependent upon uncritical realism.

Lonergan systematically formulates a version of critical realism. He begins by distinguishing between two kinds of objects. There is the object in the immediate exterior world, the reality that is there before anyone asks, "What is it?" and before anyone answers with a name, "It is an apple" or "It is sexual intercourse." Such an object is "already, out, there, now, real."[38] It is *already,* for it is prior to any human attention to it; it is *out,* for it is outside human consciousness; it is *there,* for it is spatially located; it is *now,* for it exists and is attended to in time; it is *real,* for it is bound up with human living and acting and so must be just as real as they are. There is also the object in the inner world mediated by meaning. This object is what becomes socially and scientifically understood and decided by the answer to the question: What is it? "To this type of object we are related immediately by our questions and only mediately by the [intellectual] operations relevant to the answers."[39] There are, in short, objects independent of any human cognitive activity and objects that are the result of human cognitive activity. The two should never be confused.

To these two meanings of the word *object* correspond two meanings of the word *objectivity*. In the world of immediacy, objectivity has one component; it is a characteristic of the object already, out, there, now, and real. In the world mediated by meaning, however, objectivity has three components. First, there is the experiential objectivity constituted by the facticity of objects that are already, out, there, now, and real. Second, there is the normative objectivity constituted by the human knowing and naming of these objects through attending, understanding, judging, and deciding about them. Third, there is the absolute objectivity that results from the combination of the two. Through experiential objectivity conditions for already, out, there, now, real objectivity are fulfilled, and through normative objectivity those conditions are truly linked by an attending, understanding, judging, and deciding subject to the object they condition. The combination yields a conditioned [object] with its conditions fulfilled and that, in knowledge, is a fact and, in reality, is a contingent being or event.[40] This same conclusion is articulated in the philosophy of science as "all facts

---

[38] Bernard J. F. Lonergan, *Insight: A Study of Human Understanding* (London: Longmans, 1958), 251.

[39] Ibid., 262.

[40] For a fuller exposition, see ibid., 375–83.

are theory-laden."[41] The eminent physicist Werner Heisenberg formulated this position as an uncertainty principle: our knowledge of reality is never exclusively objective but is always mediately conditioned by the knowing subject. The theory-laden nature of facts distinguishes critical realism from uncritical realism.

The tension between critical and uncritical realism in theological method is well illustrated in church statements on human sexuality. On the one hand, the United States' bishops have noted that "the gift of human sexuality can be a great mystery at times."[42] The acknowledgment of mystery, however, does not free theologians or the magisterium from the ongoing task of attempting to discern the human as sexual being and of determining the nature, meaning, and morality of sexuality and sexual acts in the context of human relationships. This acknowledgment of the mysterious nature of human sexuality indicates a commitment to critical realism and hypothetical consonance whereby we must be as cautious and tentative in our assertions about human sexuality as we are in our assertions about God. In spite of that mysterious nature, however, church teaching asserts absolute norms to control sexual behavior. The disconnect between human sexuality as a great mystery and sexual norms that imply an absolute understanding of that mystery reflects uncritical realism and literal correspondence between a mental picture of human sexual nature and all sexual persons to whom this picture refers. Critical realism's nonliteral picture allows normative claims for human sexuality to be subjected to experiential confirmation or disconfirmation. For example, Catholic teaching for centuries approved slavery, the owning of one human being by another, until, in John Noonan's cogent words, "the experience of unfreedom, in the gospel's light, made the contrary shine clear."[43] A similar statement could be made of its long-held doctrine condemning religious freedom, which was reversed only by the Second Vatican Council in 1965 in the *Declaration on Religious Freedom (Dignitatis Humanae)*, again due to the recognition that the experience of religious unfreedom in the clear light of the gospel and Catholic tradition "made the contrary shine clear" (*DH,* nos. 2, 9).

Continuing this theme, in light of human experience a number of absolute sexual norms taught by the Catholic Church and deduced from hypotheses on the nature of the sexual person do not seem to facilitate intelligibility in terms

---

[41] See, for example, Norwood Russell Hanson, *Patterns of Discovery: An Inquiry into the Conceptual Foundations of Science* (New York: Cambridge University Press, 1958); and idem, *Observation and Explanation: A Guide to Philosophy of Science* (New York: Harper and Row, 1971).

[42] USCCB, *Always Our Children* (Washington, DC: USCCB, 1997), no. 3.

[43] John T. Noonan, "Development in Moral Doctrine," *Theological Studies* 54 (1993): 674–75.

of understanding the mystery of human sexuality. In fact, they seem to assail much of the knowledge gained through the sciences and human experience. The disconnect between magisterial hypotheses on the nature of the sexual person and the capacity of those hypotheses to make the mysterious nature of human sexuality more intelligible reflects the tensions between uncritical realism and critical realism. This tension is evident in the sexual anthropologies that ignore, reduce, or distort the contributions of science and experience to theological discourse about human sexuality. Conservative and progressive virtuous perspectives on same-sex marriage illustrate this tension.

Human Experience

We agree with Catholic ethicist Servais Pinckaers that human experience has "a very important function in moral theology."[44] *Gaudium et Spes* emphasizes the relevance of human experience for theological reflection. Theologically interpreted human experience, of both past and present, helps to construct a definition of human dignity and to formulate and justify norms to facilitate its attainment; experience serves as a window onto the ethically normative. To deny the ethical relevance of human experience for assisting in the definition of human dignity reflects a reductionist methodology where the only legitimate human experience is that which conforms to, and confirms, established church norms. It was such a methodology, in large part, that allowed the magisterium's approbation of slavery until Pope Leo XIII's rejection of it in 1890 and its denial of religious freedom until the Second Vatican Council's approbation of it in 1965. John Noonan comments with respect to the magisterium's late condemnation of slavery: "It was the *experience* of unfreedom, in the gospel's light, that made the contrary shine clear."[45]

A legitimate question at this point is whose experience is to be used in the formulation of a definition of human dignity and in the formulation and justification of norms that facilitate its attainment? We emphasize that human experience is only one part of the Wesleyan Quadrilateral and never a standalone source of theological ethics. And my experience alone is never a source at all. Ethical authority is ecclesially granted only to *our* experience, to *communal* experience, as a source of ethics, and only in constructive conversation with the three other sources, scripture, tradition, and science/reason, as well as with the theological reality called *sensus fidei*, the sense of the faithful and their lived experience. First, however, we must clarify what we mean by *experience*.

---

[44] Servais Pinckaers, *The Sources of Christian Ethics* (Washington, DC: Catholic University of America Press, 1995), 91.

[45] Noonan, "Development in Moral Doctrine," 674–75.

There is little to be gained from simply encountering the world in which we live; many people have many such encounters and learn little from them. In the Wesleyan Quadrilateral experience means "the human capacity to encounter the surrounding world consciously, to observe it, be affected by it, and to learn from it."[46] It is of the essence of such experience that it is never a neutral encounter with the world. It is always encounter interpreted and socially constructed by both communities and individuals in specific socio-historical contexts. It is, therefore, also dialectical, differently construed, perhaps, by me, by you, by us, and by them (neo-Thomist and neo-Augustinian theologians, for instance). For genuine human experience as we have defined it, the dialectic is necessarily a "dialectic of reason *and* experience" and never a dialectic controlled by either reason or experience alone. It is also a dialectic that results not in an absolutist ethical code but in "various revisable rules."[47] In a church that is a communion of believers the resolution of different construals of experience to arrive at ethical truth requires a respectful, charitable, and prayerful dialogue, such as that lauded and rhetorically embraced by Pope John Paul II in *Ut Unum Sint* (nos. 28–39).[48] Charitable dialogue must occur internally, among the communion of believers, some of whom are laity, some of whom are theologians, and some of whom are bishops, including the bishop of Rome,[49] all of whom acquire knowledge through practice or action,[50] that is, through experience. It is important that dialogue take place also externally, among all people of good will. In the formation of conscience people are tasked to discern what human experience confirms or challenges their definition of human dignity and, correspondingly, to formulate and justify norms that facilitate its attainment.

Virtuous Perspective and the Selection, Interpretation, Prioritization, and Integration of the Sources of Ethical Knowledge

In Chapter 2 we argued that a virtuous perspective shapes the definition of human dignity and the formulation and justification of norms that facilitate

---

[46] Neil Brown, "Experience and Development in Catholic Moral Theology," *Pacifica* 14 (2001): 300.

[47] Edward Collins Vacek, "Catholic 'Natural Law' and Reproductive Ethics," *Journal of Medicine and Philosophy* 17 (1992): 342–43.

[48] See Salzman and Lawler, "Theologians and the Magisterium," 7–31.

[49] We shall use this tripartite division of believers throughout for purposes that will become apparent as we proceed.

[50] Richard Bernstein, *Beyond Objectivism and Relativism* (Philadelphia: University of Pennsylvania Press, 1985), 74.

attaining human dignity. So far in this chapter, we have explained the sources of ethical knowledge that justify that definition and those norms. In this section we bring together those insights to demonstrate how a virtuous perspective shapes the selection, interpretation, prioritization, and integration of those sources to define human dignity and formulate and justify norms, focusing on one of our two slides from the Introduction.[51]

Recall the example from our sexual ethics course of a gay couple marrying on a beach. One Catholic *virtuous perspective,* which we label a conservative perspective because its goal is to conserve traditional magisterial teaching, has a strict hierarchy in the selection, interpretation, prioritization, and integration of the sources of ethical knowledge. Tradition, narrowly defined as magisterial teaching, is the prioritized source and authority for the selection, interpretation, prioritization, and integration of the sources of ethical knowledge. The magisterium exercises its authority to determine the interrelationship among tradition, scripture, science/reason, and experience, to define human dignity, and to formulate and justify norms to facilitate its attainment. Another Catholic virtuous perspective we label a progressive perspective since, forewarned by errors in Catholic teaching in the past, it accepts tradition as a source, but not uncritically and not narrowly defined as magisterial teaching. A *progressive perspective* employs a dialectic among the four sources of ethical knowledge to uncover the truth attuned to contemporary reality that can then progress into the future as the best account of truth presently understood.

Both perspectives may accept the virtue of chastity[52] to guide their respective definitions of human dignity and the formulation and justification of norms on the issue of human sexuality in general and same-sex marriage in particular. Recall the *Catechism of the Catholic Church*'s definition of chastity: "the successful integration of sexuality within the person and thus the inner unity of man in his bodily and spiritual being. Sexuality, in which man's belonging to the bodily and biological world is expressed, becomes personal and truly human when it is integrated into the relationship of one

---

[51] We have chosen to address the issue of same-sex marriage because it more clearly demonstrates a contrast between two virtuous perspectives on the selection, interpretation, prioritization, and integration of the sources of ethical knowledge. In the case of Terri Schiavo, magisterial teaching on artificial nutrition and hydration is much more ambiguous and open to interpretation. For a discussion of ANH and magisterial teaching, see Salzman and Lawler, "Karl Rahner's Theology of Dying and Death: Normative Implications for the Permanent Vegetative State Patient," *Irish Theological Quarterly* 77, no. 2 (May 2012): 141–64.

[52] Both conservatives and progressives would no doubt include other virtues, such as the virtues listed in 1 Corinthians 13:4–7 and expanded upon in chapter four of Pope Francis's *Amoris Laetitia*. Even including these additional virtues, however, conservatives and progressives would maintain a similar anthropology and norms.

person to another in the complete and lifelong mutual gift of *a man and a woman*" (no. 2337, emphasis added). The two perspectives disagree on the final clause of that definition and its implications for their respective definitions of human dignity and the formulation and justification of norms for its attainment. A conservative perspective embraces the qualification "a man and a woman"; a progressive perspective revises and expands the qualification to "two people." We now present a conservative perspective on the selection, interpretation, prioritization, and integration of the sources of ethical knowledge and then critique that perspective from a progressive perspective.

A conservative perspective focuses on the virtue of chastity as defined by the *Catechism* and applies it to same-sex marriage anthropologically and normatively. Anthropologically, chastity defines sexual human beings heterosexually ("the complete and lifelong mutual gift of *a man and a woman*"); homosexual orientation is, therefore, an "objective disorder." Normatively, chastity defines sexual acts as ethically right only if they are reproductive sexual acts between a man and woman in marriage. Any other sexual acts—nonreproductive heterosexual acts or homosexual acts, for instance—are unethical based on that heterosexual anthropology.

Since the primary focus of a conservative virtuous perspective is to conserve the truth of magisterial teaching, it prioritizes that teaching and uses it as the prioritized source for selecting, interpreting, and integrating the other sources of moral knowledge. Consequently, we will present the magisterium's teaching as representative of the conservative perspective. Magisterial teaching on homosexual acts states the following: "Basing itself on Sacred Scripture, which presents homosexual acts as acts of grave depravity, tradition has always declared that 'homosexual acts are intrinsically disordered.' They are contrary to the natural law. They close the sexual act to the gift of life. They do not proceed from a genuine affective and sexual complementarity. Under no circumstances can they be approved" (*CCC*, no. 2357). This teaching indicates how the magisterium determines the selection, interpretation, and integration of the sources of ethical knowledge. It includes three sources: scripture, reason or natural law, and experience. We consider each in turn.

First, the magisterium's teaching prohibiting homosexual acts states that it bases itself on scripture and, since it also claims its interpretation of scripture is authoritative, its interpretation is definitive, regardless of what the other sources of ethical knowledge might indicate about the accuracy and applicability of that interpretation. Second, natural law, the human participation in eternal law through right reason, is used to justify the anthropology and norms derived from that interpretation. Natural law is interpreted in the direction of a binary, man-woman heterosexual anthropology that justifies the absolute norm that only heterosexual reproductive acts are morally right. Complementing natural law with his personalism, Pope John Paul II, in his June 29, 1995, "Letter to Women," introduces the concept of complementarity into magisterial teaching to defend both the anthropology and the norm. Complementarity signifies that two realities, man and woman in this case, are "complete" in themselves but "for forming a couple they are incomplete." John Paul further notes in his letter that "woman complements man, just as man complements woman. . . . Womanhood expresses the 'human' as much as manhood does, but in a different and complementary way" (no. 7). Affective complementarity is the crux of magisterial teaching on heterosexual complementarity that defines sexual human dignity because it intrinsically links biological and personal complementarity. Citing the *Catechism of the Catholic Church,* the CDF notes, negatively, that affective complementarity is lacking in homosexual acts and, therefore, these acts can never be approved. More positively, another conservative perspective argues that marital sexual acts of a reproductive kind are "biologically *and thus* personally one."[53] According to the magisterium's interpretation of experience, only reproductive marital sexual acts facilitate human dignity; all homosexual acts frustrate human dignity, because "they do not proceed from a genuine affective and sexual complementarity."

A progressive perspective may also focus on the virtue of chastity as defined by the magisterium but extends it to all persons of all sexual orientations by revising the final clause from "mutual gift of *a man and a woman*" to "mutual gift of *two people*," and applies it both anthropologically and normatively. Anthropologically, chastity defines sexual human beings whether they are heterosexual, bisexual, or homosexual; homosexual and bisexual orientations are as "objectively ordered" as heterosexual orientation. Normatively, chastity defines marital sexual acts as ethically right if they are integrated biologically, based on one's sexual orientation, and personally, based on just and loving reproductive or nonreproductive sexual acts between a married man and a woman, a man and a man, or a woman and a woman. How does a progressive virtuous perspective select, interpret, prioritize, and integrate the sources of ethical knowledge on this issue to justify its anthropological and normative claims?

First, the conservative perspective's use of scripture highlights an important point on the interrelationship between church teaching and scripture, a point that reflects the dialectic between the sources of ethical knowledge that a progressive perspective follows and a conservative perspective seems

---

[53] John Finnis, "Law, Morality, and 'Sexual Orientation,'" *Notre Dame Law Review* 69, no. 5 (1994): 1067, emphasis added.

to ignore. Up until the mid-twentieth century the primary use of scripture in Catholic ethical teaching was what is called proof texting; church authority would come to a conclusion about what is right or wrong on the basis of its interpretation of the natural law and then search scripture to find passages that would support this conclusion. Prior to *Gaudium et Spes*, for instance, natural law was used to justify the ethical claim that procreation was the primary end of marriage and, with the publication of *Humanae Vitae* in 1968, procreation was established as an intrinsic meaning of the sexual act. Since homosexual acts cannot procreate, they frustrate the natural procreative end of marriage and of the sexual act and, therefore, are always unethical. The magisterium would then look to scripture to justify this conclusion arrived at from its reading of natural law. There is a fundamental disconnect here, however, between this proof texting use of scripture to justify ethical claims and the historical-critical method that was introduced in the twentieth century in Pope Pius XII's encyclical *Divino Afflante Spiritu* and reinforced in the Second Vatican Council's *Dei Verbum* as the recognized Catholic method for interpreting scripture.

Based on the historical-critical method and its use to interpret and apply biblical passages that address homosexual acts, which we will explore in greater detail in Chapter 10, many biblical exegetes argue that the condemnation of male homosexual acts we find in scripture are based on a misunderstanding of sexual human dignity. Simply stated, the biblical authors had no understanding of sexual orientation when they wrote the scriptures. The term *homosexual,* in fact, did not exist until the mid-nineteenth century. Contemporary science reveals, and the magisterium now recognizes, that there are men and women of different sexual orientations—heterosexual, homosexual, and bisexual—and that an individual does not choose his or her sexual orientation. This knowledge was not available to the biblical authors. Their understanding was that those who engaged in homosexual acts were trading, in the words of St. Paul, "natural sexual relations," presumed to be heterosexual, for "shameful actions" (Rom 1:26–27). We now know that not all individuals are naturally heterosexual and, a progressive virtuous perspective argues, our contemporary experience of sexual orientation must factor into our contemporary application of scriptural passages on homosexual activity. The magisterium's interpretation of scripture as prohibiting homosexual acts rests on its claim to absolute authority to interpret scripture and to apply its interpretation to issues such as the ethics of homosexual acts. A progressive virtuous perspective argues for a broader method of interpreting scripture, a method that integrates contemporary scientific methods, such as the historical-critical method, and the contemporary experience of human sexual orientation and its anthropological and normative implications.

Second, prioritizing magisterial teaching on the immorality of homosexual acts, the conservative perspective labels homosexual orientation an "objective disorder" with a strong predisposition towards "intrinsically disordered acts." This language, however, disregards what secular disciplines of knowledge tell us about homosexual orientation. Credible science finds that homosexual orientation is not infrequent in creation. Peer-reviewed scientific literature has documented that human sexual practice has been incredibly varied across time and cultures[54] and has identified same-sex practice in over three hundred species of vertebrates as a natural component of the social system.[55] Based on such studies, James Alison, a Catholic priest and theologian, challenges the claim that a homosexual orientation is objectively disordered. "There is no longer," he judges, "any reputable scientific evidence of any sort: psychological, biological, genetic, medical, neurological—to back up the claim."[56] In fact, there is substantial scientific evidence to the contrary. In addition, it is accepted in contemporary scientific and theological literature, including the *Catechism of the Catholic Church* (no. 2358) and other magisterial documents[57] that people do not choose their sexual orientation. Sexual orientation, "the sustained erotic attraction to members of one's own gender, the opposite gender, or both—homosexual, heterosexual, or bisexual respectively,"[58] is given and not chosen. Such evidence leads evolutionary biologist Joan Roughgarden to assert the following: "To the extent that information about nature can inform theological discourse on human and biological diversity, the message for full and proper inclusion of gay, lesbian, and transgender persons is clear and unequivocal."[59]

A progressive perspective argues, based on the evidence of the contemporary sciences, that the conservative claim that homosexual orientation is objectively disordered in the ontological order is not justified. This theological claim, according to the CDF, is contingent on whether or not

---

[54] Michel Foucault, *The History of Sexuality*, 3 vols., trans. Robert Hurley (New York: Vintage Books, 1988–90).

[55] See Bruce Bagemihl, *Biological Exuberance: Animal Homosexuality and Natural Diversity* (New York: St. Martin's Press, 1999).

[56] James Alison, "The Fulcrum of Discovery Or: How the 'Gay Thing' Is Good News for the Catholic Church," talk given several times in 2009. A version is available at http://www.jamesalison.co.uk/texts/eng59.html.

[57] See, for example, USCCB, *Always Our Children*, no. 5.

[58] Richard C. Pillard and J. Michael Bailey, "A Biological Perspective on Sexual Orientation," *Clinical Sexuality* 18 (1995): 1.

[59] Joan Roughgarden, "Evolutionary Biology and Sexual Diversity," in *God, Science, Sex, and Gender: An Interdisciplinary Approach to Christian Ethics*, ed. Patricia Beattie Jung and Aana Marie Vigen, with John Anderson (Chicago: University of Illinois Press, 2010), 103.

homosexual acts are intrinsically immoral: "Although the particular inclination of the homosexual person is not a sin, it is a more or less strong
tendency ordered toward an intrinsic moral evil; *and thus* the inclination
itself must be seen as an objective disorder."[60] The central reason why
homosexual orientation is labeled as objectively disordered is because it
has a "strong tendency ordered toward an intrinsic moral evil." If it can be
established that homosexual acts are not intrinsically evil, then the claim
that homosexual orientation is objectively disordered and the conservative
anthropology on which it is based must be reconsidered.

The third source of ethical knowledge that the conservative perspective
relies on to condemn homosexual acts is experience. Homosexual acts, it
claims, providing no proof for its claim, "do not proceed from a genuine
affective and sexual complementarity" and, therefore, frustrate human
dignity. In the language of magisterial teaching, such acts are intrinsically
disordered and can never be morally justified. Scientific and theological
arguments have much to tell us about the morality of homosexual acts between homosexual couples. Regarding the judgment that homosexual acts
"do not proceed from a genuine affective and sexual complementarity" and
are therefore intrinsically disordered and frustrate human dignity, credible
social-scientific studies indicate that this is not the case. Lawrence Kurdek,
who has carried out extensive social-scientific research on gay and lesbian
couples for many years, reports that their levels of affective satisfaction
are similar to heterosexual couples.[61] A growing body of peer-reviewed
social-scientific data demonstrates that committed, stable, and justly loving
gay and lesbian unions are as personally complementary and affectively
fulfilling as heterosexual ones. Gay and lesbian acts of making just love are
as unitive as heterosexual acts of making just love. An equally impressive
body of social-scientific data shows that, contrary to magisterial claims

---

[60] CDF, "Letter to the Bishops of the Catholic Church on the Pastoral Care of Homosexual Persons," no. 3, emphasis added.

[61] Lawrence A. Kurdek, "What Do We Know about Gay and Lesbian Couples?" *Current
Directions in Psychological Science* 14 (2005): 251–54; "Differences between Partners from
Heterosexual, Gay, and Lesbian Cohabiting Couples," *Journal of Marriage and Family*
68 (2006): 509–28; "Lesbian and Gay Couples," in *Lesbian, Gay, and Bisexual Identities
over the Lifespan*, ed. Anthony R. D'Augelli and Charlotte J. Patterson (New York: Oxford
University Press, 1995), 243–61; and "Are Gay and Lesbian Cohabiting Couples *Really*
Different from Heterosexual Married Couples?" *Journal of Marriage and Family* 66 (2004):
880–900. See also Ritch C. Savin-Williams and Kristin G. Esterberg, "Lesbian, Gay, and
Bisexual Families," in *Handbook of Family Diversity*, ed. David H. Demo, Katherine R.
Allen, and Mark A. Fine (New York: Oxford University Press, 2000), 207–12; and Philip
Blumstein and Pepper Schwartz, *American Couples: Money, Work, Sex* (New York: Mor-
row, 1983).

with no supporting evidence, partnered gays and lesbians raise children to be every bit as healthy and heterosexual as the children of heterosexuals.[62]

Finally, the magisterium's narrow focus on tradition as magisterial teaching to justify its anthropological and normative claims ignores a broader tradition that includes the *sensus fidei* of virtually the whole church. Recall the church's definition of *sensus fidei*, "the instinctive capacity of the whole church to recognize the infallibility of the Spirit's truth."[63] One way to measure the *sensus fidei* is through sociological surveys that illuminate what faithful Catholics believe. According to recent surveys on same-sex marriage, 67 percent of Catholics in the United States support same-sex marriage.[64] Although it has become common for the magisterium and some conservative theologians to dismiss survey data as sociological and not theological data, and although theological ethicists do not argue for morality by majority consensus, this does not mean that there is no correlation whatsoever between sociological data and theological ethics. The sociological data correlate to and illuminate the *sensus fidei* in the church and, rightly discerned, are among the sources of ethics in the church. This data, allied to the legalization of same-sex marriage and its support throughout the United States, Canada, and Europe, indicate what many Catholics believe on this issue. Relying on tradition that includes the *sensus fidei* as a source of ethical knowledge, we must at least explore the reasons why those who support same-sex marriage do so and the reasons why those who oppose it do so. These reasons are closely linked to the contemporary definition of both the anthropological and normative good.

We have explored those reasons analyzing the virtuous conservative and progressive perspectives on the selection, interpretation, prioritization, and integration of the sources of ethical knowledge relating to same-sex marriage anthropologically and normatively. To summarize, the conservative method, reflected in magisterial teaching on sexual ethics in the pontificates of Popes John Paul II and Benedict XVI and in the scholarship of conservative philosophers and ethicists, has a strict interpretation of the selection, interpretation, prioritization, and integration of the sources of moral knowledge in which tradition, narrowly defined as magisterial teaching, is prioritized as the hermeneutical lens and authority for the selection, interpretation, prioritization, and integration of the sources of moral knowledge. In the conservative virtuous perspective, guided by its heterosexual understanding of the virtue of chastity, sexual human dignity

[62] See Todd A. Salzman and Michael G. Lawler, *Sexual Ethics: A Theological Introduction* (Washington, DC: Georgetown University Press, 2012), 173–75.

[63] Thiel, *Senses of Tradition*, 47.

[64] Pew Research Center, "Support for Same-Sex Marriage Grows, Even among Groups That Had Been Skeptical" (June 26, 2017).

is ordered if it is heterosexual, intrinsically disordered if it is homosexual; homosexual acts are held to be objectively sinful.

The progressive method, reflected in magisterial teaching on social ethics and also in sexual ethics in the pontificate of Pope Francis and in the scholarship of progressive Catholic ethicists, adopts a dialectical approach to the selection, interpretation, prioritization, and integration of the sources of moral knowledge. The sources serve to inform, critically analyze, and complement one another in the ongoing discernment of a definition of human and sexual dignity and in the formulation and justification of norms to facilitate the attainment of human dignity. In a progressive virtuous perspective, also guided by its understanding of the virtue of chastity, human sexual beings are naturally either homosexual, heterosexual, or bisexual, and homosexual or heterosexual sexual acts can be ethically justified when they are just and loving and contribute to a just and loving relationship.

Questions for Reflection

- What do you understand by the Wesleyan Quadrilateral? What is its function in Christian ethics?
- What are the contributions of Pope Pius XII's *Divino Afflante Spiritu* and the Second Vatican Council's *Dei Verbum* to reading the scriptures? What difference do they make to your understanding of the interpretation and application of scripture? What difference do they make to Christian ethics?
- What do you understand by the word *tradition*? What is the contribution of tradition to theological ethics? Who is gifted in the Catholic Church to interpret tradition? Please explain and discuss.
- What is the attitude of the Catholic Church to science? What is the difference between a classicist worldview and a historically conscious worldview? Does that make any difference to the relationship of science and theological ethics? Please explain.
- What do you understand by the word *experience*? How does experience relate to Christian ethics? Please explain and discuss.
- Compare and contrast conservative and progressive virtuous perspectives on the selection, interpretation, prioritization, and integration of the sources of ethical knowledge on same-sex marriage to define sexual human dignity and to formulate and justify norms that facilitate its attainment.

Suggested Readings

Bretzke, James T. *A Morally Complex World: Engaging Contemporary Moral Theology*. Collegeville, MN: Liturgical Press, 2004.

Farley, Margaret A. *Just Love: A Framework for Christian Sexual Ethics*. New York: Continuum, 2006.

Haught, John F. *Science and Religion: From Conflict to Conversation*. New York: Paulist Press, 1995.

Salzman, Todd A. *What Are They Saying about Roman Catholic Ethical Method?* New York: Paulist Press, 2003.

Salzman, Todd A., and Michael G. Lawler. *The Sexual Person: Toward a Renewed Catholic Anthropology,* Moral Traditions Series. Washington, DC: Georgetown University Press, 2008.

Schneiders, Sandra. *The Revelatory Text: Interpreting the New Testament as Sacred Scripture*. San Francisco: Harper San Francisco, 1991; Collegeville, MN: Liturgical Press, 1999.

4

Perspectives and Theological Ethics

Learning Objectives

- Explain the virtues of faith and justice and their interrelationship.
- Explain the virtuous principle "faith that sees injustice and does justice."
- Understand the theological perspective of liberation theology and how it seeks liberation from socioeconomic oppression for the poor and oppressed.
- Understand the theological perspective of feminist theology and how it seeks liberation from gender oppression for women (and men).
- Understand the theological perspective of black theology and how it seeks liberation from racial oppression for blacks and other minorities.
- Understand the theological perspective of LGBT theology and how it seeks liberation from sexual oppression for LGBT people.

We noted in Chapter 3 that a virtuous perspective shapes the lens for the selection, interpretation, prioritization, and integration of the four sources of ethical knowledge, and we investigated two perspectives, conservative and progressive, and the impact of these perspectives anthropologically and normatively on the evaluation of same-sex relationships. The four sources—scripture, tradition, science/reason, and experience—indicate methodological components to facilitate an ongoing, perspectival, and evolving understanding of human dignity and of the norms that facilitate its attainment. In this chapter we explore the virtuous principle of "faith that sees injustice and does justice" and how the principle has been incarnated in four theological perspectives to name and transform social injustice: liberation theology, feminist theology, black theology, and LGBT theology.

In the next chapter we explain the anthropological and normative implications of different theological perspectives. Before exploring the virtuous principle and the four theological perspectives we briefly explain two additional methodological dimensions that are foundational for shaping, developing, and analyzing them, culture and contextual theology.

Culture and Contextual Theology

The words of *Gaudium et Spes* on culture are perhaps more relevant today than ever before, with globalization highlighting the interrelationship and interdependence among human beings socially, politically, economically, and spiritually. This interrelatedness is manifested in and through the various world cultures. Humans, *Gaudium et Spes* teaches, "can come to an authentic and full humanity only through culture" (*GS*, no. 53), and culture reveals the nature of humanity itself where "new roads to truth are opened" (no. 44). The church must be in ongoing dialogue with culture to learn from it when it contributes to understanding human dignity and to challenge it when it assaults human dignity. *Gaudium et Spes* notes about that church that "from the beginning of her history, she has learned to express the message of Christ with the help of the ideas and terminology of various peoples" (no. 44); that is, through the particularities of cultural experience. The pastoral letters of the bishops of the United States on the economy and on nuclear war are examples of the dialectic between culture and the development of moral norms. The letters draw on the traditional Catholic virtues of justice and fairness to formulate culturally specific norms, but the understanding of justice and fairness they evince is articulated in light of the specific US cultural experiences to which they respond. Discerning the impact of culture on the definition of human dignity and the formulation and justification of norms to facilitate its attainment is an essential methodological consideration that allows for a plurality of anthropological and normative definitions in both social and sexual ethics.

One of the major developments in modern Catholic ethical method, one that flows out of *Gaudium et Spes*'s focus on human experience and culture as essential components for discerning ethical truth, has been the emphasis on doing theological ethics in context. Stephen Bevans defines contextual theology as "a way of doing theology in which one takes into account the spirit and message of the gospel; the tradition of the Christian people; the culture in which one is theologizing; and social change in that culture."[1] A strong tendency of theological ethics since the Second Vatican Council,

---

[1]   Stephen Bevans, *Models of Contextual Theology* (Maryknoll, NY: Orbis Books, 2002), 1.

which is reflected in contextual theology, is its focus less on the abstract universality of human nature and shared human experience and more on the concrete particularity of men and women and of their experience within particular cultures and societies. We are in full agreement with theologian Bryan Massingale when he states that "the only way to universal insights is through particular [cultural] perspectives."[2] Focus on contextual theology and particularity has led to different theological anthropologies and norms that facilitate attaining human dignity. These differences arise out of theological perspectives shaped by different cultures and experiences. After we explain the virtuous principle of faith that sees injustice and does justice, we consider four different theological perspectives.

Faith That Does Justice: A Virtuous Principle

The virtuous principle that shaped and was shaped particularly by the theological movement known as liberation theology is *faith that does justice*. Before considering this principle, we explain the two virtues themselves, faith and justice, particularly as shaped by the perspective of liberation theology, a theological movement developed by Latin American Catholic theologians who do theology from their contextual experience of social, political, and economic oppression and offer this contextual theology as a way to bring about the kingdom of God in the here and now. Liberation theology profoundly shaped subsequent theologies committed to faith that does justice.

The *Catechism of the Catholic Church* defines faith as "the theological virtue by which we believe in God and believe all that he has said and revealed to us" (*CCC*, no. 1814). "Gustavo Gutiérrez finds fault with th traditional concept of faith as assent. Rather than being a mere assent, he writes, it must be a warm welcome of the gift of the word," concretely incarnated through word and deed.[3] If it is not concretely incarnated, faith dissolves into abstract idealism and piety. It focuses, that is, on the human assent to God's promises without ever actively working toward the establishment of the kingdom of God through relationship with and responsibility for neighbor, especially the most vulnerable, poor, and marginalized neighbor.

---

[2] Bryan Massingale, "Beyond Revisionism: A Younger Moralist Looks at Charles E. Curran," in *A Call to Fidelity: On the Moral Theology of Charles E. Curran*, ed. James J. Walter, Timothy O'Connell, and Thomas A. Shannon (Washington, DC: Georgetown University Press, 2002), 258.

[3] In Avery Dulles, "Faith in Relationship to Justice," in *The Faith That Does Justice: Examining the Christian Sources for Social Change*, ed. John C. Haughey (New York: Paulist Press, 1977), 33.

Liberation theologians frequently describe faith as "the historical praxis of liberation."[4] For Gutiérrez, "history is the scene of the revelation God makes of the mystery of his person. His word reaches us in the measure of our involvement in the evolution of history."[5] The historical situation, Hugo Assman, agrees, is the primary source of ethical knowledge, above even scripture and tradition,[6] for these two sources must be viewed, interpreted, and applied through the lens of the historical and experiential lived reality of individuals in community.

Praxis is a technical term drawn from Marxism that philosophically influenced liberation theology and drew criticism from the magisterium as materialistic. Liberation theology, however, rejects those aspects of Marxism that conflict with the Catholic theological tradition, but that tradition itself, specifically *Gaudium et Spes*, encourages dialogue with all philosophical movements, ideas, and concepts that can open up new roads to truth. The Marxist concept of praxis, which refers to human actions that can transform reality and create a more human and humane world, is such a concept. For liberation theologians, praxis is action that seeks to overcome and transform social or structural sin in institutional structures, like oppression, poverty, racism, and misogyny, that frustrate human dignity. Praxis is revolutionary. While Marxists focus on praxis to change economic and social relationships, liberation theology focuses on it to transform any structural relationship that frustrates human dignity. For Marx, critical theory complements revolutionary praxis. It provides a "new consciousness" that can see and name the oppressive and alienating structures and give direction for praxis that will correct and humanize those structures.

Drawing from Marxist critical theory and praxis, liberation theology applies praxis to faith. Faith is a commitment to the word of God that enables us both to discern unjust social structures that frustrate human dignity and to envision a future that reflects the common good and incarnates the kingdom of God. Such a vision of faith is a corrective to an abstract notion of faith that is disengaged from both individual and social reality. Pope Francis sums up this vision well in *Gaudete et Exsultate* when he calls all people to holiness; when, quoting from *Evangelii Gaudium* in *Amoris Laetitia,* he challenges Christians to get their shoes "soiled by the mud of the street" (*AL,* no. 308); and in his address to the world's priests on March 28, 2013, to take on the "smell of the sheep." This is a praxis-oriented, engaged, and transformative faith. The term *liberation*

---

    [4] Ibid., 34.
    [5] Gustavo Gutiérrez, "Faith as Freedom: Solidarity with the Alienated and Confidence in the Future," *Horizons* 2, no. 1 (1975): 32.
    [6] Hugo Assman, *Theology for a Nomad Church* (Maryknoll, NY: Orbis Books, 1975), 104.

is deeply biblical and theological. It parallels the biblical term *salvation,* signifying the re-creation and total fulfillment of human beings both here and hereafter. In the here and now liberation is always partial and limited, but it still calls us to faith praxis that frees people from domination and exploitation by oppressive socioeconomic structures that assault human dignity. Gutiérrez summarizes a faith in Christ that embodies praxis and liberation: "The encounter with Christ in the poor constitutes an authentic spiritual experience. It is to live in the Spirit, the link of the love of the Father and the Son, God and man, between men. Christians committed to a praxis of liberation try to live in their lives this deep communion."[7] For Gutiérrez, Christ is God become poor and to know God as liberator, as he liberated the Israelites from Egypt, "is to liberate, to do justice."[8] Only in commitment to the liberation of the poor and marginalized, with whom Christ identifies himself, only in concretely and actively living our faith in praxis, can we give faith the "warm welcome" it requires.

Faith, active in praxis, must be guided by justice. The *Catechism of the Catholic Church* defines justice as the preservation of our neighbors' rights and rendering to them what is their due (*CCC,* no. 2407); justice guides our proper relationships to others. This, however, is a generic definition and does not specify what constitutes our neighbors' rights and what is their due. Just as history shapes the understanding and manifestation of the virtue of faith, so too does it shape the understanding and manifestation of the virtue of justice. Compare Pope Leo XIII's understanding that "inequality of rights and of power proceeds from the very author of nature"[9] with Vatican II's understanding that "with respect to the fundamental rights of the person, every type of discrimination, whether social or cultural, whether based on sex, race color, social condition or religion, is to be overcome as contrary to God's intent" (*GS,* no. 29). These two understandings of rights have corresponding understandings of justice. For Pope Leo justice is deductive, prioritizing divinely established legitimate authorities who institute stratified social structures and considering human dignity to the extent that it conforms to those structures. For Vatican II, justice is inductive, prioritizing the human dignity of individuals and determining whether it is facilitated or frustrated by existing authorities and structures. Both perspectives agree that justice should be grounded in gospel love, but what

---

[7] Gutiérrez, "Faith as Freedom," 40.

[8] Gustavo Gutiérrez, *The Power of the Poor in History* (Maryknoll, NY: Orbis Books, 1983), 8.

[9] Pope Leo XIII, *Quod Apostolici Muneris,* in *The Church Speaks in the Modern World,* ed. Etienne Gilson (Garden City, NY: Doubleday Image, 1954), no. 5. David Hollenbach, "Modern Catholic Teachings concerning Justice," in Haughey, *The Faith That Does Justice,* 215.

love requires in any given situation is shaped by contextual individual and social relationships and the type of justice guiding those relationships.

Catholic tradition distinguishes among three types of justice—commutative, distributive, and social—depending on the types of relationships and their interdependence.[10] As the United States Conference of Catholic Bishops (USCCB) has stated in "Economic Justice for All," "Commutative justice calls for fundamental fairness in all agreements and exchanges between individuals or private social groups" (no. 69).[11] This type of justice is guided by contracts and agreements and requires equal respect for all persons guiding economic transactions and contracts. For example, employees owe employers industrious work for their wages; employers owe employees a just and living wage and treatment with human dignity.

"Distributive justice requires that the allocation of income, wealth, and power in society be evaluated in light of its effects on persons whose basic material needs are unmet" (no. 70). This type of justice governs relationships between the state and individuals. Relationship with the state is an umbrella concept that refers to all aspects of social life; the state is more narrowly focused and pertains to the political order that formulates and enforces laws. Distributive justice is concerned with goods and burdens. A major focus in Pope Francis's pontificate has been the issue of poverty and its devastating consequences on human dignity worldwide. Goods must be more equitably distributed to ensure that every person has a decent existence in terms of food, shelter, education, healthcare, and the ability to participate in society. Burdens must be more equitably distributed to ensure that these goods are realized, and progressive taxation is one way the Catholic tradition has proposed to ensure a just distribution of burdens to meet the goods; those who have more should pay more taxes (no. 76).

Social, legal, or contributive justice "implies that persons have an obligation to be active and productive participants in the life of society and that society has a duty to enable them to participate in this way" (no. 71). In the past the focus was on the individual's obedience to just laws to ensure the common good. Today, this focus has expanded to include the responsibility of individuals to contribute to the life of a well-functioning state, including contributing to the revision of unjust laws or the formulation of more just laws, especially in evolving historical, cultural, and contextual situations. Contributive justice, for example, would require that as knowledge and understanding of human sexuality evolve, laws guiding sexual

[10] See Charles E. Curran, *The Catholic Moral Tradition Today: A Synthesis* (Washington, DC: Georgetown University Press, 1999), 120–25.

[11] USCCB, "Economic Justice for All," in *Catholic Social Thought: The Documentary Heritage*, ed. David J. O'Brien and Thomas A. Shannon (Maryknoll, NY: Orbis Books, 2000).

relationships evolve as well. So-called sodomy laws in the nineteenth and twentieth centuries that prohibited homosexual and even certain hetero-sexual acts between married couples have been revised based on evolving understandings of human sexual dignity. In 2003, the US Supreme Court invalidated all sodomy laws in the United States.

Two recent theological perspectives on justice that emerge out of the experiences of gender and racial injustice are reconciliatory justice and justice as spirituality. Reconciliatory justice, introduced by mujerista theologian Ada María Isasi-Díaz, is grounded in the reconciliatory praxis of care and tenderness.[12] This justice is radically subjective, moving the experiences of injustice of the poor and marginalized to the center of real-ity and empowering them to formulate and implement, through dialogue, concrete guides to make justice a reality in our world today. Reconciliation is both a personal and social virtue. The approach to social justice in the Catholic tradition continues to be a preferential option for the poor, which calls for the oppressors to create a more just society but allows them to maintain their privileged status, wealth, and power. Reconciliatory justice calls for conversion and repentance, where the oppressors forego their privileged status and share their wealth and power in solidarity to create a more just society for all. Tenderness, like virtue, complements reason with emotion. Both liberationist and virtue ethicists too often focus on reason to control emotion. Tenderness promotes the complementarity between reason and emotion. Emotion as tenderness and care should create empathy and compassion for one's neighbor and a pathway to justice, truth, and reconciliation. Reconciliatory justice calls for conversion and repentance to deconstruct unjust social structures, and the vision of truth that sustains them, and to reconstruct just social structures guided by truth that privi-leges the voices and participation of the poor, marginalized, and oppressed.

Justice as spirituality is developed by Bryan Massingale, a black Catholic theological ethicist, who focuses on racism in society and the church. He proposes justice as spirituality, which focuses on lament and compassion. Lament begins with the experiences of, and solidarity with, the oppressed and their cries of anguish, outrage, pain, grief, and righteous indignation over injustice and moves the oppressor also to lament as an honest confession of, and responsibility for, the oppression. Lament gives rise to compassion, a compelling response to racism and its endemic struc-tural presence, identifies with the victims of racism, and leads to healing action in solidarity with the oppressed to bring about reconciliation and

---

[12] Ada María Isasi-Díaz, "Justice as Reconciliatory Praxis," *International Journal of Public Theology* 4 (2010): 42–43. For an excellent summary of the work of Ada María Isasi-Díaz and Bryan Massingale, see Charles E. Curran, *Diverse Voices in Modern US Moral Theology* (Washington, DC: Georgetown University Press, 2018), chaps. 9 and 10.

transformation. Both reconciliatory justice and justice as spirituality are grounded in the experiences of gender and race oppression and, drawing from fundamental Christian virtues of reconciliation, conversion, empathy, and compassion, inform justice as solidarity with the Latina or African American "other" to redeem and transform the reality and structures of gender and racial injustice.

These five types of justice—commutative, distributive, social, reconciliatory, and spiritual—should guide human relationships. It is important to note, however, that depending on people's perspective and the definition, selection, and prioritization of the type of justice, they can come to very different conclusions about what is just and unjust and what justice requires in any given situation. The LGBT theological perspective argues, for example, that distributive justice requires that nondiscrimination legislation be enacted to protect against unjust discrimination against individuals based on their sexual orientation or gender in employment, housing, and healthcare. Other perspectives, such as that of the USCCB, argue that contributive justice must protect the religious freedom and the freedom of conscience of those who are morally opposed in conscience to same-sex relationships or transgender people, and allow those so opposed to deny employment, housing, or services to them. The baker in Colorado who refused to make a wedding cake for a same-sex couple is a case in point where these two interpretations of distributive and contributive justice conflict. We believe that the principle *faith that does justice* is a virtuous principle that helps to navigate the tension among different understandings of justice. We further believe that liberation theology, feminist theology, black theology, and LGBT theology provide helpful theological perspectives to incarnate Jesus's concern for "the least of these" and to ensure that faith praxis is an incarnation of justice that seeks the liberating kingdom of God in both the here and now and the hereafter.

Faith That Sees Injustice and Does Justice: The Virtuous Principle Expanded

As we noted in the Introduction, Gen Zers are committed to social justice and are more committed and active in some faith traditions than Millennials. Consequently, the virtuous principle, *faith that does justice,* which is deeply rooted in Catholic social teaching, is rooted also in their ethical perspective. Jesuit ethicists, drawing from Catholic social teaching, unite the two virtues of faith and justice to promote a theological ethical virtuous perspective. In 1974, Pedro Arrupe, superior general of the Society of Jesus, announced the 32nd General Congregation of the Society. The focus of the meeting, he declared, was to discuss how the Jesuits were responding to the radical transformation of the church called for by the Second Vatican Council. One point that was emphasized at the congregation and became a defining Jesuit charism that reflects the gospel imperative to care and seek justice for the poor was the virtuous principle *faith that does justice.* The congregation discerned that promoting justice in the world was to become the "integrating factor" of the Jesuits' work, a focus and primary expression of faith praxis.[13] It is also a central expression of faith-praxis for all those who call themselves Christian and seek to follow Jesus as the voice for the voiceless.

Faith that does justice is not a new concept in Catholic social teaching. It was expressed, though not in the same words, in the Second Vatican Council's *Gaudium et Spes,* which called for "the birth of a new humanism, one in which man is defined first of all by this responsibility to his brothers and to history," which calls Christians to give witness to "a living and mature faith" in order to "build a better world based upon truth and justice" (no. 55). Such a faith "needs to prove its fruitfulness by penetrating the believer's entire life, including its worldly dimensions, and by activating him toward justice and love, especially regarding the needy" (no. 21).[14] This virtuous principle has clear parallels with what Pope John Paul II referred to in *Sollicitudo Rei Socialis* as the Christian virtue of solidarity, which "is a firm and persevering determination to commit oneself to the common good; that is to say to the good of all and of each individual, because we are all really responsible for all" (*SRS,* no. 38). *Gaudium et Spes* defines the common good as "the sum total of social conditions which allow people, either as groups or as individuals, to reach their fulfillment more fully and more easily" (no. 26).

To *act* for justice guided by faith, by confronting poverty, for example, and creating a more equitable distribution of wealth and resources throughout the world, we must first be able to *see* injustice. Faith that does justice creates a virtuous perspective that, in turn, creates an awareness and sensitivity to the reality of the many forms of injustice in the world so that in word and, more important, in deed, we can respond to this injustice. Since seeing correctly is essential for virtue ethics and for acting justly, we expand the principle of faith that does justice to *faith that sees injustice and does justice.* Why is this an important corrective to the Jesuit principle? Years ago, Bernard Lonergan introduced the concept scotosis

---

[13] Peter-Hans Kolvenbach, SJ, "The Service of Faith and the Promotion of Justice in American Higher Education," address (2000), available online; see also Haughey, *The Faith That Does Justice,* 3.

[14] See Avery Dulles, "The Meaning of Faith Considered in Relationship to Justice," in Haughey, *The Faith That Does Justice,* 10–46.

(from the Greek *skotos*, meaning "darkness"), which produces something Lonergan called scotoma (a blind spot). Scotosis results from bias, "the love of darkness." It is not a conscious act, but it arises "in the censorship that governs the emergence of psychic contents."[15] This censorship can be either positive or negative. Positively, "it selects and arranges materials that emerge in consciousness in a perspective that gives rise to an insight"; negatively, it prevents "the emergence into consciousness of perspectives that would give rise to unwanted insights."[16] To exclude an insight "is also to exclude the further questions that would arise from the insight and the complementary insights that would carry it towards a rounded and balanced viewpoint." The lack of that more balanced viewpoint "results in behavior that generates misunderstanding *both in ourselves and in others*."[17] Scotosis is often at the root of structural sin that persists because ethical agents and institutions have blind spots that do not see the underlying structures that create and support injustice and, therefore, cannot act to transform them. A patriarchal Catholic Church that does not see any gender discrimination in a male-only clergy and white Americans who do not see any social benefits that result from being white and male are suffering from scotosis.

The virtuous perspective of faith that sees injustice and does justice aligns well with the see-judge-act model of pastoral reflection initiated by Pope John XXIII in his encyclical *Mater et Magistra*, which is grounded in experience and induction and invites an ethical response to lived experience, especially the experience of the poor, marginalized, and oppressed.[18] The perspective allows Christians first to *see* injustice, both individual and structural, then to *judge* that injustice, and finally to *act* to establish or restore justice in light of that judgment. Acts can take the form of charity or justice. Acts of charity are personal acts of service toward neighbors, especially the most-needy neighbors. Acts of justice work to reform and transform sinful structures that perpetuate poverty and any other form of oppression, to facilitate the attainment of human dignity, and to realize the common good. While individual acts of charity are necessary and important to fulfill the gospel imperative to love one's neighbor, acts of justice are essential to confront and transform unjust social structures that violate the common good and human dignity. In what follows we explore four

---

[15] Bernard J. F. Lonergan, *Insight: A Study of Human Understanding* (London: Longmans, 1957), 191.

[16] Ibid., 192.

[17] Ibid., 191, emphasis added.

[18] See also Marvin L. Mich, "Commentary on *Mater et Magistra* (Christianity and Social Progress)," in *Modern Catholic Social Teaching: Commentaries and Interpretations*, ed. Kenneth B. Himes, 191–216 (Washington, DC: Georgetown University Press, 2005).

theological perspectives that reveal social structures where human dignity is violated and, guided by faith that sees and does justice, attempt to name and transform those structures.

Liberation Theology

One of the most exciting theological movements starting in the twentieth century is liberation theology. It focuses on endemic poverty in Latin America and attempts to transform it from a virtuous perspective of faith that sees injustice and does justice is liberation theology. Liberation theology evolved out of the experiences of the poor and marginalized in Latin America and, by confronting unjust social structures that institutionalize oppression,[19] has refined the notions of faith and justice in light of those oppressive experiences. Unjust social structures include violations of commutative, distributive, and contributive justice. Such violations of commutative justice include, but are not limited to, contractual agreements between employees and employers that do not pay a just wage, exploit workers through long hours, and offer no protection for sexual or other types of harassment on the job, and practice other violations of human rights and human dignity. Violations of distributive justice include, but are not limited to, violations of basic human needs by the state or society, such as lack of food, inadequate shelter, lack of access to education and healthcare, and unequal distribution of social burdens on the most vulnerable in society. Violations of social justice include, but are not limited to, frustrating human participation in the life of society to facilitate the common good such as dictatorships or violations of subsidiarity or participatory justice that suppresses voting rights or participation in the governing process. These experiences and reflection on them provide a unique method for selecting, interpreting, prioritizing, and integrating the sources of ethical knowledge to define human dignity and to formulate and justify norms to attain it in the shadow of those experiences.

Stephen Bevans categorizes liberation theology as a praxis method of contextual theology. This method can be understood as "faith seeking intelligent action." It "understands revelation as the presence of God in history—in the events of everyday life, in social and economic structures, in situations of oppression, in the experience of the poor and marginalized."[20]

---

[19] See Gustavo Gutiérrez, *A Theology of Liberation,* 2nd ed. (Maryknoll, NY: Orbis Books, 1988).

[20] Bevans, *Models of Contextual Theology,* 73, 75. In this section we are indebted to Bevans's treatment of liberation theology as a praxis theological model.

Liberation theology proposes an inductive method of "critical reflection on praxis" grounded in the particularity of history, culture, and context. Combined with the virtuous perspective of faith that sees injustice and does justice, it is a transformative method for doing theological ethics.

Before explaining the method of liberation theology, which in many ways reflects our own method, we begin with a definition: Catholic ethical method is a theological method that proposes both an epistemology for reaching ethical truth and a normative pattern for reaching a definition of human dignity and formulating and justifying norms for its attainment. In liberation theology epistemology unifies knowledge as activity and knowledge as content, but the former precedes the latter.[21] That is, experience and action are the points of departure for constructing knowledge into content, into theological anthropology and the formulation and justification of norms, laws, and doctrines. It is the experience of unjust socioeconomic structures and relationships and reflection on them in light of the gospel that yields just action that responds to, and attempts to transform, those structures.

There are several dimensions of liberation theology's method guided by the virtuous perspective of faith that sees injustice and does justice. First, the method is historically conscious, openly acknowledging that humans, their societies, and the meanings and values they espouse are always in a process of gradual growth and change. Truth exists as much in active history as in static intellectual ideas. Pope Francis confirms this. "We can see that the word of God is not a series of abstract ideas but rather a source of comfort and companionship for every family [and, we add, person] that experiences difficulties or suffering" (*AL,* no. 22). History, within a cultural context, shapes the ongoing discernment of the truth of God's compassionate word and presence in that context.

Second, the method, therefore, looks to Catholic truths that come to us from the past not as ethical facts to be uncritically accepted as true across time and cultures but as ethical data for conscientious discernment of their possible applications in a different, contemporary, contextual situation. This approach ensures that truth can be handed on to future generations strengthened and more attuned to developing human experience and human dignity. It is indeed a *living* truth.

Third, the method provides what we designate a "unique perspective," not only for refining and combining the virtues of faith and justice as discussed above but also for guiding the Christian perspective that acknowledges Jesus Christ as liberator and calls humans to be active participants in that liberation.

---

[21] Ibid., 72.

Fourth, the method is thoroughly inductive. It begins not with a prescribed ethical norm from which it deduces the required ethical action in the contextual situation but with the contextual situation itself, including the persons involved in it, and inductively discerns a conscientious choice of the required ethical action in the situation.

Fifth, the method is a virtue ethical method. The see-judge-act formula requires first that we see injustice through the perspective of faith that does justice in order to analyze, evaluate, and act justly to liberate the poor and marginalized from unjust social structures that frustrate human dignity. In virtue ethics, as we have already stressed, action follows being. Virtue ethics focuses primarily not on the acts a person must do to be ethical and virtuous but on the person and his or her character, and only secondarily on the acts the person must do to be virtuous. Just action follows just seeing and judging.

Sixth, this method accepts the four sources of ethical knowledge for developing a normative method: scripture, tradition, science/reason, and human experience. However, the selection, interpretation, prioritization, and integration of the sources of ethical knowledge arise, inductively, out of the experiences of the poor and marginalized. The method of liberation theology does not begin with words from scripture and tradition and end with new theological words; it begins with virtuous actions for justice now and seeks to habituate those actions forward into the future. In this method the experiences of the poor and marginalized are foundational. Out of their experiences, through the lens of faith that sees injustice and does justice, liberation theology interprets the words of scripture and the insights of tradition, including the statements of the magisterium, to come to an ongoing understanding of Christ's liberating presence in the here and now that empowers humans to act to realize that presence. Bevans describes this as a dialectic spiral of theological reflection on committed and intelligent action. "Theology follows as fruit of critical reflection on socially transformative praxis. Change occurring or brought about ceaselessly in persons and societal realities dictates continuing change in our interpretation of the Bible and of Church teaching."[22] Each new experience obliges us to interpret scripture and tradition afresh, to change accordingly, and then to go back and reinterpret them again and again. The universality of this method is grounded in human experience as an ongoing source for reinterpretation. Its particularity is grounded in the distinct historical, cultural contexts that invite reinterpretation. This particularity extends the insights of liberation theology and its method to other types of structurally

---

[22] Ibid., 76.

induced oppression and suffering. It is to those other types of oppression we now turn.

Feminist Theological Perspectives

Liberation theology gave rise to not only other liberation theologies of experience sparked by socioeconomic oppression but also theologies responding to gender oppression. The focus of liberation theology is on the violation of human dignity that results from economic injustice; the focus of feminist theology is on the violation of human dignity that results from gender injustice. Gender is distinct from sex, but this distinction is often overlooked in magisterial teachings on human sexuality. The human animal is traditionally binary, divided biologically into male and female sexes. Gender concerns the historical and socially constructed structures that particularize that biological difference at different times and in different places. These social structures are almost always patriarchal and oppressive to women and they are, therefore, a central concern of feminist social criticism and feminist ethics.

Feminist theology is a direct offshoot of liberation theology and takes as its point of departure the experiences of women and their oppression throughout history.[23] These experiences challenge perceptions of principles, norms, and doctrinal teachings and attempt to refine them contextually. Lisa Sowle Cahill notes that "feminist ethics begins with the particular, with practice, with experience, with the situation—but out of the particular (not over against it) feminists recognize what furthers or damages 'full humanity' for women and men."[24] It is the experience of women, past and present, that challenges not only the perception of fundamental values but also the very definition of human dignity. The norm forbidding the ordination of women to the priesthood reaffirmed by Pope John Paul II in his 1994 apostolic letter *Ordinatio Sacerdotalis (OS)* is a specific doctrine that warrants serious reconsideration in light of these reflections.

---

[23] For an informative text on feminist thought and its implications for moral theology, see Charles E. Curran, Margaret A. Farley, and Richard A. McCormick, SJ, eds., *Feminist Ethics and the Catholic Moral Tradition: Readings in Moral Theology No. 9* (New York: Paulist Press, 1996).

[24] Lisa Sowle Cahill, "Feminist Ethics, Differences, and Common Ground: A Catholic Perspective," in Curran, Farley, and McCormick, *Feminist Ethics and the Catholic Moral Tradition*, 185. For Cahill's emphasis on experience in developing a credible (sexual) ethic, see Lisa Sowle Cahill, *Sex, Gender, and Christian Ethics* (Cambridge: Cambridge University Press, 1996).

Cahill utilizes Susan Parsons's work on Christian feminist theologies[25] as a framework to present three feminist paradigms of gender that are evident in Christian ethics: liberal, social constructionist, and naturalist.[26] The liberal paradigm emphasizes freedom and equality as foundational values for preserving human dignity, and the common good is ensured by protecting autonomy, self-determination, and human rights. Gender roles are minimized and defined in terms of equality; every person, male and female, has an equal right to education, work, pay, and a dignified living. This paradigm has little or no tolerance for the traditional gender roles assigned to men and women based on their sexual differentiation. The social constructionist paradigm recognizes and resists the social construction of ethical values. It recognizes that most ethical values are constructed by social and ethical ideologies created and perpetuated by those in power, and it resists the rampant abuses of this social construction by giving a voice to the voiceless. Men and women must redefine their identities and patterns of relationship in dialogue with those who have been marginalized. In the United States, the #MeToo movement highlights sexual abuse and harassment in all social contexts and attempts to reground men's relationship to women in human rights, human dignity, mutual equality, and respect not subject to the vicissitudes of a distorted, patriarchal, social construction. A goal of the #MeToo movement is to realize the common good by deconstructing oppressive, exploitative, patriarchal hierarchies, and reconstructing just, social structures rooted in new views of gender identity and patterns of relationship. In this paradigm gender is not "natural"; it does not have a legitimate right to define social and personal relationships.

Finally, the naturalist paradigm investigates whether or not there are certain universal experiences shared by all human beings regardless of cultural influence and socialization, and whether or not these universal values can serve as a foundation for normative ethical standards. In this paradigm one way of interpreting gender is in terms of the shared universal experience of the reproductive differences between male and female. From this shared universal experience naturalist feminist theological ethicists ask if these differences yield normative guidance for relationships and institutions and, if they do, what is the extent and nature of this guidance. There are three possible responses to the interrelationship between biological differentiation and gender. First, one can claim there is no interrelationship between the two. Second, one can claim that biological differentiation entails defining characteristics of human nature that determine intrinsic or divinely

---

[25] See Susan Parsons, *Feminism and Christian Ethics* (Cambridge: Cambridge University Press, 1996).

[26] Cahill, "Gender and Christian Ethics," in *The Cambridge Companion to Christian Ethics*, ed. Robin Gill (Cambridge: Cambridge University Press, 2001), 121–22.

established masculine and feminine roles based on that nature. Third, one can claim there is an interrelationship and that it is defined by a variety of historical, social, cultural, political, and economic institutions and realities. Radical feminists defend the first position and espouse Parsons's liberal paradigm; the second and third positions are reflected in the anthropologies of John Paul II and Lisa Cahill, respectively.

John Paul II attaches ontological meaning to male and female sex, with corresponding and absolute normative implications for gender in ethical questions, about marriage for instance. Genesis's second creation story reveals, John Paul teaches in *Mulieris Dignitatem*, "the fundamental truth . . . concerning man created as man and woman in the image and likeness of God" (*MD*, no. 6). This fundamental truth reveals the fundamental equality between man and woman,[27] but their distinct physical natures entail distinct gender roles in both marriage and the church. Marriage is defined in terms of male-female complementarity, by which women are called to bring full dignity to motherhood and the conjugal life. Though John Paul II admits that women's roles have been defined too narrowly in terms of wife, mother, and family relationships without adequate access or representation in the public sphere, he also notes that "the true advancement of women requires that clear recognition be given to the value of their maternal and family role, by comparison with all other public roles and all other professions" (*FC*, no. 23). Men are never defined primarily in terms of their roles as husbands or fathers; more emphasis is given, rather, to their social roles. Arguing from sexual complementarity to gender role complementarity perpetuates imbalances in power and perpetuates social structures that limit women's creativity and contributions in the public realm. Such distinctions between the feminine and the masculine in marriage and family life are more culturally than ontologically determined.

Biological sexual differentiation and gender complementarity are used to defend the argument that only men can be priests. Jesus was a male, the apostles were males, and throughout its two-thousand-year history only males have been ordained to the priesthood in the Catholic Church (see *OS*, no. 1; *MD*, no. 26).[28] Jesus is the bridegroom and the church is the bride, and the male priest represents Jesus as bridegroom who complements the female church as bride. Since only males can be bridegrooms, it is

---

[27] John Paul II, *Familiaris Consortio*, no. 22 (hereinafter, *FC*); *MD*, no. 16; "Letter to Women" (June 29, 1995), no. 4. See Charles Curran's explanation and critique of John Paul II's position on the dignity and equality of women in *The Moral Theology of Pope John Paul II* (Washington, DC: Georgetown University Press, 2005), 187–95.

[28] These arguments based on maleness were first articulated by the CDF in *Inter Insigniores (Declaration on the Question of the Admission of Women to the Ministerial Priesthood)* (1976).

ontologically determined also that only males can be priests. This perspective is reflected in Michael Novak's comment, "Why is the priest male? It figures. It fits. The priest's maleness is a reminder of the role played in our salvation by the sacramentality of human flesh—not flesh-in-general, but male flesh."[29] John Paul can both defend the fundamental equality of men and women and simultaneously argue that gender complementarity includes role complementarity. There are clear social and ecclesial roles grounded in masculinity and femininity; true complementarity must not entail a masculinization of the feminine or a feminization of the masculine (*MD,* no. 10). John Paul posits gender complementarity, grounded in biological differentiation, to justify clearly defined roles for men and women in both marriage and in the church.

Such definitions of complementarity have led many feminists to argue that complementarity, even under the guise of equality and dignity, always entails women's subordination.[30] Cahill proposes a more balanced approach to the interrelationship between sex and gender. It is the subordination and oppression found in traditionalist naturalist accounts of this relationship that leads her, at least in part, to consider gender as a foundational anthropological dimension in her ethical theory and to refine it in light of social and cultural critical analysis. For Cahill, biological differentiation is an essential and universal component of human experience that affects how men and women are in the world, but too much emphasis has been, and continues to be, placed on biological difference to subordinate the feminine to the masculine. This situation begs for redress. "Gender understood as ethical project entails the social humanization of biological tendencies, capacities, and differences, including the social ties that they, by their very nature, are inclined to create."[31] This social humanization must take place both in the marital relationship and in the church, and it takes place by the deconstruction and reconstruction of traditional gender roles and hierarchies. Such reconstruction challenges many of the absolute magisterial norms on sexual ethics. It also justifies arguments for the ordination of women as priests and bishops.

Margaret Farley develops a method for doing feminist ethics that explicitly relies on the Wesleyan Quadrilateral of scripture, tradition, science, and experience. Experience is common to the other three sources of ethical knowledge and serves as the foundation for her ethical method. We note once again that experience is never a standalone source of theological ethics. And my experience alone is never a source at all. Ethical authority

---

[29] Michael Novak, "Women, Ordination, and Angels," *First Things* 32 (April 1993): 32.

[30] Curran, *The Moral Theology of Pope John Paul II,* 193.

[31] Cahill, *Sex, Gender, and Christian Ethics,* 89.

is granted only to our experience, to *communal* experience, and only in constructive conversation with the three other sources and with the theological reality called *sensus fidei*, the sense of the faithful and their lived experience. Criteria are formulated for analyzing and evaluating experience and distinguishing between authentic experience that can serve as a foundation for defining human dignity and formulating and justifying norms for its attainment, and inauthentic experience that leads to violations of human dignity. For Farley, justice and love are the two virtues that shape the criteria for determining authentic and inauthentic experience and its implications for the selection, interpretation, and integration of the other sources of ethical knowledge.

Another type of feminist theology, mujerista theology, has a similar but distinct method to more traditional feminist theologies. Mujerista theology is grounded in the experience of Latinas and their struggle for liberation from oppression. This focus on liberation is an offshoot of liberation theology and shares many of the same goals and objectives of that theology. There are, however, important differences. The experience of Latinas lacks the voice, authority, and power that first-world feminists enjoy. Although first-world feminists still struggle with patriarchal structures socially and ecclesially, those structures are tempered by democratic structures and white privilege that limit the oppression they experience. White privilege provides greater social, economic, and political opportunities and benefits for white women and denies those opportunities and benefits to African Americans, Latin Americans, and other racial minorities. This is not to demean the suffering that women endure from oppressive patriarchal structures, but rather to recognize degrees of suffering and degrees of entrenched patriarchy in different cultural contexts. Latinas who live in dictatorships or machismo cultures do not have the built-in social and legislative protections that women in developed, democratic countries enjoy. As a result, their struggles to overcome oppression and realize gender equality and equal human dignity is much more profound and dangerous.

These distinctions impact the method for doing mujerista theology. The shared methodological point of departure for liberation theology and feminist theology is experience. However, experience is distinct for mujerista theology in comparison to liberation theology. Praxis or experience is primary and theological reflection follows from praxis. For mujerista theology, according to Isasi-Díaz, praxis is reflective action; the two are thoroughly integrated. Christian Latinas are "organic intellectuals"[32] who,

---

[32] Charles Curran borrows this concept from Antonio Gramsci to name Latinas who through their liberative praxis introduce new modes of thought and conceptions of a just world (Curran, *Diverse Voices in Modern US Moral Theology*, 182).

through their participation in liberative praxis, work to overcome oppressive structures and contribute to a reconstructed vision of the world by introducing and promoting new perspectives.

When scripture is used in mujerista theology, the hermeneutical lens for its reading is liberation and faith that sees injustice and does justice. The parable of the workers in the vineyard (Matt 20:1–16) offers an example. The workers arrive at various times throughout the day, beginning in the early morning and stretching out to a short time before the end of the workday. When the landowner pays the workers, he pays the same amount to all the workers, those who arrived early and those who arrived late. The common interpretation of this parable is that the landowner is being just to those who worked all day and generous to those who worked only part of the day. It is his prerogative to be generous and this generosity extends not only to the workers but to the lowliest and greatest sinners who respond to the call to tend the vineyard. From the perspective of mujerista theology, however, based on their experience of exploitation and oppressive social structures, the landowner's paying every worker the same amount is a violation of justice. From the experience and perspective of Latinas, the landowner has disrespected the workers who worked all day by not paying them more than those who worked only part of the day. The landowner disrespects them in their labor, and they protest. Even though their protest is ineffectual, by confronting the owner of the vineyard they maintain their honor, dignity, and self-respect.[33] As organic intellectuals, Latinas provide nuance to the selection, interpretation, prioritization, and integration of the sources of ethical knowledge and expand the parameters of the discipline of theology from its academic focus to a lived reality where all Latinas engage in theology through lived experience. This method is legitimized by tradition and the authority and inviolability of conscience, which applies to academically trained theologians as well as organic intellectuals trained in a lived, often oppressive, patriarchal reality.

Black Theological Perspectives

The anthropological focus of liberation theology is on the violation of human dignity that results from socioeconomic injustice, and the anthropological focus of feminist theology is on the violation of human dignity that results from gender injustice. The anthropological focus of black theologi-

---

[33] Ada María Isasi-Díaz, "A Mujerista Hermeneutics of Justice and Human Flourishing," in *The Bible and the Hermeneutics of Liberation*, ed. Alejandro F. Botta and Pablo Adriñach (Atlanta: Society of Biblical Literature, 2009), 181–95. See Curran, *Diverse Voices in Modern US Moral Theology*, 181–82.

cal perspectives is on the violation of human dignity that results from racial injustice. The greatest systemic violation of justice in the United States is racism, and black theologians see that injustice and seek to transform it into justice. The history of racism in the United States, directed primarily against black Americans but also other minorities, in both society and the Catholic Church, is a source of scandal. Racism and the prejudice that accompanies it have marked, and continue to mark, the attitude of Catholics to their fellow racial-minority Catholics. It is only relatively recently that black theology, which originated through the work of Protestant theologian James Cone and is influenced by liberation theology,[34] has gained a footing in Catholic theology in the United States, though the number of minority Catholic theologians is miniscule compared to the number of white theologians. Among the leading black American Catholic theologians are Jamie Phelps, Diana Hayes, Shawn Copeland, and Bryan Massingale.

Racism is endemic and evident throughout the history of the United States. Its most egregious manifestation was the slavery on which both the economy and white privilege were built. Slavery was first legalized by European colonists in Massachusetts in 1641 and was officially abolished by the Thirteenth Amendment in 1865 (though Mississippi ratified the amendment only in 1995). This gives some indication of how entrenched slavery was in the Southern states and what Shawn Copeland refers to as "the virulent residue of slavery,"[35] which continues to shape social and religious racist attitudes. Between 1691 and 1967 marriages between whites and non-whites were illegal, and anti-miscegenation laws were overturned by the US Supreme Court in *Loving v. Virginia* only in 1967. Jim Crow laws, which forced segregation under the racist legal principle "separate but equal," perpetuated racism in social structures. Although the civil rights movement, led by activists such as Martin Luther King, Jr., culminated in 1964 with the passing of the Civil Rights Act, which prohibited discrimination based on race and improved conditions for minority populations in the United States, systemic racism continues to flourish. It is present in our judicial, economic, and educational systems, and scandalously in our churches.

Throughout the 1980s and 1990s there was a tremendous spike in incarceration rates for black American males in the United States, largely due to racially based drug prosecutions. The crack cocaine epidemic in the 1980s was largely associated with the black population; the more expensive powder cocaine was the drug of choice for affluent whites. The disparity

---

[34] James Cone, *The Cross and the Lynching Tree* (Maryknoll, NY: Orbis Books, 2007).

[35] M. Shawn Copeland, "Theology as Intellectually Vital Inquiry: A Black Theological Interrogation," *CTSA Proceedings* 46 (1991): 51; idem, *Enfleshing Freedom: Body, Race, and Being* (Minneapolis: Fortress Press, 2010).

in incarceration for possession of crack and powder cocaine, a ratio of 100:1, reflected racial bias. The Fair Sentencing Act of 2010 reduced that ratio to 18:1, which is still a substantial ratio gap.[36] A Pew Study in 2016 found that whites, who make up 64 percent of the US population, make up only 30 percent of the prison population, while blacks, who make up only 12 percent of the population, make up 33 percent of the prison population. The #BlackLivesMatter movement, sparked by the killings of Michael Brown, Jr., in Ferguson, Missouri, Eric Garner in New York, Freddie Gray in Baltimore, and an increasing number of others, has focused on this divide. Sociological data also indicates substantial structural racism in terms of access to and success in education. Black students are substantially more likely than whites to be held back in all school grades, even though it is documented that holding children back does not benefit them academically or socially and makes them more likely to drop out later. Disparities in test scores are consistent through primary and secondary education. Black students are suspended and expelled from schools at three times the rate of white students. More black students drop out before completing high school (16 percent) than white students (8 percent), which translates to fewer black students going to college and attaining the college degree that increases the likelihood of financial stability later in life. Over 33 percent of the white population holds a college degree compared to only 19 percent of the black population. Black men and women who do hold a college degree are less likely than white men and women with the same qualifications to be called back for an interview for a job.[37]

Teachers in schools with minority populations have less experience, are less likely to be certified, and are paid less than teachers in schools with predominantly white populations. Black students are more likely to live in low-income, poor, and unsafe neighborhoods, which affects the local tax dollars available to support education. This socioeconomic fact in turn affects the quality of schools, safe learning environments, adequate nutrition for physical and mental development, all of which have a negative impact on academic and social development. Broken families, lack of parental support, domestic abuse and sexual violence are all disproportionately higher among blacks than whites. These impediments to equal education and success translate into less earning power through life. In 2016, the median household income in the United States was $81,431 for Asian households, $65,041 for white households, $47,675 for Hispanic

---

[36] Andrew Cohen, "How White Users Made Heroin a Public-Health Problem," in *The Atlantic* (August 12, 2015).

[37] Lindsey Cook, "US Education: Still Separate and Unequal," *US News and World Report* (January 28, 2015),

households, and \$39,490 for black households.[38] In 2017, blacks had the highest level of unemployment, 7.5 percent compared to the US average of 4.4 percent.[39] The US Census Bureau reports that 9 percent of whites, 22 percent of blacks, and 20 percent of Hispanics live in poverty in the United States.[40] These structural sins are evident not only in society but in the church as well.

The Catholic Church in the United States, Bryan Massingale notes, is predominantly white and racist. In one of the most cited texts in his book, he explains how the Catholic Church is racist:

> What makes the US Catholic Church a "white racist institution" is not the fact that the majority of its members are of European descent (especially since in many places, they no longer are), nor the fact that many of its members engage in acts of malice or bigotry. What makes it "white" and "racist" is the pervasive belief that European aesthetics, music, theology, and persons—and only these—are standard, normative, universal, and truly "Catholic."[41]

Massingale proposes racial reconciliation, "challenging and severing the cultural nexus between skin color and race-based systemic advantage and privilege,"[42] to transform racism in the church. This requires that people see and confront racism and see and transform the structures of white privilege that perpetuate and enable racism in the first place. Simply confronting racism without transforming the white privilege that perpetuates it is incomplete and only pushes racism more deeply into the subconscious, leaving racist structures intact.

Massingale's overarching question for Catholic black theology is this: "What would Catholic moral theology look like if it took the black experience seriously as a dialogue partner?"[43] The answer to this question demonstrates the ethical method of black theology. Massingale suggests that black theology is less interested in methodological discussions and more interested in engaging social praxis. Catholic black theology, he asserts, coincides closely with liberation theology in method and intent, sharing the

---

[38] "Median Household Income in the United States in 2016, by Race or Ethnic Group in US Dollars," *Statista*.

[39] "Unemployment Rate in the United States in 2017, by Ethnicity," *Statista*.

[40] Kaiser Family Foundation, "Poverty Rate by Race/Ethnicity (2016)."

[41] Bryan N. Massingale, *Racial Justice and the Catholic Church* (Maryknoll, NY: Orbis Books, 2010), 80.

[42] Bryan N. Massingale, "Has the Silence Been Broken? Catholic Theological Ethics and Racial Justice," *Theological Studies* 75 (2014): 142.

[43] Ibid., 141.

following dimensions: experience, induction, culture, context, and historical consciousness. Black theology is grounded in the experiences of racism
and white privilege in the United States. It is inductive, contemplating
these experiences and, through critical reflection and analysis, evaluating
the culture, its meanings, and its values that shape people's perspectives.
Black theology is contextual; its focus is on distinct communities of race,
gender, and geographical location (racism in the South is quite different
in its expression than racism in the North), and it is historically conscious
in that the seeing, judging, and acting in relation to racism is an evolving
project.

What is distinctive in the method of black theology is its emphasis on
scotosis, on the affective and emotional, and spirituality. We consider each
in turn. Massingale defines racism as

> a deep set of formative meanings and values attached to skin color
> that decisively affects group identity and social consciousness, so
> much so that race often operates as a non-conscious factor in human
> decision-making, influencing behavior and beliefs without an indi-
> vidual's conscious awareness (i.e., "unconscious racism").[44]

Unconscious racism is a result of scotosis, a blind spot that individuals and
societies have about racism and the unjust social structures it creates and
sustains. To act justly, one must first see accurately, and a methodological
focus on seeing accurately to overcome scotosis is a central consideration
in black theology. Lament and spirituality are two methodological considerations that help to confront scotosis, to see more clearly to act more
justly.

Black theology focuses on the affective and spiritual to bring the nonconscious factor of race to conscious awareness in the process of decision
making. How is this accomplished methodologically? Massingale and
Copeland critique overly rationalist approaches to ethical theory and their
application to specific ethical issues. Instead, they emphasize the need for
the affective and emotional to complement and guide the rational. Lament—expressions of righteous indignation, outrage, sorrow, and pain—is
a biblically based affective virtue and is critical to Massingale's method.
"Because racism forms people in visceral and nonconscious ways, there
are limits to the effectiveness of intellectual analysis, rational appeals, and
discursive practices in combating it." Catholic theological ethics must attend more deliberately to the nonrational. "We act justly," he opines, "not
because we are intellectually convinced, but because we are passionately

---

[44] Ibid.

moved."[45] Indeed, if we think experientially about horrific crimes that we hear about on the nightly news, such as the death of Freddie Gray, which resulted from injuries sustained in police custody, a common reaction is righteous indignation, outrage, sorrow, and pain, and then we process those emotions with rational analysis that helps to explain them. Massingale emphasizes that we should feel these emotions and allow them to permeate our being and shape our ethical perspective. We should not seek to interject reason too quickly to fix the problem by seeking solutions. It is lament that shapes our perspective, sharpens our reason, and corrects the scotosis of racial injustice. Just as emotion and reason complement one another in virtue ethics, they do so in black theology as well.

We must, however, always be critical of the emotion that arises from experience and complement it with reason. Scotosis can be an overwhelming impediment that distorts emotions and prevents us from seeing and acting justly to confront racism. Consider a member of the alt-right who sees an interracial couple holding hands and walking down the street. The emotions for that person in that situation may be similar to those of the person who hears about Freddie Gray on the news—righteous indignation, outrage, sorrow, and pain—but those emotions emerge from a subconscious or conscious racist perspective that motivates how they see and act on race. Feelings alone, then, are inadequate to direct seeing, judging, and acting. Because of scotosis and personal and structural sin, which are at the root of racism, we cannot always trust our emotional responses to ethical issues. Lament must be guided by prayerful discernment or spirituality.

A third distinct methodological component in black theology is spirituality and contemplation, which correct scotosis, dispel false consciousness, and bring to the fore a sensitivity to racial injustice and our conscious or unconscious participation in it. Massingale reviews the works of several theologians who write about spirituality and contemplation as resources for racial justice.[46] These authors highlight the importance of what we might call a sacramental presence to racial injustice. Christopher Pramuck proposes a "contemplative mirror," where one has sustained contemplative prayer and established a perspective on reality, sitting in reverence and silence, allowing God to make compassionate space in one's heart for the suffering, pain and "luminous differences" of racially and culturally diverse groups.[47] Margaret Pfeil proposes a mystical/political spirituality guided by the beatitudes to guide a response to white complicity. This spirituality is a way of being a transformative, compassionate, resistive presence in the

---

[45] Ibid., 142.

[46] Ibid., 148–49.

[47] Christopher Pramuck, *Hope Sings, So Beautiful: Graced Encounters across the Color Line* (Collegeville, MN: Liturgical Press, 2013), 45–51.

world in solidarity with the oppressed and suffering. Through contemplative action one enters into solidarity with the oppressed "other" and allows that solidarity to shape one's perspective and motivate one's actions.[48]

These methodological dimensions, combined, provide a solid foundation and means for seeing the racism that exists in our social, cultural, and religious contexts. They provide the tools for the selection, interpretation, prioritization, and integration of the sources of ethical knowledge that prioritize the experiences of oppressed races, substantiated through the social sciences, to focus on Jesus in scripture as liberator and critique tradition that, throughout history, has been far too complicit in racism. Black theology demands a thorough deconstruction of racist and white privileged structures and a reconstruction of those structures based on symbols and sacraments that incarnate justice for all created in the image and likeness of God.

LGBT Theological Perspectives

The anthropological focus of LGBT theological perspectives is on the violation of human dignity that results from sexual orientation and gender injustice against LGBT people. Before exploring this theological perspective, since at least some of the terms are relatively new in theological discourse, we first define those terms. Lesbian, gay, and bisexual designations emphasize a person's sexual orientation. Sexual orientation, in general, is defined as "the sustained erotic attraction to members of one's own gender, the opposite gender, or both—homosexual, heterosexual, or bisexual respectively."[49] Homosexual orientation, specifically, is "a *condition* characterized by an emotional and psycho-sexual propensity towards others of the same sex,"[50] and a homosexual is "a person who feels a most urgent sexual desire which *in the main* is directed towards gratification with the same sex."[51] Transgender "refers to people with a disjunction between their physical sex and gender identity."[52] Sex is determined by the

---

[48] Alex Mikulich, Laurie Cassidy, and Margaret Pfeil, *The Scandal of White Complicity in US Hyper-Incarceration: A Non-Violent Spirituality of White Resistance* (New York: Palgrave Macmillan, 2013), chaps. 5 and 6.

[49] Richard C. Pillard and J. Michael Bailey, "A Biological Perspective on Sexual Orientation," *Clinical Psychology* 18 (1995): 1.

[50] D. Sherwin Bailey, *Homosexuality and the Western Christian Tradition* (New York: Longman's, 1955), x, emphasis added.

[51] Donald W. Cory, *The Homosexual in America* (New York: Julian Press, 1951), 8.

[52] Susannah Cornwall, "Intersex and Transgender People," in *The Oxford Handbook of Theology, Sexuality, and Gender,* ed. Adrian Thatcher (Oxford: Oxford University Press, 2015), 658–59.

biological genitalia a person has at birth; gender is the cultural expression of this biological sex within a culture. Transgender people experience a disconnect between their sex and gender. The cultural interpretation and medical treatment of those characteristics often reflect the biological sexual binary of male/female or a gender cultural binary of boy/girl, man/woman. Margaret Farley asks whether the focus should be on how we treat this bisexual pathology or whether it should even be judged pathological at all.[53] This gets to the root of anthropology and what is considered "normal" and "natural" in the sexual realm.

Queer theory is a critical perspective on sex and gender, challenging what is considered normal or natural. Specifically, it "contends that identities—including identities relating to sexuality and gender—are socially constructed through the deployment of social power, including the power of discourse and naming."[54] Queer theory shares similarities with black theology in that the social prejudice associated with race and sexual identity are often a result of scotosis, which allows racist and sexually discriminatory views to predominate through social structures defined by those in power. These views protect the status quo and resist recognizing and supporting the fundamental equality and dignity of all human beings. There is a profound disconnect between official Catholic teaching on LGBT issues and the *sensus fidelium* (sense of the faithful), as is clearly evident in the social sciences.

In the last twenty years there has been a seismic cultural shift in support for homosexuals and same-sex relationships in the United States. A Pew Research survey in 2001 indicated that 57 percent of Americans opposed same-sex marriage and 35 percent supported it. A 2017 survey reported an inversion in those percentages: 62 percent of Americans supporting same-sex marriage and 32 percent opposing it. For our purposes here, two populations are highly relevant in these surveys. First, the greatest support for same-sex marriage (77 percent) came from Millennials and Gen Zers, ages eighteen to twenty-nine. This support differs based on political affiliation (87 percent of Democrats and 59 percent of Republicans in this age group support same-sex marriage), but a substantial majority of Republicans support same-sex marriage. Second, 66 percent of white Catholics support same-sex marriage and, strikingly, 80 percent of them between the ages of eighteen and twenty-nine. In one sense the support of same-sex

---

[53] Margaret A. Farley, *Just Love: A Framework for Christian Ethics* (New York: Continuum, 2006), 151.

[54] Patrick S. Cheng, "Contributions from Queer Theory," in Thatcher, *The Oxford Handbook of Theology, Sexuality, and Gender*, 153.

marriage by Millennials and Gen Zers is not surprising. These cohorts, across the political and religious spectrums, tend to be more inclusive, concerned for justice and equality, and react negatively to social injustice. In another sense the support of same-sex marriage by Catholics overall (66 percent), those sixty-five and older (53 percent), and those eighteen to twenty-nine (80 percent) is remarkable given the concerted effort by the USCCB's absolute condemnation of same-sex marriage and resistance to sexual orientation or gender nondiscrimination legislation.

Americans broadly support nondiscrimination laws that protect LGBT people in employment, housing, and public accommodations. Seventy percent of them favor such laws, 35 percent of them *strongly* favor, and only 23 percent oppose them. There is strong support among Catholics for nondiscrimination laws; white Catholics favor them (74 percent) and *strongly* favor them (35 percent) and Hispanic Catholics favor them (70 percent) and *strongly* favor them (25 percent).[55] Sociological data demonstrate a disconnect between official Catholic teaching and the beliefs of Catholics on both same-sex marriage and nondiscrimination legislation. What is this teaching, and what accounts for the disconnect?

Official Catholic teaching is that a homosexual orientation is "objectively disordered" and that homosexual acts are "intrinsically disordered." The former claim means that homosexual orientation, though not sinful, "is a more or less strong tendency ordered toward an intrinsic moral evil; and thus the inclination itself must be seen as an objective disorder." The latter claim affirms tradition that "has always declared that 'homosexual acts are intrinsically disordered.' They are contrary to the natural law and close the sexual act to the gift of life. They do not proceed from a genuine affective and sexual complementarity. Under no circumstances can they be approved" (*CCC,* no. 2357). Labeling homosexual orientation "objectively disordered" is hurtful and alienates homosexuals, their families, and friends. One reason Millennials and Gen Zers are leaving the church is because of its anti-homosexual teachings. This is a perfect example of institutional scotosis.

Catholic teaching posits an ontological gender binary between male and female that is God-given and uses the term *complementarity* to articulate its position. Complementarity posits that there are certain realities that belong together and that together produce a whole that neither produces alone. We note the following characteristics of complementarity. First, it

---

[55] Robert P. Jones et al., "Emerging Consensus on LGBT Issues: Findings from the 2017 American Values Atlas," Public Religion Research Institute (2018).

is nearly always classified along masculine and feminine lines,[56] and this classification is used metaphorically, biologically, or in a combination of both. Second, it is often formulated by Pope John Paul II as a "nuptial hermeneutics," in terms of bridegroom and bride.[57] God, Jesus, and husband are presented as masculine and bridegroom; creation, church, and wife are presented as feminine and bride. Third, in its theological anthropology, the Catholic magisterium posits an "ontological complementarity" whereby men and women, though fundamentally equal and complete in themselves,[58] are incomplete as a couple ("Letter to Women," no. 7). Heterosexual complementarity completes the couple in marriage and reproductive-type sexual acts by bringing the masculine and feminine biological and psychological elements together in a unified whole.

David Matzo McCarthy expands the church's notion of a nuptial hermeneutic that limits moral sexual relationships to heterosexual marriage and argues for a nuptial metaphor of *both* homosexual and heterosexual unions grounded in the human body. He does so in four steps. First, the beginning of all theological reflection is "God's reconciliation with the world, which, in the gathering of the church, constitutes a body."[59] Second, the church/ body of Christ generates a relationship of bodies to create a network of communion or common life. Within this network there is a "desire of the body" to enter into permanent unions, "which is drawn to God's faithfulness and patterned in mimesis of God's enduring love." Third, this desire is "matched by a thoroughgoing hermeneutics of the body" whereby, "through marriage, the body is given an identity that does not merely bring its agency to fulfillment but also locates the communicative acts of the body at the axis of a community's whole life."[60]

Fourth, McCarthy argues that although the hermeneutics of the body and the nuptial metaphor it justifies is limited to heterosexual marriage in

---

[56] It is important to note that the distinction between biological sex (male/female) and socially conditioned gender (masculine/feminine) is frequently absent in magisterial discussions of complementarity. See Susan A. Ross, "The Bridegroom and the Bride: The Theological Anthropology of John Paul II and Its Relation to the Bible and Homosexuality," in *Sexual Diversity and Catholicism: Toward the Development of Moral Theology*, ed. Patricia Beattie Jung with Joseph Andrew Coray, 39–59 (Collegeville, MN: Liturgical Press, 2001), 56n5.

[57] Ross, "The Bridegroom and the Bride"; and David Matzko McCarthy, "The Relationship of Bodies: A Nuptial Hermeneutics of Same-Sex Unions," in *Theology and Sexuality: Classic and Contemporary Readings*, ed. Eugene F. Rogers, Jr. (Oxford: Blackwell Publishing, 2002), 206–10.

[58] John Paul II, "Authentic Concept of Conjugal Love," *Origins* 28 (March 4, 1999): 655.

[59] McCarthy, "The Relationship of Bodies," 201.

[60] Ibid., 210.

the Catholic tradition, it can be extended to homosexual unions as well by integrating an adequate definition of sexual orientation into a theology of the body to develop a "nuptial hermeneutics of same-sex unions."[61] The magisterium defines heterosexual orientation as normative, the "natural" explanation of the nuptial metaphor, and defines homosexual orientation as objectively disordered. Homosexual orientation is objectively disordered in the *desire* for a person of the same sex and because it creates a "strong tendency" toward homosexual *acts* that are intrinsically evil.[62] This emphasis on desire and act highlights the disparity in magisterial teaching in the term *orientation* when applied to heterosexual or homosexual orientation. Heterosexual orientation focuses on the affective complementarity of two embodied persons;[63] homosexual orientation focuses on desire and acts.

McCarthy provides a definition of homosexual orientation, which, aside from hetero-genital complementarity, is consistent with the magisterium's understanding of heterosexual orientation:

> Gay men and lesbians are persons who encounter the other (and thus discover themselves) in relation to persons of the same sex. This same-sex orientation is a given of their coming to be, that is, the nuptial meaning of human life emerges for a gay man in relation to other men and a woman when face to face with other women.[64]

In a steadfast interpersonal union homosexual couples give their bodies to one another and are "theologically communicative," that is, they are witnesses to the community of God's "constancy and steadfast fidelity."[65] In their witness homosexual couples have "iconic significance" in their sexuality through embodied interpersonal union, just as heterosexual couples, both fertile and infertile, have "iconic significance" in their sexuality in their embodied interpersonal union. Heterosexual complementarity is not a determining factor. Rather, two embodied persons, heterosexual or homosexual, in permanent interpersonal union reflecting God's constant love and steadfast fidelity are the determining factor. In the case of fertile heterosexual couples, embodied interpersonal union is potentially procreative; in the case of infertile heterosexual and homosexual couples,

---

[61] Ibid., 212.

[62] CDF, "Letter to the Bishops of the Catholic Church on the Pastoral Care of Homosexual Persons" (October 1, 1986), no. 3; and "Vatican List of Catechism Changes," *Origins* 27, no. 15 (September 25, 1997): 257.

[63] Congregation for Catholic Education, *Educational Guidance in Human Love: Outlines for Sex Education* (Rome: Typis Polyglottis Vaticanis, 1983), 13n35.

[64] McCarthy, "The Relationship of Bodies," 212–13.

[65] Ibid., 213.

embodied interpersonal union is not potentially procreative. Embodiment and the nuptial metaphor, however, are essential to all three unions.

McCarthy proposes an incarnational sexuality directed by relationship and engaging embodiedness in a way that respects sexual orientation and sees the potential of relational fulfillment through embodied heterosexual, homosexual, or bisexual persons. This vision of embodiedness that is not attached to a gender binary also serves to reshape stances on transgender and intersex people.

Abby Wilkerson summarizes this rethinking in relation to intersex people: healthy sexualities may "encompass a range of pleasures and identities, rather than evaluating the eroticism of bodily configurations and practices on the basis of their proximity to a predetermined norm."[66] The principle applies also to transgender people.

McCarthy provides a credible theological perspective to challenge the Catholic Church's heterosexual absolutism on sexual relationships, but what justifies the church's stance and the disconnect on LGBT issues between that stance and the stance of Catholic lay people? First, guided by conscience, which we discuss in detail in Chapter 6, the *sensus fidelium* is functioning as a source of ethical knowledge on LGBT issues. As discussed in Chapter 3, the International Theological Commission teaches that *sensus fidei* is "a sort of spiritual instinct that enables the believer to judge spontaneously whether a particular teaching or practice is or is not in conformity with the Gospel and with apostolic faith."[67] That instinct enables all believers both "to recognize and endorse authentic Christian doctrine and practice and to reject what is false," and "to fulfill their prophetic calling."[68] That the vast majority of Catholics in Western culture now support same-sex marriage and nondiscrimination legislation against the LGBT population is not an argument; it is a fact. Surveys point to the fact that Catholics know their church condemns same-sex relationships and does not support nondiscrimination legislation, but they are not convinced by these teachings. As McCarthy's "iconic significance" and other arguments indicate,[69] there are substantial theological arguments challenging the church's stance on these issues and, for many Catholics, the church's

---

[66] Abby L. Wilkerson, "Normate Sex and Its Discontents," in *Sex and Disability*, ed. Robert McRuer and Anna Mollow (Durham, NC: Duke University Press, 2012), 202.

[67] International Theological Commission, Sensus Fidei *in the Life of the Church* (2014), no. 49.

[68] Ibid., no. 2.

[69] See Todd A. Salzman and Michael G. Lawler, *The Sexual Person: Toward a Renewed Catholic Anthropology* (Washington, DC: Georgetown University Press, 2008).

arguments lack credibility and appear to many to be a violation of human dignity and justice.

A second source of ethical knowledge in church teaching is its teaching on the authority and inviolability of a well-formed conscience. Conscience must be formed according to the various sources of ethical knowledge. Church tradition is one source of ethical knowledge and it requires respect,[70] not unthinking obedience, as one of many virtues that should guide Catholics in forming their consciences. That respect for church teaching has to be in dialogue with other sources of ethical knowledge in the formation of conscience, especially experience.

Experience, a third crucial source of ethical knowledge, is critical when reflecting on same-sex relationships and transgender issues. Some thirty years ago, while acknowledging that the question of same-sex relations was a question of dispute, Margaret Farley noted this homosexual experience from anecdotal sources and commented that we "have some clear and profound testimonies to the life-enhancing possibilities of same-sex relations and the integrating possibilities of sexual activity within these relations. We have the witness that homosexuality can be a way of embodying responsible love and sustaining human friendship."[71] She repeats this judgment in her book *Just Love*.[72] She concludes, logically, that "this witness alone is enough to demand of the Christian community that it reflect anew on the norms for homosexual love."[73] Her astute observation has been radically reaffirmed in the marital experience of countless homosexual couples, especially since the US Supreme Court decision of *Obergefell v. Hodges* in 2015 legalizing same-sex marriage.

Combined with other methodological considerations, the ethical sources of *sensus fidei*, conscience, and experience call for a fundamental rethinking of the anthropology grounding the church's absolute norms prohibiting same-sex relationships and the church's stance justifying unjust discrimination based on homosexual orientation and gender. It is to these considerations we turn in the next chapter.

---

[70] See Francis A. Sullivan, *Magisterium: Teaching Authority in the Catholic Church* (Dublin: Gill and Macmillan, 1985), 159–64.

[71] Margaret A. Farley, "An Ethic for Same-Sex Relations," in *A Challenge to Love: Gay and Lesbian Catholics in the Church*, ed. Robert Nugent, 93–106 (New York: Crossroad, 1983), 99–100.

[72] Farley returns to the question of gay and lesbian experience and judges that "we do have strong witnesses to the role of such relationships in sustaining human well-being and opening to human flourishing" (Farley, *Just Love*, 287).

[73] Farley, "An Ethic for Same-Sex Relations," 99–100.

Questions for Reflection

- Explain the virtue of faith and its alliance with justice in the virtuous principle *faith that sees injustice and does justice.* What do you understand by the word *praxis,* and what are its implications for theological ethics?
- Describe the various understandings of justice and how those understandings can come into conflict. List and explain criteria for resolving such conflicts. Is it just for the Colorado baker to refuse to bake a cake for a same-sex couple's wedding? Explain and discuss your answer.
- Explain the virtuous principle *faith that sees injustice and does justice.* How does this principle function in the four theological perspectives of liberation, feminist, black, and LGBT theological ethics?
- What is the oppression that liberation theology seeks to address? What methodological insights does it contribute to alleviate that oppression?
- What is the oppression that feminist theology seeks to address? What methodological insights does it contribute to alleviate that oppression?
- What is the oppression that black theology seeks to address? What methodological insights does it contribute to alleviate that oppression?
- What is the oppression that LGBT theology seeks to address? What methodological insights does it contribute to alleviate that oppression?

Suggested Readings

Cone, James. *The Cross and the Lynching Tree.* Maryknoll, NY: Orbis Books, 2007.

Copeland, Shawn, M. *Enfleshing Freedom: Body, Race, and Being.* Minneapolis: Fortress Press, 2010.

Curran, Charles E. *Diverse Voices in Modern US Moral Theology.* Washington, DC: Georgetown University Press, 2018.

Curran, Charles E., Margaret A. Farley, and Richard A. McCormick, SJ, eds. *Feminist Ethics and the Catholic Moral Tradition: Readings in Moral Theology No. 9.* New York: Paulist Press, 1996.

Gutiérrez, Gustavo. *A Theology of Liberation.* Second edition. Maryknoll, NY: Orbis Books, 1988.

Massingale, Bryan N. *Racial Justice and the Catholic Church.* Maryknoll, NY: Orbis Books, 2010.

Thatcher, Adrian, ed. *The Oxford Handbook of Theology, Sexuality, and Gender.* Oxford: Oxford University Press, 2015.

5

Anthropology
and Ethical Norms

Learning Objectives

- Understand anthropology and human dignity.
- Understand and explain the dimensions of the human person integrally considered.
- Understand what an ethical norm is and what its implications are for ethical action.
- Understand and distinguish between faculty and epistemic virtues.

Throughout this book we argue, sometimes explicitly, sometimes implicitly, that what is ethical is what validates and enhances human dignity and what is unethical is what denies and damages human dignity. The word *dignity* denotes worth, and human dignity denotes the worth of every human being—black, brown, white, Asian, Native American, bisexual, heterosexual, homosexual, transsexual, male, female. *Gaudium et Spes* suggests an approach to what must be included in any definition of human dignity when it prescribes that the ethical character of any action must be determined by objective criteria "drawn from the nature of the human person and human action" (*GS,* no. 51). The official commentary on *Gaudium et Spes* explains that this principle applies not only to marriage and sexuality about which it is formally articulated, but also to the entire realm of human activity. It is formulated as a general principle: "Human activity must be judged insofar as it refers to the human person integrally and adequately considered."[1] The human person integrally and

---

[1] *Schema constitutionis pastoralis de ecclesia in mundo huius temporis: Textus recognitus et relationes*, par. 11 (Vatican City: Vatican Press, 1965), 9.

adequately considered is defined by an anthropology. The longstanding official anthropology of the Catholic tradition holds that the human being is composed of a body and a soul that vivifies the body and makes the resulting person a human person, a rational animal. Drawing on *Gaudium et Spes*'s embodied personalist principle, Belgian theological ethicist Louis Janssens expands on that body-soul anthropology and advances a theological anthropology that embraces six dimensions of the human person and his or her dignity. The human person is a subject; in corporeality; in relationship to the material world, to others, and, we add, to self and to God; created in the image and likeness of God; a historical being; and fundamentally unique but equal to all other persons.[2] We consider each characteristic in turn.

The Human Person Integrally and Adequately Considered

First, the human person is a free and inviolable subject and should never be treated as an object or as a means to some end. Every subject-person is, at least potentially, a rational, knowing, judging, and freely deciding human being. Thomas Aquinas teaches that the human soul has two powers: intellect, which is the understanding, knowing, and judging power; and will, which is the choosing and deciding power. The will is free, and freedom to make one's own, unforced choices is an essential dimension of human anthropology; that freedom founds that most important dimension of human dignity, namely, personal conscience, which we shall consider in detail in the next chapter. For the moment we note only the teaching of *Dignitatis Humanae (Decree on Religious Freedom)* on the freedom and inviolability of conscience. It decrees that the free human being "is not to be forced to act in a manner contrary to his conscience. Nor, on the other hand, is he to be restrained from acting in accordance with his conscience, especially in matters religious" (*DH*, no. 3). Freedom of informed conscience is an essential characteristic of humans and of their intrinsic dignity and must be active in every decision for action for it to be ethical. Any decision persons are forced to against their will is not to be, *indeed* cannot be, judged an ethical decision.

Second, persons are also corporeal; they are essentially *embodied* persons. A longstanding and well known, but not so well understood Catholic teaching has been that the human being is essentially composed of body

---

[2] Louis Janssens, "Artificial Insemination: Ethical Considerations," *Louvain Studies* 8 (1980): 3–29.

and soul. That teaching poorly understood led to the negative presumption that men and women were dualistic, divided into two unequal parts, a body that was physical and of a lower order and a soul that was spiritual and of a higher order. Embedded in that presumption, James Nelson notes, was an approach to bodiliness which "distrusted, feared, and discounted our bodies,"[3] especially their sexuality understood as physical. Sandra Lipsitz Bem shows how that distrust and fear of our bodies and their perceived inadequacies is manifested in our endless attempts to improve them.[4] Those attempts, we underscore, are motivated more by our desire to improve our *gendered* bodies rather than our *physiological* bodies. Nowhere was that distrust and fear more in evidence than in matters related to sexuality. The Christian tradition has always been suspicious of embodied sexuality and has regarded it in general as "objectively disordered" as a consequence of original sin.[5] This negative tradition about the body seriously influenced ethical judgments on the dignity of embodied men and women and led to rigid sexual norms that restricted sexual activity to marriage between a man and a woman. As far back as the fifth century, St. Augustine of Hippo taught that virginity was to be preferred to marriage,[6] and that even in marriage, "in these days no one perfect in piety seeks to have children other than spiritually."[7]

After the horrors of the Second World War that presumption of the imperfection of bodily existence began to wane and was replaced by a developing and widespread theological opinion that human existence—"even in the sphere of the Spirit—is essentially bodily existence."[8] So fundamental to human existence and anthropology is bodiliness that contemporary Catholic theologians tend to say not that men and women *have* bodies but that they *are* bodies. The distrust and fear of the human body that once controlled the Christian tradition and so diminished human dignity, has given way to a positive evaluation of the human body, embodiedness, and its essential place in human reality that has greatly enhanced human

---

[3] James Nelson, *Body Theology* (Louisville, KY: Westminster/John Knox Press, 1992), 9.

[4] Sandra Lipsitz Bem, *The Lenses of Gender: Transforming the Debate on Sexual Inequality* (New Haven, CT: Yale University Press, 1993), 159–62.

[5] Mark Jordan, *The Silence of Sodom: Homosexuality in Modern Catholicism* (Chicago: University of Chicago Press, 2000), 34.

[6] Augustine, *De Bono Coniugali*, III, 3, *PL* 40, 375. The Council of Trent taught the same thing (see *Catechism of the Council of Trent*, trans. John A. McHugh and Charles J. Callan [New York: Wagner, 1945], 338–43).

[7] Augustine, *De Bono Coniugali*, *PL* 40, 387.

[8] Rudolph Bultmann, *Theology of the New Testament* (London: SCM, 1952) I, 192.

dignity. That enhancement calls for a reevaluation, we have argued, of the Catholic ethical norms that control sexuality.[9]

Third, through their bodies humans are essentially persons-in-relation, each with self, with other embodied persons, with the material world, and with God. Being in relation is an essential factor of human being and human dignity. Psychological studies repeatedly indicate that one of the greatest threats to healthy human development is poor self-esteem, and the Christian tradition has not always done an adequate job of emphasizing healthy self-esteem or self-love. Jesus's great commandment is well known: "'You shall love the Lord your God with all your heart, with all your soul, with all your mind, and with all your strength.' The second is this: 'You shall love your neighbor as yourself'" (Mark 12:28–34; Matt 22:34–40, 46b; Luke 10:25–28). Not so well known is the fact that there are *three* commandments in this text: love God, love yourself, and love your neighbor as yourself. Typically, the Christian tradition has interpreted self-love as egocentric and antithetical to the love of the gospel. While this certainly *can* be the case, and the cultures of Western countries that emphasize radical individualism encourage egocentric love, that love is not the healthy self-love demanded by the gospel. Authentic self-love first affirms oneself as a good, valuable, and lovable self-in-God and then, in alliance with love of neighbor, turns toward others and places this good, valuable, and lovable self-in-God unconditionally at their service.[10] If humans do not truly and fully accept and love themselves, in both their wholeness and their brokenness, they can neither give themselves fully to another person nor fully accept the other person.

Humans are also in relation with one another; they are, in the language of the Gospels, *neighbors*. Who, Jesus was asked, and we also ask, is our neighbor, and how are we called to love that person? As the Gospels make clear, our neighbor can be any other person, at any time, at any place. Some of the most challenging parables, like that of the Good Samaritan for example (Luke 10:29–37), concern those whom we would least likely consider to be our neighbor: "Samaritans," homosexuals, people with AIDS, people of color, the poor and marginalized, women in a patriarchal society, and very visibly in our day, refugees. Yet, it is these very people that Jesus commands us to love and to treat with compassion and mercy. The possibilities of fulfilling this command in both disposition and action are countless, but it is beyond doubt that the core of Christian ethics is that

[9] See Todd A. Salzman and Michael G. Lawler, *The Sexual Person: Toward a Renewed Catholic Anthropology* (Washington, DC: Georgetown University Press, 2008).
[10] See Darlene Fozard Weaver, *Self-Love and Christian Ethics* (Cambridge: Cambridge University Press, 2002).

we first recognize this demand for love of neighbor, that we see injustice and do justice toward our neighbors.

Humans are also in relation with the material world. As embodied persons we recognize our need for clean air and water, shelter, and healthy living conditions, and this recognition brings with it a recognition of our responsibility to care for the material world. This responsibility for our environment is a crucial issue in contemporary ethics, which we develop extensively in Chapter 7. As the world population continues to grow and the science of climate change continues to reveal calamitous effects on our environment and the survival of the human species if we do not act soon to reduce carbon emissions, this issue requires urgent attention. We need to utilize technology to develop what Edward Schillebeeckx refers to as a "meta-cosmos" that rescues humans "from their animal limitations and offers an opening for new possibilities."[11] Technology can be a positive or negative tool for humanization. It can produce nuclear bombs and it can produce clean and reusable energy, though not without risk, as tragic experiences at Chernobyl, Three Mile Island, and Fukushima have taught us.[12] It can help us harness solar and wind energy, conserve energy, and preserve natural resources to reduce carbon emissions, thereby slowing climate change. We must acknowledge both that there are a limited number of natural resources and that limited resources require not only conservation but also fair and equitable distribution throughout the world. Social and environmental ethics both rely heavily upon this dimension of human reality and dignity.[13]

Humans are also, and importantly, in relation with God, and this relationship is important throughout this book as we seek to articulate a Christian ethics for the third millennium. "Created in the image of God, the human person is called to know and worship Him . . . and to glorify Him in all their attitudes and activities."[14] Christians believe in a loving Creator God, that they are called to be in a profound relationship with this Creator God, and that their character dispositions and actions affect their relationship with this God. If they freely accept relationship with God, as they can, then they accept also that they find their ultimate well-being and doing and dignity in this relationship. This relationship, however,

---

[11] Edward Schillebeeckx, *Christ: The Experience of Jesus as Lord* (New York: Seabury, 1980), 735.

[12] See Osamu Takeuchi, "Nature, Human Beings, and Nuclear Power in Japan," in *Just Sustainability: Technology, Ecology, and Resource Extraction*, ed. Christiana Z. Peppard and Andrea Vicini (Maryknoll, NY: Orbis Books, 2015).

[13] See Pope Francis, *Laudato si'*; Richard Miller, ed., *God, Creation, and Climate Change* (Maryknoll, NY: Orbis Books, 2010); and Peppard and Vicini, *Just Sustainability*.

[14] Janssens, "Artificial Insemination," 9.

is not a divinely exclusive one; it is reflected broadly in all our human relationships. Our relationship with God and neighbor is dialectical. Pope Francis reminds us, "You cannot love God without loving your neighbor, and you cannot love your neighbor without loving God."[15] God's love for us and our love for God are foundational for all being in relationship. Love invites us to live a life of faith praxis, hope, and self-love and love of neighbor evidenced in care for ourselves, for others, and for the world we inhabit.

Our relationship with God includes various theological mysteries that shape a distinct Christian perspective. We are committed to this distinct perspective and its contributions to ethical discourse. Having explained those mysteries in Chapter 3, we now briefly explain how they influence the selection, interpretation, prioritization, and integration of the four sources of ethical knowledge to define human dignity and formulate and justify norms that facilitate and do not frustrate its attainment, especially in the areas of environmental and sexual ethics. Charles Curran argues that perspective, which he calls "stance," is drawn from "the visual experience and expresses the way we look at something that puts everything else into focus."[16] A foundational question to be asked of Christian ethical method, then, is what perspective guides Christian ethicists in their perception of reality? Metaethical objectivism justifies the claim that the good can be defined, and faith in the living Christ provides the perspective or hermeneutical lens to formulate and justify both that definition and the norms that facilitate its attainment. Drawing from what he calls the "fivefold Christian mysteries," Curran formulates a Christian perspective that serves as a paradigm and point of departure for Christian ethical method.[17] James Gustafson judges that "Curran's stance demonstrates the significance of 'postethical' levels of moral discourse or, in other words, of background beliefs and loyalties that provide a larger framework of justification and orientation for ethics without being a sufficient condition for determining particular moral action."[18] Curran proposes the following mysteries as

---

[15] Pope Francis, *The Infinite Tenderness of God: Meditations on the Gospels* (Frederick, MD: The Word Among Us Press, 2016).

[16] Charles E. Curran, *The Catholic Moral Tradition Today* (Washington, DC: Georgetown University Press, 1999), 30.

[17] Charles E. Curran, *Moral Theology: A Continuing Journey* (Notre Dame, IN: University of Notre Dame Press, 1982), 38–44; Curran, *The Catholic Moral Tradition Today*, 30.

[18] James M. Gustafson, "Charles Curran: Ecumenical Moral Theologian Par Excellence," in *A Call to Fidelity: On the Moral Theology of Charles E. Curran*, ed. James J. Walter, Timothy E. O'Connell, and Thomas A. Shannon (Washington, DC: Georgetown University Press, 2002), 225–26.

inherent in a Christian perspective: creation, sin, incarnation, redemption, and resurrection destiny.[19]

The mystery of creation nurtures the belief that God has created the universe and everything in it, including rational humans, and that God's creation is fundamentally good. Since human nature is a clearly discernible *rational* nature, to act according to their nature humans are required to act rationally, and through their rational reflection on the created world they have the capacity to discern ethical truth, that is, to discern the behavior that facilitates the attainment of human dignity. Unfortunately, however, long historical experience shows that humans do not always act rationally, and unethical behavior or sin is a demonstrable reality of their existence together; it came into and continues in creation through human actions contrary to humans' rational nature. Though the mystery of sin does not destroy the basic goodness of God's creation, it does deform it. It affects human reason, diminishing the ability to discern the meaning of human existence, the recognition of and respect for human dignity, and the call to wholeness or holiness. We note something here that is important to consider in a materialistic world. One need not accept that these religious mysteries are true in any scientifically verifiable way to accept them as satisfying and beneficial to a life in relation with other human beings. Philosopher Owen Flanagan, who certainly does not believe they are true and who asserts that "thinking about our lives in ways that incorporate superstition and wishful thinking is childish and unbecoming to rational social animals like us," still accepts them as supporting a way of social life that is "noble, honest, and worthy."[20]

For Curran, stance or perspective "serves as an interpretive tool in understanding the basic mysteries of Christian life."[21] For Philip Keane, it "is a creative, integrating, imaginative grasp of the meaning of life."[22]

---

[19] See also James M. Gustafson, *Christ and the Moral Life* (New York: Harper and Row, 1968), 242–48, and James T. Bretzke, *A Morally Complex World: Engaging Contemporary Moral Theology* (Collegeville, MN: Michael Glazier, 2004), 33–35, who have proposed Christ as the foundational stance for Christian ethics. While Christ is the *norma normans non normata* (the norming but unnormed norm), proposing him as foundational stance begs the question of Christology. We concur with Curran that, given the complexity of christological questions and the danger of a narrow Christology (Curran, *The Catholic Moral Tradition Today*, 31–32) and further, given that the mysteries Curran cites are directly related to questions of Christology, these mysteries may adequately account for a Christian stance.

[20] Owen Flanagan, *The Really Hard Problem: Meaning in a Material World* (Cambridge, MA: MIT Press, 2007), 108, 190.

[21] Curran, *Moral Theology*, 43.

[22] Philip S. Keane, *Christian Ethics and Imagination* (New York: Paulist Press, 1984), 65.

The Christian theological perspective that Christian ethicists share—the selection, interpretation, prioritization, and integration of the Christian mysteries—shapes their ethical perspectives and guides the process of their formulating a definition of human dignity and of norms that facilitate its attainment. Their perspective is often implied rather than stated in their writings. Drawing attention to perspective, however, is crucial to Christian ethical method. It may shift the focus from the formulation and justification of specific norms for the ethical life, which is often polarizing and not necessarily conducive to dialogue among Christian ethicists, to perspectives on creation, sin, incarnation, redemption, and resurrection and how those mysteries shape a perspective, provide common ground for open and charitable dialogue, and build community. The International Theological Commission's call for constructing interdisciplinary theological methods could foster such dialogue.[23]

Fourth, each corporeal human being, the Christian traditions universally hold, is brought into existence by the creative act of God:

> God created humankind in his own image,
>   in the image of God he created them;
>   male and female he created them. (Gen 1:27)

Each embodied human being, male and female alike, is created by God in the image and likeness of God. That human image and likeness of God introduces a very important, and much ignored, dimension of human dignity, namely, its historical dimension. Contemporary Catholic theology looks upon God as both transcendent *Mystery* and, on the basis of God's creation of all there is, as present in and to the world as the ground of its existence.[24] This Mystery is revealed to humans not from outside their world but from inside it and from history, especially from inside the history of the man Jesus of Nazareth. It is communicated to all persons created and born into the world and remains embedded in their world as an essential dimension at the very heart of their history. Divine Mystery is not above the historical process but at its very heart, in and through history's unfolding forward movement.

---

[23] International Theological Commission, "Theology Today: Perspectives, Principles and Criteria," *Origins* (March 15, 2012): 641–63.

[24] See, for instance, Michael H. Barnes, *In the Presence of Mystery: An Introduction to the Story of Human Religiousness* (Mystic, CT: Twenty-Third Publications, 1984); Elizabeth A. Johnson, *She Who Is: The Mystery of God in Feminist Theological Discourse* (New York: Crossroad, 1992).

When men and women cooperate with the divine Mystery, they can be converted—changed existentially, intellectually, and ethically—and move forward to a more responsible and ethical stance toward both their fellow humans and the God who created each of them. It is here that the Mystery of God present in and to God's creation makes existential contact with the mystery of the human created by God. Created in the image and likeness of divine Mystery, each human is a mystery to be plumbed to an ever-greater depth. No one person is complete at creation but is a being needing to be completed, needing to develop gradually into the person the Creator God intended that person to become, humanly, relationally, intellectually, ethically, and spiritually. That dynamic of humans awaiting gradual completion means that everything that can be said at any given time in history about them is partial, tentative, and waiting to evolve gradually as humans themselves evolve. Pope John Paul II proposed this law of gradualness in *Familiaris Consortio*, insisting that the human being "knows, loves, and accomplishes moral good by different stages of growth" (*FC,* no. 123). Pope Francis, in turn, points out in *Amoris Laetitia* that "this is not a gradualness of law but rather a gradualness in the prudential exercise of free acts on the part of subjects who are not in a position to understand, appreciate or fully carry out the objective demands of the law" (*AL,* no. 295). The full comprehension of the mystery of humanity and its relationship to the Creator God, Christian theologians teach, is *eschatological*, that is, it is achieved only at the end of life.[25]

Fifth, humans are essentially historical beings and any credible understanding of them and of their dignity must recognize the impact of history on them. This impact and its implications for defining human dignity, however, are interpreted differently according to different theoretical perspectives. Some theologians focus on a classicist, universal, and essential understanding of basic goods like life, knowledge, self-integration, practical authenticity, justice and friendship, marriage, and religion or holiness. Others focus on a historically conscious, particular, and existential understanding of these same goods. While acknowledging the universal inclination of human beings toward basic goods, the latter also recognize their particularity. As aspects of universal human dignity the basic goods are universal; as individual instantiations of basic goods that provide human beings with a rational basis for ethical choice, they are particularized by history, culture, social context, individuality, and particular relationships. We agree with Lisa Sowle Cahill that the basic goods are universal as "shared framing experiences and moral common ground" in that there is "shared human being in the world;" they are particular in that the "shared

---

[25] Schillebeeckx, *Christ,* 731.

is achieved not beyond or over against particularity but in and through it."[26] Because of the law of gradual growth noted above, historical consciousness recognizes that there is not a single absolute perspective or definition of human dignity but plural partial, adequate, and reliable perspectives that are shaped by an ongoing dialogue in the present, with the past, directed toward the future.

The sixth dimension of the human is that each and every human, corporeal person is unique and equal to all other human persons. This dimension is so universally acknowledged that we see no need to delay on it, except to emphasize that however unique every person might be not one of us is ever as fully developed and formed as we might be. An essential honoring of all persons' dignity, therefore, will mean allowing them to grow and develop gradually in every facet of their lives, as both popes John Paul II and Francis teach (*FC,*, no. 34; *AL*, no. 295).

An essential prerequisite before entering into any of the many dialogues in this book is to be again clear about how we understand what is ethical. What is ethical, good, and right is what facilitates these dimensions of the human person and of human dignity; what is unethical, bad, and wrong frustrates them. Ethical challenges abound when, as is inevitable, our actions facilitate some dimensions of human dignity but conflict with others. We can travel, for example, to a conference to discuss important ethical issues surrounding climate change and possible theological and scientific responses to it. This facilitates our relationships with colleagues, the impact we can have on religious and political groups, and perhaps creates an overall positive impact on our relationship with the material world. The material resources we use to travel to the conference by car or plane, however, and the carbon emissions from them that further pollute our atmosphere, and the services provided by workers in hotels and restaurants not paid a just and living wage, can have a negative impact on the material world and the human relationships we are hoping to improve. Such is the ethical complexity of every genuine human act.

Ethical Norms

We move on now to the consideration of Catholic norms for ethical behavior. "Moral norms are the criteria for judging the sorts of persons we ought to be and the sorts of actions we ought to perform in faithful response to

---

[26] Lisa Sowle Cahill, *Sex, Gender, and Christian Ethics* (Cambridge: Cambridge University Press, 1996), 51, 55.

God's call"[27] to love God and to love our neighbors as ourselves. Norms are either formal or material. Formal norms are moral absolutes derived from our knowledge of human nature and of God's law. Given the anthropology we have articulated, for instance, and specifically given our understanding of all humans as free and equal persons, a first formal and universal norm will be that the common good should be sought in all our actions. A second formal norm would be that we should be just always, in all circumstances, to all people, a norm that can be articulated also in the gospel injunction to love our neighbors as ourselves. Pope Francis has appropriated to himself an important teaching of Aquinas. The devil, he asserts, is always in the detail. "Although there is necessity in the general principles, the more we descend to matters of detail the more frequently we encounter defects. . . . In matters of action, truth or practical rectitude is not the same for all as to matters of detail, but only as to the general principles. . . . The principle will be found to fail according as we descend further into detail." It is true, he continues, that general rules "set forth a good which can never be disregarded or neglected, but in their formulation they cannot provide absolutely for all particular situations" (*AL*, no. 204).[28] The application of general principles and formal norms to particular situations is not a "one size fits all" but must be discerned in context and in conscience.

The application of the formal norm that the common good is to be safeguarded and promoted in all our actions, therefore, must be conscientiously discerned from the consideration of both the norm itself and the particular context and circumstance in which it is to be applied. One application of the ethical norm of the common good that is particularly pressing in our shared world today is the issue of climate change, an issue "in which humans from many nations, traditions, and generations find themselves collectively responsible for how a planetary system will function over centuries."[29] Lutheran ethicist Larry Rasmussen describes climate change as "a perfect moral storm,"[30] and it is a storm for the creation of which we are all guilty and for the resolution of which we are all ethically responsible. In their discernment today of their responsibility for the resolution of the crisis of climate change, and with the memory of the close reciprocation

---

[27] Richard M. Gula, *Reason Informed by Faith: Foundations of Catholic Morality* (New York: Paulist Press, 1989), 283.

[28] Thomas Aquinas, *Summa Theologiae Santi Thomae de Aquino* I-II, 94, 4 (hereinafter, *ST*).

[29] Willis Jenkins, *The Future of Ethics: Sustainability, Social Justice and Religious Creativity* (Washington, DC: Georgetown University Press, 2013), 1.

[30] Larry Rasmussen, "Climate Change as a Perfect Moral Storm," *Journal of Lutheran Ethics* 14 (2014): 41.

both the Old and the New Testaments make between God and God's poor,[31] when deciding for the common good Christians must always take into consideration the plight of the poor and marginalized who are always the ones who suffer most from the effects of climate change across the world.

The rule "be just" also needs to be discerned for what specific and detailed action(s) we must do to be just. The conscientiously discerned actions become material norms. Discerning the formal norm to be just toward all equal and equally free persons, we can easily deduce the material norms do not kill, do not tell a falsehood, do not steal your neighbor's goods, repay your debts. We could also deduce material norms proscribing racism toward people of color and discrimination against LGBT people and prescribing hospitality toward strangers and immigrants to be major, universal ethical issues today. Racism is not unique to America, but it has been endemic in America since it accommodated slavery, thus concretely falsifying the principle of human equality. That principle, like all formal principles, needs to be discerned and made concrete in detailed material norms and actions, norms such as people of color are not to be disrespected and discriminated against, actions such as accepting African, Mexican, and Native American peoples, educating them, hiring them, paying them just wages, and perhaps above all not gunning them down daily on our streets under the pretext of law and order. They are not "others" in our society, not enemies; they are our fellow citizens and Christian neighbors, many of whom are among the endemically poor and have given their lives to guarantee our freedom.[32]

The United States is a nation of immigrants, which renders ironic the present crisis facing recent immigrants. Christians looking for a norm to fashion their actions and reaction to immigrants need only read their Bible to find its norm of hospitality: "When a stranger sojourns with you in your land, you shall do him no wrong. . . . You shall love him as yourself" (Lev 19:33–34). Jesus validates that norm of hospitality on a number of occasions, instructing his disciples, for instance, "Whenever you enter a town and they do not receive you...I tell you it shall be more tolerable on that day for Sodom than for that town" (Luke 10:10–12; Matt 10:14–15).

---

[31] See Michael G. Lawler, Todd A. Salzman, and Eileen Burke-Sullivan, *The Church in the Modern World: Gaudium et Spes Then and Now* (Collegeville, MN: Liturgical Press, 2014), 138–63.

[32] For more detail on both institutional and individual racism, see Bryan N. Massingale, "Conscience Formation and the Challenge of Unconscious Racism/Racial Bias," in *Conscience and Catholicism: Rights, Responsibilities, and Institutional Policies*, ed. David E. DeCosse and Kristin E. Heyer (Maryknoll, NY: Orbis Books, 2015), 53–68; and Vincent W. Lloyd and Andrew Prevot, eds., *Anti-Blackness and Christian Ethics* (Maryknoll, NY: Orbis Books, 2017).

He also makes hospitality or inhospitality to strangers a major cause of salvation or damnation in Matthew's famous last judgment scene (Matt 25:34–46). The Bible prescribes more salutary ethical principles, norms, and actions than do American politicians with their prescription to build walls, both material and psychological. That is why the Bible is a major source of Christian ethics, and the political proliferation of myths and falsehoods is not.[33]

Formal norms, then, prescribe how we are to be virtuous, while material norms prescribe what we are to do to be virtuous. German theological ethicist Dietmar Mieth asserts that the only absolute ethical norm is that "good is to be done and evil left undone,"[34] and that every other ethical norm requires a subjective and discerning judgment.[35] We agree with him and with the CDF's International Theological Commission that "in the context of pluralism, which is ours, one is more and more aware that one cannot elaborate a morality based on the natural law without including a reflection on the [subjective] interior dispositions or virtues that render the moralist capable of elaborating an adequate norm of action."[36] An anthropological understanding of the human being implicitly enters into every decision about formal ethical norms and every material and action norm. In this section we have considered the ethical behavioral norms that flow from the four sources of Catholic ethics we considered in Chapter 3 and the anthropology we articulated above.

Virtue and Norms

The call for the renewal of theological ethics at the Second Vatican Council in the 1960s emphasized bringing "forth fruit in charity for the life of the world" (*Optatam Totius,* no. 16). This emphasis on the virtue of charity or love reflects earlier Catholic theological efforts to reform the traditional manual method for doing moral theology.[37] Though the council did not issue a specific call for a shift to virtue ethics from the legalistic approach of the manuals, contemporary Catholic theological ethicists have been

---

[33] For further detail on immigration, see *How Immigration and Concerns about Cultural Changes Are Shaping the 2016 Election: Findings from the 2016 PRRI/Brookings Immigration Survey*, Public Religion Research Report.

[34] See Aquinas, *ST* I-II, 94, 2, for this first principle of practical reasoning.

[35] Dietmar Mieth, *Moral und Erfahrung: Beitrage zur theologisch-ethischen Hermeneutik* (Freiburg: Herder, 1977), 34.

[36] International Theological Commission, *In Search of a Universal Ethic: A New Look at Natural Law* (May 20, 2009), no. 55.

[37] See Gerard Gilleman, *The Primacy of Charity in Moral Theology* (Westminster, MD: Newman, 1959).

developing such a shift. Catholic ethical norms initially derived from two methodological approaches, deontology and teleology. Deontology emphasizes rules, obligations, and duties: do not kill, do not commit artificial contraception, honor your father and your mother. Teleology emphasizes the consequences of actions and the maximizing of their good or value.[38] The council's call for a focus on love has been an impetus for transforming Catholic ethical method from an ethics of law or consequences to the virtue ethics of being and doing we have been developing in this book. We align with Alasdair MacIntyre and the many other contemporary ethicists who advance virtue ethics as more promising to the ethical life than deontology or teleology.[39]

The shift from deontology and teleology to virtue ethics is accompanied by a fundamental methodological shift from a focus on subjects' actions to a focus on their characters. There is what John Greco labels a shift in the "direction of analysis"[40] from rules, laws, and actions to free persons and their characters. This shift is as momentous ethically as Copernicus's shift from focusing on the earth as the center of our universe to focusing on the sun as its center was astronomically. Traditional approaches to ethics understand the normative properties of an act in terms of its intrinsic meaning or consequences; the direction of analysis is from act to person. An act is said to be right or wrong based on law or consequences, and a person's character is morally evaluated as virtuous or vicious based on the acts the person does. A virtue approach to ethics understands the normative properties and meanings of acts in terms of the normative properties and meanings of persons. The direction of analysis is from person and personal character to actions. In other words, virtue theories make rightness follow from an action's "source in a virtue, rather than the other way around."[41] This shift prioritizes free persons over the actions they do and virtues over laws and consequences.

We have stated several times in this book the common opinion that virtue ethics focuses on being and character, the being of a subject and that the deontological ethics of duty or utilitarian ethics of consequences focuses on the subject's doing or action. That assertion is true as a general

---

[38] See Todd A. Salzman, *Deontology and Teleology: An Investigation of the Normative Debate in Roman Catholic Moral Theology* (Louvain: Peeters, 1995).

[39] In addition to MacIntyre, whom most judge to be a preeminent contemporary virtue theorist, other important theorists in the field of virtue ethics will be introduced as our chapter unfolds.

[40] John Greco, "Virtue Epistemology," rev., *Stanford Encyclopedia of Philosophy* (Stanford, CA: Stanford University, 2017), 8.

[41] Guy Axtell, ed., *Knowledge, Belief, and Character: Readings in Virtue Epistemology* (Lanham, MD: Rowman and Littlefield, 2000), xiii.

statement about virtue ethics, but it is not especially clarifying of it, and indeed, if it is understood to mean that virtue ethics ignores *doing*, it is entirely untrue, for we expect the virtuous person to *do* virtuously. We expect the character with the virtue of justice to *do* just actions; we expect the character with the virtue of compassion to do compassionate actions; and so on for all the virtues. Contrary to critics who suggest that virtue ethics does not offer ethical directions or rules, it does offer rules. It offers, Rosalind Hursthouse insists, "v-rules": Do justly, do compassionately, do not do what is mean, unjust, or cruel.[42] Ethical action is action according to some virtue, while vicious action is action according to some vice. The ethics of Aristotle and Aquinas was, and contemporary virtue ethics is, an ethics of character and being, but there was and there is always the axiom: action follows being. It is, as we argued earlier, the habitual doing of acts of justice, compassion, and every other virtue that first instills and then reinforces the habits and dispositions that are virtues and the actions to which they are ordered.

The v-rules "be just" and "be compassionate" do not tell a person precisely what action to do to be just or compassionate, but neither do the ontological rules "honor your father and your mother" and "thou shalt not bear false witness." A personal process of discernment is always required to decide what ethical action is required to act justly or to honor your father and your mother. That discernment is under the control of the virtue of prudence, without which, both Aristotle and Aquinas argue, no other virtue is possible. Virtue, remember, is a mean between excess and defect. It is not, however, an arithmetic mean lying midway between excess and defect but a mean relative to the persons. There is, therefore, a range of actions lying on the continuum between excess and defect that would be just or compassionate in any specific situation, and it requires a prudence-controlled personal discernment to decide what action would, in fact, be just or compassionate or honoring of your parents.

Central to a theory of virtue is the notion that virtues are not only preconditions for human flourishing but also constituents of that flourishing. "A virtue is a character trait that human beings, given their physical and spiritual natures, need to flourish (or to do and fare well)."[43] The person with the virtue of justice, for example, will *be* a just person and will therefore *do* just acts. Character virtues, such as justice, compassion, and honesty, are bases of excellent human being and doing. So too are epistemic

---

[42] Rosalind Hursthouse, *On Virtue Ethics* (Oxford: Oxford University Press, 2002), 36–39.

[43] Rosalind Hursthouse, "Applying Virtue Ethics," in *Virtues and Reason: Philippa Foot and Moral Theory*, ed. Rosalind Hursthouse, Gavin Lawrence, and Warren Quinn (Oxford: Clarendon, 1995), 68.

or intellectual virtues, such as prudence, responsibility, and reliability "bases of excellent epistemic [being] and functioning."[44] The character virtues facilitate the attainment of human dignity; the epistemic virtues facilitate the attainment of true knowledge of both human dignity and the principles and norms that facilitate its attainment. "Moral responsibility for what we do," James Montmarquet notes, "is often dependent on epistemic responsibility for what we believe."[45]

Focus on subjective epistemic virtues has founded a relatively new movement in philosophy over the last thirty years named virtue epistemology, which includes diverse schools and methods. All the schools, however, adhere to four basic commitments. First, virtue epistemology is a discipline that yields ethical norms. Second, rational subjects are the foundation of epistemic value and the focus of epistemic evaluation.[46] Third, Greco's "shift in the direction of analysis" evident in virtue ethics is applied also to virtue epistemology, and this shift distinguishes it from traditional epistemological methods. "Non-virtue theories try to analyze virtuous character in terms of justified belief, defining the former in terms of dispositions to achieve the latter." Greco proposes a directional reversal, "defining justified belief in terms of virtuous character that itself is defined in terms of successful and stable dispositions to form belief."[47] Justified beliefs "are those that issue from responsible inquiries of virtuous inquirers. It is a mistake to put it the other way around: epistemic virtues are those habits and dispositions that lead us to have justified beliefs."[48] Fourth, the intellectual virtues are prioritized in the search for justified belief and knowledge.

An epistemic or intellectual virtue, Greco argues, is "an innate ability or acquired habit that allows one to reliably achieve some intellectual good, such as truth."[49] Epistemic virtues include both faculty virtues, like imagination, perception, memory, intuition, introspection, and character virtues, like reliability, responsibility, conscientiousness, carefulness, and open-mindedness. Faculty virtues are indispensable in accounting for knowledge from the past. Character virtues are indispensable in accounting for ongoing knowledge that presupposes past knowledge, builds on it,

---

[44] Robert C. Roberts and W. Jay Wood, *Intellectual Virtues: An Essay in Regulative Epistemology* (Oxford: Oxford University Press, 2007), 7.

[45] James A. Montmarquet, *Epistemic Virtue and Doxastic Responsibility* (Lanham, MD: Rowman and Littlefield, 1993), vii.

[46] John Greco and John Turri, eds., *Virtue Epistemology: Contemporary Readings* (Boston: MIT Press, 2012).

[47] John Greco, "Agent Reliabilism," *Philosophical Perspectives* 13 (1999): 290.

[48] Christopher Hookway, "Cognitive Virtues and Epistemic Evaluations," *International Journal of Philosophical Studies* 2, no. 2 (1994): 211.

[49] Greco, "Virtue Epistemology," 2.

and lets it develop. The development, exercise, and prioritization of the intellectual virtues in the theological ethicist affect the marshaling of evidence to justify a theological anthropology that defines human dignity and formulates and justifies principles and norms that facilitate its attainment.

Virtue epistemologists in general agree on Greco's directional shift in epistemology and the centrality of intellectual virtues in the process of coming to knowledge. They disagree on the interrelationship between virtue epistemology and virtue ethics, on whether or not and how the epistemic *ought* relates to the ethical *ought*. Lorraine Code agrees with Greco's and Ernest Sosa's directional shift in epistemology that emphasizes the cognitive activities of a subject in community guided by the social practices of investigation. She criticizes Sosa, however, for not integrating the insights from ethical virtue theory with virtue epistemology. Specifically, Code believes that epistemology should emphasize virtues that relate to subject agency in the process of attaining and justifying knowledge. To that end she proposes *responsibilism* as a virtue-epistemological theory that posits the subject's responsibility as the primary intellectual virtue. Responsibilism emphasizes both the knower as active agent and the knower's conscientious choice as essential elements in the attainment and justification of knowledge. All other intellectual virtues emanate from this central virtue.[50]

James Montmarquet agrees with Code that virtue theory and virtue epistemology should be more closely aligned, but whereas Code focuses on *responsibility* as the foundational intellectual virtue for epistemic claims, he focuses on *conscientiousness*, which he defines as an appropriate desire for truth.[51] He specifies conscientiousness in three categories of epistemic virtues. The virtue of *intellectual impartiality* includes openness to others' ideas, willingness to learn from others, suspense of personal bias toward others' ideas, and recognition of one's own fallibility. This intellectual impartiality sounds very like what Pope Francis proposes when he proposes dialogue before the articulation of any ethical norm. "Keep an open mind," he advises. "Don't get bogged down in your own limited ideas and opinions but be prepared to change and expand them. The combination of two different ways of thinking can lead to a synthesis that enriches both" (*AL*, no. 139. The virtue of *intellectual sobriety* disposes the inquirer, Montmarquet writes, "out of sheer love of truth, discovery, and the excitement of new and unfamiliar ideas, to embrace what is not really warranted, even relative to the limits of his own evidence."[52] Truth, the Second Vatican Council teaches, "cannot impose itself except by virtue of its own truth,

---

[50] See Lorraine Code, *Epistemic Responsibility* (Boston: Brown, 1987).

[51] Montmarquet, *Epistemic Virtue and Doxastic Responsibility*, 23.

[52] Ibid.

as it makes its entrance into the mind at once quietly and with power." The virtue of *intellectual courage* includes "the willingness to conceive and examine alternatives to popularly held beliefs, perseverance in the face of opposition from others (until one is convinced one is mistaken), and the determination required to see such a project through to completion" (*DH*, no. 1). Theological history is full of such intellectual courage by Catholic theologians condemned by the church for their careful and conscientious theological opinions. The different virtues of responsibility and conscientiousness account for a different selection, interpretation, prioritization, and integration of the four sources of ethical knowledge to define human dignity and to formulate and justify norms for its attainment. They also emphasize both the need to justify one's definition of human dignity and normative claims in dialogue with others and to have the courage to revise, if necessary, one's perspective based on this process of justification.

An emphasis on the responsibility and the conscientiousness of the knower is necessary in virtue epistemology but, we suggest, it is not sufficient. Persons can be very responsible and conscientious in their intellectual activity and still be incorrect in the truth they achieve. While all virtue epistemologists accept the change in the direction of analysis from act to person, defining justified belief and knowledge in reference to their source in personal virtues, they disagree on how to define virtuous character. For Greco, who is in the reliability school, virtuous character is "defined in terms of successful and stable dispositions to form belief" and a consequential focus on "reliable success in producing true belief."[53] For Hookway, who is in the responsibility school, a virtuous character decentralizes "questions of the epistemic status of beliefs in favor of questions of agency and inquiry."[54] The reliability school focuses on getting knowledge right; the responsibility school focuses on the knower's motivation for seeking knowledge.

The reliability/responsibility debate, we believe, ought not to be construed as an either/or but as a both/and debate. We believe with Guy Axtell in a dual component account of the justification of true knowledge that reflects a complementarity between reliability and responsibility. Such an account integrates, we would argue with Axtell, "constraints on the agent's faculty reliability," imagination, perception, and memory, "with constraints on the agent's responsibility in gathering and processing evidence."[55] Linda

---

[53] See Axtell, *Knowledge, Belief, and Character,* xiv.
[54] Ibid., xiii–xiv.
[55] Ibid., 188.

Zagzebski's account of the justification of true knowledge balances the *motivation* of the subject seeking knowledge with the subject's *success* in achieving true knowledge.[56] In Ernest Sosa's virtue perspectivism a proposition is known by a knower "only if *both* he is rationally justified in believing it *and* he is in a position to know . . . whether it is true."[57] Greco's and our mixed theory account of justification is that "an adequate account of knowledge ought to contain both a responsibility condition and a reliability condition. Moreover, a virtue account can explain how the two are tied together. In cases of knowledge, objective reliability is grounded in epistemically responsible action."[58] The dual-component virtue epistemology that we accept and teach seeks an integration and balance between reliability and responsibility accounts of justified belief and knowledge.

Questions for Reflection

- Discuss what you have learned in this chapter about anthropology and its relationship to human dignity.
- Outline the dimensions of human nature integrally and adequately considered. Has your understanding of them helped you to understand yourself and the demands of your ethical life?
- What do you understand by an ethical norm? Distinguish between formal and material norms and their implications for your ethical life.
- What do you understand by character virtues and epistemic virtues? Discuss character and epistemic virtues and their implications for your ethical character and action.

Suggested Readings

Greco, John, and John Turri, eds. *Virtue Epistemology: Contemporary Readings*. Boston: MIT Press, 2012.

---

[56] See Linda Zagzebski, *Virtues of the Mind: An Inquiry into the Nature of Virtue and the Ethical Foundations of Knowledge* (Cambridge: Cambridge University Press, 1996).

[57] Ernest Sosa, *Knowledge in Perspective: Selected Essays in Epistemology* (Cambridge: Cambridge University Press, 1991), 28.

[58] Greco, "Virtue Epistemology," 5.

Janssens, Louis. "Artificial Insemination: Ethical Considerations." *Louvain Studies* 8 (1980): 3–29.

Salzman, Todd A., and Michael G. Lawler. *The Sexual Person: Toward A Renewed Catholic Anthropology.* Washington, DC: Georgetown University Press, 2008.

Salzman, Todd A., and Michael G. Lawler. *Virtue and Theological Ethics: Toward a Renewed Ethical Method.* Maryknoll, NY: Orbis Books, 2018.

Snow, Nancy E. *The Oxford Handbook of Virtue* (Oxford: Oxford University Press, 2018).

PART II

Christian Formation of Conscience and Contemporary Ethical Issues

6

Conscience and Discernment

Learning Objectives

- Explain conscience.
- Explain discernment.
- Understand the interrelationship between conscience and discernment.
- Explain how to form one's conscience through the Wesleyan Quadrilateral.
- Explain how neuroscience informs ethical discourse and the formation of conscience.

In this chapter we consider both conscience and discernment. The Catholic way of choosing the good, namely, *conscience*, is a practical judgment that I must do this rather than that. The process of arriving at a practical judgment of conscience is variously called *discernment* or *discretion*. We shall treat these two words as synonymous and interchangeable. Ethics enters a human life when an individual is faced with a judgment about possible actions, goes through a process of discernment of the possible actions, makes the judgment that he or she must do this action rather than that one, and then actually does the chosen action. The process of ethically evaluating the actions is technically called discernment or discretion, and the practical judgment to do this action rather than any of the possible others is called conscience. We first consider conscience.

Conscience

Pope Francis in *Amoris Laetitia* complains that we "find it hard to make room for the consciences of the faithful, who very often respond as best they can to the Gospel amid their limitations and are capable of carrying out their own discernment in complex situations." He goes on to insist that "we have been called to form consciences, not to replace them" (*AL,* no. 37). That is good advice for Catholic teachers at all levels. Already in the thirteenth century theologian Thomas Aquinas established the authority and inviolability of conscience. Anyone, he argues, "upon whom the ecclesiastical authorities, in ignorance of the true facts, imposes a demand that offends against his clear conscience, should perish in excommunication rather than violate his conscience."[1] For any Catholic in search of the good and the true, no clearer statement on the authority and inviolability of personal conscience could be found. Aquinas goes further and insists that even the dictate of a mistaken conscience must be followed, and that to act against such a dictate is unethical and sinful. "To believe in Christ," he argues, "is good in itself and necessary for salvation; all this does not win the will unless it be recommended by reason. If the reason presents it as bad, then the will reaches to it in the light, not that it really is bad in itself, but because it appears so because of a condition that happens to be attached by the reason apprehending it."[2]

Seven hundred years later, the last hundred of which saw the rights of individual conscience essentially ignored in the Catholic Church, the Second Vatican Council's *Gaudium et Spes* issued a clarion call with respect to conscience. "Conscience is the most secret core and sanctuary of man. There he is alone with God whose voice echoes in his depth. In a wonderful manner conscience reveals that law which is fulfilled by love of God and neighbor" (*GS,* no. 16). *Dignitatis Humanae (Decree on Religious Freedom)* went further to assert the inviolability of conscience. "In all his activity a man is bound to follow his conscience faithfully, in order that he may come to God for whom he was created. It follows that he is not to be forced to act contrary to his conscience. Nor, on the other hand, is he to be restrained from acting in accordance with his conscience, especially in matters religious" (*DH,* no. 3), or, we add, ethical. In the 1960s these were words seldom voiced in Catholic magisterial circles, but they are words deeply rooted in the Catholic moral tradition and, indeed, constitutive of it.

From Aquinas we learn that conscience is related to reason, and its understanding is situated in Aquinas's anthropology. Closely following Aristotle, he considers the human person to be a unitary being endowed with a body and a rational soul that vivifies it. Reason distinguishes humans from all other animals, and the soul has two powers, intellect and will,

---

[1] Thomas Aquinas, *In IV Sent.*, dist. 38, q. 2, art. 4.

[2] Thomas Aquinas, *Summa Theologiae Sancti Thomae de Aquino* I-II, 19, 5 (hereinafter, *ST*).

intimately related and involved in the process of knowledge. All knowledge begins with experience,[3] proceeds through understanding, and arrives at judgment and decision that is then actualized in action. Conscience is the act of practical judgment that something is right or wrong, ethical or un-ethical, to be done or not to be done. Conscience binds us to do or not to do some action and, when an action has been done, "conscience is said to accuse or worry us if what has occurred is found to be out of accord with the knowledge by which it was tested, and to defend or excuse us if what has occurred is found to have turned out in accordance with the piece of knowledge."[4] It is almost universally agreed, as Robert Smith asserts, that conscience is "the act of practical judgment on a particular moral issue . . . that commands us to do this or not to do that."[5]

Conscience, then, comes at the end of a rational process of experience, understanding, judgment, decision. This process includes a natural grasp of moral principles that Aquinas calls *synderesis.* "Though the habits which inform conscience are many," he argues, "nevertheless they all take effect through one chief habit, the grasp of principles called *synderesis.*"[6] Aquinas never makes these principles clear anywhere because, as Jean Porter argues, his "general theory of goodness requires him to hold that the first principle of practical reasoning is self-evident to all."[7] Cardinal Joseph Ratzinger, in a 1991 speech, interpreted the medieval tradition as offering two levels to the concept of conscience, *synteresis* and *conscientia. Synteresis* is "an inner repugnance to evil and an attraction to the good. The act of conscience applies this basic knowledge to the particular situation."[8] To make a practical judgment of conscience, then, involves both a grasp of the first principles of practical judgment *(synteresis)* and a gathering of as much evidence as possible, consciously weighing and understanding the evidence and its implications, and finally making as honest a judgment as possible that this action must be done and that action must not be done. Since this process ends with a judgment about what is good or evil, right or wrong, we call it an *ethical* process. Conscience, we insist, is not a law unto itself; it must be as fully informed as possible to be right. That

---

[3] See *ST* I, 79, 2. For an excellent summary, see Kenneth L. Schmitz, "St. Thomas and the Appeal to Experience," *Proceedings of the Catholic Theological Society of America* 47 (1992): 1–20.

[4] Schmitz, "St. Thomas and the Appeal to Experience."

[5] Robert J. Smith, *Conscience and Catholicism: The Nature and Function of Conscience in Contemporary Roman Catholic Theology* (Lanham, MD: University Press of America, 1998), 12.

[6] *ST* I, 79, 13. The correct Greek word is actually *synteresis* and that will be used herein.

[7] Jean Porter, *The Recovery of Virtue: The Relevance of Aquinas for Christian Ethics* (Louisville, KY: Westminster/John Knox, 1990), 85–86.

[8] Cardinal Joseph Ratzinger, "Conscience and Truth," no. 8.

formation is the process from gathering the necessary evidence, discerning the evidence, to making the practical judgment that this is what I must do in this situation at this time.

Since conscience is a practical judgment that comes at the end of a deliberative process about the relationship of means to ends, it necessarily involves the virtue of prudence, by which "right reason is applied to action."[9] Aquinas locates prudence in the intellect[10] along with *synteresis* and *conscientia*. *Synteresis* provides the first formal principles of practical reason; prudence discerns those principles and translates them into a material principle and action in this particular situation and enables conscience to make practical judgments that this is the right thing to do on this occasion, toward this person, and with this good motive.[11] Prudence, therefore, needs to know "both the general moral principles of reason and the individual situation in which human actions take place."[12] It is the task of prudence to monitor the process of discernment and judgment to ensure that this is the right occasion, the right person, and the right motive, for instance, for aid to the poor. As prudence controls the right exercise of aid to the poor, so also does it control and integrate the exercise of all other ethical virtues. It is a *cardinal* virtue around which all other virtues pivot, integrating agents and their actions.[13] Because prudence controls the judgments that precede the exercise of all other ethical virtues, and must precede them if they are to be ethical, Aquinas holds that "no moral virtue can be possessed without prudence, since it is proper to moral virtue to make a right choice."[14] In the field of deliberation and choice, he argues, it is the "work of prudence which counsels, judges, and commands."[15]

Unfortunately, in the experientially demonstrated ethical weakness of human beings, all judgments, even the most prudential practical judgments of conscience, can be in error. That raises the question of the erroneous conscience and so, at this point, we need to introduce some important distinctions. Ethicists note that there are two poles in every moral judgment. It is always a free, rational human *subject* who makes a judgment, and so one pole of the judgment is a subjective pole; but every subject makes a judgment about some *objective* reality, giving alms to the poor or homosexual activity, for instance, and so there is always also an objective pole. Subjects arrive at their judgments either by following the rational process

---

[9] *ST* II-II, 47, 5.
[10] Ibid., 47, 1.
[11] See Ibid., 47, 6.
[12] See Ibid., 47, 3.
[13] See *ST* I-II, 61, 2 and 3.
[14] Ibid., 65, 1.
[15] Ibid.

outlined above or by somehow shortchanging that process. In the first case the subject arrives at a right ethical understanding and conscience judgment about the object; in the second case the subject arrives at a wrong or erroneous understanding and conscience judgment about the object. If a decision to act follows a right understanding and judgment about the object, then conscience is also said to be right; if it follows an erroneous understanding and judgment, then conscience is also said to be erroneous.

If the error of understanding and judgment can be ascribed to some ethical fault, taking "little trouble to find out what is true and good" (*GS,* no. 16), for instance, or negligent failure to be sufficiently attentive to the necessary experience, to gather the necessary evidence, to engage in the necessary discernment, to take the necessary advice, then the wrong understanding and the practical judgment of conscience flowing from it are both deemed to be culpable and cannot be ethically followed.[16] If the error cannot be ascribed to some ethical fault, then both the understanding and the practical judgment of conscience flowing from it are deemed to be nonculpable and not only can but must be followed, even contrary to church authority, as Aquinas argued above. Joseph Ratzinger, later Pope Benedict XVI, concurs. "Over the Pope as the expression of the binding claim of ecclesiastical authority there still stands one's own conscience, which must be obeyed before all else, if necessary even against the requirement of ecclesiastical authority. This emphasis in the individual, whose conscience confronts him with a supreme and ultimate tribunal, and one which in the last resort is beyond the claim of external social groups, even of the official church, also establishes a principle in opposition to increasing totalitarianism."[17] Subjects are bound not only *to* conscience but also *for* conscience, that is, they must do all in their power to ensure that conscience is right. Any culpable negligence in the search for rightness is immoral. There is one final distinction to be added here. The morality of an action is largely controlled by the subject's motive. A good motive—giving alms to the poor *because* the poor need help and to help them is the right and Christian thing to do—results in an ethical action. A bad motive—giving alms to the poor *because* I want to be seen and to be praised by others (Matt 6:2, 5; see Luke 18:10–14)—results in an unethical action for the giver of alms, even if good for the poor.

A decision of right conscience is a complex process. It is an *individual* process, but far from an *individualistic,* exclusively subjective process. The Latin word *con-scientia* literally means "knowledge together," perhaps

---

16 See *ST* I-II, 19, 6.

17 Joseph Ratzinger, "The Dignity of the Human Person," in *Commentary on the Documents of Vatican II,* vol. 5, ed. Herbert Vorgrimler (New York: Herder, 1969), 134.

better rendered in English as "to know together." It suggests what human experience universally demonstrates, namely, that being freed from the prison of one's individual self into the company of others is a surer way to come to right knowledge of ethical truth and right moral judgment of what one ought to do or not do. This community basis of the search for Christian truth, conscience, and ethical action builds a sure safeguard against both an isolating egoism and a subjective relativism that negates all universal truth. The community dimension of consciences has been part of the Christian tradition since St. Paul, who clearly believed in the inviolability and primacy of conscience (1 Cor 10:25–27; 2 Cor 1:12; 4:2; Rom 14:13–23). Bernard Häring calls this community dimension "the reciprocity of consciences."[18] It is within this reciprocity of consciences that church authority functions, not guaranteeing conscience (past errors preclude that simplistic claim) but informing it to a right practical judgment. We are instructed here by Cardinal Newman's famous comment in a letter to the Duke of Norfolk: "If I am obliged to bring religion into after-dinner toasts (which indeed does not seem the right thing), I shall drink to the pope if you please, still to conscience first and to the pope afterward."

The Catholic faithful, the International Theological Commission teaches in *Sensus Fidei* in the Life of the Church,"

> have an instinct for the truth of the Gospel, which enables them to recognize and endorse authentic Christian doctrine and practice, and to reject what is false. . . . Banishing the Catholic caricature of an active hierarchy and a passive laity and in particular the notion of a strict separation between the teaching church *(Ecclesia docens)* and the learning church *(Ecclesia discens),* the Council taught that all the baptized participate in their own proper way in the three offices of Christ as prophet, priest, and king. In particular it taught that Christ fulfills his prophetic office not only by means of the hierarchy but also via the laity. (nos. 2, 4).

The attainment of ethical truth in the Catholic tradition, therefore, involves a dialogical process in the communion-church between the "bishops down to the last member of the laity" and, when that process has been conscientiously completed, even the last member of the laity is finally "alone with God whose voice echoes in his depths" (*GS,* no. 16) and has to make that practical judgment of conscience that this is what *I* must believe or not

---

[18] Bernard Häring, *Free and Faithful in Christ: Moral Theology for Clergy and Laity,* vol. 2 (New York: Seabury, 1980), 25.

believe, do or not do. Back to Newman's dictum, and indeed also Aquinas's and Ratzinger's: first conscience, and afterward the pope.

Having made a practical judgment and decision of conscience, no Catholic is "to be forced to act in a manner contrary to his conscience. Nor . . . is he to be restrained from acting in accordance with his conscience, especially in matters religious" (*DH*, no. 3) and, we might add, ethical. Theologian Joseph Ratzinger points out that "not everything that exists in the church must for that reason be also a legitimate tradition. . . . There is a distorting as well as legitimate tradition."[19] The longstanding adherence of the church to false teachings on the taking of interest on loans, religious freedom, and slavery are well-known examples of distorting traditions that have now been corrected. Ratzinger concludes: "Consequently tradition must not be considered only affirmatively but also critically."[20] The *Catechism of the Catholic Church* places the church's teaching beyond doubt: Catholics have "the right to act in conscience and in freedom so as personally to make moral decisions" (*CCC*, no. 1782). A well-informed and therefore well-formed conscience is the Catholic way to choosing the true and the good.

Discernment

Conscience, we have argued, is a practical judgment that this action rather than any possible other is the ethical action to be done in this situation. That definition leaves a critical question: How is that practical judgment to be arrived at? Pope Francis hints at a Catholic answer in the citation we offered at the beginning of this chapter: the faithful "are capable of carrying out their own discernment in complex situations" (*AL*, no. 29). Discernment is the truly Christian way to reach a decision of conscience, and it is to discernment that we now turn.

Christian discernment, we insist from the beginning, is a thoroughly *theological* activity, at least in its Catholic use. We are not saying that non-Catholics have no need to or cannot discern, for they too can and must discern their situations and reach practical, conscience judgments for their actions to be ethical. When we say that for Catholics discernment is a *theo-logical* activity, we are saying that it is both a gift and a skill to recognize the presence and activity of God, in Greek *theos,* in every situation and decision in their lives. When Catholics discern, they are seeking two things. They are seeking, first, the presence and activity of God in their

---

[19] Joseph Ratzinger, "The Transmission of Divine Revelation," in *Commentary on the Documents of Vatican II*, vol. 3, ed. Herbert Vorgrimler (New York: Herder, 1969), 185.

[20] Ibid.

lives, especially what God is calling them to do in this particular situation. They are seeking, second, the action they must do in this situation to be aligned with God's will and, therefore, to be ethical. We say it is a gift because it is given to us at our creation by our creator God; we say it is a skill because the gift can be honed and developed by practice. As gift and skill, discernment is not unlike riding a bicycle. First, my parents give me the gift of a bicycle for my birthday, and then, by constant practice, I develop my skill until I can ride the bicycle easily.

The first thing that Catholics seek to discern is the presence and activity of God in their life. Spiritual writer Mark McIntosh distinguishes five moments in the process of discernment, the first of which is the discernment of the presence and activity of God in a person's life.[21] Trust or faith in that God, a theological virtue, provides the foundation for Christian discernment and for the ethical action that is its outcome. This first moment involves ridding my mind of all worldly distraction and ways of thinking, ridding it of what Sigmund Freud called the *superego*, prescriptions and proscriptions for doing this or not doing that from authoritarian figures in my childhood, parents, teachers, priests, so that I would become a good boy or a good Catholic. St. Paul recommended this clearance of mind to his Roman converts: "Do not be conformed to this world, but be transformed by the renewing of your minds, so that you may discern the will of God" (Rom 12:2).

The second moment in the process of discernment is the discerning of good and evil impulses and desires that distort my perceptions and make my discernment of the presence of God and God's Spirit and of my ultimate practical judgment of conscience more difficult. Again St. Paul instructs us. "The works of the flesh are obvious: fornication, impurity, licentiousness, idolatry, sorcery, enmities, strife, quarrels, dissensions, carousing. . . . The fruit of the Spirit is love, joy, peace, patience, kindness, generosity, gentleness, and self-control" (Gal 5:19–26). We can easily add our own lists of evils and goods: the evils of greed, idolatry of money, refusing to share our goods with those less privileged, digital pornography and sexting, racial hatred; the goods of mercy, loving our neighbors and enemies, feeding the hungry, sheltering the homeless, showing hospitality to refugees and immigrants, nonviolence, embracing diversity, truthfulness.

The third moment of discernment is a moment of practical wisdom that demands maturity, both human and Christian. It demands the experience-based human maturity to intuitively reach the most ethical action in a situation; and it demands the Christian maturity to recognize not only the

---

[21] Mark A. McIntosh, *Discernment and Truth: The Spirituality and Theology of Knowledge* (New York: Herder, 2004), 8.

presence of God's Spirit in our lives but also the ethical action toward which the Spirit is impelling us in every particular situation.

This recognition of both the presence of the Spirit and the action toward which the Spirit is impelling us leads into the fourth moment of discernment, the moment that *recognizes* that this action in this situation is God's will for us. This recognition in turn leads us into a broader vision of Christian truth, a larger perspective or lens with which to view our actions, a twentieth-floor rather than a third-floor window to see far beyond the ethical action toward which we are now impelled.

The fifth and final moment of discernment is the moment we *judge* that this action rather than that one is God's will for us in this specific situation, and we freely move to do it. This final moment is the moment of the practical judgment of conscience, and following that practical judgment into action is the moment we act ethically.

As developing human beings, our lives are filled with choices. To be alive is to be faced with choices, some major, some minor. Who am I? Who do I want to be? Who and what do I want to become? Where should I go to school? Who do I choose as my friends? How concerned am I for the human flourishing of my friends? How concerned am I for the human flourishing of my enemies? Should I take these jeans from the store without paying? What should I have for breakfast? Should I hook up with this person I do not even know? As we reach adulthood and seek to fashion it into a mature adulthood, there are two possible approaches to answering those questions. The first is what we shall call *personal autonomy*, the ability to stand on our own two feet and answer the questions. The second is what we shall call *interdependence*, the ability to acknowledge our need for others to help us, encourage us, sustain us as we seek Christian, ethical answers to our questions. These two approaches may at first appear to be in opposition, but they are not. To be in interdependent relationship with others is not to be thought of as an abdication of our autonomy; rather, it is to be recognized as an autonomous choice, a willingness to forego an individualistic, stubborn, and ultimately childish willfulness to do our own individualistic thing. Conscience, we explained above, is knowing together; discernment, we now explain, is knowing and deciding together. It cannot be otherwise, for discernment is the prelude to the practical judgment of conscience. For Christians in general, among those on whom we may freely choose to depend is the Holy Spirit of God, and discernment is ultimately the process of uncovering both the presence of the Spirit in our lives and where the Spirit is leading us in any situation.

Exercising personal adult autonomy, making one's own decision based on conscious rather than unconscious factors is never easy, for we all have parental, clerical, and cultural authoritarian hangovers from childhood, which Freud called the *superego*. The superego is frequently confused with conscience, but there is a vast difference between them. The superego is the remains of childhood training that was intended to guide our religious and social behavior when we were as yet unable to make our own proper ethical choices. That childhood training, however, took place at a time when our dependence on adult authority was necessary, but that authority for our choices was never intended to be permanent. It was always intended to give way to the autonomous practical judgments of our informed conscience when we had reached the personal and cognitive maturity to be autonomous. St. Paul's instruction to the Corinthians accurately describes the difference between the superego and conscience: "When I was a child, I spoke like a child, I thought like a child, I reasoned like a child; when I became a man, I gave up childish ways" (1 Cor 13:11). Among the childish ways adults must give up are the remnants of the superego. That is not to say that all childhood instructions are to be overthrown in our maturity. As a mature Catholic adult I still should not tell a lie, should not steal my sister's things, should be nice to that old grinch Mr. O'Driscoll who refused to return every ball that found its way into his backyard, but not because my mother or Father Burke said so. No, I should not tell a lie or steal or swear at Mr. O'Driscoll because in my maturity I am able to discern the practical conscience judgment that this is what I must and must not do to be an adult and mature Catholic.

Discernment is a critical process for everyone seeking to make ethical choices and to do ethical actions. It is also a difficult process, and everyone needs help with it. For Catholics, that help is found abundantly in the Wesleyan Quadrilateral we dealt with in Chapter 3. The Wesleyan Quadrilateral embraces scripture, tradition, science/reason, and experience. In scripture, Deuteronomy says it all when it says that "the word is very near to you; it is in your mouth and in your heart, so that you can do it" (30:14). The word, God's Word, which the apostle John will later testify "became flesh and dwelt among us" (John 1:14) in Jesus, and God's Spirit are in our hearts, waiting to be discerned there, waiting to speak God's will for every moment of our lives if we only take the time and find the quiet to listen. Proverbs teaches that "the wise of heart is called a man of discernment" (Prov 16:21), and Isaiah might have been speaking of us when he complained of his compatriots that "this is a people without discernment" (Isa 27:11). We have already seen Paul's New Testament words on discernment, and there is no need to repeat them again, though they are certainly to be noted as an important contribution from scripture to the Catholic theory of discernment. We add only his further instruction to the Corinthians, for it became enormously influential in the early Christian Church and especially in the early monastic tradition, the second source of ethical knowledge.

The instruction in question is given in the context of a discussion of the variety of gifts given by the Spirit of God. "There are varieties of gifts but the same Spirit. . . . There are varieties of working but it is the same God who inspires them in everyone" (1 Cor 12:4–6). Only one gift concerns us here, "the ability to distinguish between spirits" (1 Cor 12:10). The interpretation of this text by the influential Alexandrian catechist Origen (ca. 185–254) and later by the even more influential Alexandrian theologian Athanasius (ca. 296–373) was one to encourage an ascetical life. They argued that the ability to distinguish between spirits was given only to those whose ascetical lives prepared them to exercise this gift most acutely. The early desert monks offered a different interpretation of Paul's text. The gift of discerning spirits, they argued, was given to and could be exercised by every Christian. Joseph Lienhard comments that in the early monastic tradition the distinguishing or discerning of spirits "ceases to be viewed as an exceptional gift or charism and is treated as a virtue, even a necessary virtue"[22] for every Christian wishing to advance in the Christian life. A virtue in Aristotle's definition, remember, is "a state of character concerned with choice, lying in a mean,"[23] and in Thomas Aquinas's definition a habit or a disposition ordered to an act.[24] We combine those two definitions and understand *a virtue to be a state of character, a habit, or a disposition that enables a person to perform an ethically good act.* The person with the virtue of justice will be enabled to perform just acts; the person with the virtue of prudence will be enabled to perform prudent acts; the person with the virtue of discerning spirits will be enabled to discern spirits. In the history of the Roman Catholic Church, this virtue, as with so many others, was generally—and we suggest mistakenly—linked with clerics.

The history and development of this idea is vast, too vast for adequate treatment in this short section, and we content ourselves by picking out two very influential persons in that development.[25] The first is the medieval Cistercian monk Bernard of Clairvaux (1090–1153). In his *Sermons* Bernard argues that discernment, which he often calls discretion, is not only a virtue but "the mother of the virtues." He adds that "without the fervor of charity the virtue of discretion is lifeless, and intense fervor goes headlong without the curb of discretion. Praiseworthy the man who possesses both, the fervor that enlivens discretion, the discretion that regulates fervor."[26]

---

[22] Joseph T. Lienhard, "On 'Discernment of Spirits' in the Early Church," *Theological Studies* 41 (1980): 528–29.

[23] Aristotle, *Nicomachean Ethics*, II, 6.1106b.

[24] Thomas Aquinas, *ST* I-II, q. 49, a. 1; ibid., a.3.

[25] For a full development, see McIntosh's *Discernment and Truth*.

[26] Bernard of Clairvaux, *On the Song of Songs 2.23.8* (Kalamazoo: Cistercian Publications, 1976), 32.

Bernard underscores this balancing role for discernment/discretion in a subsequent sermon. Discretion, he argues, "regulates every virtue. . . . Discretion therefore is not so much a virtue as a moderator and guide of the virtues. . . . Take it away and virtue becomes vice, and natural affection itself a force that disturbs and destroys nature."[27] Both fervor and discretion in balance, Bernard argues, are necessary for genuine spiritual life. They are necessary also, we argue, for genuine ethical life, if spiritual and ethical lives can even be separated. Everyday human experience teaches us here the truth of Bernard's insights. The virtue of love and fervor, for instance, can easily be misdirected and corrupted; the virtue of a passionate love can easily become self-focused and self-satisfying rather than other-focused and other-satisfying. In the Catholic tradition that situation is itself inchoately unethical and can lead to unethical actions. How often do the media report murders because of unbalanced love and suicides because of unrequited love? One only has to be alive and conscious to grasp the importance of balance in a human life, and the Catholic tradition teaches that balance is achieved with the help of the Spirit-assisted discernment or discretion of the various spirits that clamor for our attention and choice.

The second influential figure we deal with comes three hundred years after Bernard, Ignatius of Loyola, founder of the Society of Jesus or the Jesuits (1491–1556). Ignatius was born during the European Renaissance and, through his new Society, helped greatly in the Renaissance of both the Catholic Church and the discernment of Spirits. After a mystical experience in 1521, he put together a series of notes intended to guide those who were guiding others in the discernment of God's will for them. We know those notes today as the *Spiritual Exercises*.[28] A core contribution of the *Exercises* is the introduction of a step in the discernment process that we will call alignment with Jesus's understanding of God's will for him. This alignment with Jesus the Christ is advanced as the chief means by which the virtue of Christian discernment grows. There is a need in the process of discernment to which we have alluded several times, the need not only to discern the will of God but also to discern the spirits or impulses that distract us from the will of God, that distract us from ethical choice and action. Let us say that the will of God for us is that we give alms to the poor, and in the Christian tradition that is universally accepted as the will of God for us, but we still have a choice to make to be ethical. Are we going to give alms to the poor to help the poor or are we going to give alms to the poor to help ourselves, perhaps as a needed deduction on our income

---

[27] Ibid., *3.49.5*, 25.

[28] For an excellent extended analysis of Ignatius and discernment of spirits, see Jules J. Toner, *A Commentary on Saint Ignatius' Rules for the Discernment of Spirits* (St. Louis: Institute of Jesuit Sources, 1982).

taxes or perhaps, as the Gospel says, that we "may be praised by men" (Matt 6:2)? Ignatius's answer is that, if we allow our lives to be animated by the same Spirit who animated Jesus in his search for the will of God his Father, both our inner and outer lives will inevitably become more spiritual. Our life will also become, we add again, more ethical. At the beginning of this section we cited Pope Francis's assertion that the faithful "are capable of carrying out their own discernment in complex situations" (*AL,* no. 37). The pope clearly stands firmly in the long Catholic tradition of the earliest monks that *all* the disciples of Jesus and not only clerics are capable of carrying out their own discernment of spirits. As a Jesuit, he stands equally clearly in the tradition of Ignatius of Loyola.

The third source for theological ethics, we asserted, is science/reason. Again, the scope of the influence of science is too vast for a brief treatment here, and so we choose to focus on a single question that has great importance for discernment, the question of attention. Pope John Paul II insists in *Familiaris Consortio* that the church values scientific research "when it proves helpful in understanding the historical context in which pastoral action has to be developed and when it leads to a better understanding of the truth" (*FC,* no. 5). We agree with the pope and suggest that the data of contemporary neuroscience on the bicameral brain is enormously helpful in leading to a broader understanding of human emotion, thought, disposition, and action, and that therefore it should be of interest to theological ethicists.

In the early days of emotion research it was assumed that emotion and cognition resulted from separate brain processes. Theological ethicists, accepting that assumption, have always privileged reason over emotion. Contemporary neuroscience has now exploded that assumption and has shown "the overlap between circuitry involved in cognitive and affective [emotional] processing,"[29] thereby demonstrating that "emotion really amounted to cognition, in the definition of cognitive neuroscience, because emotion entailed information processing and transformation." There is mounting evidence that emotion is "constitutive of, and not separate from, the reasoning and decision making that people do about their own values and the preferences and values of others."[30] Emotion serves to guide, control, and even on occasion inhibit attention. The brain, theologian-scientist Andrew Newberg writes, "places functional restrictions on all thought

---

[29] Richard J. Davidson, "Seven Sins in the Study of Emotion: Correctives from Affective Neuroscience," *Brain and Cognition* 52 (2003): 129; see also Neil Messer, *Theological Neuroethics: Christian Ethics Meets the Science of the Human Brain* (London: Bloomsbury, 2017).

[30] Michael L. Spezio, "The Neuroscience of Emotion and Reasoning in Social Contexts: Implications for Moral Theology," *Modern Theology* 27 (2011): 346, 342.

processes, and hence [on] how we experience religion, spirituality, and theology."[31] Neurotheology fashions a method that opens the insights of one theological ethicist to the insights of others, thereby eliminating the unnecessary and unhelpful polarity that presently separates them.[32] For theological ethicists to ignore neuroscience and its data, we suggest, is to ignore a sure foundation in which to root their ethical theories.

Attention and Free Will

The issue of attention, "the selective prioritization of the neural representations that are most relevant to one's current behavioral goals,"[33] is an important one in both science and theology. Prioritization of data is always necessary, for despite its billions of neurons the human brain is still a limited information system and external and internal stimuli compete for its resources. Attention resolves that competition in favor of the data that is most relevant to the task and goal at hand. It is also, as we shall see in a moment, an essential element of free will and choice. Early neuropsychological literature distinguished several types of attention, two of which are important for our purposes here, sustained attention and focused attention.[34]

Experimental data indicate that sustained attention is predominantly right-hemisphere reliant and focused attention is predominantly left-hemisphere reliant. Since, however, the two hemispheres are connected and involved together in every brain activity, we are to understand this data as predominance and not as exclusive action by one hemisphere or the other. Scanning studies clearly indicate that focused attention is reliant on the left frontal cortex,[35] and that deficits in focused attention result from left-hemisphere lesions.[36] There is also evidence of right-hemisphere

---

[31] Andrew B. Newberg, *Principles of Neurotheology* (Burlington, VT: Ashgate, 2010), 84.

[32] At the November 2016 Consistory creating new cardinals, Pope Francis called polarity "a virus" that "compromises the universality of the church" (see Inés San Martín, "As Bishops Joust, Pope Francis Calls New Cardinals to Spurn Polarization," *Crux* (November 19, 2016).

[33] Timothy J. Buschman and Sabine Kastner, "From Behavior to Neural Dynamics: An Integrated Theory of Attention," *Neuron* 88 (2015): 127.

[34] Adriaan H. van Zomeren and Wiebo H. Brouwer, *Clinical Neuropsychology of Attention* (Oxford: Oxford: Oxford University Press, 1994).

[35] Maurizio Corbetta et al., "Selective and Divided Attention during Visual Discriminations of Shape, Color, and Speed: Functional Anatomy by Positron Emission Tomography," *Journal of Neuroscience* 11 (1991): 2383–402.

[36] Walter Sturm and Andr Büssing, "Einfluss der Aufgabenkomplexität auf hirnorganische Reaktionsbeeinträchtigungen—Hirnshädigungs oder Patienteneffkt?," *European*

predominance for broad, global attention.[37] Executive attention is the name given to the resolution of "conflicts among the many brain areas that may be active simultaneously, in order to maintain a coherent direction of behavior," and has been associated with the prefrontal cortex areas of the brain.[38]

The age-old question of free will, so crucial in judging ethical responsibility, arises at this point.[39] Free will implies the ability to choose freely one thing rather than another and is the sine qua non of morality. Without free will we would not have the ability to choose our actions freely and would consequently have no ethical responsibility for them. Our actions would be predetermined, and we would never be responsible for them. Neuroscience raises serious questions about free will. Many brain studies show an association between volitional processes and increased energy in the brain's frontal lobes. "Right here," researcher and psychiatrist Jeffrey Schwartz asserts, "you can say while pointing to the bright spots on the PET scan, volition originates."[40] The critical question, of course, is which comes first, the increased frontal lobe energy or the volitional act? If the brain energy comes first, then it can be argued that our actions are determined by our brains; if the volitional act comes first, then we exercise free will. As a result of his extensive experiments with obsessive-compulsive disorder (OCD) patients, whom he found can be trained to choose and to have thoughts other than their obsessive ones, Schwartz argues that humans do have free will and are responsible for their actions. He explains his conclusion by arguing for what he calls mental force, "a physical force generated by mental effort" which is "the physical expression of will . . . [and] . . . physically efficacious."[41] Mental force enables humans to make a free choice of this action or that. There is no determinism.

Schwartz traces the cause of this mental force to the outcome of what is called in neurocognitive science "effortful attention." The causal efficacy of will, he argues, "is a higher-level manifestation of the causal efficacy of attention. To focus attention on one idea, on one possible course of action

---

Archives of Psychiatry and Neurological Sciences 235 (1986): 214–20.

[37] Richard B. Ivry and Lynn C. Robertson, *The Two Sides of Perception* (Cambridge, MA: MIT Press, 1998); Lynn C. Robertson, Marvin R. Lamb, and Robert T. Knight, "Effects of Lesions of Temporal-parietal Junction on Perception and Attentional Processing in Humans," *Journal of Neuroscience* 8 (1988): 3757–69.

[38] Michael I. Posner, *Attention in a Social World* (New York: Oxford University Press, 2012), 19–21 (and the other researchers cited there).

[39] See Messer, *Theological Neuroethics*, 71–104.

[40] Jeffrey M. Schwartz and Sharon Begley, *The Mind and the Brain: Neuroplasticity and the Power of Mental Force* (New York: Harper, 2002), 294.

[41] Ibid., 295.

among the many bubbling up inchoate in our consciousness, is precisely what we mean by volition."[42] Volition acts through attention that focuses on and makes predominant one thought or one action out of the many that are possible. Attention, however, is only the first part of what "will" means. There is a second part, James argued and Schwartz has shown to be true, namely, consent to the reality that is attended to. Schwartz found in his experiments that "for the stroke victim, the OCD patient, and the depressive, intense effort is required to bring about the requisite refocusing of attention."[43] Intense effort, we suggest, is required also for everyone seeking the discernment of spirits. Freely chosen effortful attention generates the mental force that is required for any discernment and choice. Personal *intention*, that is, is made causally efficacious through personal effortful *attention*.

It is neuroscientifically clear that, notwithstanding the overlap between emotional and cognitional brain circuitries, emotional understanding occurs predominantly in the right hemisphere;[44] the left hemisphere is not as concerned about others and their feelings. Neuropsychologist Larry Schutz demonstrated that, absent the right hemisphere, "social intercourse is conducted with a blanket disregard for the feelings, wishes, needs, and expectations of others."[45] Persons with deficit in the right frontal lobe but not the left undergo a personality change that includes an incapacity for empathy,[46] "the ability spontaneously to reconstruct in oneself what another is feeling, thinking, and intending."[47] Pope Francis insists in *Evangelii Gaudium* that mercy, which is preceded by empathy, must always be pastorally active when judging ethical situations (*EG,* no. 44; also *AL,* nos. 308–11). Empathy and mercy, therefore, must be active also in theological ethicists. If emotions rely more strongly on a right-hemisphere hub, explicit, logical reasoning relies more strongly on a left-hemisphere hub, though the less-explicit reasoning that is involved in science and theology is predominantly a right-hemisphere activity. Noted French physicist Henri Poincaré judged that the subliminal right-hemisphere self is in no way inferior to the conscious left-hemisphere self. It is capable of discernment

[42] Ibid., 324–25.

[43] Ibid., 360.

[44] Georg W. Alpers, "Eye-catching: Right Hemisphere Attentional Bias for Emotional Pictures," *Laterality* 13 (2008): 158–78.

[45] Larry E. Schutz, "Broad-perspective Perceptual Disorder of the Right Hemisphere," *Neuropsychology Review* 15 (2005): 11–27.

[46] Richard J. Perry et al., "Hemispheric Dominance for Emotions, Empathy, and Social Behavior: Evidence from Right and Left Handers with Frontotemporal Dementia," *Neurocase* 7 (2001): 145–60.

[47] Spezio, "The Neuroscience of Emotion," 351.

and knows how to intuit and choose.[48] Poincaré wrote at the beginning of the twentieth century, but there is now an extensive body of research showing that insight and problem solving is associated with activation in the right anterior temporal area.[49]

Experience and Ethics

We consider finally the fourth aid for those seeking discernment. Ethicist Joseph Selling declares that paragraph 46 of *Gaudium et Spes* "stands as a milestone in the evolution of Roman Catholic moral theology."[50] The paragraph states that "there are a number of particularly urgent needs characterizing the present age, needs which go to the roots of the human race. To a consideration of these in the light of the Gospel and of *human experience*, the Council would now direct the attention of all." This paragraph shifts method in Catholic ethics by rooting it not exclusively in scripture but also in human experience. A legitimate question, however, immediately arises: Whose experience is to be used in the formulation of a Christian ethics?

We emphasize again that experience is never a standalone source of theological ethics; it is only one part of the Wesleyan Quadrilateral to be considered in discerning an ethical judgment and action. Individual experience alone is never a source at all. Ethical authority in the Catholic Church is granted only to *communal* experience, and only in constructive conversation with the three other sources, scripture, tradition, and reason. We mean by experience "the human capacity to encounter the surrounding world consciously, to observe it, be affected by it, and to learn from it."[51] Contemporary theological ethicists espouse an inductive methodology that begins with this human experience and they seek a common experience on which to found and formulate ethical norms.

Lisa Cahill states well the relationship between human experience and ethical norms. "The essential point to emphasize for an ethics which begins with, and remains respectful of, differences in experience, while not giving up the possibility of normative ethics, is that the 'shared' is not achieved

---

[48] Brewster Ghiselin, ed., *The Creative Process* (Berkeley and Los Angeles: University of California Press, 1992), 28.

[49] John Kounios et al., "The Origins of Insight in Resting-state Brain Activity," *Neuropsychologia* 46 (2008): 281–91; Simone Sandkühler and Joydeep Bhattacharya, "Deconstructing Insight: EEG Correlates of Insightful Problem Solving," *PLoS One* 3 (2008): 1459.

[50] Joseph Selling, "*Gaudium et Spes: A Manifesto for Contemporary Moral Theology*," in *Vatican II and Its Legacy*, ed. Leo Kenis and Matthew Lamberigts (Leuven: Peeters Press, 2003), 151.

[51] Neil Brown, "Experience and Development in Catholic Moral Theology," *Pacifica* 14 (2001): 300.

beyond or over against particularity [experience], but rather in and through it."[52] Human realities do not always conform to some theoretical ideal, and, therefore, ethically right choices will often depend more on conscientious discernment and prudent, practical adaptation of an ideal to the particular experiential reality rather than on the ideal itself. The challenge is to discern carefully what constitutes authentic experience that may revise the definition of human dignity and norms that facilitate attaining it, and what constitutes inauthentic experience that must be judged by an established definition of human dignity and its corresponding norms. Theological ethicists, we have suggested, consider a quadrilateral of sources to discern that definition and to formulate and justify those norms.

Questions for Reflection

- What is the role, function, and authority of conscience in the Catholic tradition?
- How have Bernard of Clairvaux and Ignatius of Loyola influenced the Catholic tradition's understanding of discernment? How does discernment help to guide one's ethical decision-making process?
- What is the interrelationship between conscience and discernment?
- How do the sources of ethical knowledge help to inform one's conscience?
- What can we learn from neuroscience to inform us about ethics in general and the formation of conscience in particular?

Suggested Readings

Curran, Charles, E., ed. *Conscience: Readings in Moral Theology No. 14.* New York: Paulist Press, 2004.

Lawler, Michael G., and Todd A. Salzman. "In *Amoris Laetitia*, Francis' Model of Conscience Empowers Catholics." *National Catholic Reporter*, September 7, 2016.

McIntosh, Mark A. *Discernment and Truth: The Spirituality and Theology of Knowledge.* New York: Herder, 2004.

---

[52] Lisa Sowle Cahill, *Sex, Gender, and Christian Ethics* (Cambridge: Cambridge University Press, 1996), 55.

Smith, Robert J. *Conscience and Catholicism: The Nature and Function of Conscience in Contemporary Roman Catholic Theology.* Lanham, MD: University Press of America, 1998.

Toner, Jules J. *A Commentary on Saint Ignatius' Rules for the Discernment of Spirits.* St. Louis: Institute of Jesuit Sources, 1982.

7

Ecology and Climate Change

Learning Objectives

- Explain the causes and effects of climate change.
- Explain the four types of conversion—religious, intellectual, psychic, and moral—and their relevance for a response to climate change.
- Analyze and evaluate climate change from an ecological conversion virtuous perspective.
- Explain the implications of a Christian perspective for a response to climate change.
- Explain the ethical implications of Pope Francis's *Laudato Si'* as a response to climate change.

Over five hundred scientists and religious leaders from Massachusetts, including Boston's Sean Cardinal O'Malley, recently signed a joint appeal for climate action, noting that "climate change is an ecological and moral emergency that impacts all other aspects of our shared lives and requires us to work together to protect our common home."[1] This call for action reflects the international recognition in the Paris Climate Agreement, ratified by 175 countries, of the pending disaster that climate change poses for the planet and its people, especially the vulnerable poor. It also emphasizes the need for a cooperative national and international effort to reduce greenhouse gases to preserve the planet and its inhabitants. In this chapter we follow the see-judge-act model of Catholic social teaching to explore the issue of ecology and climate change. To analyze, evaluate, and propose responses to this crisis we rely both on the four sources of ethical

---

[1] Woods Hole Research Center, "Faith and Science Joint Appeal for Climate Action," May 23, 2018.

knowledge, scripture, tradition, science/reason, and human experience, as most recently formulated in Pope Francis's *Laudato Si' (On Care for Our Common Home)*, and on an ecological virtuous perspective grounded in personal conversion.

Jeffrey Sachs, one of the world's leading economists, has described *Laudato Si'* as "magnificent—absolutely magnificent." He declares: "I often say that I can assign it to first-year graduate students in earth sciences, biology, theology, diplomacy, or political science. It's so completely holistic that it can be read from all these crucial points of view, so therefore it inspires in its profundity and *it speaks to our urgent needs* in a very direct way."[2] Before examining *Laudato Si',* however, we first explain the foundational metaethical, anthropological, and normative issues that have created the climate crisis and how we respond to it by integral ecology and the see-judge-act method of Catholic social ethics guided by a virtuous perspective.

Catholic Teaching on the Environment

Two ethical misperceptions have led to the present ecological crisis. The first is metaethical relativism, a "disorder which drives one person to take advantage of another, to treat others as mere objects" (*LS*, no. 123). This relativism extends to the environment, which humans objectify and treat as a mere means to fulfilling their own immediate needs, convenience, and personal satisfaction, without care, concern, or regard for the environment. In a recent documentary Pope Francis asserts this disregard emphatically, declaring that "the poorest of the poor is planet earth."[3] The second ethical misperception is a distorted anthropology at the root of the ecological crisis, what Pope Francis calls a "misguided anthropocentrism" that "leads to a misguided lifestyle" (*LS*, no. 122). For Francis, the distortion is a fundamental anthropology that displaces and opposes cosmology and creation and puts anthropology and humans at the center of all reality. *Laudato Si'* summarizes the consequences of this anthropological relativism:

> When human beings place themselves at the center, they give absolute priority to immediate convenience and all else becomes relative. Hence, we should not be surprised to find, in conjunction with the omnipresent technocratic paradigm and the cult of unlimited human power, the rise of a relativism which sees everything as irrelevant unless it serves one's own immediate interests. (LS, no. 122)

---

[2] Cited in *Crux,* June 30, 2018, emphasis added.
[3] *Pope Francis: A Man of His Word* (2018), directed by Wim Wenders.

The distortion is not only between humans and the material world but also among humans themselves. In the economic disparities between developed and developing countries and between the rich and the poor within those countries, "some consider themselves more human than others, as if they had been born with greater rights" (*LS*, no. 90). Such an anthropology is a violation of several dimensions of the human person integrally and adequately considered, as we discussed in Chapter 5. It violates proper relationships between humans and the material world and between neighbors and social groups, especially the poor who suffer the most from the devastating consequences of climate change. It also denies the proper relationship between humans and God, denying that we are not absolute but creatures created by and in the image and likeness of God. The implications of relativism and misguided anthropocentrism lead to ethical norms that disregard the common good and focus on fulfilling only immediate personal desires and needs (*LS*, no. 123).

To correct these foundational ethical misperceptions, we must embrace a perspectivism which recognizes "objective truths" and "sound principles" (*LS*, no. 123). We must foster an anthropology that reflects the human person integrally and adequately considered, for "there can be no ecology without an adequate anthropology" (*LS*, no. 118). We must propose ethical norms rooted in the common good as human dignity and guided by the virtuous perspective of an "integral ecology that is one of the central theological themes of *Laudato Si'*. Pope Francis describes integral ecology as follows: "Since everything is closely interrelated, and today's problems call for a vision capable of taking into account every aspect of the global crisis, I suggest that we now consider some elements of an *integral ecology*, one which clearly respects its human and social dimensions" (*LS*, no. 137). Integral ecology asserts that everything is interconnected, and therefore we must analyze and evaluate the current crisis from an interdisciplinary and interrelational perspective. We propose in this chapter a twofold approach for analyzing and evaluating the ecological crisis; the see-judge-act method of Catholic social teaching, and a virtuous perspective that begins with ecological conversion.

The ecological virtuous perspective of what we shall later call soteriology, and faith that sees the injustice of the ecological crisis and seeks to do justice, aligns well with the see-judge-act method of pastoral reflection initiated by Pope John XXIII in his encyclical *Mater et Magistra*.[4] The perspective allows Christians to *see* injustice at the root of the ecological

---

[4] See also Marvin L. Mich, "Commentary on *Mater et Magistra*," in *Modern Catholic Social Teaching: Commentaries and Interpretations*, ed. Kenneth B. Himes (Washington, DC: Georgetown University Press, 2005), 191–216.

crisis, both individual and structural, to *judge* that injustice, and to *act* to establish or restore justice in light of that judgment. To guide us in this method we propose "ecological virtues," first and foremost the virtue of conversion and other virtues that inform *Laudato Si'* and that we shall specify as we go along. In *Laudato Si'* Pope Francis focuses on virtues that shape one's perspective to restore creation, the most fundamental virtue being *ecological conversion.* He notes that many otherwise prayerful Christians ridicule concern for the environment or remain passive and do nothing to change their habits to live out their Christian faith consistently. He calls Christians to "'ecological conversion,' whereby the effects of their encounter with Jesus Christ become evident in their relationship with the world around them. *Living our vocation to be protectors of God's handiwork is essential to a life of virtue*; it is not an optional or a secondary aspect of our Christian experience" (*LS*, no. 217, emphasis added). The connection between a life of virtue and care for God's creation is essential to a virtuous ecological perspective. We turn now to a detailed explanation of the ecological conversion perspective that guides our see-judge-act method.

See: Science

The Catholic Church has an abysmal record of integrating scientific method and conclusions into its theological, cosmological, and anthropological understandings of reality. One need only look to its condemnation of Galileo for defending Copernicus's heliocentric model of the solar system or the rejection and suspicion of science in Pope Pius IX's *Syllabus of Errors*. More recently, however, as we discussed in Chapter 3, a respect for and methodological integration of the sciences have been promoted by both Pope John Paul II and Pope Francis. Pope John Paul II highlights the need for intense dialogue between science and theology. Theology and science must enter into a "common interactive relationship" whereby, while maintaining its own integrity, each discipline is "open to the discoveries and insights of the other."[5] Pope Francis's *Laudato Si'* insists on an interdisciplinary approach, which includes "an intense dialogue between science and religion" (*LS*, no. 62). The encyclical's use of the natural sciences and its exploration of related environmental questions are unprecedented in magisterial statements. Specifically, it draws from the science of environmental studies and climate change and presents a harsh but accurate indictment of the current situation: the earth is becoming "an immense pile of filth" (*LS*, no. 22). Pope Francis articulates a theological understanding of humans'

---

[5] See John Paul II, "The Relationship of Science and Theology: A Letter to Jesuit Father George Coyne," in *Origins* 18, no. 23 (November 17, 1988): 375.

relationship to creation and the world and draws out the theological, anthropological, and normative implications of that relationship based on what the sciences tell us about climate change.[6] To fully understand him and his argument we must now ask: What do the sciences tell us about climate change?

The Intergovernmental Panel on Climate Change, a nonpartisan organization, concludes that "scientific evidence for warming of the climate change is unequivocal."[7] There is overwhelming consensus among climate scientists (97%) that global warming is occurring and that humans are responsible for it. Since the late-nineteenth century the average surface temperature of the planet has risen two degrees Fahrenheit, an increase largely due to increased levels of carbon dioxide (CO_2) in the atmosphere. Carbon dioxide is a heat-trapping gas caused by human activities like burning fossil fuels in automobiles and by deforestation. Burning fossil fuels releases carbon dioxide into the atmosphere, and the gas then traps the sun's heat; deforestation causes the loss of a natural filtering and reduction source for the gas. The end result, now well documented, is an increase in surface temperatures on both land and sea.[8] Most of this warming has occurred in the last thirty-five years; sixteen of the seventeen warmest years on record have occurred since 2001. Currently, the world is in a race to limit global warming to 2° Celsius (3.6° Fahrenheit) above temperatures at the beginning of the Industrial Revolution. Pre–Industrial Revolution levels of CO_2 were 280 parts per million (ppm); currently we are at 407 ppm. A sustainable level is 350 ppm.[9] The increase in CO_2 levels is paralleled by an increase in global temperatures. The year 2016 was the hottest year on record (since records started being recorded in 1880), 1.1° Celsius (2° degrees Fahrenheit) above pre–Industrial Revolution levels.[10] At the current rate of warming, anything less than 2° Celsius of warming by 2100 is unlikely.[11]

The 2° Celsius mark in global temperature increase is a threshold established by Yale economist William Nordhaus in 1977 and a marker set by the Paris Agreement in 2015. The impact of current and increasing CO_2

---

[6] See Celia Deane-Drummond, "*Laudato Si'* and the Natural Sciences: An Assessment of the Possibilities and Limits," *Theological Studies* (2016): 392–415. Although she claims that this encyclical's use of the natural sciences is "unprecedented" in magisterial statements, she still believes that Francis's position on ecology is "idealized" (414).

[7] NASA, "Climate Change: How Do We Know?" *Global Climate Change: Vital Signs of the Planet* (June 12, 2018).

[8] Ibid.

[9] NASA, "Global Climate Change: Vital Signs of the Planet" (April 2018).

[10] Nicola Jones, "How the World Passed a Carbon Threshold and Why It Matters," *Yale Environment 360* (January 26, 2017).

[11] Adrian E. Raftery et al., "Less than 2° Warming by 2100 Unlikely," *Nature Climate Change* 7 (2017): 637–41.

levels and global temperatures for the earth are devastating for the planet and all its inhabitants. If we reach that threshold, "life on our planet will change as we know it."[12] Seas will continue to rise, wiping out coastal cities. There will be mass extinctions, more intense and prolonged droughts, increased wildfires, more frequent and intense hurricanes. Shifts in weather patterns will reduce crop production and availability of fresh water. In addition, even if there is a drastic reduction in greenhouse gases, the negative environmental effects of current levels on the environment will only gradually reduce given the "shelf life" of these emissions. Drastic measures must be taken to avoid these increases to prevent these consequences. Climate-change scientists emphasize the need for public policy to shift from fossil fuels to renewable sources of energy such as sun, wind, and water. Bill McKibben notes: "We're a long ways down the path to disastrous global warming, and the policy response—especially in the United States—has been pathetically underwhelming."[13] Given the overwhelming scientific evidence for climate change and its disastrous effects on all creation and the underwhelming response to it in many countries, including the United States, we now ask: What accounts for the lack of leadership among policymakers to address this crisis?

Science, Ethics, Scotosis, and Conversion

James Hansen of NASA's Goddard Space Center, one of the world's leading climate scientists, notes a disconnect between the overwhelming scientific evidence documenting climate change and the general public's awareness of this evidence. "A wide gap has developed between what is understood about global warming by the relevant scientific community and what is known by policymakers and the public."[14] Elsewhere in this book we have discussed Bernard Lonergan's theory of scotosis, an ethical blind spot that arises "in the censorship that governs the emergence of psychic contents."[15] When it comes to the science of climate change and the general population's awareness of climate change, there is substantial scotosis. There is, therefore, also a need for what Pope Francis labels "ecological conversion" (*LS*, nos. 216–22), the need to *see* the unjust treatment of our

---

[12] Ashley Strickland, "Earth to Warm 2 Degrees Celsius by the End of This Century, Studies Say," *CNN Health* (July 31, 2017).

[13] In ibid.

[14] Guest Opinion, "Global Warming Twenty Years Later: Tipping Points Near," *Worldwatch Institute: Vision for a Sustainable World* (June 12, 2018).

[15] Bernard J. F. Lonergan, *Insight: A Study of Human Understanding* (London: Longmans, 1957), 191.

planet and its ecological implications, to *judge,* and to *act* to preserve the planet. We consider scotosis and conversion in turn.

Scotosis

First, what accounts for the disconnect between the scientific community's findings on global warming and the general public's awareness of those findings? Theologian Richard Miller proposes four reasons for the disconnect.[16] *First, human experience, a foundational source of ethical knowledge, does not necessarily affirm global warming.* In the United States in 2017–18, the Midwest experienced a very long and cold winter. The upper Midwest had a snowstorm in mid-April that broke records; the total accumulation of snow in Minneapolis for that April was 26.1 inches, breaking the previous record of 21.8 inches set in 1983. This longer and colder winter and record snowfall led the general population to question scientific claims about global warming. Although people's experience is certainly an important source of ethical knowledge, this 2018 experience must be interpreted in light of and not despite the scientific evidence. Episodic experience alone, mine, yours, or that of the good people of Minnesota, does not provide sure evidence that runs counter to the established scientific conclusions about global warming. As we write this, despite the local experience of people in the American Midwest, another enormous iceberg has broken away from the northern ice mass and is seriously threatening the existence of the equally human people of Greenland.

There are important distinctions to make to grasp the disconnect between people's experiences and the scientific reality. First, there is a problem of language and perception. The terms *weather* and *climate* are often used interchangeably, but they are distinct. *Weather* refers to atmospheric conditions over short periods of time, minutes, hours, or days, and is measured locally. *Climate* refers to global average temperatures, humidity, or storm patterns over longer periods, seasons, years, even decades. People are tempted to interpret their experiences of cold weather in the short term as a challenge to scientific evidence about global climate patterns. The phrase *global warming* does not help this confusion, since the climate's warming seems counterintuitive to people's experience of colder weather. This confusion is exemplified in one of Donald Trump's 2013 tweets that climate change is a hoax. "Ice storm rolls from Texas to Tennessee—I'm in Los Angeles and it's freezing. Global warming is a total, and very expensive, hoax!" As president, he has continued to deny human contributions to

---

[16] Richard W. Miller, ed., *God, Creation, and Climate Change: A Catholic Response to the Environmental Crisis* (Maryknoll, NY: Orbis Books, 2010), 2–7.

climate change, though he has softened his rhetoric somewhat.[17] Personal experience that is not interpreted in dialogue with the scientific experience may often confuse and distort scientific claims and the theological and/or ethical conclusions that can be deduced from them, especially when we remember the influence of the selection, interpretation, prioritization, and integration of the sources of ethical knowledge.

This confusion between what episodic personal experience indicates and what long-term scientific knowledge demonstrates may explain, in part, the shift in media terminology from *global warming* to *climate change* to designate what is happening to the planet. Global warming refers to the temperature increase across the earth since the 1900s, and especially since the 1970s, largely due to greatly increased automobile fossil-fuel emissions. Climate change refers to a wide range of phenomena that result from burning fossil fuels, including not only increased temperatures (global warming) but also changes in sea level, loss of ice in places like Antarctica, shifts in plant blooming, species extinction, and extreme weather occurrences. Global warming is more focused on global temperatures and climate change is more comprehensively focused on the impact of climate changes on the ecosystem as a whole. Indeed, even in 2017–18, while the Midwest was experiencing longer and colder weather, the overall climate temperatures continue to rise. March 2018 was one of the warmest Marches on global record.[18] Human experience must be seen and interpreted in a broader context. While most people trust the scientific method and its conclusions in many daily activities—they will, for instance, take a sick child to the doctor to be diagnosed and treated—there is personal inconsistency in that trust. Such inconsistency is evident in the disconnect between human experience of local weather and scientific knowledge of global climate change.

A second reason for the disconnect between ordinary and scientific experience is the intentional effort by those with vested economic and political interests to promote skepticism of scientific conclusions when it serves those interests. Oil and coal companies have funded "research groups" to spread disinformation about climate change. ExxonMobil is one of the world's largest fossil-fuel corporations, and it has not only spread such disinformation for years, but a Harvard study in 2017 found that it has done so knowing that climate change is in fact real.[19] It continues to

---

[17] Ryan Teague Beckwith, "President Trump Won't Say If He Still Thinks Climate Change Is a Hoax. Here's Why," *Time* (September 27, 2017).

[18] NASA's Goddard Institute for Space Studies, "March 2018 Was One of the Six Warmest Marches on Record" (April 16, 2018).

[19] See Tom DiChristopher, "Exxon Mobil Misled the Public on Climate Change, Harvard Study Finds," *CNBC* (August 23, 2017).

fund climate-change-denial groups such as the National Center for Policy Analysis and the Heritage Foundation. The coal industry has also given millions of dollars to lobby groups, such as the American Coalition for Clean Coal Electricity, promoting so-called clean coal that will not increase CO_2 emissions and contribute to global warming and climate change. These claims of clean coal are largely fictitious. The most promising development of a sustainable clean coal plant in Kemper County, Mississippi, turned into a financial and engineering debacle, losing hundreds of millions of dollars for investors and taxpayers.[20] Yet this project was promoted by politicians who benefit from coal-industry lobbying money.

Third, the climate issue has become a politically partisan issue. Unaware of the scientific data themselves, people trust that politicians they support are giving them accurate information about fossil fuels and climate change. In his State of the Union Address in 2018, President Donald Trump declared: "We have ended the war on American energy and we have ended the war on beautiful, clean coal."[21] His comment and persistent denial of climate change, as well as his announced intention to withdraw the United States from the Paris Climate Agreement, indicate the politically partisan nature of discussion about climate change that is introduced into public discourse and misinforms the public. For most of his presidency George W. Bush censored James Hansen from NASA.[22] And Senator James Inhofe from Oklahoma, chairman of the Senate Committee on the Environment and Public Works from 2003 to 2007, referred to global warming as the greatest hoax ever perpetrated on the American people.[23] Inhofe gets the majority of his campaign contributions from oil and gas companies and is the second-largest political recipient of that money.[24] Politicians like Trump, Bush, and Inhofe have access to, and sometimes control over, the media to shape or at least influence the public narrative on climate change. Too often, this narrative is grounded in alternative facts and misinformation about climate change, which are suspiciously linked to money, lobbyists, and corporate interests. In *Laudato Si'*, which we will discuss in detail below, Pope Francis notes and critiques this political and economic alliance

---

[20] See Sharon Kelly, "How America's Clean Coal Dream Unraveled," *The Guardian*, March 2, 2018. Petra Nova coal plant in Texas uses carbon capture and storage technology, but it is not sustainable (James Conca, "The Largest Clean Coal Power Plant in America Turns to Natural Gas," *Forbes* [July 11, 2017]).

[21] See Umair Irfan, "Trump's Perennial 'War on Coal' Claim, Fact-Checked," *Vox* (January 31, 2018).

[22] See Mark Bowen, *Censoring Science: Inside the Political Attack on Dr. James Hansen and the Truth of Global Warming* (New York: Dutton, 2008).

[23] See James Inhofe, *The Greatest Hoax: How the Global Warming Conspiracy Threatens Your Future* (Washington, DC: WND Books, 2012).

[24] Miller, *God, Creation, and Climate Change*, 5.

(*LS*, nos. 26, 54), which often distorts the truth about climate change and prevents popular support and political action, both national and international, to address the issue.

Fourth, the media too often serves as the mouthpiece for this unholy alliance between politicians and corporate interests. In 2009, Eric Pooley wrote an extensive critique of the media's coverage of global warming in which he demonstrates how the media has essentially functioned as a stenographer, merely "presenting a nominally balanced view of the debate [over global warming] without questioning the validity of the arguments, sometimes even ignoring evidence that one side was twisting truth. . . . [This] actually helped opponents of climate action stifle progress."[25] Media coverage on climate change has improved, and there is greater attention to a shift from the media as stenographer to the media as interrogator seeking truth, at least within some news outlets, but recent studies still find a political bias in the media that promotes a certain corporate-driven narrative when reporting on climate change. In Aaron Huertas's and Rachel Kreigsman's study in 2013 gauging the accuracy of three major cable news networks (CNN, Fox, and MSNBC) when reporting on climate change, they discovered the following: "70 percent of climate-science-related segments on CNN were accurate, 28 percent of Fox News Channel segments were accurate, and 92 percent of such segments on MSNBC were accurate."[26]

Despite political and media misinformation, overall public awareness on the reality of climate change has improved dramatically; 73 percent of registered voters in the United States believe global warming is real, and 59 percent believe that it is caused primarily by human activities. However, there is a stark political divide in those numbers: "95% of liberal Democrats, 88% of moderate/conservative Democrats and 68% of liberal/moderate Republicans believe it is real, but only 40% of conservative Republicans" believe it. There is a similar political divide among those who believe humans are the primary cause of global warming: "84% of liberal Democrats, 70% of moderate/conservative Democrats, and 55%

---

[25] Eric Pooley, "How Much Would You Pay to Save the Planet? The American Press and the Economics of Climate Change," Joan Shorenstein Center on the Press, Politics and Public Policy (January 2009), 5.

[26] Aaron Huertas and Rachel Kriegsman, "Science or Spin? Assessing the Accuracy of Cable News Coverage of Climate Science" (April 2014); see also Michael Svoboda, "Media Coverage of Climate Change: Key Books and Reports on Climate Change and the Media, 2003–2011 (Part 1)" and "Media Coverage of Climate Change: Key Books and Reports on Climate Change and the Media, 2012–2017 (Part 2)," Yale Climate Connections (March 3, 2017).

of liberal/moderate Republicans believe it but only 26% of conservative Republicans" believe it. [27]

In addition, only 13 percent of Americans know that more than 90 percent of climate scientists (the actual number is now closer to 97 percent) agree that global warming is happening and that humans are causing it. [28] These statistics indicate a deep and pervasive political divide on the issue of climate change that can be traced, at least in part, to the four reasons given for the disparity between the scientific evidence and political and public knowledge of that evidence: experience of local weather patterns, the concerted effort by fossil-fuel industries to spread misinformation on global warming, the political divide on the issue, and various media outlets that promote disinformation or, at least, do not challenge misinformation. We are not in a position to judge the degree of scotosis of those who deny the overwhelming scientific evidence for climate change or the awareness or moral culpability of those who promote misinformation about global warming, but the scotosis does highlight the need for Pope Francis's "ecological conversion" to *see* correctly in order to *judge* responsibly and *act* justly.

Ecological Conversion: A Virtuous Perspective

At a General Audience on January 17, 2001, Pope John Paul II introduced the phrase "ecological conversion" into official church teaching, intending by it humans' deepened sensitivity to the ecological disaster confronting humanity. Pope Francis's *Laudato Si'* focuses on the need for ecological conversion in humans' relationship with, and attitude toward, the environment. To understand Francis's call for ecological conversion, however, we must first understand ecology. The term derives from the Greek *oikos*-home, as in *Laudato Si'*'s English title, *On Care for Our Common Home*, but it has both a narrow biological and a broader theological meaning in *Laudato Si'*. Biologically, it designates the interrelationship of all natural organisms, including humans, and their natural environment. Theologically, it acknowledges and admires the goodness of God's creation and calls for humans to care for it, guided by the ecological virtues of gratitude for creation, love for that creation, solidarity in our common home, mutual responsibility for it, prudent use of it, and justice for all who share it, especially for the poor and vulnerable who are always the most damaged when

---

[27] Anthony Leiserowitz et al., "Politics & Global Warming, March 2018," *Yale Program on Climate Change Communication* (March 2018).

[28] Anthony Leiserowitz et al., *Climate Change in the American Mind: October 2017.*

creation is damaged. It calls also for the recognition of the essential inter-relationships that exist among all the organisms that inhabit our common home and for consideration of the social, economic, and political realities that affect these interrelationships.[29]

For Francis, ecological conversion calls for

> a number of attitudes which together foster a spirit of generous care, full of tenderness. First, it entails gratitude and gratuitousness, a recognition that the world is God's loving gift, and that we are called quietly to imitate his generosity in self-sacrifice and good works. . . . It also entails a loving awareness that we are not discon-nected from the rest of creatures but joined in a splendid universal communion. As believers, we do not look at the world from without but from within, conscious of the bonds with which the Father has linked us to all beings. By developing our individual, God-given ca-pacities, an ecological conversion can inspire us to greater creativity and enthusiasm in resolving the world's problems and in offering ourselves to God "as a living sacrifice, holy and acceptable (*Rom* 12:1)." (*LS*, no. 220)

While conversion is at the core of Christian theology, turning away from sin, including the sin of violating and selfishly exploiting our com-mon home, it is also an epistemological concept that shapes how we see, judge, and act. Neil Ormerod and Cristina Vanin argue that the ecological conversion called for in *Laudato Si'* is somewhat vague and ambiguous and requires detailed analysis and explanation to draw out its full epis-temological and ethical implications. In their analysis and explanation they turn to Bernard Lonergan and his major interpreter, Robert Doran, to explain conversion and interpret *Laudato Si'* in light of it.[30] Lonergan introduced the notion of the conversion of the knowing subject in his magisterial *Insight*, and further developed it in his *Method in Theology*.[31] Conversion is a process that involves "a radical about-face in which one repudiates characteristic features of one's previous horizon,"[32] or what we

---

[29] Deane-Drummond, "*Laudato Si' and the Natural Sciences*," 392–93. In theological literature the terms *ecology* and *environment* are often used interchangeably.

[30] In this section on conversion we are indebted to Neil Ormerod and Cristina Vanin, "Ecological Conversion: What Does It Mean?" *Theological Studies* 77, no. 2 (2016): 328–52.

[31] Lonergan, *Insight*, esp. 431–87; idem, *Method in Theology* (New York: Herder, 1972), 270–71.

[32] Robert M. Doran, *Theology and the Dialectics of History* (Toronto: University of Toronto Press, 1990), 35.

called earlier one's perspective. It is a turning away from "self-absorption" and "self-enclosure" to "self-transcendence."[33]

For Lonergan, such conversion can be threefold: *intellectual, moral,* or *religious.* Intellectual conversion abandons "the myth that fully human knowing is to be conceived on an analogy with seeing and replaces it with the affirmation of a self that knows because it understands correctly."[34] Such conversion is an "effort to reach cognitive integrity in one's intellectual positions"[35] by shifting from the perception of human knowledge as a mode of seeing to the perception of it as a mode of understanding. Moral conversion is "a shift in the criterion of one's decisions and choices from satisfaction to values."[36] A value "is the good as the possible object of rational choice;"[37] the value or good available for ecological choice is directly the lowering of both greenhouse-gas emissions and global temperatures and indirectly the preservation of our common home. We emphasize here the notion of possible choice. Currently all rational human beings have a choice between using creation either for self-satisfaction, personal pleasure, or economic profit, a choice that is already leading the earth to disaster, or for the creation's preservation for the common good. When we consider this possible choice, again, we have to be especially mindful of its possible implications for the poor, the most disadvantaged and vulnerable of our neighbors whom the Christ commands us to love "as yourself" (Mark 12:31). We suggest that the ethical choice of the value, good, and action demanded of Christians is clear. We further suggest that when values/goods are chosen and acted on, like the virtues we explained in Chapter 2, they are strengthened and solidified in us, making it easier to further act on them in the future.

Religious conversion is simply "falling in love with God,"[38] which for human beings faced with myriad distractions is not so easy. In the climate case under discussion in this chapter, it is easy to be distracted from the love of God and God's creation by the love of mastery and selfish use of creation for our own benefit. Doran adds a fourth type of conversion that he calls *psychic conversion.* In psychic conversion one converts one's preconscious sensor, which allows images to emerge into consciousness, from a repressive role that suppresses disturbing images to a facilitative role that promotes a conscious and intentional search for images that convey

---

[33] Robert M. Doran, "What Does Bernard Lonergan Mean by 'Conversion?'" lecture, University of St. Michael's College, Toronto, Ontario, Canada, July 15, 2011).

[34] Doran, *Theology and the Dialectics of History,* 36.

[35] Doran, "What Does Bernard Lonergan Mean by 'Conversion?'"

[36] Doran, *Theology and the Dialectics of History,* 36.

[37] Lonergan, *Insight,* 601.

[38] Ibid.

truth, meaning, and goodness.[39] We consider each of these conversions in relation to *Laudato Si'* and climate change. These four conversions are all interrelated, but three of them, intellectual, religious, and psychic, entail seeing and judging from a virtuous perspective so that moral conversion becomes a guide to act from that perspective.

In relation to ecology, *religious conversion* calls Christians to recognize the sacredness of God's creation and to live in intimate awe in relationship to it. Ecological conversion is situated within a Christian soteriological and faith perspective on the world and its climate considered in toto and identifies a specific conversion toward the world as part of one's Christian vocation. Soteriology derives from the Greek *soter* ("savior"), and soteriological culture draws its meanings and values from a transcendent divine ground believed by those who are religiously converted to be the ground of all being, meaning, value, and human salvation. In relation to the environment, religious conversion calls us to fall in love not only with God but also with God's creation, and to recognize and repent "our errors, sins, faults and failures . . . and desire to change" (*LS*, no. 218). The ultimate goal is to be so converted that "we are not disconnected from the rest of creatures but joined in a splendid universal communion" (*LS*, no. 220). All Christians are called "to recognize and to live fully this dimension of their conversion" (*LS*, no. 221).

Lonergan articulates his understanding of value in relation to the personal feelings or emotions that might be distractions to a rational choice. The objects of desires, feelings, and emotions, he notes, are manifold, but this feeling-manifold "is part and parcel of the *total manifold*, and it is in the total manifold that concretely and effectively the potential good resides."[40] In terms of our present discussion of ecological ethics, personal desires or feelings for personal pleasure or economic profit from our use of our creation-home must be evaluated in terms of the outcomes of our use on the total manifold that includes creation itself and the humans who inhabit it, especially the poor humans who are most disadvantaged and vulnerable. The consistent scientific data on those outcomes is that our self-serving misuse of creation is severely damaging to all those manifold stakeholders. "Feelings reveal values to us," Lonergan correctly judges. "They dispose us to commitment. But they do not bring commitment about."[41] No personal commitment can be brought about by anyone or anything other than a

---

[39] Doran, *Theology and the Dialectics of History*, 42–63; see also Ormerod and Vanin, "Ecological Conversion," 332.

[40] Lonergan, *Insight*, 606, emphasis added.

[41] Bernard Lonergan, "Natural Right and Historical Mindedness," in *A Third Collection: Papers by Bernard Lonergan,* ed. Frederick E. Crowe (New York: Paulist Press, 1985), 173.

person's own free choice. A person's choice is ineluctably free, and that is why every individual must make a choice about our environmental home. That is also why all Christians, marshalling all that they have learned from the Christ and truly believe, must make a choice for our home, irrespective of any contrary feeling/emotion. Recalling our earlier discussion of virtue and emotion, we now affirm again that the feeling/emotional dimension of the human person is not totally separated from the rational dimension but allies with it to shape together a virtuous perspective that defines the good as human dignity and the environmental good as human dignity within a whole and healthy creation-home.

Doran notes that *psychic conversion* embraces two types of consciousness. The first type is directly related to what we propose as the process for the selection, interpretation, prioritization, and integration of the sources of ethical knowledge to define human dignity and formulate and justify norms to facilitate its attainment. This consciousness inquires "into the data of our experience as we seek to understand it, weighing the evidence as we determine if our understanding is correct, making judgments, raising questions for deliberation, and making decisions that lead to actions."[42] The second type of consciousness is a passive sensing and imagining of desires, delights and joys or fears, sorrows, and sadness. This second type can prevent us from raising relevant questions by creating a fear that these questions and the ethical issues they raise, in conjunction with intellectual, moral, and religious conversion, will require authentic individual and social conversion that will fundamentally change our perspective and how we live our lives. Psychic conversion establishes the link between these two ways of being conscious so that we can see-judge-and act in an ethical way.

Intellectual conversion can aid in understanding ecological conversion in several ways.[43] First, it helps to ground values objectively by knowing correctly and combats "practical relativism," which promotes a "misguided anthropocentrism" that often "leads to a misguided lifestyle" (*LS*, nos. 122–23) and exacerbates the ecological crisis. Objective values like human dignity in relationship promote individual and social conversion to a simpler lifestyle in harmony with nature. Second, intellectual conversion helps to shift from merely descriptive to explanatory understanding. A key aspect of *Laudato Si'* in respect to ecological conversion is to see the interconnectedness of all things, what we have already called the total manifold. Without explanatory understanding, analysis, and evaluation of climate change, responses to it remain fragmented and ineffective. Third,

---

[42] Ormerod and Vanin, "Ecological Conversion," 346; see Doran, "What Does Bernard Lonergan Mean by 'Conversion?'"

[43] Ormerod and Vanin, "Ecological Conversion," 344–46.

as discussed at the beginning of this chapter, intellectual conversion can help to overcome scotosis and the disconnect between science and public knowledge by recognizing the objectivity of science that comes about "in the communal self-correcting process of learning with its mix of immanently generated knowledge and reasonable belief in the results of others."[44] Fourth, intellectual conversion can correct the current tendency of a hyper-anthropological culture, which is cut off from an adequate understanding and integration of cosmological culture and interprets reason only instrumentally as humans' ability to dominate and exploit the natural order. *Laudato Si'* promotes intellectual conversion to facilitate ecological conversion by relying on the sciences to analyze the current crisis and provide solutions to that crisis, although Francis also recognizes the limits of science in this endeavor: "Many problems of today's world stem from the tendency, at times unconscious, to make the method and aims of science and technology an epistemological paradigm which shapes the lives of individuals and the workings of society" (*LS*, no. 107). Intellectual conversion provides a balance in the dialogue between science and theology embraced and taught by popes John Paul II and Francis. The three conversions, intellectual, religious, and psychic, generate a virtuous perspective for seeing and understanding correctly, which then effectively guides the selection, interpretation, prioritization, and integration of the sources of ethical knowledge to judge and act correctly. We now explore those sources.

Judge: Sources of Ethical Knowledge

Ecological conversion, through intellectual, religious, and psychic conversions, gives us the courage and insight to ask difficult questions about our current relationship with the environment and to use the sources of ethical knowledge to seek answers to those questions through evaluative judgment that guides human acts. When addressing environmental ethics in general, and climate change specifically, ethical method may select all four sources of ethical knowledge and prioritize them in the following order, reason or the sciences, experience, tradition, and scripture, to define human dignity in relation to the environment and to formulate and justify norms that facilitate its attainment. This prioritization of these sources, we warn, is not a general ranking of the importance of the sources of ethical knowledge but a ranking of importance for the particular issue of ecological ethics.

---

[44] Ibid., 345.

First, ethical method must consult the natural sciences to gain a scientifically informed perspective on the actual and projected threat of climate change. To repeat, there is indisputable scientific evidence[45] that climate change is occurring, that the actions of humans significantly contribute to it, and that if nothing is done to address it in the near future, the consequences for humanity, especially for the poor in developing countries, will be catastrophic in terms of extreme weather patterns, famine, displacement, and violence. Second, experience confirms the scientific evidence: widespread drought, famine, and starvation throughout Africa; drought, wild fires, and an increase in the number and severity of hurricanes in North America; more severe flooding in Asia. All of these events point to at least a correlation, if not causation, between climate change, its impact on local ecosystems, and its devastating effects on millions of people.[46] Science, however, Pope Francis notes, cannot provide a complete explanation of life; it must be complemented with other sources of ethical knowledge (*LS*, no. 199). Tradition in the form of recent Catholic teaching based on scientific data and experience affirms that climate change or global warming is a reality and calls for the international community, especially wealthier countries that are in economic conditions to effect substantial reduction in greenhouse-gas emissions, to work toward reducing these emissions. A report by the working group commissioned by the Pontifical Academy of Sciences states the following on global warming:

> We call on all people and nations to recognize the serious and potentially irreversible impacts of global warming caused by the anthropogenic emissions of greenhouse gases and other pollutants, and by changes in forests, wetlands, grasslands, and other land uses. We appeal to all nations to develop and implement, without delay, effective and fair policies to reduce the causes and impacts of climate change on communities and ecosystems. . . . By acting now, in the spirit of common but differentiated responsibility, we accept our

---

[45] See James Hansen, "Global Warming Twenty Years Later: Tipping Points Near" (June 23, 2008); Peter T. Doran and Maggie Kendall Zimmerman, "Examining the Scientific Consensus on Climate Change," *Eos Transaction American Geophysical Union* 90, no. 3 (January 20, 2009): 22–23.

[46] There is debate among scientists about whether we have adequate scientific evidence to determine a correlation or causation between global warming and more severe weather patterns. The debate focuses on the lack of collected data to scientifically substantiate the claim, not on the probability that climate change will lead to more severe weather patterns, which many scientists already accept. See "Forum: Is Extreme Weather Linked to Global Warming?" *Yale Environment 360* (June 2, 2011).

duty to one another and to the stewardship of a planet blessed with the gift of life.[47]

The sure data and evidence of science, experience, and tradition must be accepted, interpreted, prioritized, and integrated into the selection and interpretation of scripture, the fourth source of ethical knowledge, to discover its true understanding of the relation between humans and creation and to formulate and justify norms that facilitate attaining human dignity for all in that environment. Fifty years ago, in a now-classic and prophetic article, Lynn White recognized the ecological crisis and explored the interpretations of the creation stories in Genesis that have, in part, led to the crisis.[48] *Laudato Si'* focuses on Genesis in its depiction of humans' relationship with the earth (*LS*, nos. 65–75).[49] In the later Priestly account of creation (Gen 1:1–2:4), God creates human beings on the sixth day and gives them "dominion *(radah)* over the fish of the sea, the birds of the air, and all the living things that crawl on earth" (Gen 1:28). The Hebrew verb *radah* can be interpreted in a strong sense as "subdue, rule over" or in a weaker sense as "govern." The strong sense of *radah* emphasizes humans' total dominion over creation and is often used to justify exploitation and disregard for it.[50] We see the consequences of this disregard in environmental devastation and the current ecological crisis.

The strong sense of *radah*, Francis says, "has encouraged the unbridled exploitation of nature by painting him [that is, humankind] as domineering and destructive by nature" (*LS*, no. 67). He teaches that, according to the church, the strong sense is not the correct interpretation of *radah*.

> The biblical texts are to be read in their context with an appropriate hermeneutic, recognizing that they tell us to "till and keep" the garden of the world (cf. Gen 2:15). "Tilling" refers to cultivating, ploughing or working, while "keeping" means caring, protecting, overseeing and preserving. This implies a relationship of mutual responsibility between human beings and nature. (*LS*, no. 67)

---

[47] "Fate of Mountain Glaciers in the Anthropocene," Pontifical Academy of Sciences Glacier Report (May 11, 2011).

[48] Lynn White, "The Historical Roots of Our Ecological Crisis," *Science* 155, no. 3767 (March 10, 1967): 1203–7.

[49] Though, as Brendan Byrne points out, Paul's letter to the Romans (at 9:18–22) could complement Genesis. See "A Pauline Complement to *Laudato Si'*," *Theological Studies* 77, no. 2 (2016): 308–27.

[50] Daniel J. Harrington and James F. Keenan, *Jesus and Virtue Ethics: Building Bridges between New Testament Studies and Moral Theology* (Lanham, MD: Sheed and Ward, 2002), 185.

The weaker sense of *radah* interprets it as situating humans in relationship with and caring for creation, emphasizing "responsible stewardship" (*LS*, no. 166) over creation, though Francis prefers throughout *Laudato Si'* the term *care* to the term *stewardship*.[51] Care is a broader concept than stewardship. It includes humans' relationship with and care for the environment, but it also includes care for the neighbor, for the vulnerable, for poor indigenous communities, for health, and for the nobility of all human activity. Scientific evidence that proves the damage humans have done to the environment, the manifold experiences of manifold peoples, and traditions that call for correcting past and lessening future damage all justify the weaker interpretation of *radah* over the strong interpretation. An integrated and dialectical hermeneutic of the selection, interpretation, prioritization, and integration of the four sources of ethical knowledge, as reflected in *Laudato Si'*, has both anthropological implications for defining human dignity and normative implications for human relationship with the environment.

Faithfully following Genesis, human dignity has to be defined in relationship with, not over and above, creation. Humans throughout the world must recognize their dependence on creation for their very survival. Among the normative implication of this dependence is that they must love and care for creation. What love and care for the environment mean concretely and presently is a concerted effort to address the present climate crisis and reduce greenhouse-gas emissions that are endangering the very survival of humanity. The human dignity of all is clearly facilitated to the extent that they respond to the current crisis; it is clearly frustrated to the extent that they do not respond to it.[52]

Additional methodological considerations aid in the selection, interpretation, prioritization, and integration of the four sources of ethical knowledge. In the case of climate change and ecological ethics, an inductive approach highlights the importance of the natural sciences for providing a factual assessment of the environmental situation. This factual assessment

---

[51] Kevin W. Irwin, *A Commentary on* Laudato Si': *Examining the Background, Contributions, Implementation, and Future of Pope Francis's Encyclical* (New York: Paulist Press, 2016), 119–20.

[52] For theological reflections on environmental ethics, see Miller, *God, Creation, and Climate Change*; Cristina L. H. Traina, "Creating a Global Discourse in a Pluralistic World: Strategies from Environmental Ethics," in *Christian Ethics: Problems and Prospects*, ed. Lisa Sowle Cahill and James F. Childress, 250–64 (Cleveland: Pilgrim Press, 1996); William C. French, "Natural Law and Ecological Responsibility: Drawing on the Natural Law Tradition," *University of St. Thomas Law Journal* (2008): 12–36; and "With Radical Amazement: Ecology and the Recovery of Creation," in *Without Nature? A New Condition for Theology*, ed. David Albertson and Cabell King, 54–79 (New York: Fordham University Press, 2010).

is to be prioritized as the point of departure for reflecting theologically on the environmental crisis and its ethical implications for human dignity and for formulating a normative response to the crisis. Historical consciousness recognizes the evolving nature of human knowledge and understanding in all four sources of ethical knowledge. The contributions of the sciences to human knowledge and understanding of the environment are crucial for the ongoing ethical reflection to address challenges that the sciences reveal. Contextual theology highlights the cultural, historical, contextual, and socioeconomic challenges that confront attempts to respond to the crisis. The virtues of love and care will have very different specific normative implications in a country like the United States, which has the economic and technological resources to effect climate change nationally and internationally, compared to a country like Sudan, which has limited economic and technological resources to effect climate change. The ability to respond to particular ethical issues is always context dependent. The four sources of ethical knowledge combine to provide an evaluative perspective to judge the current ecological crisis in order to act responsibly and justly to address it. Moral conversion, the shift from self-satisfaction to values, reveals different values and, in alliance with *Laudato Si'*, also different ecological virtues to help realize those values.

Act: A Virtuous Perspective

Moral conversion opens up a virtuous perspective for ecological conversion. The moral shift from self-satisfaction to value enables one, first, to see injustice and, then, to act justly, reasonably, and responsibly.[53] To understand the relationship between moral conversion and ecological conversion, Ormerod and Vanin divide moral conversion into four categories of values. We associate those values with particular ecological virtues and propose actions corresponding to the values and virtues to address the cataclysmic consequences of climate change, to help stop the damage humans are doing to the earth, and to restore our creation-home. A major value is the human dignity of all human persons; a second is the value of all creatures (plants and animals) that have "value in themselves" (*LS*, no. 33); and a third is a healthy interrelationship among them all. Humans, other creatures, and the shared environment are all being negatively affected by climate change that yields changes in weather patterns that, in turn, have an impact on crop and food production and cause more frequent and more severe storms and rising sea levels that threaten coastal areas. Mountains of toxic waste, a

---

[53] Doran, "What Does Bernard Lonergan Mean," 14; see *LS*, no. 123.

result, at least in part, of pollution that results from uninhibited production and consumerism, are released into water systems, landfills, and seas, causing further environmental damage. Much of this toxic waste is being shipped to developing countries, whose poor citizens are most vulnerable to its devastating health and environmental effects. "Both everyday experience and scientific research show that the gravest effects of all attacks on the environment are suffered by the poorest."[54] Moral conversion calls for values and virtues that love and care for the dignity of every human being, especially the poor and most vulnerable, who suffer debilitating poverty and injustice; for all of God's creatures, for their sane, responsible, and healthy interrelationship; and for corrective and preventive measures to protect their environment. We choose at this point to emphasize especially the gospel value of love for all our fellow creatures and neighbors and the virtue of justice for all, for "our vital well-being is inextricably linked to the well-being of the whole planet."[55]

Focusing on the virtue of care, *Laudato Si'* addresses the need to protect and preserve vital values, especially the human dignity of the poor, who suffer the most from any environmental damage. The two assaults on vital human values, climate change and environmental pollution, cause numerous health hazards and millions of premature deaths across the world (*LS*, no. 20). They also cause the ongoing extinction of plants and animals, which unbalances the ecosystem on which all life depends (*LS*, no. 36). *Laudato Si'* highlights also another vital value, the interrelationship and interdependence of all creation. "Because all creatures are connected, each must be cherished with love and respect, for all of us as living creatures are dependent on one another" (*LS*, no. 42). When this relationship is threatened, as it is currently, humans can attempt to compensate for the imbalance through science and technology, but these interventions have other consequences on the ecological system, many of them unforeseen and potentially deleterious. A just response to protect vital values must be twofold. Humanity must immediately cease its assault on the environment through pollution and toxic waste to allow it to heal, and it must do so through technological and scientific solutions that do not further destabilize an already unstable ecosystem. This requires careful planning and national and international cooperation to address very complex issues.

Lonergan argues that social values are values "such as the good of order which conditions the vital values of the whole community" and that such values take precedence over any vital values of individual members within

---

[54] Bolivian Bishops' Conference, "Pastoral Letter on the Environment and Human Development in Bolivia *El universo, don de Dios para la vida*" (March 23, 2012), no. 17; *LS*, no. 48.

[55] Ormerod and Vanin, "Ecological Conversion," 337.

the community.[56] This argument is the common-good argument in Catholic social thought, expressed, for example, in *Gaudium et Spes,* which defines the common good as "the sum of those conditions of social life which allow social groups and their individual members relatively thorough and ready access to their own fulfillment" (*GS,* no. 26). Human dignity is foundational to the common good, but it can be realized integrally and adequately only in relationships that put restraints on what any individual can demand of the community. Moral conversion and the realization of social values require an inversion of the prioritization of the individual over the community. Too often, individualism shapes culture and promotes a distorted prioritization of the relationship between the individual and the community. This distorted prioritization of the individual over the community and individual profit over societal preservation and sustainability has led, at least in part, to the ecological crisis we now face. *Laudato Si'* notes that the economy (and, we add, individuals who have the power to shape the economy) "accepts every advance in technology with a view to profit, without concern for its potentially negative impact on human beings" (*LS,* no. 109). The prioritization of profit and those who benefit from profit over the vital and social values realized by promoting the common good and protecting the environment demands moral conversion. Such conversion itself demands "profound changes in 'lifestyles, models of production and consumption, and the established structures of power which today govern societies'" (*LS,* no. 5). There must be moral conversion individually, socially, and politically. Each individual human being is called to embrace a simpler life in the manner of St. Francis of Assisi (*LS,* no. 10), for whom "less is more" (*LS,* no. 222), or, in the manner of Mahatma Gandhi, who invited all humans to "live simply so that others can simply live." Pope Francis argues in favor of social connectedness:

If everything is related, then the health of a society's institutions has consequences for the environment and the quality of human life. "Every violation of solidarity and civic friendship harms the environment." In this sense, social ecology is necessarily institutional, and gradually extends to the whole of society, from the primary social group, the family, to the wider local, national and international communities. Within each social stratum, and between them, institutions develop to regulate human relationships. Anything which weakens those institutions has negative consequences, such as injustice, violence and loss of freedom. Several countries have a relatively low level of institutional effectiveness, which results in greater problems

---

[56] Lonergan, *Method in Theology,* 31.

for their people while benefiting those who profit from this situation. (*LS*, no. 142)

Virtues guiding social value are, for instance, solidarity, justice or, as the *Catechism of the Catholic Church* says, the "firm will to give their due to God and neighbor" (*CCC*, no. 1807) and, we add, to God's creation in which all neighbors live and love, effectively willing the good of the other as well as of oneself, mutual care, and subsidiarity. All are called to be in solidarity with both the earth, which Francis describes as the poorest of the poor, and the poor and vulnerable, whom he describes as suffering most from the devastating effects of climate change (*LS*, no. 132) and who suffer the injustice of an unjust distribution of the world's goods (*LS*, nos. 152, 232). Christians all need to be well aware of their summons to adhere to Jesus's great commandment to "love the Lord your God with all your heart, and with all your soul, and with all your mind, and with all your strength" and to "love your neighbor as yourself" (Mark 12:30–31). One way to love God concretely and effectively is to love and care for God's creation, and one way to love our neighbors as ourselves concretely and effectively is to love and care for their creation-*oikos*-home. We must be careful here that we do not love and care for the poor and vulnerable only by giving alms for their support. Though we must certainly do that, we must also seek to raise them out of their poverty and vulnerability by providing them with education and job training to enable them to enter into and help contribute to their societies. Subsidiarity is another way to transform not only the poor but all citizens into effective members of society. The principle of subsidiarity, according to John Paul II in *Centesimus Annus*, prescribes that "a community of a higher order should not interfere in the internal life of a community of a lower order, depriving the latter of its functions, but rather should support it in case of need and help it to coordinate its activity with the activities of the rest of society, always with a view to the common good" (*CA*, no. 48). The ecological crisis we have been discussing is a clear case in which the lower, smaller, and less powerful societies in the nations of the earth are helpless before the ecological crisis and desperately need the help of the higher and more powerful political and economic societies to resolve the crisis. It is also a clear case for the conversion of the unjust social structures that are generated and controlled by the political and economic elites (*LS*, no. 196).

Another way in which all individuals can concretely and effectively exercise solidarity and subsidiarity is by pressuring institutions—such as local, national, and international businesses and universities—to divest from technologies and resources like fossil fuels, which are known to harm the environment. The Global Catholic Climate Movement is one example of an organization that individuals can join in this effort. Pope Francis wisely counsels that "caring for ecosystems demands far-sightedness, since no one looking for quick and easy profit is truly interested in their preservation" (*LS*, no. 36). Our local, national, and international institutions can and must implement and support regulations that first heal and then protect the healed environment. Contrary to the obvious common good, "many of those who possess more resources and economic or political power seem mostly to be concerned with masking the problems or concealing their symptoms" (*LS*, no. 26).

We have witnessed continued assaults on the environment and a lack of political protection for it in the United States with the deregulation of laws by the Environmental Protection Agency and the Trump administration's budget cuts to NASA's Carbon Monitoring System, which seeks to improve the ability to monitor global carbon emissions. This exemplifies and verifies Pope Francis's judgment that "politics and business have been slow to react in a way commensurate with the urgency of the challenges facing our world" and that the "post-industrial period may well be remembered as one of the most irresponsible in history" (*LS*, no. 165). President Trump's declared intention to withdraw from the Paris Climate Agreement indicates the administration's lack of commitment to address climate change and its worldwide impacts. Such disregard for the science that demonstrates climate change and offers solutions to correct it is way beyond scotosis. It calls for not only intellectual conversion to see the overwhelming scientific evidence for humanly caused climate change but also, indeed even more so, for moral conversion and commitment to act on the evidence responsibly. The virtues of solidarity, justice, love of neighbor, honesty, and subsidiarity can all facilitate that process.

Lonergan advances cultural values as higher values than both vital and social values, for beyond mere living and operating, he argues, all humans have to find a meaning and value in their living and operating. Ormerod and Vanin examine cultural values in three types of culture, cosmological, anthropological, and soteriological, and explore their relevance for moral conversion. "Cosmological culture draws meaning and value from the natural rhythms of the cosmos, the cycles of nature, and a cosmic hierarchy of being."[57] It derives from a preexisting social order that shapes an existing society, such as an indigenous or an agrarian society, and mirrors a cosmic or heavenly order. An example of this mirroring is the Christian celebration of Easter at the time of spring fertility and rebirth. As Ormerod and Vanin note, "Anthropological culture draws its meanings and values from a world-transcendent source of reason, reflected in the reason of the

---

[57] Ormerod and Vanin, "Ecological Conversion," 341.

individual."[58] Aristotle's virtuous individual conform his or her reason to this transcendent source, and society, in turn, conforms itself to the paradigmatic virtuous person. For Aristotle, virtuous leaders create virtuous societies. In the Old Testament the paradigmatic virtuous person is the prophet, Moses for instance, or Isaiah, and the covenanted community is modeled after the prophet. In the New Testament the paradigmatic virtuous person and prophet is Jesus the Christ, and the Christian community is modeled after him.

There has always been a tensive and creative dialectic between the cosmological and the anthropological cultures, but the Enlightenment upset this dialectic, prioritizing anthropological cultural meanings and values and deriding cosmological meanings and values. We in the West presently live in a super-anthropological culture that has humankind at its center and cuts off dialogue with cosmological culture. This is where soteriological culture becomes important. Soteriology, as we explained earlier, derives from the Greek *soter* ("salvation"), and soteriological culture draws its meanings and values from a transcendent divine ground believed by those who are religiously converted to be the ground of all being, meaning, value, and human salvation. The dialectic between cosmological and anthropological cultures, which has been so important for the emergence of meanings and values that promote and sustain human dignity, and which has been ruptured by the prioritization of a super-anthropological culture, can be restored by the integration of divine meanings and values embedded in soteriological culture. Our present super-anthropological culture tends toward the denial of the existence of any divine ground of being, meaning, and value, but for the religiously converted, those who have fallen in love with God, soteriological culture offers meanings and values to both this super-anthropological culture and cosmological culture, establishing them once again in dialectical and creative tension.

For Christians, those soteriological meanings and values are incarnated in Jesus, whom they believe to be the Christ, the anointed one of the Divine, whom they follow. The meanings and values incarnated in him, they believe, are to be incarnated also in them. For Christians, the search for meaning, value, and direction of life, therefore, in Doran's words, "becomes assent to his claim, I am the way, the truth, and the life."[59] "When human beings place themselves at the center," Pope Francis teaches, "they give absolute priority to immediate convenience and all else becomes relative. Hence, we should not be surprised to find, in conjunction with the omnipresent technocratic paradigm and the cult of unlimited human power,

---

[58] Ibid.
[59] Doran, *Theology and the Dialectics of History*, 488.

the rise of a relativism which sees everything as irrelevant unless it serves one's own immediate interests" (LS, no. 122). When human beings, Christians, we teach, imitate the meanings and values incarnated in Jesus, they are living by meanings and values more than sufficient to resolve every human crisis, cosmological, anthropological, or ecological. In Chapter 2 we characterized virtue as a personal habit or disposition ordered to an act. We now underscore the single virtue that should characterize Christians, namely, responsibility to imitate Jesus; responsibly and honestly following Jesus in all things will enable Christians to resolve every human crisis.

Reading the signs of the times, *Laudato Si'* recognizes the ecological crisis, noting that an "excessive anthropocentrism" has created a distorted understanding of humans' relationship with the material world, one of the dimensions of the human person integrally and adequately considered.[60] Pope Francis fundamentally challenges this distorted anthropology and the severed relationship among the anthropological, cosmological, and soteriological cultures. He posits a corrective to *dominion* as control over and exploitation of the earth to *dominion* as responsible government of and loving care for creation and our environment. Ecological conversion and care for our creation-*oikos*-home must facilitate a recognition of the interdependence of humans and their material environment and, guided by the solidarity, faith, hope, and love of soteriological culture, reestablish the dialectic between anthropological and cosmological cultures based on this revision. Such a revision helps to create a revised perspective and ecological culture that provides "a distinctive way of looking at things, a way of thinking, policies, an educational programme, a lifestyle, and a spirituality which together generate resistance to the assault of the technocratic paradigm" (*LS*, no. 111). This revised perspective is grounded in the virtues of humility, solidarity, honesty, care, hope, and prudence.

Personal value, Lonergan argues, "is the person in his self-transcendence, as loving and being loved, as originator of values in himself and in his milieu, as an inspiration and invitation to others to do likewise."[61] From a Christian perspective, personal value is beautifully summarized in Jesus's moral command, "Go and do likewise" (Luke 10:37); it is a paradigm of discipleship, imitation, and effective witness from a Christian virtuous perspective. Personal value and meaning invite us to see and internalize our fundamental human dignity as created in the image and likeness of God, to integrate this soteriological insight into both cosmological and anthropological cultures, re-relating *cosmos*-planet and *anthropos*-humankind, to

---

[60] See also *Schema constitutionis pastoralis de ecclesia in mundo huius temporis: Textus recognitus et relationes*, par. 11 (Vatican City: Vatican Press, 1965), 9.

[61] Lonergan, *Method in Theology*, 32.

internalize this integration and live it out in in witness to all our neighbors. In this process people develop "ecological virtues, patterns of life designed to lessen their damaging footprints upon the planet, which embody the values inherent in ecological conversion."[62] Personal values and meanings call for conversion from super-anthropocentrism, which is dominated by hubris and sin against God, fellow humans, and the environment, and is manifested in the destruction of the environment. The environmental sin is "evident in the soil, in the water, in the air and in all forms of life. This is why the earth herself, burdened and laid waste, is among the most abandoned and maltreated of our poor" (*LS*, no. 2). "Only by cultivating sound virtues," Francis asserts, "will people be able to make a selfless ecological commitment" (*LS*, no. 211).

Among the "sound virtues" that make up a virtuous ecological perspective we name especially prudence, responsibility, courage, humility, honesty, care, faith, hope, love, solidarity, subsidiarity, and reconciliation, all of which pervade *Laudato Si'*. Though we have focused on ecological conversion as the virtuous perspective to address the ecological crisis and to guide the see-judge-act method of Catholic social teaching, Pope Francis has recourse to other virtues that complement conversion and highlight the radical response individuals and local, national, and international communities must take to address the crisis. For Christians, Pope Francis voices a particularly urgent moral imperative, grounded in the imitation of Jesus, to respond to this issue in faith and humility:

> Various convictions of our faith . . . can help us to enrich the meaning of this conversion. These include the awareness that each creature reflects something of God and has a message to convey to us, and the security that Christ has taken unto himself this material world and now, risen, is intimately present to each being, surrounding it with his affection and penetrating it with his light. Then too, there is the recognition that God created the world, writing into it an order and a dynamism that human beings have no right to ignore. We read in the Gospel that Jesus says of the birds of the air that "not one of them is forgotten before God" (Lk 12:6). How then can we possibly mistreat them or cause them harm? I ask all Christians to recognize and to live fully this dimension of their conversion. May the power and the light of the grace we have received also be evident in our relationship to other creatures and to the world around us. In this way, we will help nurture that sublime fraternity with all creation which Saint Francis of Assisi so radiantly embodied. (*LS*, no. 221)

---

[62] Ormerod and Vanin, "Ecological Conversion," 343.

Pope Francis's focus on virtue to address the ecological crisis is a profound methodological development in Catholic ethical teaching. Catholic social teaching and ecological ethics have often been ethically analyzed and evaluated in official church statements from a virtuous perspective, but Catholic sexual teaching has focused almost exclusively on acts that are proscribed and absolute norms that prescribe moral action. In the next chapter we investigate "hookup" culture, relying on the human person integrally and adequately considered and a virtuous perspective to evaluate this issue and to provide general norms to facilitate just and loving acts.

Questions for Reflection

- What is the difference between climate and weather? Discuss the causes and effects of climate change.
- What is the difference between environmental ethics and ecological ethics? Why does Pope Francis focus on "integral ecology" in *Laudato Si'*?
- How do you understand ecological conversion? Do you see conversion in your own perspective on climate change intellectually, morally, religiously, and psychically? In what way?
- How do the four sources of ethical knowledge—scripture, tradition, reason/science, and experience—help you to see and judge the ethical issue of climate change? What acts can individuals and national and international political bodies take to address climate change?
- Discuss the three types of cultures, cosmological, anthropological, and soteriological, and give examples of how each could address climate change. Do you use any values from these cultures to guide your own acts when addressing climate change? Explain.
- Explain the specific contribution of a Christian perspective to climate change. Do you presently adhere to such a perspective?
- Discuss Pope Francis's *Laudato Si'* as a response to climate change.

Suggested Readings

DiLeo, Dan, ed. *All Creation Is Connected: Voices in Response to Pope Francis' Encyclical on Ecology*. Winona, WI: Anselm Academic, 2018.

Irwin, Kevin W. *A Commentary on* Laudato Si': *Examining the Background, Contributions, Implementation, and Future of Pope Francis's Encyclical*. New York: Paulist Press, 2016.

Miller, Richard W., ed. *God, Creation, and Climate Change: A Catholic Response to the Environmental Crisis*. Maryknoll, NY: Orbis Books, 2010.

Miller, Vincent J., ed. *The Theological and Ecological Vision of* Laudato Si': *Everything Is Connected*. London: Bloomsbury T & T Clark, 2017.

Ormerod, Neil, and Cristina Vanin. "Ecological Conversion: What Does It Mean?" *Theological Studies* 77, no. 2 (2016): 328–52.

8

Hookup Culture

Learning Objectives

- Define *hookup*.
- Explain the psychological, emotional, and relational effects of hookups.
- Ethically analyze and evaluate hookups on the basis of the human person integrally and adequately considered.
- Ethically analyze and evaluate hookup culture from a just and loving virtuous perspective.
- Evaluate hookups on the basis of Margaret Farley's seven norms guiding sexual acts.

A relatively recent phenomenon on college and university campuses is the hookup culture, which is today's "culture of courtship."[1] This culture is based on casual sexual encounters that span the sexual spectrum from kissing to oral, vaginal, and anal sexual intercourse and are understood not to include any psychological or emotional connection or relational commitment. In this chapter we first explain sources of ethical knowledge for analyzing and evaluating hookup culture. Second, we describe hookup culture from the perspective of those who participate in it and analyze and evaluate it based on the dimensions of the human person integrally and adequately considered, which we explained in Chapter 5.[2] Third, we propose the virtuous perspective of just love as an approach to premarital sexual relationships and present norms to guide those relationships. In

---

[1] Michael Kimmel, *Guyland: The Perilous World Where Boys Become Men* (New York: Harper, 2008), 213.

[2] See *Schema constitutionis pastoralis de ecclesia in mundo huius temporis: Textus recognitus et relationes*, par. 11 (Vatican City: Vatican Polyglot Press, 1965), 9.

Chapter 9 we explore the contemporary process of marrying and analyze and evaluate what we call nuptial cohabitation.

Hookup Culture and the Sources of Ethical Knowledge

Sociological data indicates that in the United States there is growing acceptance of premarital sex. These rates have shifted from a minority view (28 percent in 1972; 38 percent in 1978; 41 percent in 1982; 44 percent in 2004) to a majority view (58 percent in 2012).[3] This majority perspective is reflected also in Catholic views on premarital sex. Young Catholics aged 18–23 engage in oral sex (53 percent of practicing Catholics, 77 percent of sporadic Catholics, and 84 percent of disengaged Catholics) and vaginal intercourse (61 percent of practicing Catholics, 79 percent of sporadic Catholics, and 81 percent of disengaged Catholics) in defiance of church teaching that absolutely prohibits any premarital sex.[4] The *Catechism of the Catholic Church* teaches that premarital sexual intercourse, which it calls fornication, "is gravely contrary to the dignity of persons and of human sexuality which is naturally ordered to the good of spouses and the generation and education of children" (*CCC,* no. 2353). Sexual intercourse, the church teaches, can take place only in marriage and must include two intrinsic meanings in every act, a unitive meaning and a procreative meaning. Any sexual acts outside of marriage or any nonreproductive type sexual acts in marriage are condemned as gravely disordered. The statistics just cited reveal a serious disconnect between Catholic teaching about premarital sex and the lived experience of young Catholics, and that disconnect requires interpretation and clarification.

We must distinguish between different types of premarital sex and their evaluations, for not all premarital sex is equal from an ethical perspective. Among those who support the possibility that premarital sex can be ethical, Jennifer Beste's recent study concludes that 81 percent of women and

---

[3] J. M. Twenge, R. A. Sherman, and B. E. Wells, "Changes in American Adults' Sexual Behavior and Attitudes, 1972–2012," *Archives of Sexual Behavior* 44, no. 8 (2015): 2273–85. See also Public Religion Institute, "Millennials, Sexuality, and Reproductive Health Survey" (March 2015), which largely affirms these percentages among Millennials. In the survey question on the ethical evaluation of "sex between two adults who have no intention of establishing a relationship" (hookups), responses were as follows: 37 percent ethically wrong; 21 percent depends on the circumstances; 37 percent ethically acceptable; 7 percent other or refused. A recognized tendency of Millennials is to take circumstances into consideration before making an ethical judgment ("depends on the circumstances").

[4] Christian Smith et al., *Young Catholic America: Emerging Adults In, Out of, and Gone from the Church* (New York: Oxford, 2014), 224–25.

68 percent of men believe that hookups are not just.[5] Her findings parallel other studies[6] that support the conclusion that hookups are unjust (and we add, therefore unethical), since they lack mutuality, equality, and/or free consent and tend to objectify the other person, using that person as a mere means to a sexual end. When Beste asked her students what context would constitute the most pleasurable and just sexual activity, sex in a hookup with an acquaintance or a stranger received very low scores (0 percent for men and 2 percent for women), while sex in a committed relationship of four or more months (men 69.2 percent; women 35.3 percent) and sex in marriage (men 7.7 percent; women 56.9 percent) received the majority of positive responses.[7] The results from this small sample of students affirm the findings of other surveys that some level of commitment is necessary for sexual intercourse to be just and ethical. To understand why Millennials and Gen Zers on college campuses both engage in hookups and find them ethically problematic, we explore the nature of this culture and ethically analyze it using the dimensions of the human person integrally and adequately considered.

Hookup Culture and the
Human Person Integrally and Adequately Considered

We have several times advised that theological ethics must be in dialogue with culture, and that at times culture can provide new roads to truth; at other times, theological ethics must raise a prophetic voice challenging culture. Hookup culture is a reality that theological ethics challenges. To do so, however, we must first understand that culture, what drives it, who participates in it, and what are its psychological, emotional, relational, and spiritual impacts on individuals who participate in it and on their perspectives on relationships, commitment, and marriage. We consider these questions under the light of the human person integrally and adequately considered. Hookup culture has become a common college and university

---

[5] Jennifer Beste, *College Hookup Culture and Christian Ethics: The Lives and Longings of Emerging Adults* (New York: Oxford University Press, 2018), 225.

[6] See Lisa Wade, "Are Women Bad at Orgasms?" in *Gender, Sex, and Politics*, ed. Shira Tarrant (New York: Routledge, 2016), 227–58; Laura Hamilton and Elizabeth A. Armstrong, "Gendered Sexuality in Young Adulthood: Double Binds and Flawed Options," *Gender and Society* 23, no. 5 (2009): 589–616; Elizabeth L. Paul and Kristen A. Hayes, "The Casualties of 'Casual' Sex: A Qualitative Exploration of the Phenomenology of College Students' Hookups," *Journal of Social and Personal Relationships* 19, no. 5 (2002): 639–61; Caroline Helmand and Lisa Wade, "Hookup Culture: Setting a New Research Agenda," *Sexuality Research and Social Policy* 7, no. 4 (2010): 323–33.

[7] Beste, *College Hookup Culture and Christian Ethics,* 250.

experience, as common as freshman orientation, Greek life, study halls, dances, and sporting events. Students engage in academic, social, and hookup events or parties. Sociologists have studied the prevalence of hook-ups on colleges and universities, and their findings tell us much about the correlations among religious belief, ethics, and ethical practice. Hookups involve sexual intercourse (35–40 percent), oral sex without intercourse (15 percent), kissing and non-genital touching (31 percent), and manual stimulation of genitalia (19 percent).[8] In a survey of four thousand under-graduate students from five US colleges and universities, approximately 75 percent of students engaged in a hookup at least once during their col-lege experience and 28 percent engaged ten or more times.[9]

Although many contemporary college students may see the value of sociological research on hookup culture, they often do not find this data reflects the complexity of their lives and experiences. The majority of col-lege students may participate in hookup culture, but that does not mean they find this participation meaningful or fulfilling. An accurate ethical analysis and evaluation of hookup culture must consider their perspectives. Beste, using an ethnographic method that asks students in her classes to attend hookup parties and analyze and evaluate those experiences, has provided a fascinating account of those who participate in and experience hookup culture.[10] There are several aspects of her study that give insight into the complex lived reality of college students, why they engage in the hookup culture, and how ethics can serve to navigate this complexity and address the psychological, emotional, and relational goals that many college students seek, but do not find, in hookup culture. We consider her study throughout this chapter.

Donna Freitas, a leading voice in the analysis and evaluation of hookup culture, describes three major criteria for a hookup. First, it involves some type of sexual activity; second, it is brief, lasting as little as a few minutes or as long as several hours; and third, it is a purely physical exchange and discourages any communication that might lead to a psychological or emotional connection.[11] Considering the first criterion, her survey of

---

[8] See Amy M. Burdette et al., "'Hook Up' at College: Does Religion Make a Differ-ence?" *Journal for the Scientific Study of Religion* 48 (2009): 535; and Kimmel, *Guyland*, 195.

[9] Paula England, Emily Fitzgibbons Shafer, and Allison C. K. Fogarty, "Hooking up and Forming Romantic Relationships on Today's College Campuses," in *The Gendered Society Reader*, ed. Michael S. Kimmel and Amy Aronson (New York: Oxford University Press, 2007), 531–46.

[10] Beste, *College Hookup Culture and Christian Ethics*, 1.

[11] Donna Freitas, *The End of Sex: How Hookup Culture Is Leaving a Generation Un-happy, Sexually Unfulfilled, and Confused about Intimacy* (New York: Basic Books, 2013), 25.

college students asks whether those students had ever had oral, anal, or vaginal sex: 77 percent answered yes,[12] a datum that closely parallels the data of other hookup studies (75 percent). It also parallels the percentages of young people (18–23) in the overall population who engage in oral sex (71 percent) and sexual intercourse (73 percent).[13] Although these statistics inform us that the majority of young people are engaging in some type of sexual activity, it does not tell the whole story in terms of the *meaning* of the sexual activity for them. To be useful as a source of ethical knowledge, this sociological data must be complemented with more detailed reflection on the entire hookup experience. The data merely reveal that hookups entail sexual acts between two partners and are common among young people and college students. As we have indicated throughout this book, acts are important for virtue ethics, but they are secondary. What is primary is the virtue or vice from which the acts emanate and that directs the meaning of the acts, which, in turn, reinforce or violate the virtue. What is the *motive* for and *quality* of the sexual experience in a hookup, how does the person *feel* afterward, and what are the short-term and long-term *relational consequences* of sexual experience devoid of psychological, emotional, and relational connection?

That hookups are brief conveys their casual nature; they are accomplished with a minimal investment of personal time and emotion. Prime goals are to avoid extended interaction after the hookup, to avoid waking up the next morning with one's hookup partner and any awkward morning-after interactions, and to avoid the "walk of shame" back to one's dorm following a one-night stand (disproportionately an experience for women). The social contract for a hookup demands no emotional connection to one's partner and a clear line of demarcation between physical and relational intimacy, both of which can be more easily achieved and maintained if there is limited contact after the hookup. To analyze and ethically evaluate hookup culture specifically, and premarital sex in general, we apply the dimensions of the human person integrally and adequately considered and propose just love as a virtuous perspective to guide people toward more fulfilling and life-giving sexual relationships. To recall the dimensions of the human person integrally and adequately considered, that person is a subject; in corporeality; in relationship to the material world, to others, to self, and to God, and created in the image and likeness of God; a historical being; and fundamentally unique but equal to all other persons.[14] We consider each in turn.

---

[12] Ibid., 25–26.

[13] Smith, *Young Catholic America*, 224–225.

[14] Louis Janssens, "Artificial Insemination: Ethical Considerations," *Louvain Studies* 8 (1980): 3–29.

The Human Person Is a Free Subject

First, every person is a subject, not an object. Perhaps the greatest violation of human dignity in hookup culture is that it reduces the partner to an
object or a *mere* means to one's own sexual gratification, devoid of any
psychological, emotional, or relational connection. To experience any such
connection is, in fact, to violate the implied contract of the hookup culture.
"Hookups are a quick way to get an animalistic need for sex fulfilled."[15]
A dimension of the person as subject is that he or she is a conscious, free,
knowing human being capable of making responsible decisions. A common phenomenon of hookup culture is alcohol consumption and/or drug
use. Amy Burdette reports that the median consumption of alcohol before
a hookup is six drinks for men and four drinks for women.[16] What is the
relationship between alcohol consumption and hookup culture and how
does it affect responsible decision making?

Hookup parties often begin with "pre-game" drinking because "no one
wants to show up at a party sober."[17] Drinking before the party serves
several purposes. First, it creates a social mood among participants. For
men, they spend the "pre-game" time drinking and socializing about
how they want to "score" and with whom. They spend very little time on
physical appearance; dressing and preparation take ten minutes or so. For
women, drinking is accompanied with extensive preparation, two or three
hours to fix hair, apply makeup, and try on various outfits to find which
one looks the "hottest, sexiest, or 'sluttiest.'"[18] Second, drinking reduces
inhibitions for interacting with other people at the party and paves the
way for a hookup. It clouds the judgment of both partners and expands the
parameters of sexual attractiveness.[19] Third, drinking reduces or eliminates
culpability for ethical decision making. Catholic teaching has consistently
taught that impediments, circumstances, or character traits that limit or
eliminate decision-making capacity, such as alcohol or drugs, limit freedom
and therefore ethical culpability for decisions. Clouding judgment through
drinking is especially important for women in preparation for a hookup.
It is better to be labeled a drunk, than a slut, which is a gender disparity
of hookups we address below. A hangover is judged to be a small price to
pay for ethical exoneration. The free decision when sober to drink or take
drugs before and/or during hookup parties, however, frequently is ethically
culpable. The hookup culture that ritualizes drinking at the "pre-game" and

---

[15] Beste, *College Hookup Culture and Christian Ethics*, 151.
[16] Burdette et al., "'Hook Up' at College," 535.
[17] Beste, *College Hookup Culture and Christian Ethics*, 19.
[18] Ibid., 20.
[19] Kimmel, *Guyland*, 200.

hookup party itself can function as an impediment and affect decision-making capacity of whether, and how much, one drinks.

No person as subject should ever be treated as an object. Hookups entail objectification of both women and men. For women, the decision to dress "slutty" or provocatively demonstrates a lack of self-love. Women who hook up are buying into the commodification of femininity, that is, gendered marketing practices construct femininity as a commodity to be objectified and consumed in order to sell beauty products including makeup, hair-styling paraphernalia, clothes, and accessories that communicate beauty and desirability as defined by the industry. One student articulates this well: "As college students, we are bombarded by media that tells us we are not worth it until we buy this product or that item. We are told to doubt ourselves, our bodies, and our hearts."[20] On their part, men objectify women by participating in this commodification, paying attention to and interacting with women who present as sluts, and not interacting with women who have not invested in the accessories, do not possess the desired physical characteristics, or are simply "plain."

Michael Kimmel's *Guyland* provides an example that epitomizes the objectification of women on college campuses. On an unnamed campus a sorority has pledges lie on the floor, blindfolded, in their panties. In a ritual referred to as "circle the fat," men from a fraternity enter the room and mark the pledges with permanent markers. After the men leave the room, the women are taken to another room with mirrors and told to remove their blindfolds. The marks they discover on their bodies indicate parts of their bodies that "need some work" to make them look better.[21] Both men *and* women participate in this objectification of women. When one of the young women began to sob after the humiliating event, a sister demeaned her, "Don't be a ninny," this will "make you a better person."[22] Hookup culture reflects a similar objectification by buying into vary narrow definitions of what constitutes physical beauty and how this beauty should be packaged through physical appearance, hairstyle, makeup, and clothes to be consumed. In sum, hookups violate the person as subject by using a person as a means for personal physical gratification, limiting or eliminating freedom and decision-making capacity, and objectifying the partner.

The Human Person Is an Embodied Subject in Corporeality

The second dimension of the human person integrally and adequately considered is the person as embodied subject, an integrated body and

---

[20] In Beste, *College Hookup Culture and Christian Ethics*, 161.

[21] Kimmel, *Guyland*, 243–44.

[22] Ibid., 244.

spirit. The contractual agreement of hookup is that there is to be physical sexual *engagement* of one's body and psychological, emotional, relational, and spiritual *disengagement* of one's mind. This bifurcation of the inter-relationship between body and spirit is a form of dualism; hookups reduce embodied subjects to only their bodily dimension. Hookups fundamentally violate a theological anthropology that sees the person as an integrated human being and human sexuality as a form of communicating through, with, and between integrated beings. We explore here the integrated dimensions of the sexual human being, which include *physical, emotional,* and *psychological* dimensions.

We deal first with physical union, the joining of bodies. In their excellent treatment of human sexuality, Masters and Johnson explain four phases in the physical process of sexual intercourse. These phases can be extended to other types of sexual intimacy between both heterosexual and homosexual couples. Phase One is the excitement phase, in which, for the man, the penis becomes erect due to the flow of blood into the penile tissues, and for the woman, there is moistening of the vagina, enlarged breasts, and tensing of the muscles with increased breathing and heart rate. Phase Two is the plateau phase, in the case of sexual intercourse, the entry of the penis into the vagina, further quickening of the heart and breathing, mounting erotic pleasure, and the appearance of a flush on both bodies. Phase Three, the climax, the discharge of semen by the male and a number of orgasmic muscle spasms by the female, is the moment of greatest pleasure and ecstasy, the moment sought in every act of intercourse. This pleasure is, of course, quite individual, and it is part of the ambiguity of sexuality and sexual intercourse that, in the climactic moments of orgasm, the act intended to be the giving of one person to the other throws each back on himself or herself in a solitude of pleasure. In hookups, there is not supposed to be a "giving of one person to another"; there is, rather, only consumption of one person by the other for personal sexual gratification. Phase Four is the resolution phase, in which the couple relax and blood pressure and respiration return to normal.[23]

Though these four phases are in no way to be "used as a check list against which to measure sexual performance,"[24] every sexually active couple can, at least sometimes, identify them in their sexual activity, a natural fact that offers profound evidence for the natural pleasure of the sexual act that has been so suspect in Christian history. Pleasure unites with the relational dimension of humanity to draw us toward another person

---

[23] W. H. Masters and Virginia E. Johnson, *Human Sexual Response* (Boston: Little, Brown, 1966), 3–8.

[24] June M. Reinisch and Ruth Beasley, *The Kinsey Institute New Report on Sex: What You Must Know to Be Sexually Literate* (New York: St. Martin's Press, 1990), 84.

in the most profound way through sexual activity. It is a good created by God, given as a gift to humans, and, like all gifts, it can be used for either good or ill. The abuses of pleasure and the danger of an ethic based purely on pleasure, are fully evident in the socio-historical past and present. Such abuses, however, cannot and do not diminish the valuable and essential role of integrating pleasure as a natural component of human theological sexual ethics. The lack of recognition in traditional Catholic teaching of the value of sexual foreplay and/or intimacy apart from vaginal intercourse, in oral or anal sex for example, and their condemnation as unethical, could be interpreted, at least in part, as a failure to appreciate sexual pleasure as a natural, intrinsic, and healthy component of human sexuality and sexual activity.

An essential component of the ethical evaluation of sexual acts, then, we suggest, must be a deeper understanding of the naturalness of pleasure and its function in human sexuality, as well as the development of parameters for its responsible and ethical expression. Considering pleasure in sexual intimacy, therefore, must avoid two extremes, the "too little" appreciation and integration of pleasure evidenced in the Christian tradition and the "too much" exclusive focus on pleasure, as in hookups. Like virtue, pleasure must exist as a mean between these two extremes.

The emotional dimension of human sexuality must necessarily be included in any consideration of the human being. Emotions—strong, generalized feelings with both physical and psychological manifestations—may be either positive or negative, and both positive and negative emotions occur in the human sexual being. Positive emotions include love, joy, hope, anticipation, humor, trust, happiness, passion, and inquisitiveness; negative emotions include hatred, sadness, despair, anxiety, anger, guilt, regret, resentment, hurt, dissatisfaction, and brokenness. These positive and negative emotions are further influenced and have unique expression and importance in the light of culture, ethnicity, gender, history, and experience. In the act of just and loving sexual intercourse, there is a complex combination and expression of emotions that unite two individual persons into one coupled person in an act that can heal, comfort, and create wholeness or, on occasion, affirm and console woundedness, anxiety, or brokenness. Either way, the sexual act reveals the wide spectrum of human emotions and brings out total vulnerability in both the positive and negative emotions. Indeed, analyzing human sexuality and the sexual act in terms of its emotional dimension entails a glorious mystery of wounded persons in their ongoing search for wholeness in intimate relationship.

Two aspects of hookups violate the appreciation and integration of emotions in the sexual person. First, one criterion guiding a hookup is that it is meant to be purely physical and devoid of emotional connection.

Attempting to suppress emotion from sexual intimacy, however, is thoroughly inauthentic and a violation of the embodied subject whose sexual being is designed to engage with another sexual being both physically and emotionally. Second, the emotions that frequently follow from a hookup are often negative, including regret, shame, and guilt.[25] These emotions tell us something about the meaning of these sexual encounters for human beings; they often frustrate and do not facilitate emotional human dignity for the participants.

Emotions are a unique expression of a person's basic and stable human identity, and the psychological and emotional dimensions of human sexuality are intimately related. Psychiatrist Jack Dominian presents an excellent synthesis of several psychological dimensions that illustrate the sexual act between a loving couple, which may not be present in a hookup.[26] First, through sexual intimacy a couple affirms each other's identity. The sexual act is symbolic in that, when we become sexually intimate with another person, we become vulnerable. Hookups try to suppress all vulnerability. They are an attempt to escape the suffering that inevitably comes with vulnerability, and with a successful escape they suppress the symbolism associated with sexual acts and the imagination that constructs and participates in that symbolism. In a very real sense the sexual act and relationship become symbols, sacraments the Catholic Church teaches,[27] of the embodied reality of God's unconditional love for human beings. God accepts us totally and unconditionally in our strengths and weaknesses, and sexual partners are invited to unconditionally accept each other in their strengths and weaknesses. Both these acceptances are symbolized in and through sexual intimacy for the duration of the relationship. As sacrament and symbol the sexual act shares in the common characteristic of all symbols. It is "characterized not by its uniformity [as is a simple sign] but its versatility. It is not rigid or inflexible but mobile."[28] It is also opaque and difficult to discern, and this opacity, Paul Ricoeur comments, "constitutes the depth of the symbol which . . . is inexhaustible."[29] That

---

[25] See Garcia et al., "Sexual Hookup Culture: A Review," 170–71. In one study the number of women expressing guilt is twice that of men.

[26] In this section we are indebted to Jack Dominian's excellent "Sexuality and Interpersonal Relationships," in *Embracing Sexuality: Authority and Experience in the Catholic Church*, ed. Joseph A. Selling (Burlington, VT: Ashgate, 2001), 12–15.

[27] See Michael G. Lawler, *Marriage and Sacrament: A Theology of Christian Marriage* (Collegeville, MN: Liturgical Press, 1993); and idem, *Marriage in the Catholic Church: Disputed Questions* (Collegeville, MN: Liturgical Press, 2002), 1–26.

[28] Ernst Cassirer, *An Essay on Man: An Introduction to Philosophy* (New Haven, CT: Yale University Press, 1944), 36.

[29] Paul Ricoeur, *The Symbolism of Evil*, trans. Emerson Buchanan (New York: Harper and Row, 1967), 15.

the act of sexual intimacy is symbolic and dense with opaque meanings is one more reason for its essential mystery and ambiguity. To suppress the symbolism of sexual acts, as hookups do, is to dehumanize both oneself and one's partner.

Second, the sexual act reflects, affirms, and creates gender identity, a fundamental dimension of sexual identity. Gender is concerned with the socially constructed meanings of femininity and masculinity. It is determined not only by individual sexuality but also by culture, ethnicity, and experience, and it is expressed in actions, interactions, social roles, and their expression in sexual acts. Dominian describes this gender expression as a liturgy of exchange, a divine language,[30] in which two people communicate with each other through sexual desire. In the formation and development of sexual identity through a recognition and embodiment of gender roles, it is crucial that sexual activity be a form of loving, just, open, honest, and authentic human communication. If it is, then the act becomes humanly communicative at the deepest level; if it is not, then the same act can stagnate, even block, future possibilities for communication and formation of healthy sexual identity.

There is irony in hookup culture and the gender stereotypes that it enculturates and perpetuates among participants. On the one hand, Millennials and Gen Zers are sensitive to social justice concerns. One of these concerns is the commitment to the full equality of all persons, including gender equality, and resistance to gender stereotypes that would demean or devalue a person based on those stereotypes. On the other hand, hookups incarnate the very gender stereotypes that, ideologically, Millennials and Gen Zers say they resist. Hookups attempt to ensure traditional views of dominance and submission in sexual relationships. The man pursues the woman in whom he is interested and determines the context of sexual activity: where, what, when, and most important, with whom. One of the students in Beste's study sums up the gender disparity: "These men players are . . . often praised and admired for their exploits. Women who engage in such an activity with even one male fear being labeled 'whores' or 'sluts.'"[31] In sum, hookup culture displays a gender binary that is more reflective of the early twentieth-century rather than the early twenty-first century. It places women's self-love and psychological, emotional, relational, and physical health at great risk.[32] It also damages men's gender identity by promoting

---

[30] Dominian, "Sexuality and Interpersonal Relationships," 20.

[31] Beste, *College Hookup Culture and Christian Ethics*, 86.

[32] See Laura Sessions Stepp, *Unhooked: How Young Women Pursue Sex, Delay Love, and Lose at Both* (New York: Riverhead Books, 2007); and Kathleen A. Bogle, *Hooking Up: Sex, Dating, and Relationships on Campus* (New York: New York University Press, 2008).

and reinforcing an image of masculinity that is preoccupied with physical sexual fulfillment and attempts to disconnect the physical from the psychological, emotional, and relational dimensions of human sexuality.

Kimmel seems to challenge portrayals of a strict gender binary in hookup culture, asserting that both men *and* women are seeking pleasure in hookups.[33] It may be that it is reverse gender discrimination to paint women as subordinate and passive in the hookup relationship and men as dominant and active. Our informal survey of students in our classes supports a view that women can also feel empowered by being able to participate in hookup culture, control sexual activity, and have no deep psychological or emotional connection with the men with whom they hook up. While men have traditionally been dominant in sexual relationships and women submissive, dominance can be a goal of both genders. One way women feel empowered in hookups is that they have just as much control as men in negotiating the terms and conditions of the hookup. Equality and mutuality between two persons in an intimate relationship are replaced with dominance and control by both persons. Some women defend hookups, explaining that women are empowered to control and decide their terms and conditions in a way that men have controlled and decided the terms and conditions of sexual activity throughout history. The sad irony of this empowerment and control is that women are doing to men what they loathe and resent about men doing to women. Historical male dominance is now shared with females, but it leaves the relationship void of shared vulnerability and intimacy and reduces it to an exercise in power and control. From our ethical perspective, such empowerment is merely accepting the myth that a physical sexual act can be detached from all psychological, emotional, and relational implications, no matter whether it is men or women who are constructing and living out the myth.

Third, another psychological dimension of sexual intercourse is that it is therapeutic and relieves stress. The embodied human person is a psychosomatic unity, an intrinsic union of *soma* and *psyche* (body and spirit). There is distinction between body and spirit in the human being but there is no separation, and there is ongoing and constant dialogue between the two. When a couple makes love, each brings to the experience all the psychological burdens that accompany daily life. A common reason given for participating in hookups, in fact, is to relieve stress and pressure from school, grades, parental expectations, and insecurities about future job and relationship prospects. Hookups provide an escape from these pressures.[34] The act of sexual intercourse makes possible the suspension of

---

[33] Kimmel, *Guyland*, 212–13.

[34] See Beste, *College Hookup Culture and Christian Ethics*, 151–54.

those anxieties and worries, at least for the moment, and can have a healing effect on the individual. This relief of stress, however, depends on the nature of the relationship. If the relationship is just, loving, committed, and honest, relief of stress is often an intrinsic component of sexual activity. If, however, the relationship is promiscuous, inauthentic, or dishonest, while the physical act can still suspend stress for the moment, the consequences of that experience can cause even greater stress in the form of regret or guilt. These consequences are commonly cited by participants in hookups, especially by women.

There is a strange paradox about human sexuality in the West in general and in hookup culture in particular. On the one hand, access to casual sexual activity is at an all-time high; on the other hand, so too is the occurrence of depression. Though this correlation may be purely descriptive and in no way prescriptive, it still suggests that facile sex alone does not provide relief of stress or depression. Only sex within a just, loving, and mutual human relationship does that. Sexual intercourse can be therapeutic in a healthy, just, loving, committed relationship; in an unhealthy, unjust, unloving, uncommitted relationship its psychic impact can be greater stress engendered by regret, disappointment, guilt, and a sense of objectification. The intrinsic psychosomatic integration of the human person, and therefore of human sexual activity, underscores the potential of that activity for generating healing or stress, the discrimination between the two being the nature and meaning of the relationship for the persons involved.

Fourth, sexual intimacy can be reconciling. There are no completely conflict-free relationships in human lives. Frictions, disagreements, and misunderstandings are all inevitable aspects of any human relationship, and any experience can create hurt, stress, and general distrust of the partner in the relationship. One is not likely to find couples who desire sexual intimacy at the peak of such quarrels. Intimacy comes after the resolution of the quarrel and may be an intrinsic component of that resolution. Some couples, indeed, claim that the best sex they have is after an intense argument. This is because sexual intimacy heals the wounds and reaffirms the bond and commitment that may have been threatened by a quarrel. It is difficult for a couple to have a fulfilling sexual experience if the other dimensions of the relationship are not in sync. Sexual intercourse affirms self, other, and the relationship through healing and reconciliation. Hookups are not meant to realize the mutual reconciling component since there is no relational history, by definition, between the hookup partners. In a sense, hookups are meant to be a *tabula rasa,* a blank emotional slate before and after the hookup. Because there is no past mutual emotional connection, it is difficult to build a future emotional connection in and through a hookup. Too often the emotional aftermath of a hookup is focused on the individual;

manifests itself in negative emotions such as regret, shame, guilt; and is not processed or shared with the intimate partner.

Fifth, sexual intercourse can be a profound act of thanksgiving or eucharist. The embodied nature of human persons binds them to bodily expression that is best exemplified, though by no means limited to, verbal language. Beyond verbal language there is body language, and beyond body language there is ritual language, symbolic actions filled with culturally approved meanings. Couples can say to one another "I love you" or "I thank you" or "I forgive you," and in the spoken words they are reaching to meanings far beyond the words. They can say the same things in culturally approved actions, by looks, by touches, by gifts, and in all these actions they are similarly reaching far beyond the actions to express mutual love, forgiveness, reconciliation, affirmation, and thanksgiving. In the physical action of sexual intimacy, an action as symbolic as any spoken word, they express all these things in the most profound and total way available to an embodied human being, namely, through the completely unmasked and therefore totally vulnerable body. The thanksgiving embodied in sexual activity is yet one more profound affirmation of the self, of the other, and of the relationship. Hookups attempt to avoid vulnerability and often to avoid any discussion of the relational implications of a hookup. This is the "define the relationship" conversation after a hookup or "the talk," a conversation, usually initiated by women and avoided by men, that attempts to determine whether the hookup is going anywhere in terms of relationship and commitment.[35] Avoidance of or resistance to the talk demonstrates inequality in the relationship and violation of psychologically, emotionally, integrated sexuality.

These five psychological dimensions that are communicated and experienced in just and loving sexual acts—affirm self and other, create and affirm gender identity, relieve stress, restore and reconcile persons, and embody thanksgiving—create, contribute to, and sustain the psychosomatic and spiritual dignity of sexual persons. Hookups threaten human dignity by reducing both partners to emotion-free objects; reinforcing and exploiting gender stereotypes; distancing persons from one another through regret, shame, and guilt; and denying the symbolic and shared eucharistic meaning of sexual intimacy.

The Human Person Is in Relationship

A third dimension of the human person integrally and adequately considered is relationship. We first consider relationship with self since one's

---

[35] Kimmel, *Guyland*, 204–5.

relationship with self is both a motivating source for hookups and also is influenced by hookups. To do so, however, we must first contextualize this dimension with two other dimensions: relationship with the material world and with humans as historical. We are all in relationship with the material world, and it is important to explain how this relationship, part of which is the historical evolution and influence of culture, has shaped the worldview of Millennials and Gen Zers and why hookup culture has become "culturally normative" for sexual relationships.[36] Researchers opine that hookup culture "is best understood as the convergence of evolutionary and social forces during the developmental period of emerging adulthood."[37] Cultural shifts in dating, which began in the 1920s, help to explain the evolution that has resulted in hookup culture. These shifts are attributable, in part, to increased access to, and use of automobiles and novel forms of socializing and entertainment that moved dating from the milieu of parents to a more autonomous milieu guided by the mores of peers and media. Visual media during this period introduced images of erotic sex and its commercialization, though these images pale in comparison to today's cyberporn.

Although censorship laws in the 1930s attempted to curb what was perceived as prurient influence, they had a limited impact, especially with the onset of the sexual revolution in the 1960s. The sexual revolution arose from feminism and an appreciation of gender equality, availability of birth control (condoms and pills), access to college education, changing gender demographics with more women than men on college campuses, college parties, and less parental influence on the process of dating and marriage. With the explosive growth of the Internet in the 1990s, sexual images in general and pornography specifically reached epidemic proportions. These influences, combined with the normalization of casual sex, both heterosexual and homosexual, in popular culture in television *(Jersey Shore, Queer as Folk, The L-Word)*, movies *(Hooking Up and No Strings Attached)*, and books *(The Happy Hook-Up: A Single Girl's Guide to Casual Sex; 11 Points Guide to Hooking Up: Lists and Advice about First Dates, Hotties, Scandals, Pickups, Threesomes, and Booty Calls; and Fifty Shades of Grey)* have shaped the perspectives of Millennials and Gen Zers. They are the greatest consumers of popular culture and social media and most profoundly influenced by these modes of communication and their messages about sex, sexuality, and relationships.

In addition to the historical evolution of the influences of popular culture and social media, there are changing socioeconomic factors that put

---

[36] See Justin R. Garcia et al., "Sexual Hookup Culture: A Review," *Review of General Psychology* 16, no. 2 (2012): 161.

[37] Ibid.

intense pressure on young people to succeed in an increasingly competitive, consumer society. In part, due to a lack of coping skills and a countercultural perspective to resist these pressures, Millennials and Gen Zers seek to escape them by engaging at times in risky behavior and relationships that anesthetize them to these pressures and anxieties. Hookups, and the drinking and drugs that frequently accompany hookup parties are a common expression of escapism. Anxieties are summed up well by some of the ethnographers in Beste's study. "College students have become slaves of anxiety, from sources such as homework loads, employment, friendships, romantic relationships, family pressures, the fear of missing out, the fear of being left behind, and lack of sleep while they try to balance it all." Or again, "My greatest obstacle and the obstacle of many of my college peers is that we have 'become the slaves of anxiety.' We are all scared of amounting to nothing, so much so that we fill our voids with a 'false sense of security.'"[38] These anxieties, and the attempt to cope with them through a hookup, reveal a deeper human reality about the meaning and nature of human suffering.

The reality of suffering is an intimate part of human life and has become overwhelming for many young people. Rather than seeking to understand and embrace suffering as part of life and developing coping skills to address it in a healthy, constructive manner, which many religious traditions and authentic relationships offer, they seek to suppress suffering and escape its reality through hookups, alcohol, and drugs. The vicious cycle of these coping mechanisms is evident when, the morning after indulging in these activities, the emotions or anxieties the partners are fleeing return, often intensified and compounded by regret, guilt, remorse, doubts about self-worth (especially for women),[39] and quite possibly a hangover, from the experiences the night before.

> The fun does not last when the night is over. Hangovers are never fun the next day. On many occasions, my friends have suffered the damages of drunk texting, such as starting arguments or embarrassing themselves. When people hook up I hear about all the regrets the next morning. All of these consequences lead me to believe that these people really are not happy and fulfilled with their lives. What happy and fulfilled person includes hangovers and drama and regrettable sex in his or her life?[40]

---

[38] Beste, *College Hookup Culture and Christian Ethics*, 169.

[39] Ibid., 99; see also Stepp, *Unhooked*; and Bogle, *Hooking Up*.

[40] In Beste, *College Hookup Culture and Christian Ethics*, 106.

Regret is a common emotion to describe the aftermath of a hookup. As one of Beste's ethnographers comments: "Regret is hard to live with for the rest of your life and can really damage someone's self-worth and respect."[41] The vicious cycle often continues with attempts to suppress the regret, stress, anxiety, guilt, and unhappiness that result from hookups, drinking and drugs by engaging in more of the same; one hookup develops into serial hookups with the same negative psychological, emotional, and relational consequences. Einstein is said to have defined insanity as "doing the same thing over and over again and expecting different results." Whether the attribution is correct, the sentiment certainly is correct in the case of hookups, yet the repetitive cycle is often difficult to break for many young people due to peer pressure and fear of "missing out." Many sociological surveys and anecdotal accounts of the unhappiness that accompanies hookups psychologically, emotionally, and relationally confirm the insanity of hookups as a response to human suffering and anxiety.

In the historical and cultural context of hookups, what does it mean to love oneself? Psychological studies repeatedly indicate that one of the greatest threats to healthy human development, including sexual development, is poor self-esteem.[42] Consumer society does not promote healthy self-love.

> As teenagers and young adults, the dominant message we are bombarded with via the internet, media, social networking, and advertising, is that we can "be better," look better, be more successful, and be more popular. We set the ideals as our goals and desire to achieve them in a state of neediness, seriously believing that by achieving them we will feel satisfaction. In reality, these "achievements" are short lived and leave us wanting more. When we fail to achieve these far-fetched goals, we are discontent and can even begin to hate ourselves and who we are. If we focus on perfecting ourselves to this important, ideal person, we begin to push ourselves away from who we really are; we are running from our true self.[43]

Hookups are one way that young people run from their true selves. They are the incarnation of the consumer perspective that prepares one person to be consumed by the other and to consume the other in a physical sexual relationship devoid of relational meaning or depth. This superficial perspective of self and others drives the consumer perspective, perpetuates the

---

[41] In Ibid., 109.

[42] Dominian, "Sexuality and Interpersonal Relationships," 14.

[43] In Beste, *College Hookup Culture and Christian Ethics*, 159.

hookup culture, and frustrates the love of self that human dignity requires so that one may truly love and respect one's neighbor in a just and loving committed relationship.

As we noted in Chapter 5, the Christian tradition has not always done enough to emphasize the importance of healthy self-love. Jesus's great commandment is well known: "'You shall love the Lord your God with all your heart, with all your soul, with all your mind, and with all your strength.' The second is this: 'You shall love your neighbor as yourself'" (Mark 12:28–34; Matt 22:34–40, 46b; and Luke 10:25–28). Not so well known, as we pointed out earlier, is that there are *three* commandments in this text: love God, love yourself, and love your neighbor as yourself. The Christian tradition has tended to interpret love of neighbor as altruistic and agapaic and self-love as egocentric and antithetical to the love of the gospel. But while this *can* be the case, and the cultures of many developed countries that emphasize radical individualism do encourage egocentric love, egocentric love is not the healthy self-love demanded by the gospel. Authentic self-love first affirms oneself as a self-in-God, good, valuable, and lovable, and then, in alliance with love of neighbor, turns toward the other and gives this good, valuable, and lovable self-in-God unconditionally to the other. As Aquinas might argue: *Nemo dat quod non habet* ("No one gives what is not possessed"). If we do not truly and fully accept ourselves, in both our wholeness and our brokenness, we can neither give ourselves fully to other persons or fully accept other persons.

This is the type of self-giving to another that is reflected in a profound way through sexually intimate acts, the giving of self that affirms the desired goodness and uniqueness of both the self and the other and affirms also the self-esteem of both the giver and the recipient. It also creates genuine communion. This is a major reason why it is so crucial that the other in sexually intimate acts must never be objectified, as is the case in hookups and promiscuous sexual encounters. Many people, unsure of themselves, seek affirmation of who they are and strive to build self-identity and self-esteem through hookups. But because hookups are not an unconditional giving of self to the other, the search is frustrated and neither self-identity nor self-esteem is ever truly affirmed or established. To repeat our assertion from Chapter 5, if humans do not truly and fully accept and love themselves, in both their wholeness and their brokenness, they can neither give themselves fully to another person nor fully accept another person.

Self-love, then, is directly related to love of other(s), love of neighbor. Thomas Merton sums up this interrelationship well.

A man who is not at peace with himself necessarily projects his interior fighting into the society of those he lives with and spreads a contagion of conflict all around him. Even when he tries to do good to others his efforts are hopeless, since he does not know how to do good to himself. In moments of wildest idealism he may take it into his head to make other people happy: and in doing so he will overwhelm them with his own unhappiness. He seeks to find himself somehow in the work of making others happy. Therefore, he throws himself into the work. As a result, he gets out of the work all that he put into it: his own confusion, his own disintegration, his own unhappiness.[44]

Hookups manifest not only a distorted sense of self-love but also a distorted sense of love of neighbor. By objectification of both the self and the other, they obscure the full humanity of both and, therefore, also the ability to enter into an authentic relationship that accepts and loves each other's graces, gifts, strengths, and talents, and also each other's sins, anxiety, weakness, and brokenness.

The Human Person Is a Historical Being

Another important dimension of humans is that we are historical in our relationships with self and neighbor, and this historicity is central from a virtuous perspective as well. While hookups are ethically problematic in and of themselves, perhaps they are most problematic in their lasting impact in shaping one's outlook on intimate relationships. The experiences of regret, shame, guilt, remorse, objectification, with all their psychological, emotional, and relational implications, do not end the morning after a hookup. From a virtuous perspective they shape participants' perspectives on sexual relationships and intimacy now and in the future. That is one of the profound insights of virtue ethics: Our actions are not only manifestations of virtue (or vice) now but also shapers of virtue (or vice) for the future. Repeated experiences of objectification of ourselves and others do not immediately end and transform into authentic love of self and other when we meet the "right" person. Those experiences shape our lasting relational perspectives on the nature of love, relationship, commitment, honesty, and authenticity. If these perspectives are distorted by the hookup culture, which they are, then this may and oftentimes will carry over into future relationships.

Another relationship to consider in hookup culture is relationship with God and the impact of religion on that culture. In her study of hookup culture at seven colleges and universities, Donna Freitas focuses on four types

---

[44] Thomas Merton, *No Man Is an Island* (New York: Harcourt Brace, 1955), 127.

of institutions: private-secular, public-secular, evangelical, and Catholic. Her conclusion is that hookup culture is dominant in private-secular, public-secular, and Catholic colleges and universities, and virtually nonexistent in evangelical colleges.[45] More recent research indicates that "the odds of 'hooking up' are actually much higher at religion-affiliated schools than at secular educational institutions," especially among women.[46] Researchers offer three reasons for this, at least in terms of Catholic institutions. First, Catholic schools bring together students who have more in common religiously and socially, and young people are more likely to date or hook up with those with whom they share a common background. Second, Catholic schools place an emphasis on marriage and family and sponsor activities that promote social interactions on a regular basis. Third, Catholic schools often have limited rules regulating alcohol on campus, which is very much a part of the hookup culture. On the other hand, at evangelical colleges there is a "purity culture," in which there is a focus on marriage; sex, even a kiss, is most often postponed until marriage.[47]

Jason King has explored the hookup culture on Catholic campuses and finds that there is an "anti-hookup culture" at "very Catholic" colleges and universities more in line with evangelical than secular schools.[48] He categorizes schools as "very Catholic" if 80 percent or more of the students identify as Catholic; the core curriculum requires at least three theology classes; mass is celebrated daily, and students attend mass regularly; there are few, if any, coed residence halls; and coed visitation is strictly limited. Less than 30 percent of students hook up on these campuses. On campuses that are "mostly Catholic" and "somewhat Catholic" the hookup rates are 55 percent and 45 percent, respectively. The possibility of a hookup developing into an actual relationship at "mostly Catholic" schools may account for the higher percentage of hookups, whereas demographic variables of students at "somewhat Catholic" schools, such as rural and economically disadvantaged students, may account for lower percentages of hookups at those schools.[49] Regardless, it seems that the variables that affect hookup culture at Catholic schools may be minimally related to church teaching that absolutely prohibits premarital sex, and more related to active

---

[45] Freitas, *The End of Sex*, xi–xii.
[46] Burdette et al., "'Hook Up' at College," 545–46.
[47] Freitas, *The End of Sex*, xi–xii.
[48] Jason King, "How Does Catholic Identity Effect Hookup Culture?" *First Things* (February 9, 2017); and idem, *Faith with Benefits: Hookup Culture on Catholic Campuses* (New York: Oxford University Press, 2017).
[49] King, "How Does Catholic Identity Effect Hookup Culture?"

participation in church life.[50] This indicates the need for families to promote active participation in the life of the church at a young age, both liturgically and in church activities like youth ministry. It also indicates the need for the church to approach the issue of human sexuality more comprehensively and positively. Merely reciting absolute condemnations of premarital sex does not convey a positive meaning about the beauty of human sexuality and the need for a committed, loving context to share that beauty. From a virtuous perspective the church must emphasize the *meaning* of sexual acts for human persons. Such a virtuous perspective might include a catechumenate for marriage, such as we develop in Chapter 9, to ritualize the lived human experience of the majority of young couples today. The meaning of sexual experience from this perspective is very different from the perspective of hookup culture.

Other researchers have taken up the question of religion and its influence on hookup culture, and their findings indicate that attending religious services, rather than religious affiliation or subjective religiousness, has the greatest impact on reducing participation in the hookup culture.[51] This conclusion affirms the importance of the ethical perspectives that we explored in Chapter 4 and the virtue perspective we explained in Chapter 3. There is an important causal relation between virtue and action, being and doing. It is not necessarily the case that attending religious services is essential to live out one's faith and commitment to see injustice and do justice, but the active participation in a religious tradition is important as both an expression and a reinforcement of those virtues. Sociological studies indicate the influence of such participation in life decisions, such as whether to participate in hookup culture or what hookup culture means to the people who participate in it.[52]

The Human Person Is Unique and Equal to Every Other Human Person

The final dimension of the human person integrally and adequately considered in relation to hookup culture is that the human person is unique and equal to every other human person, a fact that is especially important in sexual intimacy. Recognizing the fundamental equality of another human person requires respect and, in sexual intimacy, mutuality. Hookups are frequently about self-gratification with little or no concern for either mutuality

---

[50] See Burdette et al., "'Hook Up' at College"; Smith et al., *Young Catholic America*, 229.
[51] Burdette et al., "'Hook Up' at College"; Smith et al., *Young Catholic America*, 229.
[52] Burdette et al., "'Hook Up' at College."

or for gratification of the other person. There is fundamental inequality built into the hookup culture. One of Beste's male students sums up the impact of inequality in sexual expression: "I have experienced unequal, non-mutual sex. It sucks. Despite the injustice and inequality it brings to the relationship, it is hard to relate to somebody when you don't see them as your equal or they don't see you as their equal. . . . To be quite honest, it's a total boner killer."[53] This student's insight about the importance of equality between human beings is not only an important theological truth, because all people are equally created in the image and likeness of God, but is also an important relational truth. Pope Francis shares concerns about relational inequality in *Amoris Laetitia*: "When reciprocal belonging turns into domination, 'the structure of communion in interpersonal relations is essentially changed.' It is part of the mentality of domination that those who dominate end up negating their own [we add, and the other's] dignity" (*AL*, no. 155). Gender, ethnic, sexual, and relational equality are foundational for realizing human dignity; hookups profoundly jeopardize this dignity.

A Virtuous Perspective for Norms Guiding Just and Loving Sexual Relationships

Following our consideration of the hookup culture from the perspective of the dimensions of the human person integrally and adequately considered, and guided by Margaret Farley, we now propose seven norms to guide people to make just and loving decisions for engaging in sexual relationships. First, however, we explore the virtuous perspective of just love that guides us toward those norms.

To fulfill the dimensions of the human person integrally and adequately considered, and to be authentically human, heterosexual and homosexual activity must be *just and loving*. That "just and loving" needs explanation. The search for ethical judgment in sexual matters today frequently ends with the claim that sexual activity is ethical when it is loving, a claim that is vapid because it is usually devoid of content. We agree with Farley: "Love is the problem in ethics, not the solution,"[54] and it is the problem to the extent that it lacks content. Our task here is to give it content. We begin with an ancient definition: *amare est velle bonum* ("to love is to will the good of another").[55] Love is an activity of the will, a decision to will the

[53] In Beste, *College Hookup Culture and Christian Ethics*, 246.
[54] Margaret Farley, "An Ethic for Same-Sex Relations," in *A Challenge to Love: Gay and Lesbian Catholics in the Church,* ed. Robert Nugent (New York: Crossroad, 1983), 100.
[55] See Thomas Aquinas, *Summa Theologiae* I-II, 28, 1c.

good of another human being. True love, as every lover knows, is *ec-static*, that is, in love a person goes out of self to another person who is unique and equal. That there are two absolutely unique and equal, and yet like, selves in any loving relationship introduces the cardinal virtue of justice, "the virtue according to which, with constant and perpetual will, someone renders to others their due rights."[56] If asked what justice—rendering to others their due rights—has to do with sexual acts, we respond that, since sexual acts are between two, equal personal selves, justice has everything to do with them. Farley proposes seven norms that are all part of justice.[57] These are not absolute norms, like magisterial norms that absolutely prohibit certain actions regardless of the context, circumstances, or intention. Rather, they are norms that admit of degrees, depending on the context, and can reflect "minimal" or "maximal" justice, depending on that context and also depending on the ability to see injustice and do justice. We first explain the norms and then consider them in reference to hookup culture.

The first norm is "do no unjust harm." We must treat ourselves and others with profound respect and avoid violating human dignity. Human sexuality and its sexual expression are particularly susceptible to harm because of the vulnerability associated with them. Karen Lebacqz notes that "sexuality has to do with vulnerability. Eros, the desire for another, the passion that accompanies the wish for sexual expression, makes one vulnerable . . . capable of being wounded."[58] The depth of vulnerability in sexual expression requires a similar depth of sensitivity to the myriad ways in which vulnerability can be violated and unjust harm inflicted on another in the sexual realm. Some of these violations are obvious, such as rape, violence, sadomasochism, enslavement, and sexual assault. Other violations are subtler and require a depth of sensitivity to discern the meaning of sexual expression for the self, the other, and third parties. Is this sexual activity respectful of the other? Does it communicate openly and honestly meaning and a level of commitment to the other? Does it receive openly and honestly that meaning and level of commitment from the other? Does it do unjust harm to third parties, possible offspring from a sexual relationship, for instance, or future partners that might be affected by sexually transmitted diseases (STDs)? Might psychological or emotional damage occur because of this relationship and its impact on future relationships? Seeing injustice in the sexual realm requires sensitivity and maturation

---

[56] Thomas Aquinas, *Summa Theologiae Sancti Thomae de Aquino*, II–II, 58, 1.

[57] Margaret A. Farley, *Just Love: A Framework for Christian Sexual Ethics* (New York: Continuum, 2006), 215–32.

[58] Karan Lebacqz, "Appropriate Vulnerability: A Sexual Ethic for Singles," *Christian Century* (May 6, 1987): 436.

that comes with growth, development, and experience. That sensitivity, however, can also be severely damaged in and through experience.

*A second norm is that **free consent** is essential in every just and loving sexual relationship,* which parallels everything we said above about the person as subject. In every relationship between free human subjects, sexual or otherwise, consent must be free and uncoerced. A challenge that hookup culture faces is that the consumption of alcohol and the use of drugs seriously diminish free consent. While no means no, does yes actually mean yes, and does silence imply consent? The increasing frequency of sexual assaults both on and off college campuses puts increasing pressure on individuals, even intoxicated individuals, to discern consent and clearly to offer or to refuse it. If there is any ambiguity about whether free consent was given to engage in sexual activity, one should assume that consent has not been given and therefore should refrain from sexual activity. The burden of proof is on the person who initiates sexual contact to determine whether or not consent is given. Even when this burden of proof appears to have been met, the determination of free consent will remain complex when alcohol, drugs, and any form of gender or power disparities are present, for all of these affect a person's capacity to give free consent.

*A third norm is that just and loving sexual activity requires **mutuality**,* and *a fourth norm is that it requires **equality**.* These two norms go hand in hand. Mutuality in sexual relationships is grounded in equality and requires a shift in the traditional perspective of active/dominant and passive/submissive partners in a sexual relationship to a perspective grounded in fundamental equality between two persons. Farley refers to this changed perspective as "active receptivity and receptive activity."[59] Just and loving sex requires the mutual exchange of willing participation that celebrates the gift of sexuality in its various expressions. Mutuality fundamentally challenges gender and ethnic power disparities.

One modern characteristic guiding sexual relationships, perhaps the greatest and most difficult characteristic to realize, especially in patriarchal cultures, is the fundamental equality of all persons. For Christians, that equality takes on a deeply religious character because it is believed to be the creative plan of the God who created *'adam* male and female, blessed them, and named them together *'adam* (Gen 5:1). A sexual act that is just and loving seeks the good of equality and renders all the rights flowing from equality to both partners. Any sexual act that involves inequities— of power, social or economic status, ethnic origin, level of maturity, for example—is ipso facto an unethical sexual act. Flowing from personal

---

[59] Farley, *Just Love*, 221.

equality is personal freedom. A sexual act that is just and loving renders to the partner in the act the rights associated with freedom and seeks the good of freedom for both partners. That means, in the concrete, that a just and loving sexual act requires the free consent of both partners, and that any sexual act that subverts free consent is ipso facto an unethical sexual act. The use of power, violence, and rape is never ethical. With the modern "discovery" that women are as free as men, free consent may be seriously interfered with or even precluded entirely by any sexual activity that is marked by socially constructed male domination or female subordination. The same reasoning applies to anyone of diminished capacity, the immature, the dependent, the drugged, and the drunk, for example, for diminished capacity automatically means diminished consent.

Unfortunately, a lack of equality, often grounded in gender disparities, is so ingrained in Western culture that seeing those disparities and responding to them to realize equality requires a process of growth and development, both individually and communally. Scotosis—an ethical blind spot—regarding gender disparities and gender inequality affects relationships and power structures within relationships. Through the process of education and advocacy scotosis can be confronted and patriarchal and discriminatory cultures transformed to help realize equality between gendered persons. This is an ongoing process that takes time to see injustice and to do justice.

A fifth norm is that **commitment** *is foundational for just and loving sexual relationships.* Farley notes what the evidence reveals, that "sexual desire without interpersonal love leads to disappointment and a growing disillusionment."[60] No commitment is a condition of hookups and is also one of the main reasons why people who engage in hookups often feel objectified and used in the experience. The Christian tradition has always required from the partners some form of long-term commitment, some kind of solemn promise or covenant, for sexual intercourse to be ethical. That this covenant was traditionally linked to marriage, and that marriage was primarily linked to procreation, are not reasons to reject commitment as a reasonable and ethical norm for sexual activity, heterosexual or homosexual.

To be just, therefore, any sexual act requires a level of commitment consonant with the maturity of the persons engaging in it. Responsible sexual activity should be approached with a level of maturity that appreciates and respects the other as equally human and gives evidence of a level of commitment appropriate for the depth of the sexual experience. Serial hookups do not promote the virtue of commitment. Rather, they damage

---

[60] Ibid., 225.

the ability to commit and to integrate sexuality into "a shared life and an enduring love."[61]

*A sixth norm is that long-term commitment is required for a just and loving relationship to mature into **fruitfulness** for both individual and common good.* That fruitfulness—which may include the love and communion between the partners, heterosexual, homosexual, or bisexual; offspring; and the common good of the community in which the partners and any children live—requires a long-term commitment to be nourished into maturity.[62] Fruitfulness includes both the possibility of the procreation of children and the possibility of love and communion between the partners, both of which expand the wider social community. Fruitfulness as interpersonal love and communion is like throwing a large rock into a small pond. The initial splash is the intimate communion of the couple in the sexual act. The ripple effect extends to and affects all their other human relationships and experiences. Genuinely just and loving sexual acts ripple out in a similar way to create and enhance virtues such as love, commitment, integrity, reconciliation, forgiveness, and justice that then influence other social relationships.

*The seventh and final norm is **social justice**,* which applies more to the societal structures in which sexual relationships take place than to the sexual partners themselves. Social justice refers us back to Chapter 4, where we discussed different theological perspectives that can see injustice and do justice. Social justice challenges us to see structures of injustice in sexual activity—structures of gender inequality, domestic violence, the commercialization of sexuality, sexual exploitation of all kinds, homophobia, patriarchy—and to transform those structures to facilitate just and loving sexual relationships. One other structure of injustice that demands transformation, we suggest, is the hookup culture we confront in this chapter.

Can Hookups Fulfill These Norms?

As theological ethicists we do not believe that hookup culture fulfills all of these norms, though it may fulfill some of them. First, if the rules for a hookup are followed, sexual contact and activity with no emotional connection, then there may be, at the time, "no unjust harm" in a hookup. The criteria for a hookup, however, we argue, are themselves unethical. If the rules for the hookup are adhered to, then the implied contract between the partners has not been violated. The relational *meaning* of sexual activity, however, especially as it relates to the various dimensions of the human

---

[61] Ibid., 225.

[62] For a fuller development of this point, see Michael G. Lawler, *Family: American and Christian* (Chicago: Loyola University Press, 1998), 166–74.

person integrally and adequately considered has been violated, and unjust harm has been done to both partners, however unintentionally, in violating this meaning. Free consent may sometimes be fulfilled, though we remain seriously concerned about the impact of alcohol and drugs on that free consent. Mutuality and equality may also be fulfilled, though the sociological data indicate that, after the hookup, women often have a more negative perception of the experience than men. This would seem to indicate that there is a gender disconnect between the hookup and its fulfillment of expectations and that the disconnect is linked to gender expectations. These unfulfilled expectations may translate into gender inequality.

Commitment is lacking in the very definition of hookup, though King's research indicates that, at Catholic institutions, there appears to be an at least implicit hope that the hookup will lead into a more permanent commitment down the road.[63] This may or may not be a realistic expectation, but it can guide the perspectives of those engaging in hookups and create more just sexual activity, even if it violates the fundamental contractual agreement of the hookup. Fruitfulness, biological and relational, seems not to be fulfilled in hookups. Even if a woman gets pregnant from a hookup, this is an unintended outcome and becomes a problem rather than a joyous celebration of just and loving sexual acts. The complications of pregnancy from a hookup are clear and evident. Relational fruitfulness in both the short term and the long term is questionable. In the short term a hookup must not include relational fruitfulness that brings two people together in a mutually binding relationship; this would be a violation of the implied hookup contract. In the long term this suppression of relational fruitfulness, especially from a virtuous ethical perspective, suppresses honesty, justice, love, care, commitment, and fidelity. This suppression is evident not only in any particular hookup but extends to subsequent relationships and partners. Hookups lay a relational foundation for future relationships where the vices of a hookup are hard to convert into the virtues of a fruitful, interpersonal relationship.

Social justice must look seriously at how third parties and the common good are affected by hookup culture. The risk of contracting and spreading STDs increases in direct proportion to the number of sexual partners one has. Hookup culture promotes increasing the number of partners and thus risks spreading STDs and causing depression in participants, especially women,[64] which endangers not only individuals but also the common good. Any pregnancy that results from a hookup can have devastating effects on

---

[63] See King, *Faith with Benefits.*

[64] Robyn L. Fielder et al., "Sexual Hookups and Adverse Health Outcomes: A Longitudinal Study of First-Year College Women," *The Journal of Sex Research* 51, no. 2 (2014): 131–44.

the two partners, the child, the partners' families and friends, and society. Overall, from an ethical perspective, hookups violate several of the norms for just and loving sexual acts, and the ethical disvalues of hookups far outweigh their values. Hookups differ fundamentally, relationally, and ethically from the nuptial cohabitations to which we turn in the next chapter.

Questions for Reflection

- Explain Donna Freitas's three criteria for a hookup. Do they accurately reflect hookup culture?
- Is it possible to separate the physical, psychological, emotional, and relational dimensions of human sexuality in a hookup?
- What are the dimensions of the human person integrally and adequately considered that hookups fulfill? What dimensions do hookups violate? Are there other dimensions we have not discussed that hookups violate or fulfill?
- Explain the virtuous perspective of just love in terms of human sexuality. Apply this perspective to hookup culture. How does a virtuous perspective affect your understanding of hookup culture?
- Evaluate hookups on the basis of Margaret Farley's seven norms. Are there additional norms that are relevant to evaluate hookups? Explain.

Suggested Readings

Beste, Jennifer. *College Hookup Culture and Christian Ethics: The Lives and Longings of Emerging Adults*. New York: Oxford University Press, 2018.

Bogle, Kathleen A. *Hooking Up: Sex, Dating, and Relationships on Campus*. New York: New York University Press, 2008.

Farley, Margaret A. *Just Love: A Framework for Christian Sexual Ethics*. New York: Continuum, 2006.

Freitas, Donna. *The End of Sex: How Hookup Culture Is Leaving a Generation Unhappy, Sexually Unfulfilled, and Confused about Intimacy*. New York: Basic Books, 2013.

King, Jason. *Faith with Benefits: Hookup Culture on Catholic Campuses*. New York: Oxford University Press, 2017.

9

Cohabitation and the Process of Marriage

Learning Objectives

- Define *cohabitation.*
- Distinguish between nuptial and non-nuptial cohabitation.
- Explain commitment and its relationship to cohabitation and marriage.
- Understand the historical evolution of the process of marriage in the Christian tradition.
- Explain the marriage catechumenate.

When the *Lineamenta* for the 2015 Synod on Marriage and Family was distributed, the group charged with the marriage preparation of those wishing to marry in the Catholic Church in England, Marriage Care, responded that nearly every couple attending their courses was already cohabiting. Indeed, couples seeking to be married in the church and not already living together were a rarity, not only in England, but throughout the Western world. The sharp increase in cohabitation is one of the most fundamental social changes in Western countries today. Over half of all first marriages in the United States are preceded by cohabitation.[1] Studies find a similar trend in

---

[1] Larry L. Bumpass, "The Declining Significance of Marriage: Changing Family Life in the United States," NSFH working paper no. 66, Center for Demography and Ecology (Madison: University of Wisconsin-Madison, 1995), 8; L. Bumpass and Hsien-Hen Lu, "Trends in Cohabitation and Implications for Children's Family Contexts," Center for Demography and Ecology (Madison: University of Wisconsin-Madison, 1998), 7; Gail Risch et al., *Time, Sex, and Money: The First Five Years of Marriage* (Omaha, NE: Center for Marriage and Family, Creighton University, 2000).

Great Britain,[2] Norway,[3] Sweden,[4] the Netherlands,[5] France,[6] Belgium and Germany,[7] Ireland,[8] Canada,[9] and Australia.[10] Surveys in France, the Netherlands, Austria, and Great Britain indicate that cohabitation before first marriage reaches levels between 40 and 80 percent for recent marriages.[11]

A 2004 PSC Research Report documented the continuing "normality" of cohabitation; in 1960, the number of cohabiting households in the United States was "less than half a million"; in 2000, "there were nearly five million such households,"[12] a tenfold increase. A 2013 report from the Centers for Disease Control further documented the trend: 48 percent of women interviewed in 2006–10 cohabited as a first union compared with 34 percent of women in 1995; 40 percent of those cohabitations transitioned to marriage within three years. Kathleen Kiernan reported in 2004 that cohabitation similarly continues to increase in Western Europe, reaching the same level as in the United States.[13] Cohabitation, therefore, is an in-

[2] John Haskey, "Pre-Marital Cohabitation and the Probability of Subsequent Divorce: Analyses Using the New Data from the General Household Survey," *Population Trends* 68 (1992): 10–19.

[3] Oystein Kravdal, "Does Marriage Require a Stronger Economic Underpinning than Informal Cohabitation?" *Population Studies* 53 (1999): 63–80.

[4] Neil G. Bennett, Ann Klimas Blanc, and David E. Bloom, "Commitment and the Modern Union: Assessing the Link between Premarital Cohabitation and Subsequent Marital Stability," *American Sociological Review* 53 (1988): 127–38; Ann-Zofie E. Duvander, "The Transition from Cohabitation to Marriage: A Longitudinal Study of the Propensity to Marry in Sweden in the Early 1990s," *Journal of Family Issues* 20 (1999): 698–717.

[5] Aart C. Liefbroer, "The Choice between a Married or Unmarried First Union by Young Adults," *European Journal of Population* 7 (1991): 273–98.

[6] Henri Leridon, "Cohabitation, Marriage, Separation: An Analysis of Life Histories of French Cohorts from 1968 to 1985," *Population Studies* 44 (1990): 127–44.

[7] R. Lesthaeghe, G. Moors, and L. Halman, "Living Arrangements and Values among Young Adults in the Netherlands, Belgium, France and Germany, 1990," Paper presented at the annual meetings of the Population Association of America, Cincinnati (April 1–3, 1993).

[8] John Mee, "Cohabitation Law Reform in Ireland," *Child and Family Law Quarterly* 23 (2011): 323–43.

[9] Charles Hobart and Frank Grigel, "Cohabitation among Canadian Students at the End of the Eighties," *Journal of Comparative Family Studies* 23 (1992): 311–37.

[10] Michael Bracher, Gigi Santow, S. Philip Morgan, and James Trussell, "Marriage Dissolution in Australia: Models and Explanations," *Population Studies* 47 (1993): 403–25.

[11] John Haskey, "Patterns of Marriage, Divorce, and Cohabitation in the Different Countries of Europe," *Population Trends* 69 (Autumn 1992), 30; and Duncan Dormor, *Just Cohabiting: The Church, Sex and Getting Married* (London: Darton, Longman, Todd, 2004), 3.

[12] Pamela M. Smock and Wendy D. Manning, "Living Together Unmarried in the United States: Demographic Perspectives and Implications for Family Policy," PSC Research Report no. 04-555 (March 2004): 2.

[13] Kathleen E. Kiernan, "Unmarried Cohabitation in Britain and Europe," *Law and Policy* 26 (2004): 33–55.

creasing phenomenon in our human experience, and human experience is a long-established ground for Catholic ethical reflection and judgment.[14] The reality of cohabitation that may or may not lead to marriage poses a challenge for Catholic ethical teaching, which condemns premarital sex as intrinsically immoral. How do we navigate, from a Christian virtuous perspective, the disconnect between the reality of the lived experience of the majority of couples and Catholic teaching?

In this chapter, inspired by Pope Francis's Apostolic Exhortation *Amoris Laetitia* and relying on experience, reason, and tradition, we reflect on that phenomenon and seek to make "faith sense" of it; that is, we come to the experience of cohabitation with a faith nourished in the Catholic tradition and attempt to allow that faith to enter into dialogue with the experience of cohabitation and the effect it has on the Christian lives of cohabiting couples. Readers will find as the chapter unfolds that cohabitation occupies the foreground of our reflection, but they should not miss the important background that is marriage, for which cohabitation is now an established proving ground and preparation. We have much to say about cohabitation and marriage preparation in our final section.

The chapter develops in four cumulative sections. The first section considers the contemporary phenomenon of cohabitation; the second considers Pope Francis's treatment of cohabitation in *Amoris Laetitia*; the third unfolds the Western and Christian historical tradition as it relates to cohabitation and marriage; the fourth formulates a church response to cohabitation based on our theological reflection on it and advances a plea for the establishment of a marriage catechumenate for cohabiting couples. We are not the first to propose a marriage catechumenate; it has been proposed before by English theologians Paul Holmes and Adrian Thatcher.[15] We are the first, however, we believe, to propose it to the Catholic Church after the loving, merciful, and thoroughly Catholic treatment of cohabitation by Pope Francis in *Amoris Laetitia* and his recommendations for the accompaniment, integration, instruction, and nurture of cohabitors. Francis's exhortation, we believe, marks a clear turning point in the magisterial approach to cohabitation, after which the ethical evaluation of what we will call nuptial cohabitation has evolved.[16]

---

[14] See Michael G. Lawler and Todd A. Salzman, "Human Experience and Catholic Moral Theology," *Irish Theological Quarterly* 76 (2011): 35–56.

[15] Paul A. Holmes, "A Catechumenate for Marriage: Presacramental Preparation as Pilgrimage," *Journal of Ritual Studies* 6 (1992): 93–113; Adrian Thatcher, *Living Together and Christian Ethics* (Cambridge: Cambridge University Press, 2002).

[16] See Stephan Goertz and Caroline Witting, Amoris Laetitia: *Wendpunkt für die Moraltheologie* (Freiburg: Herder, 2016).

Cohabitation in the Contemporary West

Before embarking on our analysis, it is important to define precisely what we mean by the term *cohabitation*. The word derives from the Latin *co-habitare*, "to live together." It applies in general to all situations in which persons live together, in a marriage, in a family, in a dormitory, in a boarding house. An added specification, therefore, is necessary to distinguish the meaning of the word in both contemporary usage and this chapter. *Cohabitation* here means the situation of a man and a woman who, though not husband and wife, live together and enjoy intimate sexual relations. Cohabitation so understood raises a crucial Catholic red flag, for it is contrary to traditional Catholic teaching, expressed in the Congregation for the Doctrine of the Faith's *Persona Humana*, that prescribes that to be moral "any human genital act whatsoever may be placed only within the framework of marriage" (*PH*, no. 7). We shall return to that contradiction later.

We introduce here an important distinction, for not all cohabitors and not all cohabitations are alike. In 2007, we submitted to the American church a twofold typology of cohabitors and their cohabitations: there are cohabitors who intend to marry each other in the future and cohabitors who do not intend to marry each other. The cohabitation of the former we named *nuptial cohabitation*, the cohabitation of the latter *non-nuptial cohabitation*.[17] We are happy to see Pope Francis embrace this distinction, if not our terminology. In *Amoris Laetitia* he makes a distinction between "cohabitation which totally excludes any intention to marry" (*AL*, no. 53)—our non-nuptial cohabitation—and cohabitation dictated by "cultural and contingent situations" (*AL*, no. 294) that can lead to marriage when circumstances permit it—our nuptial cohabitation. The two types of cohabitation have seriously different effects on any subsequent marriage.

Two social scientific facts about cohabitation are well known and frequently mentioned by Catholic ethicists. *The first is that unmarried heterosexual cohabitation increased dramatically in the Western world in the last quarter of the twentieth century.* For couples marrying in the United States in the decade between 1965 and 1974, the percentage of marriages preceded by cohabitation was 10 percent; for couples marrying between 1990 and 1994, that percentage dramatically quintupled to 50 percent.[18] Between 1987 and 1995 there was an equally striking increase for the number of women reporting that they had cohabited at least once. In 1987,

---

[17] Michael G. Lawler and Gail S. Risch, "A Betrothal Proposal," *US Catholic* (June 2007): 18–22.

[18] Larry L. Bumpass and James A. Sweet, "National Estimates of Cohabitation," *Demography* 26 (1989): 615–25; Bumpass and Hsien-Hen Lu, "Trends in Cohabitation and Implications for Children's Family Contexts."

30 percent of women in their late thirties reported they had cohabited; in 1995, 48 percent reported they had cohabited. As marriage rates have declined, cohabitation rates have increased, especially among cohabiting adults fifty and older. Those rates increased 75 percent, from 2.3 million in 2007 to 4 million in 2016.[19] These increases did not leave the social climate in which cohabitation flourished untouched. Rather, as cohabitation cohorts became more and more homogenized, cohabitation itself became more and more conventional and socially endorsed. It also accounted for the noted and, in church quarters lamented, decrease in marriages.

The second fact often mentioned is that premarital cohabitation tends to be associated with a heightened risk of divorce, a fact on which there was consensus from a large variety of different researchers, samples, methodologies, and measures.[20] This second fact has become a favorite of Catholic commentators on unmarried heterosexual cohabitation and its implications for subsequent marriage, which leaves both them and their pastoral responses at risk of being uninformed and outdated.[21] More recent studies on more recent cohorts report more nuanced data about the relationship of cohabitation and marital instability.

As early as 1992, Robert Schoen showed that the inverse relationship between premarital cohabitation and subsequent marital stability was minimal for recent birth cohorts, a result which he linked to the growing prevalence of cohabitation. "As the prevalence of cohabitation rises sharply, the instability of marriages preceded by cohabitation drops markedly."[22] In 1997, Susan McRae demonstrated the common negative association between premarital cohabitation and marital stability when she analyzed her British sample in toto. When, however, she analyzed her sample by age cohort, her findings supported Schoen: "Younger generations do not show the same link between pre-marital cohabitation and marriage dissolution." She agreed with Schoen's conclusion that "as cohabitation becomes

---

[19] Renee Stepler, "Number of US Adults Cohabiting with a Partner Continues to Rise, Especially among those 50 and Older," Pew Research Center (April 6, 2017).

[20] Larry L. Bumpass, R. Kelly Raley, and James A. Sweet, "The Changing Character of Stepfamilies: Implications of Cohabitation and Nonmarital Childbearing," *Demography* 32 (1995): 425–36; Robert Schoen, "First Unions and the Stability of First Marriages," *Journal of Marriage and Family* 54 (1992): 281–84; David R. Hall and John Z. Zhao, "Cohabitation and Divorce in Canada: Testing the Selectivity Hypothesis," *Journal of Marriage and Family* 57 (1997): 421–27.

[21] See, as an example replicated in diocesan policies across the United States, United States Conference of Catholic Bishops, Committee on Marriage and Family, *Marriage Preparation and Cohabiting Couples* (Washington, DC: USCCB, 1999), 10. See also Pontifical Council for the Family, *Marriage, Family, and "De Facto" Unions* (Rome: Vatican Polyglot Press, 2000), 4.

[22] Schoen, "First Unions and the Stability of First Marriages," 283.

the majority pattern before marriage, this link will become progressively weaker."[23] That majority pattern, as already noted, has now arrived. When they analyzed their results in toto, Lakeesha Woods and Robert Emery uncovered much the same data as McRae: "Premarital cohabitation had a small but significant predictive effect on divorce." When they controlled for personal characteristics, however, premarital cohabitation had no predictive effect on divorce.[24]

In a sophisticated study of an Australian sample that controlled for age at union formation, educational level, importance of religion in the relationship, parental divorce, and having a child before marriage (all strong predictors of divorce), David de Vaus and his colleagues found the link between cohabitation and marital instability was apparent only for earlier cohorts.[25] When cohabitation alone was considered, the greater risk of marital separation of couples who cohabited prior to marriage than couples who did not cohabit was 11 percent for those who married in the 1970s and only 2 percent for those who married in the early 1990s. When the other above-cited control variables were added to the analysis, those who cohabited prior to marriage in the 1970s had a 6 percent higher risk of divorce than those who did not, and those who cohabited prior to marriage in the early 1990s had a 3 percent lower risk of divorce than those who did not, though that difference was not statistically significant. Jay Teachman replicated that result in 2002, showing that when a woman has cohabited only with her husband such nuptial cohabitation is not associated with increased likelihood of divorce.[26] Sheri Stritof reported the same datum from Europe in 2017.[27]

Linda Waite, one of America's most respected marriage researchers, endorses our thesis that all cohabitors and all cohabiting relationships are not equal. Waite explains that "couples who live together with no definite plans to marry are making a different bargain than couples who marry or than engaged cohabitors," and adds that "those on their way to the altar look and act like already-married couples in most ways, and those with

---

[23] Susan McRae, "Cohabitation: A Trial Run for Marriage?" *Sexual and Marital Therapy* 12 (1997): 259.

[24] Lakeesha N. Woods and Robert E. Emery, "The Cohabitation Effect on Divorce: Causation or Selection?" *Journal of Divorce and Remarriage* 37 (2002): 101–21.

[25] David de Vaus, Lixia Qu, and Ruth Weston, "Does Pre-Marital Cohabitation Affect the Chances of Marriage Lasting?" paper presented at the Eighth Australian Institute of Family Studies Conference, Melbourne, February 2003.

[26] Jay Teachman, "Premarital Sex, Premarital Cohabitation, and the Risk of Subsequent Marital Dissolution among Women," *Journal of Marriage and the Family* 65 (2002): 444–55.

[27] Sheri Stritof, "Cohabitation Facts and Statistics You Need to Know" (updated April 27, 2018), https://www.thespruce.com/cohabitation-facts-and-statistics-2302236.

no plans to marry look and act very different. For engaged cohabiting couples, living together is a step on the path to marriage, not a different road altogether."[28] In our terminology, nuptial cohabitors have already committed to one another and to the process of gradually becoming married, following both John Paul II's (in *Familiaris Consortio*) and Francis's (in *Amoris Laetitia*) "law of gradualness" in the knowledge that the human being "knows, loves, and accomplishes moral good by different stages of growth" (*FC,* no. 34; *AL,* no. 295). We will return to that law of gradualness. Waites's conclusion from her data is of the utmost importance, and we fully embrace it and recommend it to the church's ministers: "Compared to marriage, *uncommitted cohabitation*—cohabitation by couples who are not engaged [our non-nuptial cohabitation]—is an inferior social arrangement."[29] Commitment is one of the topics that participants reported they want to focus on in marriage preparation programs and that they rate as most helpful when done well.[30] We focus now on the meaning and nature of commitment.

John Paul II teaches that conjugal love "aims at a deeply personal unity, a unity that, beyond union in one flesh, leads to forming one heart and soul; it demands indissolubility and faithfulness in definitive mutual giving; and it is open to fertility" (*FC,* no. 13). We submit that this describes the situation not only of married couples but also of nuptial cohabitors who have committed to such a loving relationship with each other and who later will come to the church seeking to be married. They come to the church to celebrate publicly the gift of their love for each other and to give it renewed stability and permanence through the solemn and public commitment of marital vows to each other, to the church, and to God. Their gradual and growing *commitment* in love to one another and, ultimately, their fully grown commitment to one another in marriage are not just abstract notions; they have a very concrete, specific, and recognizable face. Marriage researcher Scott Stanley has brilliantly analyzed this commitment.

Stanley distinguishes two kinds of commitment: commitment as *dedication,* defined as "an internal state of devotion to a person or a project," and

---

[28] Linda J. Waite, "Cohabitation: A Communitarian Perspective," in *Marriage in America: A Communitarian Perspective,* ed. Martin King Whyte (Lanham, MD: Rowman and Littlefield, 2000), 26, 18. See also Susan L. Brown and Alan Booth, "Cohabitation Versus Marriage: A Comparison of Relationship Quality," *Journal of Marriage and the Family* 58 (1996): 668–78; David Popenoe and Barbara Defoe Whitehead, "Ten Important Research Findings on Marriage and Choosing a Marriage Partner: Helpful Facts for Young Adults," The National Marriage Project (New Brunswick, NJ: Rutgers University, November 2004).

[29] Waite, "Cohabitation, 26, emphasis added.

[30] Center for Marriage and Family, *Marriage Preparation in the Catholic Church: Getting It Right* (Omaha, NE: Creighton University, 1995), 3.

commitment as *constraint*, which "entails a sense of obligation."[31] Those who lose the sense of dedication and retain only the sense of constraint, he reports, "will either be together but miserable...or come apart."[32] We consider here what we believe to be the more important sense of commitment, namely, commitment as dedication, which we define as *a freely chosen and faithful devotion to a person or project.* Applied to relationships, including both nuptial cohabitation and marriage, commitment as dedication is twofold: commitment to the partner and commitment to the relationship. Commitment to the partner entails those virtues that John Paul lists or implies, namely, love, fidelity, loyalty, compassion, mercy, and fortitude amid the messiness and inevitable struggles of the relationship. Commitment to the relationship entails exclusivity, indissolubility, and fertility as fruitfulness.[33] Couples who share this double commitment manifest it in various ways. They give evidence of a strong couple identity, "a strong orientation toward 'us' and 'we.'" They "make their partner and marriage [or, we would add, nuptial cohabitation] a high priority." They "protect their relationship from attraction to others." They are willing to "sacrifice for one another without resentment." They take a long-term view, "they invest themselves in building a future together."[34] Such double commitment, Stanley and others show, is the surest path to the intimacy that all partners and spouses seek.

Couples with such double commitment report that they feel comfortable revealing their deepest desires, failings, and hurts to one another.[35] They do not think about possible alternatives to their partner; they are more satisfied with their relationship in general and their sex life in particular; and they have no need to consider adultery.[36] They are more willing to give up things important to them for the sake of their relationship, and they report higher levels of happiness and stability than do partners who do not regularly sacrifice for the sake of their relationship.[37] These couples have a strong sense of their future together and are more likely to speak of that future and of their dreams for it than of their past conflicts, failures, and disappointments.[38] It is such commitment, we suggest, that nuptial cohabitors

---

[31] Scott M. Stanley, *The Power of Commitment: A Guide to Active, Lifelong Love* (San Francisco: Jossey-Bass, 2005), 23, emphasis added.

[32] Ibid., 24.

[33] See Blaine J. Flowers, *Beyond the Myth of Marital Happiness* (San Francisco: Jossey-Bass, 2000).

[34] Stanley, *The Power of Commitment*, 24.

[35] Ibid., 62–63.

[36] Ibid., 93–95. See also W. Bradford Wilcox, *Soft Patriarchs, New Men: How Christianity Shapes Fathers and Husbands* (Chicago: University of Chicago Press, 2004).

[37] Stanley, *The Power of Commitment*, 126.

[38] Ibid., 176–79.

exhibit, albeit in seed at the beginning of their cohabitation together but in full flower when they come to the church to seek sacramental marriage. It is precisely the seedling love and commitment becoming a flower that need to be acknowledged, celebrated, accompanied, and nurtured in the marriage catechumenate we propose, which is geared to the nurturing of a healthy Christian marriage.

Pope Francis on Cohabitation

As noted in our opening section, couples seeking to be married in the church and not already living together are a rarity today. The "Final Report" of the Synod on Marriage and Family condemned all cohabitation as immoral, guided by the established Catholic tradition that, to be moral, "any human genital act whatsoever may be placed only within the framework of marriage" (*PH,* no. 7). Pope Francis ought also to condemn it for the same reason, but he does not. Instead, in *Amoris Laetitia*, he does three eminently Catholic things. First, he makes a distinction with respect to cohabitation; second, he invokes a long-established Catholic ethical tradition that teaches that circumstances can extenuate and even nullify moral culpability; third, he firmly invokes another long-established Catholic ethical tradition, namely, the authority and inviolability of individual conscience

First, Francis distinguishes between "cohabitation which totally excludes any intention to marry" (*AL,* no. 53) . . . our non-nuptial cohabitation, and cohabitation "not motivated by prejudice or resistance to a sacramental union, but by cultural or contingent situations" (*AL,* no. 294), our nuptial cohabitation. Among contingent situations he singles out the material poverty in some countries that leads couples to judge that "celebrating a marriage is too expensive in the social circumstances . . . and drives people into *de facto* unions" (*AL,* no. 294) like cohabitation. "*De facto* unions may not simply be equated with marriage" (*AL,* no. 52), but they require a constructive response seeking to transform them into opportunities that can lead to the full reality of marriage and family in conformity with the gospel. "These couples need to be welcomed and guided patiently and discreetly" (*AL,* no. 294); they need to be *accompanied* by church ministers, *integrated* into the church community, and *pointed to* the full reality of Christian marriage. Marriage, we insist, and not "irregular situations" (*AL,* no. 301) like cohabitation and divorce and remarriage, is the focus and goal of every consideration in *Amoris Laetitia.* "Today, more important than the pastoral care of failures is the pastoral effort to strengthen marriages and thus to prevent their breakdown" (*AL,* no. 307). The church, Francis argues, must "never desist from proposing the full ideal of marriage, God's plan in all its grandeur" but neither must it ever desist from *accompanying* "with mercy and patience the eventual stages of personal growth as these progressively appear" (*AL*, no. 307).

Second, the pope sprinkles *Amoris Laetitia* with another firmly Catholic teaching articulated clearly, for example, in the *Catechism of the Catholic Church:* "Imputability and responsibility for an action can be *diminished and even nullified* by ignorance, inadvertence, duress, fear;" and "affective immaturity, force of acquired habit, conditions of anxiety or other psychological or social factors *lessen or even extenuate* moral culpability" and therefore grave sin (*CCC*, nos. 1735, 2352, emphasis added). Taking his stand firmly in that long-established Catholic tradition, Francis specifically draws attention to the nullifying and extenuating circumstances of "dire poverty and great limitations" (*AL*, no. 50), as well as drug use and family and societal violence (*AL*, no. 51). He complains, justly, of those Christians who "feel that it is enough to apply moral laws to those living in 'irregular situations' as if they were *stones to throw at people's lives*. This would bespeak the closed heart of one used to hiding behind the church's teachings, 'sitting on the chair of Moses and judging at times with superiority and superficiality difficult cases and wounded families'" (*AL*, no. 305). At times, he continues, "we find it hard to make room for God's unconditional love in our pastoral activity. We put so many conditions on mercy that we empty it of its concrete meaning and real significance. That is the worst way of watering down the Gospel" (*AL*, no. 311). "It can no longer simply be said," he argues, "that all those in any irregular situation are living in a state of mortal sin and are deprived of sanctifying grace." A cohabitor may be "in a concrete situation which does not allow him or her to act differently and decide otherwise without further sin. . . . Factors may exist which limit the ability to make a decision" (*AL*, no. 301). This all applies to nuptial cohabitors and to the challenging circumstances that may have forced them to begin their marital union before their ceremonial wedding. For those who have qualms about the extenuating force of circumstances, he transmits the judgment of the International Theological Commission expressed in *The Hope of Salvation for Infants Who Die without Being Baptized* to all Catholics: "We should always consider 'inadequate any theological conception which in the end puts in doubt the omnipotence of God and, especially, his mercy'" (*AL*, no. 311).

Third, Francis acknowledges and employs throughout *Amoris Laetitia* the standard Catholic teaching on the authority and inviolability of individual conscience we discussed in Chapter 6. He insists that "we have been called to form consciences not to replace them" (*AL*, no. 37) and that "individual conscience needs to be better incorporated into the Church's praxis in certain situations which do not objectively embody our understanding of marriage" (*AL*, no. 303). The church, he urges, must never desist from proposing the full reality and grandeur of Christian marriage. Neither must it ever desist, however, we urge, from granting the authority and inviolability that Vatican II granted to a properly informed personal conscience. The traditional Catholic approach to making ethical decisions in both grave and non-grave ethical matters acknowledges the authority and inviolability of personal conscience. Cohabitors are not to be forced to act contrary to their conscience or to be restrained from acting in accordance with their conscience, especially in matters religious and, we add, sexual.

Historical Considerations

Since theology is and must be rooted in human reality, the relationship between the secular reality of cohabitation and the religious theology of marriage must be carefully informed by all available and appropriate sources of ethical knowledge. It is that task we seek to fulfill in this chapter by considering the history of marriage in the Christian tradition. Contemporary Christians, especially fundamentalist Christians, both Catholic and Protestant, too easily assume that the nuclear family of the twenty-first century, the so-called traditional family, is both biblical and natural. It is always a surprise to them to discover that it is neither.[39] There is a similar problem with the contemporary phenomenon of cohabitation. Again, it is easily assumed to be a new phenomenon, and again, it is not.

Two imperial Roman definitions have dominated the Catholic discussion of marriage. The first is found in Justinian's *Digesta* (23, 2, 1) and is attributed to the third-century jurist Modestinus: "Marriage is a union of a man and a woman, and a communion of the whole of life, a participation in divine and human law." The second is found in Justinian's *Instituta* (1, 9, 1) and is attributed to Modestinus's contemporary Ulpianus: "Marriage is a union of a man and a woman, embracing an undivided communion of life." These two definitions, which are really no more than descriptions of marriage as culturally practiced in imperial Rome, controlled every subsequent discussion of marriage in the Western tradition. They agree on the bedrock: marriage is a union between a man and a woman embracing the whole of life.[40]

---

[39] See Michael G. Lawler, *Marriage and the Catholic Church: Disputed Questions* (Collegeville, MN: Liturgical Press, 2002), 193–219.

[40] It is of note that in 1996, under the pressure of the movement to legalize same-sex marriages, the United States Congress passed the Defense of Marriage Act, which repeated the assertions of these Roman definitions that marriage was a union between a *man* and a *woman*.

Marriage, in both the Western legal and Christian theological traditions, is the union of a man and a woman. But how is marriage effected in the eyes of these two traditions that up to the Reformation, were identical? In the sixth century Justinian's *Digesta* (35, 1, 15) decreed the Roman tradition: the only thing required for a valid marriage was the mutual consent of both parties. The Northern European custom was different; there penetrative sexual intercourse after free consent made a valid marriage. This different approach to what made marriage valid provoked a widespread legal debate in Europe. Both the Roman and the Northern opinion had long histories, sound rationale, and brilliant proponents in twelfth-century Europe. The debate was ended in mid-century by Gratian, master of the Catholic University of Bologna, who proposed a compromise solution. Mutual consent *initiates* a marriage or makes it *ratum*; subsequent sexual intercourse completes it or makes it *consummatum*. This settlement continues to be enshrined in the *Code of Canon Law*: "A valid marriage between baptized persons is said to be merely ratified *(ratum)* if it is not consummated; ratified and consummated *(ratum et consummatum)* if the spouses have in a human manner engaged together in a conjugal act in itself apt for the generation of offspring" (canon 1061). To be underscored here is the *process* character of valid, indissoluble marriage, *matrimonium ratum et consummatum*, in the Catholic Church, for that process character is central to the argument presented in our next section. The present law requires for valid, indissoluble marriage two distinct acts; first, the publicly given and witnessed mutual free consent of the couple and, second, their subsequent, penetrative sexual intercourse. How the law was followed in practice is a part of both the Western and Catholic historical marital tradition that has long been ignored. It is grossly ahistorical to assume that the current practice and understanding of marriage are what they have always been.

The pre-Tridentine sequence has been well documented in historical sources. Lawrence Stone describes the situation in England and its empire. "Before the tightening up of religious controls over society after the Reformation and the Counter-Reformation in the mid-sixteenth century," he emphasizes, "the formal betrothal ceremony seems to have been at least as important, if not more so, than the wedding. To many, the couple were from that moment man and wife before God."[41] Alan Macfarlane emphasizes that "the engaged lovers before the nuptials were held to be legally husband and wife. It was common for them to begin living together immediately after the betrothal ceremony."[42] In 1754, this marital process changed in

---

[41] Lawrence Stone, *The Family, Sex, and Marriage in England: 1500–1800* (London: Weidenfeld and Nicolson, 1979), 626.

[42] Alan Macfarlane, *Marriage and Love in England: Modes of Reproduction 1300–1840* (Oxford: Blackwell, 1987), 291.

England and, ultimately, in America with the passing of the Hardwicke Act. After Hardwicke, no marriage would be valid in England other than the one performed by an ordained Anglican clergyman, on premises of the Church of England, after the calling of banns for three successive weeks.

The reality of nuptial cohabitation is true for half of contemporary couples in the modern West, Catholic and non-Catholic alike. The sequence for them has reverted to the pre-Tridentine sequence: cohabitation, sexual intercourse, wedding. Neither church nor state was satisfied with this marital process, but neither had any choice but to recognize the validity of marriages thus effected. Church law, accepted by European states as binding in marital affairs, was clear. Free consent to marry, whether articulated publicly or privately, initiated marriage; sexual intercourse after the giving of consent consummated it and made it indissoluble. In the eyes of the church, marriages that were the result of free consent and subsequent consummation had to be held as valid marriages and, therefore, when the spouses were baptized, as also valid sacraments.

The present Catholic process of marriage, specifically the focus on the wedding ceremony as the beginning of marriage, has been in effect, then, since only the sixteenth century. The present practice of the English-American civil law has been in effect only since 1754. In both institutions the present process procedure was instituted, not for some grand theological or legal reason, but to put an end to the scourge of clandestine or secret marriages. Since the *process* of marriage was otherwise prior to Trent and Hardwicke, it is not unthinkable that in the present circumstances it could be otherwise again. The parallel between the pre-Tridentine, pre-Hardwicke, and premodern process and the modern or postmodern process is striking. Premodern betrothal led to full sexual relations and pregnancy, which, in turn, led to indissoluble marriage; modern nuptial cohabitation leads to full sexual relations and, in turn, to indissoluble marriage, with or without pregnancy. Adrian Thatcher insists that in pre-Tridentine and pre-Victorian times "the full sexual experience practiced by betrothed couples was . . . *emphatically premised by the intention to marry.*"[43] In what follows it is only those nuptial cohabitors with an emphatic intention to marry who are our concern, though a full marriage ministry would also seek out non-nuptial cohabitors to prepare them for marriage if and when circumstances permit.

The stumbling block to granting ethical legitimacy to any premarital sexual activity in the Catholic tradition, and in all the Christian traditions, is the exclusive connection they have established between sexual intercourse and marriage. "Every genital act must be within the framework

---

[43] Adrian Thatcher, *Marriage after Modernity: Christian Marriage in Postmodern Times* (Sheffield: Academic Press, 1999), 119.

of marriage" (*PH,* no. 7). Outside of marriage, genital activity is always *objectively* sinful and is *subjectively* sinful when this is consciously understood and intended. That teaching certainly appears to be a major stumbling block to the claim of this chapter that the intimate sexual activity of nuptial cohabitors is ethically legitimate. Why is it, we ask, that sexual activity must always take place exclusively within marriage? We submit that the answer to that question is that sexual intercourse so radically involves all the potential of a human person that it is best expressed and safeguarded in *a stable and lasting relationship* between two people. That stable, lasting, and legally guaranteed relationship has traditionally been called marriage.

What has happened in the modern age is that nuptial cohabitors are beginning their stable marital and sexual relationship prior to their wedding ceremony. They are undoubtedly committed to one another, though they have not articulated that commitment in a public and legal ritual; they fully intend to marry when the restrictions modern society puts upon their right to marry are removed. Their nuptial cohabitation, perhaps even their engaged cohabitation, is the first little step in their journey toward marriage. In the canonico-legal words of the received tradition, their commitment and/or engagement to each other *initiates* their marriage; their subsequent ceremonial wedding, before or after the birth of a child, *consummates* their marriage and makes it indissoluble. Since their commitment to one another initiates their marriage, their cohabitation is no more premarital than that of a pre-Tridentine and pre-Hardwicke couple. Their cohabitation and intercourse are certainly before a ceremonial wedding, but they are far from premarital.

A major change in the approach of Catholic ethicists to sexual sin parallels the change in the approach to marriage.[44] The majority of Catholic ethicists have agreed for years that decisions of morality or immorality in sexual ethics should be based on *interpersonal relationship* and not simply on *physical acts* like masturbation, kissing, petting, premarital, marital, and extramarital sexual intercourse, both heterosexual and homosexual.[45] Lisa Cahill argues: "A truly humane interpretation of procreation, pleasure and intimacy will set their moral implications in the context of enduring personal relationships, not merely individual sexual acts. If human identity

---

[44] See Kevin Kelly, "Cohabitation: Living in Sin or Occasion of Grace?," *The Furrow* 56 (2005): 652–58.

[45] Christine E. Gudorf, *Body, Sex, and Pleasure* (Cleveland: Pilgrim Press, 1994), 14–18; Charles E. Curran, "Sexuality and Sin: A Current Appraisal," in *Dialogue about Catholic Sexual Teaching: Readings in Moral Theology No. 8*, ed. Charles E. Curran and Richard A. McCormick, 405–17 (New York; Paulist Press, 1993), 411–14; Vincent Genovesi, *In Pursuit of Love: Catholic Morality and Human Sexuality* (Wilmington, DE: Glazier, 1987), 154–55; Xavier Lacroix, *Le Corps de Chair: les dimensions éthique, esthétique, et spirituelle de l'amour* (Paris: Editions du Cerf, 1992), 346–50.

and virtue in general are established diachronically, then this will also be true of sexual flourishing."[46] Serious sexual immorality, traditionally called mortal sin, is no longer decided on the basis of an individual act against "nature," that is, the biological, physical, natural processes common to all animals. It is decided on the basis of human goods and human relationship built upon them. Cahill suggests such human goods as "equality, intimacy, and fulfillment as moral criteria."[47] We would add the virtues of love and justice to make more fully explicit what she clearly intends. Sexuality has three bodily meanings: intimacy of bodily contact, even bodily interpenetration; pleasure; and reproduction or procreation. All of these meanings are realized and developed over time and in the social institutions that a given society recognizes. Unethical or less than ethical behavior is defined not exclusively by any sexual act related to these three, but rather by any less than loving, just, equal, faithful, compassionate, and mutually fulfilling act.

In the case of nuptial cohabitors, a man and a woman who are deeply committed to one another and to a future marriage when circumstances permit it, and whose nuptial sexual intercourse takes place in this context of personal commitment to a future marriage, the moral theological argument proceeds along these lines. A man and a woman have a fundamental freedom to marry, but modern society has established socioeconomic conditions for marriage that they are presently unable to achieve. These circumstances surrounding the intercourse of this couple who are deeply committed to each other, who are in right relationship to both one another and God, and who fully intend to marry, Philip Keane writes, "may render their premarital intercourse an ontic evil but not a moral evil." That such intercourse is not a moral evil would appear to be true especially, Keane argues, "when the committed couple whose rights are unreasonably prejudiced by society do not experience themselves as genuinely free to marry and to abstain from intercourse until marriage."[48]

We accept the probative value of this argument. In the proposal we are presenting, however, the mutually committed nuptial cohabitors are already, if inchoately, married, and their intercourse, therefore, is not strictly pre-marital but inchoately marital, as it was in the pre-Tridentine Catholic Church and pre-Hardwicke England. Our proposal envisages a marital journey that is initiated by mutual commitment and consent, is lived in mutual love, justice, equality, intimacy, fidelity, and fulfillment in a nuptial

---

[46] Lisa Sowle Cahill, *Sex, Gender, and Christian Ethics* (New York: Cambridge University Press, 1996), 112.

[47] Ibid., 11.

[48] Philip Keane, *Sexual Morality: A Catholic Perspective* (New York: Paulist Press, 1977), 107.

cohabitation pointed to a wedding which consummates the *process* of becoming married in a mutually just, human, and public manner. In such a process, we believe, sexual intercourse meets the legitimate Catholic and social requirement that the sexual act must take place exclusively within a stable marital environment.

Catechumenate for Marriage

English expert on the theology of Christian marriage Adrian Thatcher proposes a "catechumenate for marriage."[49] We extend his proposal to propose that any catechumenate for marriage should embrace nuptial cohabitors. A catechumenate for marriage would be one way for the church to respond to Pope Francis's directive that it should *accompany* nuptial cohabitors, *integrate* them into the church, and *lead them* to the fullness of marriage, emphasizing the importance of marriage by establishing a mandatory preparation for it (*AL*, no. 204–16). Among other things, such a catechumenate would seek to elucidate a historically conscious view of, first, marriage, and then, marriage as sacrament. A catechumenate for marriage is, of course, an alternative name for what is commonly called marriage preparation, but casting marriage preparation as a catechumenate situates it in a long-established Catholic catechumenal tradition.[50] A catechumen is a person receiving religious instruction in the Catholic faith with a view to being baptized, and the catechumenate is the body of catechumens awaiting baptism and full initiation into the Catholic Church. Historically, catechumens preparing for baptism in the Catholic Church were always considered already Christians, because they had already made their commitment in faith to Christ. A catechumen who died before water baptism would, therefore, be given a Christian burial.[51] Though the sacrament of water baptism had not been received, baptism of desire had been (*CCC*, nos. 1258–59), and the grace of God was already offered to the catechumen in the begun but not completed journey of the catechumenate. Nuptial cohabitors, who have committed to each other in a subsequent marriage, have received, we argue, marriage of desire, and they are, therefore, the

---

[49] Adrian Thatcher, *Living Together and Christian Ethics* (Cambridge: Cambridge University Press, 2002), 237–53.

[50] Though our focus in this chapter is on specifically nuptial cohabitors readying themselves for marriage, there is no theological reason, we believe, why non-cohabiting couples readying themselves for marriage should not also be required to participate in the catechumenate for marriage, just as they are presently required to participate in a program of marriage preparation. Even cohabiting couples uncertain of their marriage intentions could be embraced into and thus accompanied in the catechumenate.

[51] Thatcher, *Living Together and Christian Ethics*, 242.

recipients of all the marital graces that God assuredly gives to all believers. The seven sacraments are believed to be channels of grace in the Catholic tradition, but they are not believed to be the only channels of grace.

According to Thatcher, the term *catechumenate* when used in relation to marriage "is intended to emphasize the parallels between the 'in-between' state of Christians seeking baptism, and the 'in-between' state of persons who are no longer single and who wish to bind themselves to one another unreservedly in marriage."[52] This "in-between" state is reflected in the committed, interpersonal relationship of nuptial cohabiting couples. Implementing the catechumenate for marriage "requires a paradigm shift, from treating the ceremony as the beginning of marriage, to treating it as the confirmation, celebration, and blessing of it."[53] Olivier Bressoud argues, and we agree, that it is the gradual maturation of both their relationship and their faith during their mentored nuptial cohabitation that permits a couple's relationship to attain the fullness of marriage and therefore also of sacrament. This point of view makes the sacrament of marriage an important and "privileged stage" in the journey toward the fullness of marriage.[54]

Conclusion

In this chapter we considered the widespread phenomenon of cohabitation in the contemporary world and how it parallels the phenomenon of cohabitation in both the pre-Tridentine church and pre-Victorian England and America. We considered also Pope Francis's crucial distinction between non-nuptial cohabitors (cohabitors not interested in marrying one another) and nuptial cohabitors (cohabitors who are committed to marry one another but cannot do so now because of restricting circumstance). We examined also his instruction to the church that cohabitors are not to be isolated from the church but are to be "welcomed and guided patiently and discreetly" (*AL*, no. 294). They are to be accompanied in their premarital lives by church ministers, instructed in the full grandeur of Christian marriage, integrated into Christian marital life, and pointed to the full reality of Christian marriage when circumstances permit it. As a strategy for the accompaniment, instruction, and integration of nuptial cohabitors, we proposed a marital catechumenate, which we intend to be understood in parallel with the baptismal catechumenate. Ultimately, we propose that an option for the *process of marrying* in the Catholic Church, a process that follows Popes John Paul II's and Francis's "law of gradualness" that

---

[52] Ibid., 252.

[53] Ibid.

[54] Bressoud, "Église catholique et couples non mariés," 108.

acknowledges that the human being "knows, loves, and accomplishes moral good by different stages of growth" (*FC,* no. 34; *AL,* no. 295). We describe that process schematically as follows.

Enrollment in the Catechumenate. Enrollment, which could be either verbal or written, would be witnessed on behalf of the church community and, as public betrothal did in the pre-Tridentine church, would confer on the couple the status of committed, catechumenal spouses with all the rights the church grants to full spouses, including the right to sexual intercourse and procreation. Theologically, the time of the marriage catechumenate would be as much a time of God's graciousness as the baptismal catechumenate. As baptismal catechumens are already inchoate Christians, so also marriage catechumens are already inchoate spouses.

Nuptial cohabitation. In this period the couple would live together as inchoate spouses, would have marital intercourse, including sexual intercourse, with each other in a community-approved, stable environment, and would begin the lifelong process of establishing their marital relationship as one of mutual love, justice, equality, intimacy, fidelity, and fulfillment. This inchoate-marriage period would be a perfect time for the church community to assist the couple in honing both their relationship and their faith with an ongoing catechumenate or marriage preparation program aimed precisely at this maturation.[55] This pre-wedding period of marital instruction is the marriage catechumenate, analogous to the established period of doctrinal instruction required of catechumens prior to their baptism.[56] It is theologically unthinkable that either catechumenate could happen without the grace of God. Given the expected lifelong character of Christian marriage, the marriage catechumenate is vitally important; social-scientific data indicate that committed relationship is the core of long-term spousal and parental success and a reality that can be dangerously flawed by the self-selecting factors that directed the couple to cohabitation in the first place.

Fertility. We are fully cognizant that this part of our proposal will cause unease among Christians of all denominations, for sexuality and sexual activity have been treated with suspicion in the Catholic Church since the days of the early, Stoic-influenced Christians. That suspicion led to the exclusive focus on procreation that once characterized church teaching and

---

[55] See Center for Marriage and Family, *Marriage Preparation in the Catholic Church;* Scott M. Stanley, "Making a Case for Premarital Education," *Family Relations* 50 (2001): 272–80.

[56] For suggestions for the content to be covered in the marriage catechumenate, see Michael G. Lawler and Gail S. Risch, "Time, Sex, and Money: The First Five Years of Marriage," *America* (May 14, 2001), 20–22. The nature and meaning of the *sacrament* of marriage should be added to the suggestions found there.

continues to characterize it officially, even now, when moral approaches among many of its leading ethicists have changed. We have argued, in concert with other Catholic scholars, that this focus on procreation needs to yield to another focus, namely, the focus on the interpersonal relationship that is at the very root of all spousal and parental success in marriage and family. We believe that the moral implications of sexual intercourse, sexual pleasure, and procreation leading to parenthood are best set in the context of a committed interpersonal *relationship* and not in the context of mere sexual *acts*. The context of the nuptial cohabitors with whom we are concerned in this proposal is a context of committed, stable, and intentionally lifelong relationship. Following the public enrollment, it is a context that meets the Catholic requirement that sexual intercourse be exclusively within the stable relationship of marriage. It is also a context in which the three dimensions of sexual activity we have mentioned—personal and not just bodily intercourse, mutual pleasure, and procreation leading to not only the biological birth of a child but also long-term motherhood and fatherhood—might intersect to the benefit of the marital relationship. Parenthood, particularly *shared* parenthood, expresses and realizes the union of the spouses as much as sexual intercourse and pleasure. In our proposal it can be the task of nuptial cohabitors as much as of married couples in the received tradition.

Wedding. There will come a time under the grace of God when the committed nuptial cohabitors have overcome the restrictions imposed on them by society. There will come a time under the grace of God when their relationship has reached such a plateau of interpersonal communion that they will wish to ceremonialize their loving, just, and equal relationship. That is the time for their wedding, when, with their families, friends, and Christian community, they will publicly renew their consent and commitment to each other and celebrate their union for what it has gradually become, namely, a visible symbol or sacrament of the loving union between God and God's people, between Christ and Christ's church. Their wedding can then be considered the consummation of their marriage, the consummation of a relationship they have sought to make as humane and as Christian as possible. The gradual process of marrying would then be complete: *matrimonium ratum* would become *matrimonium ratum et consummatum*.

Questions for Reflection

- What do you understand by the word *cohabitation*? In your judgment, what are the reasons for the great growth of cohabitation in the Western world?

- This chapter distinguished between *nuptial* and *non-nuptial* cohabitors. Does your experience confirm or reject this as a realistic distinction? Is it true that cohabitation before marriage increases the risk of divorce after marriage?
- What do you understand by commitment? What are the requirements for and implications of commitment for every relationship, including marriage?
- Has the legal wedding ceremony as we know it today in the Western world always been practiced in the Catholic Church in its present form? If not, why and when did it arise? How did the early practice of betrothal fit into the Catholic notion of marriage?
- What are the implications of our distinction between classicism and historical consciousness for the sacrament of marriage?
- What is your judgment about our suggestion that *nuptial cohabitation*, perhaps following engagement or betrothal, is a beginning stage in the process of becoming married and is a sufficiently stable marital stage for sexual intercourse to be ethical? Would you personally be interested in enrolling in a marriage catechumenate, with or without the betrothal ceremony we suggest?

Suggested Readings

Gudorf, Christine E. *Body, Sex, and Pleasure*. Cleveland: Pilgrim Press, 1994).

Kelly, Kevin. "Cohabitation: Living in Sin or Occasion of Grace?" *The Furrow* 56 (2005): 652–58.

Lawler, Michael G., and Gail S. Risch. "A Betrothal Proposal." *US Catholic* (June 2007): 18–22.

Salzman, Todd A.. and Michael G. Lawler. "*Amoris Laetitia* and the Development of Catholic Theological Ethics: A Reflection." In *A Point of No Return? Amoris Laetitia on Marriage, Divorce and Remarriage*, edited by Thomas Knieps-Port le Roi. Münster, Germany: LIT Verlag, 2017.

Thatcher, Adrian. *Living Together and Christian Ethics*. Cambridge: Cambridge University Press, 2002.

10

Homosexuality

Learning Objectives

- Understand the terms *sexual orientation, homosexuality,* and *homosexual.*
- Understand how to interpret and apply scripture to the ethical issue of homosexuality.
- Explain and critically analyze magisterial teaching on the immorality of homosexual acts.
- Explain how experience can influence your ethical evaluation of same-sex marriage.
- Articulate your understanding of Pope Francis's definition of marriage in *Amoris Laetitia* and explain its ethical implications for same-sex marriage.

The ethical issue of homosexual acts is continuing to divide Christians and their churches today at a time when they should be in undivided solidarity. The received tradition of the Catholic Church, expressed by the Congregation for the Doctrine of the Faith (CDF) in *Persona Humana* and in the *Catechism of the Catholic Church,* condemns homosexual acts as "intrinsically disordered" (*PH,* no. 8; *CCC,* no. 2357) and gravely unethical and does so on the basis of three sources of ethical knowledge: scripture, tradition narrowly defined as magisterial teaching, and tradition broadly defined as *sensus fidelium* (sense of the faithful), which includes experience. First, the teaching of scripture in which such acts "are condemned as a serious depravity and even presented as the sad consequence of rejecting God"; second, "the constant teaching of the Magisterium"; third, "the moral sense of the Christian people" (*PH,* no. 8). In this chapter we critically analyze each of these sources and attempt to clarify them so that readers might be

231

sufficiently informed to make a conscientious ethical judgment about both the homosexual condition and homosexual acts.

Having already established the scriptures as a source of ethical knowledge, we first examine the scriptural texts the CDF advances as showing a clear consistency "for judging the moral issue of homosexual behavior."[1] It lists the texts in which this clear consistency is found: Genesis 19:1–11; Leviticus 18:22 and 20:13; Romans 1:26–7; 1 Corinthians 6:9; and 1 Timothy 1:10.[2] We believe that, when read as the Catholic Church requires them to be read, that is, according to *Dei Verbum,* in the "literary forms" of the writer's "time and culture" (*DV,* no. 12)[3] "contextually" as Gerald Coleman puts it,[4] the texts that are advanced as a clear and unambiguous foundation of the Catholic teaching on homosexual acts are far from clear and unambiguous. They are, rather, complex and socio-historically conditioned literary forms that demand careful historical analysis, which then raises questions in the informed and inquiring theological mind. Three questions are central to this issue. First, does the Bible say anything about homosexuality as we understand it today? Second, if it does say something, what does it say, and what does it mean? Third, can the Bible speak to and enlighten the anguish and confusion that characterize contemporary Christian dialogue about homosexuality? Ultimately, the real issue here is not the issue of homosexuality and what the Bible says or does not say about it, but rather of how to read the Bible in order to inform our contemporary Christian ethical lives. We now confront our three questions in turn.

Homosexual Orientation and the Bible

The first question, does the Bible say anything about homosexuality as we understand it today, is a question of definition. What do we mean today by the words *homosexuality* and *homosexual*? The answer to that question is embedded in what contemporary science and the Magisterium of the Catholic Church now take for granted, namely, the existence in some men and women of a homosexual *orientation.*[5] In contemporary scientific and

---

[1] *Letter to the Bishops of the Catholic Church on the Pastoral Care of Homosexual Persons*, 5, *AAS* 79 (1987): 545.

[2] Ibid., 546.

[3] See also Pius XII, *Divino Afflante Spiritu* (September 30, 1943).

[4] Gerald D. Coleman, "The Vatican Statement on Homosexuality," *Theological Studies* 48 (1987): 727–34. A similar point is made by Richard B. Hays, "Relations Natural and Unnatural: A Response to John Boswell's Exegesis of Romans 1," *Journal of Religious Ethics* 14 (1986): 184–215.

[5] See Pim Pronk, *Against Nature? Types of Moral Argumentation regarding Homosexuality* (Grand Rapids, MI: Eerdmans, 1993); Richard C. Pillard and J. Michael Bailey,

theological-ethical literature, the noun *homosexuality* and the adjective *homosexual* are used to refer to a person's *psychosexual condition*, produced by a mix of genetic, psychological, and social "loading."[6] As we discussed in Chapter 4, sexual orientation, in general, is defined as "the sustained erotic attraction to members of one's own gender, the opposite gender, or both—homosexual, heterosexual, or bisexual respectively."[7] Homosexual orientation, specifically, is "a *condition* characterized by an emotional and psycho-sexual propensity towards others of the same sex,"[8] and a homosexual is "a person who feels a most urgent sexual desire which *in the main* is directed towards gratification with the same sex."[9] In its modern, scientific connotation, homosexuality is a way of *being* before it is a way of *behaving*. Stephen Donaldson, president of Stop Prisoner Rape, was therefore correct in 1994 to challenge the *New York Times'* characterization of rape within American prisons as "homosexual rape" and to point out that prison rape is predominantly "heterosexual rape," that is, rape committed by those who have a heterosexual orientation.[10]

Neither the Bible nor Christian tradition rooted in it prior to the twentieth century ever considered the homosexual condition; they took for granted that everyone was heterosexual. To look for any mention in the biblical texts of what today is called "homosexual orientation" is simply anachronism. One might as well search the Bible for advice on how to deal with Amazon or Google. The biblical passages most frequently cited as condemning *homosexuality* actually condemn homosexual *behaviors*, and they condemn these behaviors specifically as a *perversion* of the heterosexual condition they assume to be the natural condition of every human being. In its modern meaning, homosexuality is not a perversion of the heterosexual condition because homosexuals, both gays and lesbians, by

---

"A Biological Perspective on Sexual Orientation," *Clinical Sexuality* 18 (1995): 1–14; Lee Ellis and Linda Ebertz, *Sexual Orientation: Toward Biological Understanding* (Westport, CT: Praeger, 1997); Richard C. Friedman and Jennifer I. Downey, *Sexual Orientation and Psychoanalysis: Sexual Science and Clinical Practice* (New York: Columbia University Press, 2002); CDF, *Letter to the Bishops of the Catholic Church on the Pastoral Care of Homosexual Persons*; USCCB (United States Conference of Catholic Bishops), *Always Our Children* (Washington, DC: USCCB, 1997).

[6] This terminology articulates our position that homosexual orientation is neither exclusively genetic nor exclusively social in origin. See John E. Perito, *Contemporary Catholic Sexuality: What Is Taught and What Is Practiced* (New York: Crossroad, 2003), 96.

[7] Pillard and Bailey, "A Biological Perspective on Sexual Orientation," 1.

[8] Derrick Sherwin Bailey, *Homosexuality and the Western Christian Tradition* (New York: Darton, Longmans, Green, 1955), x, emphasis added.

[9] Donald W. Cory, *The Homosexual in America* (New York: Julian Press, 1951), 8.

[10] See Maria Harris and Gabriel Moran, "Homosexuality: A Word Not Written," in *Homosexuality and Christian Faith: Questions of Conscience for the Churches*, ed. Walter Wink (Minneapolis: Fortress Press, 1999), 33.

natural orientation, do not share the heterosexual condition. Homosexuality is, rather, an *inversion* of the heterosexual condition that psychosexual homosexuals, by no choice of their own, do not naturally share, and they cannot be held morally accountable for something they did not choose.[11] The context in which both Old and New Testaments condemn homosexual acts includes a universal and false assumption, shaped by the socio-historical conditions of the times in which they were written, that all human beings naturally have a heterosexual orientation and that, therefore, any homosexual behavior is a perversion of nature and thus immoral. Since that biblical assumption is now scientifically shown to be incorrect, the Bible has little to contribute to the discussion of the homosexual condition and homosexuals as we understand them today. That conclusion will become clearer when we consider our second question: What does the Bible say about homosexual behavior, and what does it mean when it says that?[12] We might add, with theologian Edward Vacek, that the Bible contains many questionable ethical teachings, such as about sex during menstruation, stoning adulterers, women's subservient roles, slavery, and not eating pork, all of which have been rejected by modern Catholic theological ethics.[13]

Interpreting the Bible on Homosexuality

The Old Testament

The single most influential biblical text leading to the condemnation of homosexual acts is probably the *interpretation* given to the biblical story of Sodom. Christian churches have consistently taught that the destruction of Sodom was caused by the unethical male homosexual behaviors practiced there, and understandably Christians have believed what their churches taught them. Two reasonable questions may be raised with respect to this widespread interpretation, the first about its accuracy, and the second about its basis in the biblical text. Our contextual exegesis will show that the interpretation of the Sodom story as condemning homosexual acts as

---

[11] See *Humanae Vitae*, no. 8; and USCCB, *Always Our Children*.

[12] Our argument in what follows is in full agreement with Gareth Moore: "There are no good arguments, from either scripture or natural law, against what have come to be known as homosexual relationships. The arguments put forward to show that such relationships are immoral are bad. Either their premises are false or the argument by means of which the conclusion is drawn from them itself contains errors." See Gareth Moore, *A Question of Truth: Christianity and Homosexuality* (London: Continuum, 2003), x. See also Robin Scroggs, *The New Testament and Homosexuality* (Philadelphia: Fortress Press, 1983).

[13] See Edward Vacek, "A Christian Homosexuality," *Commonweal* (December 5, 1980): 681–84.

understood today is not accurate and is not supported by a reading of the text in its socio-historical context.

The biblical story is not as straightforward as it appears to the untrained reader. The context of the story and its meaning begin in chapter 18 with the story of Abraham's hospitality to "three men," one of whom is soon identified as "the Lord" (Gen 18:20–22). Three "men" pass by Abraham's house on their way to Sodom, and Abraham offers the strangers the hospitality required by the Levitical law: "When a stranger sojourns with you in your land, you shall not do him wrong" (Lev 20:33–34). Abraham invites the strangers to his house. "Let a little water be brought and wash your feet . . . while I fetch a morsel of bread that you may refresh yourselves" (Gen 18:4–5). Abraham has his wife Sara bake cakes for them. He kills a calf "tender and good" for them, and he serves them himself. Abraham's hospitality and goodness are established by his reception of the three strangers, and so too will his nephew Lot's be established in the sequel. After they were fed, two of the men left for Sodom, while the Lord remained behind with Abraham.

"Two angels came to Sodom in the evening and Lot was sitting in the gate of Sodom" (19:1). Lot offered the two angels the required hospitality, bringing them to his house and feeding them, but before they retired for the night the men of Sodom surrounded the house and called for Lot to bring the two men out "that we may know them [*yadha*]" (19:5). That word *yadha* is critical for understanding what the men of Sodom were asking. *Yadha* is the ordinary Hebrew word for the English *know*, but it is also used on occasion to mean specifically sexual intercourse. Which meaning is intended in this text? The *Hebrew-English Lexicon of the Old Testament* notes that *yadha* is used 943 times, and in only 10 of those time is it used with any sexual connotation. Taking his stance on this datum, G. A. Barton argues that in this text it is not clear that *yadha* is used with any sexual connotation and that it could just as easily mean that the men of Sodom simply wished to get to know the two strangers.[14] We do not find Barton's interpretation convincing. The sexual meaning of the word seems to be insinuated by two facts. First, if all the men of Sodom wanted to do was to learn the identity of the strangers, why would Lot beg them "do not act so wickedly" (Gen 19:7); second, the word *yadha* is used in a clearly sexual sense when Lot offers his two daughters to the crowd: "Look, I have two daughters who have not known a man *(yadha)*, let me bring them out to you. . . . Only do nothing to these men *for they have come under the*

---

[14] G. A. Barton, "Sodomy," in *Encyclopedia of Religion and Ethics*, ed. James Hastings (Whitefish: Kessinger Publishing, 2003), 11, 672. Bailey advances the same argument; the men of Sodom simply wanted to know the identity of the strangers (Bailey, *Homosexuality in the Western Christian Tradition*, 1–6).

shelter of my roof" (Gen 19:8, emphasis added).We believe there is clear insinuation of homosexual intent against the two strangers at Sodom; this, however, does not necessarily mean that the sin of the men of Sodom was the sin of homosexual behavior.

The clearer sin in the Hebrew context is the sin of inhospitality. That Lot is concerned about hospitality is made evident in the phrase we have emphasized above, "for they have come under the shelter of my roof," that is, under the shelter of my hospitality, which embraces protecting them against the perverted sexual designs of the crowd. The men of Sodom are as bound by the law of hospitality as is Lot, but they demonstrate their wickedness by not living up to the law. If *yadha* is to be understood in its sexual connotation, and we are convinced it is, then the men of Sodom demonstrate the extent of their inhospitality by seeking violent *homosexual* rape of the strangers. If any action is condemned in the text, it is the crime of homosexual rape carried out by perverted *heterosexual*—not homosexual—men. If the act of homosexual rape carried out by *perverted heterosexual* men is condemned in this text, that is a long way from a condemnation of loving homosexual acts of men with a homosexual orientation.

The interpretation of the text we propose is supported by the fact that in the rest of the Old Testament, where Sodom is regularly mentioned, not once is its crime said to be homosexual behavior. Ezekiel describes it as "pride, surfeit of food, and prosperous ease, but did not aid the poor and the needy" (10:49). Isaiah advises the rulers of Sodom to "seek justice, correct oppression, defend the fatherless, plead for the widow" (1:17). Wisdom explicitly charges both the men of Sodom and the Egyptians with inhospitality: "Others [the men of Sodom] had refused to receive strangers when they came to them, but these [the Egyptians] made slaves of guests who were their benefactors" (Wis 19:14). For Christians, a prime argument in support of our interpretation that the sin of Sodom is inhospitality is Jesus's mention of Sodom in the same breath as the inhospitality accorded his disciples. "Whenever you enter a town and they do not receive you, say 'Even the dust of your town that clings to our feet we wipe off against you. . . . ' I tell you it shall be more tolerable on that day for Sodom than for that town" (Luke 10:10–12). Jesus also makes hospitality or inhospitality a major cause of salvation or damnation in the great judgment scene in Matthew 25:34–46.

If the Sodom story is ultimately about inhospitable and not homosexual acts, no such reservation can be made about the prescriptions of the Holiness Code in Leviticus. "You shall not lie with a male as with a woman; it is an abomination" (18:22). What the Holiness Code says could not be clearer: *homosexual behavior* of men presumed to be heterosexual is an abomination. Note that it is *male* acts that are prohibited in this text; female acts are not part of the prohibition. In English the word *you* in "you shall not lie" applies indiscriminately to both males and females; in Hebrew the word that is used is used only of males. It is the homosexual acts of heterosexual men that Leviticus says are an abomination, and that restriction yields some insight into both the socio-historical context in which Leviticus says what it says and what it might mean when it says it.

The first thing to be noted about the Hebrew context of the time is bad biology. The ancient Hebrew, Greek, and Roman understanding was that the male provided seed that contained the whole of life; the female simply provided the ground or the field in which the seed was sown to develop into a fully-fledged human.[15] To spill that seed anywhere it could not develop properly, on the ground or in a male body, for instance, was regarded as tantamount to murder, and murder was always held to be an abomination. Those guilty of murder suffered the same penalty as our present text prescribes for men who are heterosexual but performing homosexual acts, namely, death (Lev 24:17, 21; Num 35:30; Ex 20:13). Since they waste no life, and perhaps also because women in that patriarchal society simply do not count, heterosexual females' homosexual acts are not considered worthy of consideration in the Holiness Code or anywhere else in the Old Testament. The fact that it is only homosexual acts by heterosexual men that are declared an abomination introduces another contextual consideration, that of male honor and the actions appropriate to it.

Extended family was and is "the primary economic, religious, educational, and social network"[16] in Mediterranean society. Within the social network, family was the locus of honor, carried exclusively by males, particularly the patriarch who headed the family and to all intents and purposes owned the females in it, whether they were wives or daughters. For a male to "lie with" another male, that is to act passively and allow himself to be penetrated like a female, compromised male honor, not only that of the male being penetrated but also that of every male in the family or clan. The passivity of a male, who was expected to be active in all things, including the sexual, was always abhorred and dishonorable. In such a socio-historical context, homosexual acts by heterosexual men would be

---

[15] For Greek society, see Paige duBois, *Sowing the Body: Psychoanalysis and Ancient Representations of Women* (Chicago: University of Chicago Press, 1988), 39–85. For Jewish society, see Sirach 26:19; *Mishna*, Ketuboth, 1, 6. For Muslim society, see Carol Delaney, *The Seed and the Soil: Gender and Cosmology in Turkish Village Society* (Berkeley and Los Angeles: University of California Press, 1991).

[16] Bruce J. Malina and Richard L. Rohrbaugh, *Social Science Commentary on the Synoptic Gospels* (Minneapolis: Fortress Press, 1992), 202. See also Carolyn Osiek and David L. Balch, *Families in the New Testament World: Households and House Churches* (Louisville, KY: Westminster/John Knox Press, 1997).

an abomination, not because they are homosexual acts but because they are dishonorable acts that threatened the patriarchal and hierarchical sexual arrangement that pervaded the Old Testament.[17]

What, however, of an utterly different social context, a context in which not every human being is presumed to be by nature heterosexual, but some are known to be by nature homosexual; a context in which honor is not a dominant concern; a context in which male and female are understood to contribute equally to the procreation of new life? In such a context male homosexual behavior need not be judged as dishonorable and ipso facto unethical. Just and loving homosexual behavior, flowing from an innate homosexual orientation, cannot be regarded as a perversion of a universal heterosexual condition and, therefore, cannot be judged ipso facto unethical; and the spilling of male semen or seed would no longer be regarded as the spilling of life, murder, and an abomination. In short, when the interpreter considers what the Bible says about homosexual behavior by men presumed to be heterosexual and the socio-historical context in which it says it, it is difficult to consider the Bible as saying anything more instructive in the present socio-historical context than what it says about kosher laws. "The hare, because it chews the cud but does not part the hoof, is unclean to you. And the swine, because it parts the hoof and is cloven-footed but does not chew the cud, is unclean to you. Of their flesh you shall not eat and their carcasses you shall not touch; they are unclean to you" (Lev 11: 6–8). No Catholic ethicist would ever think of those biblical prohibitions when dining on rabbit stew or succulent pork chops. As homosexual orientation is understood today, male homosexual behavior may or may not be moral, but contemporary judgment of its morality cannot be based on what the Old Testament says about it in the context of its socio-historical time and place.

The New Testament

Many Christians consider the Old Testament to have been superseded by the New Testament and they give more credence to what the New Testament says about homosexual acts than what the Old Testament says. We must, therefore, now consider what many believe to be the centerpiece of the New Testament on homosexual behavior, namely, Paul's letter to the Romans. It is important, again, to note the context of Paul's remarks,

---

[17] The same system of honor and shame existed among the Greeks. Though it was acceptable for a young boy to behave passively sexually, it was not acceptable for an adult man. Taking the passive, female role in sexual activity brought him dishonor and negatively affected his status and role in society. See Michel Foucault, *The Use of Pleasure: The History of Sexuality,* vol. 2, trans. Robert Hurley (New York: Pantheon, 1985), 187–225.

which is an attack, not on homosexual acts in particular, but on degenerate, idolatrous, Gentile society in general. Paul makes the standard Jewish accusations about Gentile idolatry, as when he says that "what can be known about God is plain to them [Gentiles] because God has shown it to them" (Rom 1:20). But, however plain the existence of the true God of Israel might be, Gentiles did not acknowledge God, they "did not honor God as God or give thanks to God." Rather, "they exchanged the glory of the immortal God for images resembling a mortal human being or birds or four-footed animals or reptiles" (Rom 1:23). What is radically wrong with Gentiles, Paul says, is that they are idolaters, and he describes the behavior of such idolaters. *Because* they are idolaters, in some divine punishment "God *gave them up* in the lusts of their heart to impurity, to the dishonoring of their bodies.... God *gave them up* to dishonorable passions. . . . God *gave them up* to a base mind and to improper conduct" (Rom 1:24–28). What are presumed to be impure homosexual acts, though the text does not mention such acts, performed again by *perverted heterosexuals*, are God's punishment on Gentiles for their idolatry. But it is Gentile *idolatry* that is directly at stake in this Pauline text, and the gay and lesbian acts of perverted heterosexuals to which it is presumed to lead, not the gay and lesbian acts of those who by nature have a homosexual orientation and the just and loving homosexual acts in which it might issue.[18] Paul is not talking of, because he has no concept of, relationships between modern homosexual couples who might justly love one another and might be committed to one another as faithfully as any heterosexual couple. The condemnation of the homosexual actions of perverted heterosexuals does not easily translate across time to the condemnation of the just and loving actions of those whose condition is by nature homosexual.

The two remaining texts cited by the CDF as solid foundation for the church's teaching on the immorality of homosexual acts, 1 Corinthians 6:9–10 and 1 Timothy 1:10, present a serious difficulty of translation, and we shall not consider them here.[19] We lose nothing with this approach because they add nothing to what we have already discovered, that the Christian scriptures condemn as unethical the homosexual actions of *perverted heterosexuals*, not the loving sexual actions of those who *by nature*, not by any choice of their own, share the homosexual condition.

---

[18] See Dale B. Martin, "Heterosexism and the Interpretation of Romans 1:18–31," *Biblical Interpretation* 3 (1995): 332–55. For a contrary reading, see Richard B. Hays, "Relations Natural and Unnatural," 184–215.

[19] For our exegesis of these two texts, see Todd A. Salzman and Michael G. Lawler, *The Sexual Person: Toward a Renewed Catholic Anthropology* (Washington, DC: Georgetown University Press, 2008), 222–23.

The Bible and Contemporary Discourse on Homosexuality

This leads us to our third question and its answer: Can the Bible speak to the confusion that characterizes contemporary Christians with respect to homosexuality? It should first be noted that homosexual action is not a prominent biblical concern. There is no mention of it in Israel's earliest moral codes, there is nothing about it in the Decalogue, the Gospels record no saying of Jesus about it; there is not even a word for it in either Hebrew or Greek. Bruce Malina's conclusion about Paul's text in Romans is difficult to gainsay. "If we return to the twenty-first century after this excursion into the first century we can see that Paul's perspectives, if taken consistently, simply do not make sense."[20] Paul does not live in our context, in which homosexuality is scientifically recognized as a *natural* condition; we do not live in Paul's context of bad biology and cultural value; and the ancient context does not translate easily to the modern context on most issues, including homosexuality. The same conclusion applies to the even more distant texts of the Old Testament. They are articulated in the same context as Paul's texts. Everyone is presumed to be heterosexual and, therefore, any male homosexual act is a freely chosen perversion; the male is the sole source of life and, therefore, any spilling of the seed in a place where it cannot develop is murder and an abomination; the male is also the source of honor in the society, and for a male to behave as a female, sexually or otherwise, shames not only him but every other male in the family or corporate clan. "The Old Testament narratives about the men of Sodom in Genesis 19 and the Levite's concubine in Judges 19 are more concerned with egregious failures in hospitality and gang rape than with homosexuality *per se*."[21]

The Christian traditions today are moving away from a *biblical rules* approach to ethical judgments and are exploring a more profound inter-relationship among rules, norms, values, virtues, and *persons*. There is a movement away from the simplistic judgment that what the Bible says is definitive for all time and is, therefore, the universal ethical norm. Contemporarily, Lisa Cahill puts the matter succinctly. "Realizing the impossibility of transposing rules from biblical times to our own, interpreters look for larger themes, values or ideals which can inform moral reflection without

---

[20] Bruce J. Malina, "The New Testament and Homosexuality," in *Sexual Diversity and Catholicism: Toward the Development of Moral Theology*, ed. Patricia Beattie Jung with Joseph Andrew Coray (Collegeville, MN: Liturgical Press, 2001), 168.

[21] Daniel Harrington and James Keenan, *Jesus and Virtue Ethics: Building Bridges between New Testament Studies and Moral Theology* (Lanham, MD: Sheed and Ward, 2002), 166.

determining specific practices in advance."[22] Victor Furnish articulates well the larger theme that we can abstract from both the Old and New Testament texts on homosexual behavior. "Paul, in common with the tradition by which he was influenced and in accord with the wisdom of his day, saw the wickedness of homosexual practice to adhere in its lust and its *perversion* of the natural order."[23] Those judgments against uncontrolled lust of heterosexual men and a perversion of the natural order cannot automatically be applied to just and loving homosexual acts in persons whose natural sexual orientation is to persons of the same sex. Richard Sparks's judgment is also ours: "On scriptural evidence alone we are left short of a clear and clean condemnation of what might be called committed or covenantal homosexual acts."[24]

Magisterial Teaching on Homosexual Acts and Relationships

Our reading of the biblical texts, which can be extended to the equally socially constructed ethical texts of the magisterium, points to the direction of ethical discernment we propose as a way to arrive at a conscientious judgment about the morality or immorality of homosexual acts. Tradition teaches that homosexual acts are intrinsically disordered for the following reasons: they "are contrary to the natural law," the principles of which are reflected in human nature itself; "they close the sexual act to the gift of life"; and "they do not proceed from a genuine affective and sexual complementarity" (*CCC*, no. 2357; *CRP*, no. 4).[25] We will consider each of these teachings in turn.

Natural Law Argument

First, every human being has a nature that is always interpreted and socially constructed by reason. There may be, therefore, different cultural interpretations of what constitutes human nature. The meaning of the phrase *sexual orientation* as part of nature is not universally agreed upon, but the Catholic Church distinguishes between "a homosexual 'tendency,' which proves to be 'transitory,' and 'homosexuals who are definitively such because of some kind of innate instinct.' . . . It seems appropriate to

---

[22] Lisa Sowle Cahill, "Is Catholic Ethics Biblical?" Warren Lecture Series in Catholic Studies, no. 20 (Tulsa, OK: University of Tulsa Press, 1992), 5–6.

[23] Victor Paul Furnish, *The Moral Teaching of Paul: Selected Issues* (Louisville, KY: Abingdon, 1985), 78, emphasis added.

[24] Richard Sparks, *Contemporary Christian Morality* (New York: Crossroad, 1996), 81.

[25] *CRP* refers to the CDF's document *Considerations regarding Proposals to Give Legal Recognition to Unions between Homosexual Persons* (June 3, 2003).

understand sexual orientation as a *deep-seated* dimension of one's personality [or nature] and to recognize its *relative stability* in a person."[26] Sexual orientation is predominantly heterosexual, homosexual, or bisexual. This natural, historically, socially, and experientially revealed reality may be obscured by the statistical preponderance of persons of heterosexual orientation, but it is in no way negated by that statistical preponderance. We are in complete agreement with the CDF when it teaches that "there can be no true promotion of man's dignity unless the essential order of his nature is respected" (*PH,* no. 3). We disagree with the CDF, however, on its exclusively heterosexual interpretation of that "essential order of [human] nature."

Humans have no access to pure, unembellished nature. Nature reveals to their attention, understanding, judgment, and decision only its naked facticity. Everything beyond that facticity is the result of interpretation by attentive, intelligent, rational, and responsible persons; we experience nature only as rationally interpreted and socially constructed. Our sexual anthropology, then, recognizes sexual orientation as an intrinsic dimension of human nature, and what is accepted as natural sexual activity will vary depending on whether a person's orientation is homosexual or heterosexual. Homosexual acts are natural for people with a homosexual orientation; heterosexual acts are natural for people with a heterosexual orientation. They are natural because they reflect the person's fundamental human nature as understood by right reason. We are not to be understood as arguing here that homosexual activity is ethical simply because it is natural for those with a homosexual orientation; that would be to treat natural facts as moral justification and to commit the naturalistic fallacy. To be ethical, we stipulate, every sexual act, homosexual or heterosexual, must be not only natural but also free, just, loving, and respectful of the human dignity and flourishing of both partners.

Procreation Argument

We consider, second, the claim that homosexual acts "close the sexual act to the gift of life." If one explores the Catholic Church's concept of "openness to the transmission of life" in biological terms, then potentially reproductive and permanently or temporarily nonreproductive heterosexual acts are essentially different types of acts. "A sterile person's genitals," Andrew Koppleman points out, "are no more suitable for generation than a gun with a broken firing pin is suitable for shooting." It is a conceptual stretch, he goes on, "to insist that the sexual acts of the incurably infertile

---

[26] USCCB, *Always Our Children*, 4–5, emphasis added; see also *PH,* no. 8.

are of the same kind as the sexual acts of fertile organs that occasionally fail to deliver the goods."[27] Both gays and lesbians are naturally sexed human beings, and their sexual activity is as incurably infertile as the acts of permanently infertile married heterosexuals, which the Catholic Church recognizes as legitimate and ethical. If we explore "openness to the transmission of life" not in biological but in metaphorical relational terms, then both homosexual and heterosexual couples can exhibit just and loving significance in their unions and sexual acts.[28]

Complementarity Argument

We consider, third, the church's teaching that gay and lesbian acts "do not proceed from a genuine affective and sexual complementarity." The church consistently condemns homosexual acts on the grounds that they violate heterosexual and reproductive complementarity, but it never attempts to explain why they also violate *personal* complementarity other than to assert, with no supporting evidence, that they "do not proceed from a genuine affective and sexual complementarity" (*CCC,* no. 2357). The church may nowhere have confronted this question of affective complementarity but monogamous, just, loving, mutually committed homosexual couples have confronted it experientially, and they testify that they do experience affective and personal complementarity in and through their homosexual acts. Margaret Farley notes that the experiential testimonies of such couples witness "to the role of such loves and relationships in sustaining human well-being and opening to human flourishing."[29] This coincides precisely with our foundational principle on the immediate and mediate relational impact of truly human sexual acts as stated in *Gaudium et Spes.* "Expressed in a manner which is truly human, these actions signify and promote that mutual self-giving by which spouses enrich each other and enrich their family and community with a joyful and a thankful will" (*GS,* no. 49).

---

[27] Andrew Koppleman, "Natural Law (New)," in *Sex from Plato to Paglia: A Philosophical Encyclopedia*, ed. Alan Soble (Westport, CT: Greenwood Press, 2006), 2:708.

[28] For development and detail, see Todd A. Salzman and Michael G. Lawler, "*Quaestio Disputata*: Catholic Sexual Ethics: Complementarity and the Truly Human," *Theological Studies* 67 (2006): 631–35; and David Matzko McCarthy, "The Relationship of Bodies: A Nuptial Hermeneutics of Same-sex Unions," in *Theology and Sexuality: Classic and Contemporary Readings*, ed. Eugene F. Rogers, Jr. (Oxford: Blackwell, 2002), 200–216.

[29] Margaret A. Farley, *Just Love: A Framework for Christian Sexual Ethics* (New York: Continuum, 2006), 287. Frans Vosman affirms this claim as well, noting that homosexuals contribute to the "social good" in terms of "mutual support, care, and justice" ("Can the Church Recognize Homosexual Couples in the Public Sphere?" *Intams Review* 1, no. 12 [2006]: 37).

Some thirty-five years ago, while acknowledging that the question of same-sex relations is a question of dispute, Farley, focusing on experience as a source of ethical knowledge, noted the anecdotal experiences of homosexual couples and commented that we "have some clear and profound testimonies to the life-enhancing possibilities of same-sex relations and the integrating possibilities of sexual activity within these relations. We have the witness that homosexuality can be a way of embodying responsible love and sustaining human friendship." She concluded, logically, that "this witness alone is enough to demand of the Christian community that it reflect anew on the norms for homosexual love."[30] Her judgment accords with that of Bernard Ratigan, a gay consulting psychotherapist, who notes that "the gap between the caricature of us in Church documents and our lived reality seems so huge." He asks legitimately, "On what evidence does the Vatican base its assertions about us?" and goes on to point out that psychoanalysis "has moved on from being solely concerned with genital sex to thinking much more about human relationships and love."[31] So, too, has Catholic theological ethics.

Lawrence Kurdek has supported Farley's anecdotal evidence with extensive social-science research on gay and lesbian couples that demonstrates that they tend to have a more equitable distribution of household labor, demonstrate greater conflict resolution skills, have less support from members of their families but greater support from friends, and, most significantly, experience similar levels of relational satisfaction compared to heterosexual couples.[32] On the basis of this supporting evidence, we conclude this section by endorsing Farley's judgment:

---

[30] Margaret A. Farley, "An Ethic for Same-Sex Relations," in *A Challenge to Love: Gay and Lesbian Catholics in the Church*, ed. Robert Nugent (New York: Crossroad, 1983), 99–100. In a more recent book Farley returns to the question of gay and lesbian experience and judges that "we do have strong witnesses to the role of such relationships in sustaining human well-being and opening to human flourishing" (Farley, *Just Love*, 287).

[31] Bernard Ratigan, "When Faith and Feelings Conflict," *The Tablet* (December 10, 2005), 13.

[32] Lawrence A. Kurdek, "What Do We Know about Gay and Lesbian Couples?" *Current Directions in Psychological Science* 14 (2005): 251; idem, "Differences between Partners from Heterosexual, Gay, and Lesbian Cohabiting Couples," *Journal of Marriage and Family* 68 (May 2006): 509–28; idem, "Are Gay and Lesbian Cohabiting Couples *Really* Different from Heterosexual Married Couples?" *Journal of Marriage and Family* 66 (2004): 880–900. See also R. C. Savin-Williams and K. G. Esterberg, "Lesbian, Gay, and Bisexual Families," in *Handbook of Family Diversity*, ed. David H. Demo, Katherine R. Allen, and Mark A. Fine (New York: Oxford University Press, 2000), 207–12. For further social-science evidence on the character of gay and lesbian couples, see Salzman and Lawler, *The Sexual Person*, 228–30.

Sex between two persons of the same sex (just as between two persons of the opposite sex) should not be used in a way that exploits, objectifies, or dominates; homosexual (like heterosexual) rape, violence, or any harmful use of power against unwilling victims (or those incapacitated by reason of age, etc.) is never justified; freedom, integrity, privacy are values to be affirmed in every homosexual (as heterosexual) relationship; all in all, individuals are not to be harmed, and the common good is to be promoted.[33]

French theologian Xavier Lacroix explains what all Catholic theological ethicists accept, that "ethics can have for its object only acts that are free, acts that can be imputed to personal responsibility. Whatever is determined, *in so far as it is determined*, is neither moral nor immoral; it simply *is*."[34] Heterosexual orientation is an innate and stable orientation to, predominantly, persons of the opposite sex; homosexual orientation is a similarly innate and stable orientation to, predominantly, persons of the same sex. Sexual orientation is neither chosen nor easily changeable; it simply is. It is, therefore, in itself neither ethical nor unethical. The sexual acts that flow from it, however, may be ethical or unethical according to their circumstances.

The Ethics of Homosexual Acts

Sexual acts are ethical when they are natural, reasonable, free, and expressed in a truly human, just, and loving manner that promotes human dignity and flourishing. All the terms of this articulation are important and must be carefully understood. Sexual acts are ethical when they are *natural*, and they are natural when they coincide with the *nature* of the human person.[35] For men and women who are by nature heterosexual, heterosexual acts are natural and therefore ethical when they are freely chosen, truly human, just, loving, and a promotion of human dignity and flourishing; for them homosexual acts are unnatural, unreasonable, and therefore unethical, even if all other requirements for ethical acts are safeguarded. For those who are by nature homosexual, it is the reverse. For them, homosexual acts are natural, reasonable, and ethical when they are free, truly human, just, loving, and a promotion of human dignity and flourishing; for them

---

[33] Farley, "An Ethic for Same-Sex Relations," 105.

[34] Xavier Lacroix, "Une Parole Éthique Recevable par Tous," in *L'amour du semblable: Questions sur l'homosexualité* (Paris: Cerf, 1995), 148.

[35] See Stephen J. Pope, "Scientific and Natural Law Analyses of Homosexuality: A Methodological Study," *Journal of Religious Ethics* 25 (Spring 1997): 110–11.

heterosexual acts are unnatural, unreasonable, and unethical, even when all other requirements for ethical acts are safeguarded. Sexual acts are ethical when they are *reasonable*, and they are reasonable when careful attention to and understanding of all the relevant human circumstances leads a person to make an informed judgment of conscience that a given sexual action is according to right reason and facilitates mutual human dignity and flourishing. Sexual acts are ethical when they are *truly human*, that is, when they fulfill all the requirements of orientation, interpersonal, and affective complementarities[36] and when they promote human dignity and flourishing. Sexual acts are *just* when they are performed by mutual, *free* agreement, and when they do no harm either to the persons involved or to the common good. Sexual acts are *loving* when each person wills the flourishing of the other person.

Our final judgment on the ethics of homosexual acts can be succinctly stated. *Some* homosexual and *some* heterosexual acts, those that take place in a stable human relationship and are natural, reasonable, free, and expressed in a truly human, just, and loving manner for the promotion of mutual dignity and flourishing are ethical; any coercion or violence automatically makes a sexual act unethical. *Some* homosexual and *some* heterosexual acts, those that do not take place in a stable human relationship and are not natural, reasonable, free, and expressed in a truly human, just, and loving manner for the promotion of mutual dignity and flourishing are unethical; again, any coercion or violence automatically makes a sexual act unethical.

Among the criteria we have listed for an ethical sexual act is that the act takes place in a stable human relationship. That raises an issue that is much debated in the contemporary world, the issue of same-sex marriage. Same-sex marriage is now legal throughout North America, Europe, and a large part of South America. As of our writing, South Africa is the only African country to have legalized it, and Taiwan is the only Asian country where the Supreme Court has declared it legal, though it has not yet been enacted into law. In a worldwide Univision survey, 30 percent of Catholics worldwide approved of same-sex marriage. In the United States 54 percent of Catholics approved and 40 percent disapproved of it, with men disapproving of it more than women, 70 percent of men and 61 percent of women opposing it.[37] This puts men more in agreement than women

---

[36] See Todd A. Salzman and Michael G. Lawler, "New Natural Law Theory and Foundational Sexual Ethical Principles: A Critique and a Proposal," *Heythrop Journal* 47 (2006): 182–205; Salzman and Lawler, *Quaestio Disputata*, 625–52; and James F. Keenan, "Can We Talk? Theological Ethics and Sexuality," *Theological Studies* 68 (2007): 113–31.

[37] Julie Clague, "Catholics, Families, and the Synod of Bishops: Views from the Pews," *Heythrop Journal* 55 (2014): 995–96.

with the teaching of the Catholic Church on the issue. More recently, since the legalization of same-sex marriage by the US Supreme Court in 2015, surveys in the United States indicate that 67 percent of Catholics support same-sex marriage.[38]

Catholic Teaching on Same-Sex Marriage

Before beginning our discussion of the teaching of the church on same-sex marriage, we make a major stipulation. The discussion that follows is not a discussion about the relative merits of heterosexual and homosexual marriage; it is a discussion only about whether stable same-sex unions may be legally institutionalized and called marriage. It is not a discussion about whether homosexual marriage can be equated with heterosexual marriage, for it obviously cannot in the sense that homosexual marriage can in no way be biologically procreative, which is a central component in the Catholic Church's argument against same-sex marriage. Marriage, the church teaches

> is not just any relationship between human beings. It was established by the Creator with its own nature, essential properties, and purpose. . . . Marriage exists solely between a man and woman, who by mutual personal gift, proper and exclusive to themselves, tend toward the communion of their persons. In this way, they mutually perfect each other, in order to cooperate with God in the *procreation and upbringing of new human lives*. (*DRP,* no. 2, emphasis added)

Given that definition of marriage, same-sex unions can never qualify as marriage.

In the contemporary Catholic Church there are two competing models of marriage, a *procreative institution* model that has its roots in the first chapter of Genesis (1:28) and in which procreation is the primary end of marriage, and a *spousal union* model that has its root in the second chapter of Genesis (2:18) and in which the mutual love of the spouses and their marital life together is a primary end of marriage. For centuries in the Christian churches the procreative union model dominated all ethical thinking, but at the Second Vatican Council in the 1960s the Catholic Church officially established the model of spousal union as at least equal to the model of procreative institution for explaining marriage in the

---

[38] Pew Research Center, "Support for Same-Sex Marriage Grows, Even among Groups That Had Been Skeptical" (June 26, 2017).

contemporary world. Marriage, the council taught in *Gaudium et Spes*, is a "communion of love . . . an intimate partnership of life and love," declaring the mutual love of the spouses and their intention to be best friends for life to be of the very essence of marriage (*GS,* nos. 47–48). The spouses, it further taught, "mutually gift and accept one another" (*GS,* no. 48). The focus on animal bodies and acts characteristic of the procreative union model is replaced by a focus on persons and their relationship. In their marital covenant spouses create not a procreative institution but a loving spousal union that might be procreative in their youth but is covenanted to last long after procreation is biologically possible. This marital love is "eminently human," "involves the good of the whole person," and is "steadfastly true." Marriage and spousal love are still said to be "ordained for the procreation of children," but that "does not make the other ends of marriage of less account," and "marriage to be sure is not instituted solely for procreation" (*GS,* nos. 48, 50). The Catholic Church revised its teachings about marriage in the twentieth century to bring them into line with its developing theology of marriage, moving beyond the model of marriage as an exclusively procreative institution to embrace a model of marriage as spousal union including both the mutual love of the spouses and the possibility of procreation but not primarily defined by procreation. Given the dedicated and loving experience of gay and lesbian unions noted by Farley and supported by the research of Kurdek, it appears to us that a good case can be made for arguing that homosexual unions can be as marital as heterosexual ones.

What about, however, the teaching of the CDF cited above that spouses "mutually perfect each other, in order to cooperate with God in the *procreation and upbringing of new human lives*?" That clearly comes from the perspective of the procreative institution model of marriage and comes up against a teaching of Pope Pius XII that is rarely mentioned in any discussion of marital morality. In a speech to midwives on October 29, 1951, Pius taught that with "grave reasons" it was was not necessarily unethical to intentionally avoid procreation in a marriage, but that it was unethical to artificially prevent procreation in any act of intercourse. Pope Paul VI repeated this teaching in 1968 in *Humanae Vitae* (*HV,* no. 10) and Pope John Paul II repeated it again in *Familiaris Consortio* (*FC,* no. 32). Pius teaches that non-procreation even for the lifetime of a marriage is ethical for "grave reasons" of a "medical, eugenic, economic, or social kind," with no specification of what such serious reasons might be. The obligation to procreate, Pius argued, rests not on individual couples but on the entire human race. We ask, therefore, if married heterosexual couples can ethically avoid procreation for the lifetime of their marriage, why should homosexual couples be banned from marriage because they will naturally avoid procreation for a lifetime, but still be "an intimate partnership of life and love" and helpmates to one another to human and Christian flourishing? We answer that we cannot see any rational argument to prohibit marriage to them except the long-rooted Catholic perspective of marriage as a procreative institution, the absoluteness of which has been negated by the teaching of three modern popes, Pius XII, Paul VI, and John Paul II.

Pope Francis's response to the two synods on marriage and family (2014 and 2015) and his Apostolic Exhortation *Amoris Laetitia (Joy of Love)* express the softening of Roman Catholic attitudes toward homosexuals. "Every sign of unjust discrimination," he teaches, "is to be carefully avoided, particularly any form of aggression or violence" (*AL,* no. 250). To the question of same-sex marriage he gives an unequivocal response: "*De facto* or same-sex unions . . . may not simply be equated with marriage," and there are "absolutely no grounds for considering homosexual unions to be in any way similar or even remotely analogous to God's plan for marriage and family" (*AL,* no. 251). It is crucial to note what he says and does not say. He does not say that same-sex unions are unethical; he says only that they are not to be equated or even thought to be analogous to heterosexual marriages. We believe that the pope must have written that judgment before he later wrote that God "dwells deep within the marital love that gives him glory" (*AL,* no. 314). That teaching is deeply rooted in the scriptural tradition, which holds that "God is love" and that "if we love one another, God lives in us and his love is perfected in us" (1 John 4:8, 12). We cannot imagine the pope denying that Christian tradition by asserting that God dwells in the love of heterosexual spouses but not in the love of homosexual couples; that would be a betrayal of a longstanding Catholic teaching. No, if God is love, then God inevitably dwells in the love of homosexual partners. Their unions may or may not be called marriage in the Catholic Church, though they are so called by civil law across a wide swathe of the world, but there can be no doubt that God dwells in the love of the homosexual partners and that the mutual love of the partners images God's love for humankind and impels them mutually toward God.

What finally, then, do we say about the ethics of same-sex unions? We say, first, that the research data from Lawrence Kurdek and others show that gay and lesbian couples experience similar levels of mutual relational satisfaction as heterosexual couples.[39] We reject, second, the claim of the CDF and others that "as experience has shown, the absence of sexual complementarity in these unions creates obstacles in the normal

---

[39] Kurdek, "What Do We Know about Gay and Lesbian Couples?," 251; Kurdek, "Are Gay and Lesbian Cohabiting Couples *Really* Different from Heterosexual Married Couples?"

development of children who would be placed in the care of such persons" (*CRP*, no. 7). That claim is not only unsubstantiated by any evidence but is also refuted by the evidence. The preponderance of the evidence led the American Psychological Association in 2004 to approve and disseminate an important resolution: because research has shown that "the children of lesbian and gay parents are as likely as those of heterosexual parents to flourish," the association opposes any discrimination based on sexual orientation.[40] Since human experience is a source of ethical knowledge, we also oppose any discrimination based on sexual orientation. We say, third and finally, that everything we said in Chapter 6 about the authority and inviolability of a carefully informed and discerned conscience applies as much to the decision of gays and lesbians to enter a stable loving union and possibly to adopt children as it applies to any other decision of conscience.

Questions for Reflection

- What do you understand by the terms *sexual orientation, homosexuality,* and *homosexual*?
- Does the Bible have anything to say about those terms and their contemporary meanings? If yes, what does it say? If no, why do you give that answer?
- The Vatican Congregation for the Doctrine of the Faith teaches that homosexual acts are intrinsically disordered because they are contrary to the natural law, they close the sexual act to the gift of life, and they do not proceed from a genuine affective and sexual complementarity. Are you or are you not convinced by those arguments? Explain why.
- Lawrence Kurdek has done extensive research on gay and lesbian couples and reports that they experience similar levels of relational satisfaction compared to heterosexual couples. Does this information have anything to contribute to the debate about same-sex marriage? Why or why not?
- How does the Catholic Church now define marriage? Pope Francis states in *Amoris Laetitia* that there are no grounds for considering homosexual unions to be even remotely analogous to God's plan for marriage and family. Is his statement in any way helpful to you when you consider the pros and cons of same-sex marriage?

---

[40] American Psychological Association, "Sexual Orientation, Parents, and Children," resolution (July 28 and 30, 2004). For more data and detail, see Salzman and Lawler, *The Sexual Person,* 229–30.

Suggested Readings

Beattie Jung, Patricia, with Joseph Andrew Coray, eds. *Sexual Diversity and Catholicism: Toward the Development of Moral Theology.* Collegeville, MN: Liturgical Press, 2001.

Firer Hinze, Christine, and J. Patrick Hornbeck, II, eds. *More Than a Monologue: Sexual Diversity and the Catholic Church.* Vol. 1, *Voices of Our Times.* New York: Fordham, 2014.

Hornbeck II, J. Patrick, and Michael A. Norko, eds. *More Than a Monologue: Sexual Diversity and the Catholic Church.* Vol. 2, *Inquiry, Thought, and Expression.* New York: Fordham, 2014.

Salzman, Todd A., and Michael G. Lawler. *The Sexual Person: Toward a Renewed Catholic Anthropology.* Moral Traditions Series (Washington, DC: Georgetown University Press, 2008.

11

Economics and Justice

Learning Objectives

- Explain the virtuous perspective "faith that sees injustice and does justice."
- Distinguish between acts of charity and acts of justice toward the poor.
- Explain the scriptural teachings on charity and justice for the poor.
- Explain the scriptural teachings on wealth.

In this chapter we consider the relationship of theological ethics and economics. The word *economics* derives from two Greek words, *oikos* meaning "a house or household" and *nemein,* meaning "to manage." Literally, therefore, economics means managing a household, but it has come to mean more broadly managing the production, distribution, and consumption of wealth in a household or a society, and we state at the outset our belief as Catholic theological ethicists that the distribution, consumption, and management of wealth in our world is totally and sinfully unbalanced. There are a few people who are very rich and many people who are very poor and struggle every day just to survive. In the United States, for instance, 1 percent of the population controls 43 percent of the wealth, the next 4 percent controls an additional 29 percent, and 0.01 percent of the population controls wealth that is beyond imagining for the vast majority of people.[1] These figures are more or less replicated for the world population.

Pope Francis writes of this inequality in his encyclical letter *Laudato Si':*

We should be particularly indignant at the enormous inequalities in our midst, whereby we continue to tolerate some considering

---

[1] Alan Dunn, "Average America vs the One Percent," *Forbes* (March 21, 2012).

themselves more worthy than others. We fail to see that some are mired in desperate and degrading poverty, with no way out, while others have not the faintest idea of what to do with their posessions. (*LS,* no. 9)

He returned to the same theme, with a real-life example, in his Apostolic Exhortation *Amoris Laetitia:*

Here I would like to mention the situation of families in dire poverty and great limitations. The problems faced by poor households are often all the more trying. For example, if a single mother has to raise a child by herself and needs to leave the child at home while she goes to work, the child can grow up exposed to all kinds of risks and obstacles to personal growth. (*AL,* no. 49)

There are serious ethical issues entwined in the gap between the rich and the poor, for both individuals and nations. In this chapter we confront those issues by focusing on both scripture as a source of ethical knowledge from the virtuous perspective of faith that sees injustice and does justice[2] and on the two dyads poverty and wealth, poor and rich.

Virtuous Perspective:
Faith That Sees Injustice and Does Justice

Two central virtues we have already explored in this book are the theological virtue of faith and the cardinal virtue of justice. The *Catechism of the Catholic Church* defines faith as "the theological virtue by which we believe in God and believe all that he has said and revealed to us" (*CCC,* no. 1814). It defines justice as the preservation of our neighbors' rights and rendering to them what is their due (*CCC,* no. 2407). The Jesuits, drawing from Catholic social teaching, unite these two virtues to promote a theological ethical virtuous perspective, "faith that does justice." We added an important corrective to this principle in Chapter 4, "faith that sees injustice and does justice," that flows from a virtuous perspective and recognizes scotosis, a blind spot. Scotosis results from bias, "the love of darkness." It is not a conscious act, but it arises "in the censorship that governs the

---

[2] See John C. Haughey, SJ, ed., *The Faith That Does Justice: Examining the Christian Sources for Social Change* (Eugene, OR: Wipf and Stock, 1977); and Roger C. Bergman, *Catholic Social Learning: Educating the Faith That Does Justice* (New York: Fordham University Press, 2011).

emergence of psychic contents."[3] This censorship can be either positive or negative. Positively, "it selects and arranges materials that emerge in consciousness in a perspective that gives rise to an insight"; negatively, it prevents "the emergence into consciousness of perspectives that would give rise to unwanted insights."[4] A virtuous perspective can illuminate scotoma, aiding us in seeing insightfully and comprehensively, so that we can act responsibly and justly.

In order to *act* for justice guided by faith, confronting poverty, for example, and creating a more equitable distribution of wealth and resources throughout the world, we must first be able to *see* injustice. Faith that sees injustice and does justice creates a virtuous perspective that, in turn, creates an awareness and sensitivity to the reality of human suffering in the world so that in word and, more important, in deed we can respond to this suffering. This virtuous perspective aligns well with the see-judge-act model of pastoral reflection noted by Pope John XXIII in *Mater et Magistra*, which is grounded in experience and induction and invites an ethical response to lived experience, especially the experience of the poor and oppressed.[5] Faith that sees injustice and does justice allows Christians first to *see* injustice, both individual and structural, then to *judge* injustice through analysis and evaluation, and finally to *act* to establish or restore justice in light of that analysis and evaluation. Acts can take the form of charity or justice. Acts of charity are personal acts of service toward neighbors, especially the neediest neighbors. Acts of justice work to reform and transform sinful structures that perpetuate poverty and any other form of oppression, to facilitate the attainment of human dignity, and to realize the common good. While individual acts of charity are necessary and important to fulfill the gospel imperative to love one's neighbor, acts of justice are essential to confront and transform unjust social structures that violate the common good and perpetuate the endemic poverty we see throughout the world. We now turn to that specific violation of the common good and the scriptural response to it.

Poverty

Poverty is not a new reality in world history, and neither is the deep inequality between rich and poor. We would expect it, therefore, to feature

---

[3] Bernard J. F. Lonergan, *Insight: A Study of Human Understanding* (London: Longmans, 1957), 191.

[4] Ibid., 192.

[5] See also Marvin L. Mich, "Commentary on *Mater et magistra* (Christianity and Social Progress)," in *Modern Catholic Social Teaching: Commentaries and Interpretations*, ed. Kenneth B. Himes, 191–216 (Washington, DC: Georgetown University Press, 2005).

in the scriptural sources of Christian ethics, and so it does. To understand the meanings of the ideas expressed in the Christian scriptures, we must first understand the differences between the culture of the times in which they were written and American culture today. American culture is highly individualistic, holding to the unrealistic value that every person should be able to stand unaided and generating cultural norms to enforce this value. The "real American—in the nineteenth century the rugged, individual male, but in our day the individual male or female—ought to be self-reliant. The Mediterranean culture in which the scriptures were written is quite different. It values not individualism but communal belonging to some family, some society, some group. The members of a family, a society, or a group are honor bound to help the other members of the family, society, or group, including economically. Two principles, one theological and the other anthropological, underlie everything that is said about poverty and wealth in both Old and New Testaments. The theological principle is that everything in the world that the God of Israel created belongs to God, and men and women are only stewards of the things they own. The anthropological principle is a principle of kinship or belonging to a group or society or, most fundamentally, a nuclear family in which parents and their children are bound tightly together as mother, father, brothers, and sisters.

In ancient Israel that fundamental family kinship was extended to embrace as brothers and sisters all members of Israelite society, all those who were descended from the slaves God liberated from Egypt under Moses, led through the desert, and settled in the land where "milk and honey flow" (Deut 26:9). The followers of Jesus, originally Jews, extended family kinship to embrace all those who believed in Jesus as the Christ, the anointed one of God, and embraced one another as brothers and sisters (Matt 25:40; Luke 6:41–42; 1 Cor 8:13). This pattern is very much in play in everything the scriptures of both Old and New Testaments say about poverty and the obligation Christians have to care for one another. The God in whom both Jews and Christians believe is a God who acts in human history; who liberated Israel from Egypt; and who raised Jesus from the dead, validating his life and everything he said about how to be "rich toward God" (Luke 12:21). Jews and Christians are both called to respond to God's saving actions in history with ethical actions in their own history, specified by the observance of God's commandments. When we ask what those actions are to be, both the Jewish and Christian scriptures leave us in no doubt.

The Old Testament reveals that the power of the God who led Israel from slavery in Egypt will continue to be in defense of "slaves," God's defenseless poor and excluded. God is

Father of the orphans and protector of widows. . . .
God gives the desolate a home to life in. (Ps 68:5–6)

To know God is not, as it is in ancient Greece and modern America, to know *that* God is and *what* God is; it is to love God and act like God. As Gustavo Gutiérrez declares, "To know God as liberator is to liberate, is to do justice";[6] to know God as Father of the poor is to act on behalf of the poor, always remembering how God intervened in Egypt on behalf of Israelite slaves. That memory and the actions in history that it demands return again and again. The book of Deuteronomy instructs:

You shall remember that you were a slave in Egypt and the Lord your God redeemed you from there; therefore, I command you to do this. When you reap your harvest in your field and have forgotten a sheaf in the field, you shall not go back to get it; it shall be for the sojourner, the fatherless, the widow; that the Lord your God may bless you in all the works of your hands. When you beat your olive trees, you shall not go over the boughs again; it shall be for the sojourner, the fatherless, the widow. (Deut 24:18–22)

What Jesus in the New Testament would later advance as a reciprocal relationship between God and "the least of these who are members of my family" (Matt 25:40) has always been embedded in his Jewish tradition as a reciprocal relationship between God and the poor and excluded. The prophets consistently link these two and proclaim that truly to know and love God demands action on behalf of the poor and against the injustice perpetrated against them. Jeremiah, for instance, proclaims this prophetic message.

Thus says the Lord of hosts, the God of Israel: Amend your ways and your doings, and let me dwell with you in this place. . . . For if you truly amend your ways and your doings, if you truly act justly with one another, if you do not oppress the alien, the orphan, and the widow, or shed innocent blood in this place . . . then I will dwell with you in this place, in the land that I gave of old to your ancestors forever. (Jer 7:2–7)

The reciprocation could not be made clearer: knowledge and love of God is proved in practice by action on behalf of justice for the poor, those whom

---

[6] Gustavo Gutiérrez, *The Power of the Poor in History* (Maryknoll, NY: Orbis Books, 1983), 8.

Pope Francis calls the "excluded." Proverbs offers an axiomatic statement about this preferential option for the poor: "He who mocks the poor insults his creator" (17:5).

Isaiah's messianic formulation of the intimate connection between God and justice for the poor and excluded leads us into the New Testament, for in Luke's Gospel, Jesus chooses it for commentary in his home synagogue of Nazareth. "The Spirit of the Lord God is upon me, because the Lord has anointed me to bring good tidings to the afflicted; he has sent me to bind up the brokenhearted, to proclaim liberty to the captives . . . to comfort all who mourn. . . . For I the Lord love justice, I hate robbery and wrong" (Isa 61:1–8). This predilection for the poor and excluded, Isaiah prophetically proclaims, will be characteristic of the coming Messiah, the ultimately righteous one of Israel. That the Messiah has come in Jesus is proclaimed in Luke's commentary on the text: "Today this scripture has been fulfilled in your hearing" (Luke 4:21).

The confession of the followers of Jesus was and is that he is the promised Messiah—in Greek, the Christ (Mark 1:1; Matt 1:1)—the one anointed by God "to bring good tidings to the afflicted." The Gospels announce that he is the Messiah in the passage that narrates his baptism by John the Baptizer, the descent of the Holy Spirit upon him, and his designation as "beloved Son" (Mark 1:9–11; Matt 3:13–17; Luke 3:21–22). Immediately following his baptism, Jesus proclaims the advent of the kingdom or the reign of God (Mark 1:15), a reign of justice in favor of the poor and the excluded. Jesus's proclamation of this reign, not only in words but, more important in deeds, is what led him to his death on the cross and then to his being raised by God (1 Cor 15:4; Rom 6:4; 8:4; Col 2:12; Acts 2:24, 32; 3:15). For all his disciples, dispirited by his death, and not just for the two on the road to Emmaus, "their eyes were opened" (Luke 24:31) by his being raised from the dead by God (Acts 2:24, 32; Rom 6:4; 1 Cor 15:15). In the resurrection God verified both that the words and deeds of Jesus were right with God and that he was, indeed, the "holy and righteous one" (Acts 2:14).

The eyes of Jesus's followers were so well and truly opened by his resurrection that, ultimately, they confessed not only that he was the Christ, the righteous and just one sent by God, but also that he was God in human form pitching his tent among God's people (John 1:14). The universal biblical reciprocation between God and the poor reaches an unsurpassable personification and high point in Jesus who, in Gutierrez's powerful phrase, is "God become poor."[7] It is in his life on behalf of his poor and excluded brothers and sisters that Jesus is finally recognized as God's beloved Son.

---

[7] Ibid.

It is in their lives on behalf of his poor and excluded brothers and sisters that Christians, too, will be recognized as God's beloved children, for, as *Gaudium et Spes* reminds us, Jesus "clearly taught the sons of God to treat one another as brothers" (*GS,* no. 32). In our twenty-first century world there is great need for such Christian ethical action; our streets are full of the homeless needing to be housed, of the hungry needing to be fed, of the poor of every color needing help.

Like every good Jew of his time Jesus upheld the reciprocal relationship between God and the poor and insisted that to know and love God is to act on behalf of the poor and excluded and against every injustice perpetrated against them. Matthew makes his position clearest in his Sermon on the Mount: "Not everyone who says to me 'Lord, Lord' shall enter the kingdom of heaven, but only the one who does the will of my Father in heaven" (Matt 7:21). That will is to care for the poor and excluded. The disciples who responded to Jesus's invitation to "follow me" (Mark 1:17; Matt 4:18), and that includes every person today who claims to be a Christian, were and are bound to uphold the same reciprocal relationship and to ensure that it is lived not only in words but also in deeds. Matthew makes this clearest in his powerful final judgment scene:

> Then he will say to those at his left hand, "You that are accursed, depart from me into the eternal fire prepared for the devil and his angels; for I was hungry and you gave me no food, I was thirsty and you gave me nothing to drink, I was a stranger and you did not welcome me, naked and you did not give me clothing, sick and in prison and you did not visit me." Then they also will answer, "Lord, when was it that we saw you hungry or thirsty or a stranger or naked or sick or in prison, and did not take care of you?" Then he will answer them, "Truly I tell you, just as you did not do it to one of the least of these, you did not do it to me." (Matt 25:41-45)

Matthew's final comment is a chilling condemnation for those who, both then and now, do not recognize the reciprocation between God and the poor and excluded, and a blessing for those who do: "They will go away into eternal punishment, but the righteous into eternal life" (Matt 25:46). The righteousness that God and God's Christ demand of their followers is not easy, for "although he was made by God in a state of holiness, from the very dawn of history man abused his liberty at the urging of personified evil. . . . Therefore man is split within himself. As a result, all of human life, whether individual or collective, shows itself to be a dramatic struggle between good and evil, between light and darkness" (*GS,* no. 13). It is the great mystery of sin against which every human being struggles. Christians,

260 Introduction to Catholic Theological Ethics

however, share the promise of Christ, who gives them "power to become children of God, who were born, not of blood or of the will of the flesh or of the will of man, but of God" (John 1:12–13).

James, as radically Jewish as Jesus and Matthew, has his own formulation of the reciprocation between God and the poor:

> What good is it, my brothers and sisters, if you say you have faith but do not have works? Can faith save you? If a brother or sister is naked and lacks daily food, and one of you says to them, "Go in peace; keep warm and eat your fill," and yet you do not supply their bodily needs, what is the good of that? So faith by itself, if it has no works, is dead. (Jas 2:14–17)

Gaudium et Spes also has its own formulation of this sentiment, borrowed from twelfth-century Gratian: "Feed the man dying of hunger, because if you have not fed him you have killed him." Martin Luther sparked a long and false debate between Lutherans and Catholics about the respective values of faith and good works, as if Lutherans valued *only* faith and Catholics valued *only* good works. That debate was formally laid to rest in 1999 by the agreement between the Lutheran World Federation and the Catholic Church articulated in the *Joint Declaration on the Doctrine of Justification*. The theological reality is that Luther and the theologians who follow him never doubted that faith is proved in deeds, that is, that faith must work; and the Catholic Church never doubted that faith made concrete in works is necessary for salvation.

Another Christian pattern highlighted throughout the New Testament is intimately related to the universal reciprocation among God, God's Christ, and God's poor. That pattern is the pattern of service to others, especially to the poor and the excluded, which Jesus exemplifies in his life and unceasingly strives to inculcate in his disciples. The Christ of the Gospels articulates the perspective unequivocally: "The Son of Man came not to be served but to serve and to give his life as a ransom for many" (Mark 10:45; Matt 20:28). Service of others is Christ's way of relating to others; service of others is what he strives to inculcate in his disciples of every generation. He instructs them patiently that those who have authority over the Gentiles lord it over them. "But it shall not be so among you. Whoever would be great among you must be your servant, and whoever would be first among you must be the slave of all" (Mark 10:42–44; Matt 20:25–27). *Gaudium et Spes*'s interpretation of that perspective is that

> the fundamental purpose of productivity must not be the mere multiplication of products. It must not be profit or domination. Rather it

must be the *service* of man and, indeed, of the whole man, viewed in terms of his material needs and the demands of his intellectual, moral, spiritual, and religious life. And when we say man, we mean every man whatsoever and every group of men of whatever race and from whatever part of the world." (*GS*, no. 64)

How far Christians are from being truly Christian today is summed up in that same document: "If the demands of justice and equity are to be satisfied, vigorous efforts must be made . . . to remove as quickly as possible the immense inequalities which now exist" (*GS*, no. 66). Those immense inequalities are starkly highlighted by the fact that "while an enormous mass of people still lack the absolute necessities of life, some, even in less advanced countries, live sumptuously or squander wealth. Luxury and misery rub shoulders" (*GS*, no. 63). Present-day Christians must shoulder a great deal of blame for this situation. There are even some, comfortably middle class, who chastise Pope Francis for his support of the poor and who invite him to return to the business of the gospel. Either they have scotoma with respect to the clear gospel teaching that we have just exposed or they have chosen to ignore it.

The evangelist John's last-supper narrative highlights this Christian emphasis on service. The narrative describes Jesus washing his disciples' feet, a prophetic action that reveals Jesus's will to be remembered as servant and challenges those who remember him at the supper to be and do the same. Lest this point be missed, as it has been regularly missed in Christian history, John's Jesus underlines the challenge in his final testament. "I have given you an example that you also should do as I have done to you" (John 13:15). Jesus, he of righteousness and ethical action, who lived a life of love of neighbor (Lev 19:18; Mark 12:31) in service to others, challenged his disciples, then and now, to do the same. The memory of Jesus that Christians celebrate in the Eucharist recalls them to the care of their brothers and sisters, God's poor and excluded.

Ministry to the poor is already evident in the earliest Jerusalem church that devoted itself to "the apostles' teaching and communion" (Acts 2:42) and "everything they owned was held in common" (Acts 4:32). Paul makes clear that communion is not just among the members of a local community but reaches out to embrace all the churches, telling us that the poor churches in Macedonia and Achaia "have been pleased to make communion" for the church at Jerusalem (Rom 15:26; see 2 Cor 8:4) and praising "the generosity of your communion" (2 Cor 9:13). Such communion among disciples sharing the eucharistic meal, Paul argues, is a necessary precondition for authentically celebrating the Lord's Supper. When there is no such communion among believers, as there is not at Corinth, for instance, neither is there communion with the Christ whom they *say* they confess as Lord. In such circumstance, Paul judges, it is not really to eat the Lord's Supper that they came together (1 Cor 11:20). That judgment ought not to come as a surprise given the declaration that "as you did not do it to one of the least of these, you did it not to me" (Matt 25:45). When there is no servant-communion in the church, including the poor and excluded, neither is there communion with Christ and Christ's God. Leaning on this notion of communion, *Gaudium et Spes* teaches that in our world "it grows increasingly true that the obligations of justice and love are fulfilled only if each person" contributes to the common good "according to his own abilities and the needs of others" (*GS,* no. 30).

Liberation Theology and Poverty

The commitment of Christians to the service of the poor has continued throughout the Christian tradition to the present day. The modern theologians who have most detailed the connections among Eucharist, church communion, and common Christian life are liberation theologians. What came to be known as liberation theology was spawned in the poor barrios of South America on behalf of the multitudinous poor in its various countries. Liberation theologians correctly interpreted the biblical data we have considered as a preferential option for the poor and enunciated this option first as a theological doctrine that later was verified as a church doctrine of the South American Catholic Church. It is not a surprise that an Argentinian Pope Francis would highlight this doctrine in his papal words and deeds. The doctrine of the preferential option for the poor came to preeminence at two conferences of Latin American bishops, the first at Medellín in Colombia in 1968, the second at Puebla in Mexico in 1979. Medellín foreshadowed the phrase *preferential option for the poor*, and Pueblo explicitly adopted it. Among the signs of authentic Christianity, the bishops taught, are "preferential love and concern for the poor." They pledged themselves and their churches "to make clear through our lives and attitudes that our preference is to evangelize and serve the poor." They also taught that a "preferential option for the poor represents the most noticeable tendency of religious life in Latin America."[8] The questions being asked today about the "novel" words and actions of Pope Francis with respect to a church of the poor and a poor church are all answered for those with eyes to see in *Gaudium et Spes*, Medellín, and Puebla.

---

[8] Puebla Final Document, nos. 382, 707, 733. The Puebla Conference is analyzed in contextual depth in John Eagleson and Philip Scharper, eds., *Puebla and Beyond* (Maryknoll, NY: Orbis Books, 1979).

Asian liberation theologian Tissa Balasuriya writes that Eucharist is

spiritual food in so far as it leads to love, unity, and communion among persons and groups. Today this requires love among persons and effective action for justice. The eucharist must also lead us to a response to the suffering of the masses, *often caused by people who take a prominent part in the eucharist.* Unless there is this twofold dimension of personal love and societal action, the eucharist can be a sacrilege.[9]

The phrase we have emphasized, and which is demonstrable throughout the Christian world without debate, illustrated the Second Vatican Council's confession, stated in *Lumen Gentium,* that the church is a church of sinners in its membership and is, therefore, "at the same time holy and always in need of being purified" and renewed in its commitment to the Christ and to the God he reveals (*LG,* no. 8). It is a sad commentary on the Catholic Church that several liberation theologians so dedicated to the poor and excluded were condemned for teachings contrary to church doctrine, though their condemnations were later lifted thanks to the influence of Pope John Paul II. Pope Francis speaks out of the biblical tradition, the best of the church tradition, and *Gaudium et Spes* when he teaches, as Bishop McElroy points out, that "alleviating the grave evil of poverty must be at the very heart of the Church's mission. It is neither optional nor secondary."[10]

Pope John Paul II draws attention in *Christifideles Laici* to a temptation that Christians "have not always known how to avoid," the temptation to separate their Christian faith from their everyday life, to separate their acceptance of the gospel from "the actual living of the Gospel in various situations in the world." The pope implies that to be faithful to their vocation to follow Christ, Christians need to reach out in active love to those around them, preferentially to the poor and marginalized. This chapter underscores that the demand to do so does not come from Pope John Paul or Pope Francis, who do no more than interpret the ancient Jewish-Christian scriptural teaching for the situations of their time and place. No, the demand comes from Jewish Jesus and the Christian tradition that follows him as servant of God's poor and marginalized. Pope Francis, a faithful interpreter of both the gospel and the Second Vatican Council, puts this pointedly in *Evangelii Gaudium:* "How can it be that it is not

---

[9] Tissa Balasuriya, *The Eucharist and Human Liberation* (Maryknoll, NY: Orbis Books, 1979), 22, emphasis added.

[10] See Bishop Robert W. McElroy, "A Church for the Poor," *America* (October 21, 2013), 13.

a news item when an elderly homeless person dies of exposure, but it is news when the stock market loses two points? This is a case of exclusion. Can we continue to stand by when food is thrown away while people are starving? This is a case of inequality" (*EG,* no. 53). *Gaudium et Spes* has the final word in this section:

> Mindful of the Lord's saying: "By this will all men know that you are my disciples, if you have love for one another" (John 13:35), Christians cannot yearn for anything more ardently than to serve the men of the modern world with mounting generosity and success. . . . Not everyone who cries "Lord, Lord" will enter into the kingdom of heaven, but those who do the Father's will and take a strong grip on the job at hand. (*GS,* no. 92)

Wealth

We switch focus now from an ethical consideration of poverty and the demands it makes on every Christian to an ethical consideration of wealth. The switch is a critical one from the ethical obligations of Christians toward others who happen to be poor to the ethical obligation of Christians toward themselves if they happen to be wealthy. Everything we have already argued, of course, is still relevant; wealthy followers of Jesus have the obligation to act in charity to provide for the poor followers of Jesus and, indeed, of all the world's poor, and to act in justice to transform unjust social structures that perpetuate poverty. Jesus's attitude to wealth, especially great wealth or "great possessions," as we shall see, is very clear and is articulated in all three Synoptic Gospels—Matthew, Mark, and Luke—in the story of the rich young man. We start with Mark's version, which is probably the original version. As he was setting out on a journey, a man ran up and knelt before him, and asked him, "Good Teacher, what must I do to inherit eternal life?" Jesus said to him, "Why do you call me good? No one is good but God alone. You know the commandments: 'You shall not murder; You shall not commit adultery; You shall not steal; You shall not bear false witness; You shall not defraud; Honor your father and mother.'" He said to him, "Teacher, I have kept all these since my youth." Jesus, looking at him, loved him and said, "You lack one thing; go, sell what you own, and give the money to the poor, and you will have treasure in heaven; then come, follow me." Mark concludes by noting, "When he heard this, he was shocked and went away grieving, for he had many possessions (Mark 10:17–22). Luke's version is slightly different and has a dramatically different ending. It is a ruler who poses the question to Jesus and, when Jesus gives the same answer as in Mark, the ruler "became sad; for he was very rich" (Luke 18:23). Notice that the ruler does not go away in Luke as the young man does in Mark and that Jesus further responds to him with a dramatic pronouncement: "How hard it is for those who have wealth to enter the kingdom of God! Indeed, it is easier for a camel to go through the eye of a needle than someone who is rich to enter the kingdom of God" (Luke 18:24–25).

We note that Jesus says, "How *hard* it is" not "How *impossible* it is" for those with wealth to enter the kingdom of God. The ethical issue is not the possession of riches but the rich person's attitude to riches, to the poor, and to God. In an earlier story Luke had called a rich man a fool "who lays up treasure for himself and is not rich toward God" (Luke 12:21). Riches, especially great riches as with the young man in Mark's story and the ruler in Luke's, can be deceptive. They can deceive the rich into believing that, since their riches enable them to buy anything they want in this life, they can also enable them to buy salvation in the next. Riches can become idols that are worshiped instead of the one true God, who alone can grant the gift of salvation. The one true God is worshiped by rich Christians when they share their riches with the poor, not so that their situations become socioeconomically reversed, that the rich become poor and the poor become rich, but so that the rich feed the hungry, clothe the naked, provide shelter for the homeless and healthcare for the sick, and educate the illiterate to the level that enables them to function as contributing members of their society. If all this sounds overwhelming, and in our world it *can* sound overwhelming, there are many organizations that make acts of charity as easy as writing and mailing a check or acts of justice calling your congressional representative to advocate for structural changes in policy that reflect and promote justice and the common good.

That only God can grant salvation is the meaning of an earlier story in Luke of yet another man, this time a landowner, with great possessions. His land, we are told, had "produced abundantly. And he thought to himself, 'What should I do, for I have no place to store my crops?'" (Luke 12:16–17). Then he hit on an idea of what to do with his crops to his benefit: "I will pull down my barns and build larger ones, and there I will store all my grain and my goods. And I will say to my soul, Soul, you have ample goods laid up for many years; relax, eat, drink, be merry" (Luke 12:18–19). God then visits him and tells him, "You fool. This very night your life is being demanded of you. And the things you have prepared, whose will they be?" (Luke 12:20). Excessive possessions or excessive wealth can never buy salvation; God alone can grant it. Jesus comments, "So it is with those who store up treasures for themselves but are not rich toward God" (Luke 12:21). We again that anyone, rich or poor, becomes ethically rich toward the God in whom Christians profess belief by following the Jewish-Christian scriptural tradition that demands care for God's poor and marginalized. There is no ethical problem with being rich; wealth becomes unethical only when it usurps "God's role as source and measure and guarantor of life."[11]

There is another story of a rich man and his fate in Luke, who was a great one for parables. There was a rich man "who was clothed in purple and fine linen and who feasted sumptuously every day. And at his gate lay a poor man named Lazarus, full of sores, who desired to be fed with what fell from the rich man's table" (Luke 16: 20–21). The poor man, we are led to believe, went unfed, died, and "was carried by the angels to Abraham's bosom"; he must have been rich toward God. The rich man, who must not have been rich toward God, also "died and was buried" and "in Hades, being in torment, he lifted up his eyes and saw Abraham far off and Lazarus in his bosom" (Luke 16:22–23). In anguish in the flames of hell, he calls out to Abraham to have mercy on him and to help him, but Abraham is unbending in his reply: "Child, remember that during your lifetime you received good things, and Lazarus in like manner evil things; but now he is comforted here, and you are in agony" (Luke 16:25). The rich man then asked Abraham to send Lazarus to warn his brothers to pursue a different course of life, one that would include feeding and caring for the likes of Lazarus so that they might avoid the torment he was suffering. Again, Abraham is unbending: "They have Moses and the prophets," he replied. "They should listen to them" (Luke 16:29). He goes on to state what he takes to be obvious: "If they do not listen to Moses and the prophets, neither will they be convinced even if someone rises from the dead" (Luke 16:31).

Biblical scholar Raymond Collins points out that there is a concrete echo in this story of Luke's abstract version of the Beatitudes.[12] Luke's Jesus has a blessing for the poor and a woe for the rich. "Blessed are you poor," he proclaims, "for yours is the kingdom of God" (Luke 6:20), but "woe to you that are rich, for you have received your consolation" (Luke 6:24). The name Luke gives to the poor man in his story, Lazarus, means "God helps," and that is exactly what happens in the story: God helps Lazarus, so needy in life, to salvation after death. We are not to assume that Lazarus was saved because he was poor; there is no merit in being poor. No, if he

---

[11] Sandra Ely Wheeler, *Wealth as Peril and Obligation: The New Testament on Possessions* (Grand Rapids, MI: Eerdmans, 1995), 81. See also Luke Timothy Johnson, *Sharing Possessions: What Faith Demands* (Grand Rapids, MI: Eerdmans, 2011).

[12] Raymond F. Collins, *Wealth, Wages, and the Wealthy: New Testament Insight for Preachers and Teachers* (Collegeville, MN: Liturgical Press, 2017), 181.

merited salvation, it was because he heeded the demands of Moses and the prophets. The rich man is unnamed, though the Christian tradition has named him Dives, which is simply the Latin word meaning "rich." He is not condemned to hell because he is rich, but rather because of how he used his riches for his own sumptuous lifestyle, ignoring the demands of Moses and the prophets to care in justice for God's poor and excluded. "Heeding the biblical tradition with its reiterated demand that the needs of the poor be taken care of as a first demand of justice," Collins comments, "is something that the rich man's brothers need to do."[13] It is something that all who *say* they believe in Jesus also need to *do* to live a fully Christian and ethical life. It is something the rich man did not do, and his fate is advanced as a warning to all who ignore the biblical and traditional demands for justice for the poor and marginalized.

The short epistle of James, written toward the end of the first century, knows these biblical demands. "Be a doer of the word," James urges, "and not a hearer only, deceiving yourselves" (Jas 1:22). There is an echo here of a crucial statement of Jesus in Matthew's Gospel: "Not everyone who *says* to me 'Lord, Lord,' shall enter the kingdom of heaven, but he who *does* the will of my Father who is in heaven" (Matt 7:21). It is not enough to *say* I believe in Jesus and the God he reveals and then skip off and *do* nothing. I must also *do* what that faith demands, and what faith in Jesus demands is amply delineated by the demands of Moses and the prophets and Jesus himself: care for God's poor and marginalized. James puts this demand concretely and starkly. "If a brother or sister is naked or in lack of daily food," he asks, "and one of you says to them 'Go in peace, be warmed and filled,' without giving them the things needed for the body, what does it profit? So faith by itself, if it has no works, is dead" (Jas 2:15–17). James's question is purely rhetorical, for its answer is obvious: it profits nothing, for it leaves the naked and hungry person, like Lazarus, still naked and hungry. That answer is as true in the twenty-first century as it was at the end of the first century. Given the increased number of the worldwide ill clad, hungry, and homeless in our day, we could say that it is even more crucially true and makes an inescapable ethical demand on all faithful Christians: feed the hungry, clothe the naked, care for the sick and dying, house the homeless and the refugees. All of this can be done with two different intentions, one good, one bad. The good intention, one that is ethical and rich toward God, is to feed the hungry, clothe the naked, care for the sick and dying because they need to be fed and clothed and cared for; the bad intention, one not rich toward God, is to feed and clothe

---

[13] Ibid., 183.

and care so that you "may be seen by others." Those who do that, Jesus declares, "have received their reward" (Matt 6:5).

Having offered privileged Christians advice on how their wealth should be used, not only for themselves but also for their unprivileged brothers and sisters, James goes on to comment on rich persons and on their wealth itself. "Come now, you who say 'Today or tomorrow we will go to such and such a town and spend a year there doing business and making money.' Yet you do not even know what tomorrow will bring. What is your life? For you are a mist that appears for a little time and then vanishes" (Jas 4:13–14). The case here is an echo of Luke's story of the rich man and Lazarus, though there is no mention of riches. We can imagine those who are involved in this passage as merchants, traveling from city to city in search of profit, but the advice given to them is advice for all human beings, rich and poor alike. We are but mists inhabiting the world, here this morning, blown away by an afternoon wind, and so too therefore is any wealth we spend so much of our time amassing. James does not condemn the merchants' plan to make money, and he does not say that making money is unethical in itself. He says only that wealth, like life itself, is fleeting, something every human being can confirm, having experienced the death of a loved one. Wealth can, of course, be left to some loved one; that is taken for granted in American tradition. The Christian tradition articulated from the ancient biblical tradition down to the present day is that leaving wealth to one's family or one's friends is entirely ethical, but that what is far from ethical is ignoring the Christian tradition to feed the hungry, clothe the naked, house the homeless, care for the sick and dying. To do these things is to be truly "rich toward God" (Luke 12:21).

There is one final economic question we wish to raise before concluding this chapter, a question frequently raised across the world: Am I ethically bound to pay taxes? In the Mediterranean society of Jesus's time, it was a hotly debated question, for Jesus lived in a country occupied by the all-conquering Romans. Any taxes to be paid were to be paid to the hated Nero, the emperor at the time, and tax collectors were generally corrupt and equally hated. Jesus, perhaps, signaled his approval of paying taxes by calling a tax collector, Levi, as one of his disciples and then eating in Levi's house with him and other tax collectors (Matt 9:9–13; Mark 2:14–16; Luke 5:27–32). But he made his approval of paying legitimate civil taxes explicit and unequivocal in a passage reported by all three Synoptic Gospels. "Some of the Pharisees and some of the Herodians," groups who were opposed to the life Jesus led and the doctrines he taught, seeking to entrap him in his talk and to make him look bad in the eyes of his fellow citizens, asked him, "Is it lawful to pay taxes to Caesar or not?" (Mark

12:14; Matt 22:17; Luke 20:23). "Knowing their hypocrisy," he asked them to bring him the coin with which the tax to Caesar was paid and asked them, "Whose likeness and inscription is this?" They had, of course, no option but to reply, "Caesar's." Jesus then rendered his judgment on paying legitimate taxes: "Render to Caesar the things that are Caesar's and to God the things that are God's" (Mark 12:17). This dispute, important enough to be recorded in all three Synoptic Gospels, makes it clear to all the followers of Jesus that they should pay their civil taxes, no matter how much they might despise those who levy them.

Beyond his "render to Caesar the things that are Caesar's," Jesus offers no further explanation of why his followers should pay taxes. Some ten years earlier than Mark, the earliest Gospel, the apostle Paul had given much the same instruction to the followers of Jesus to pay their taxes, and he offered two reasons for paying: "for the sake of conscience," and because "the authorities are ministers of God attending to this very thing" (Rom 13:5–6). Civic authorities impose taxes of various kinds; the followers of Jesus are ethically obliged under God to pay them. There is often complaint in America about the complexity of the tax code. The Roman tax code was no simpler, but Jesus, Paul, and later the Christian who wrote 1 Peter 2:13–17 all assert that taxes are to be paid. With our knowledge of the cultural kinship norms of the time, we can offer a good reason for the obligation to pay taxes. We are all God's creatures and, therefore, brothers and sisters of one another. We are ethically obliged to care for those who are in need, the hungry, the inadequately clothed, the homeless, the refugee, all God's poor we have enumerated several times already. Civic taxes help to provide the money needed for such social services, and the followers of Jesus who *say* they desire to be like him are obliged to *do* as he did, care for the poor as he did. Paying their taxes is one social and institutional way to do so.

Conclusion

In conclusion, we wish to introduce a caveat. In this chapter we focused on the ethical source that is the sacred scripture, not because it is the only source for the Christian ethical obligation to care for the poor and marginalized of every race, color, and creed, but because it is a fundamental source for this particular ethic, which came to be known under the general heading of Catholic social teaching. This chapter demonstrates that ethics has been a staple of the Christian tradition since its beginning. At the end of the twentieth century, several authors wrote books under the general rubric of one hundred years of Catholic social thought, and they gave unintended support to the assumption that Catholic social teaching had begun only with Pope Leo XIII's 1891 epic encyclical letter *Rerum Novarum* and had ended one hundred years later with Pope John Paul II's celebration of its hundredth anniversary in his 1981 encyclical letter *Centesimus Annus*. One of those authors, Jesuit John Coleman, however, laid that assumption to rest with his acknowledgment that "Catholic social thought is much older than one hundred years. Its roots go back to the life and words of Jesus."[14] It is precisely that judgment that this chapter seeks to support and elucidate.

Questions for Reflection

- How do you understand the virtuous principle of "faith that sees injustice and does justice"? In what way does this virtuous perspective aid in the analysis, evaluation, and response to poverty? Give specific examples.
- What is the difference between charity and justice? What is structural sin? How can acts of charity and justice affect structural sin that perpetuates poverty?
- What does scripture teach about justice for the poor? Who are the poor in our society and how should we interpret and apply scripture in the twenty-first century to realize justice for the poor?
- What does scripture teach about wealth? How should a virtuous perspective, guided by faith that sees injustice and does justice, view wealth?

Suggested Readings

Bergman, Roger C. *Catholic Social Learning: Educating the Faith That Does Justice*. New York: Fordham University Press, 2011.

Coleman, John A., ed. *One Hundred Years of Catholic Social Thought*. Maryknoll, NY: Orbis Books, 1991.

---

[14] John A. Coleman, ed., *One Hundred Years of Catholic Social Thought* (Maryknoll, NY: Orbis Books, 1991), 2. See also Donal Dorr, *Option for the Poor: One Hundred Years of Catholic Social Teaching* (Maryknoll, NY: Orbis Books, 1992); David J. O'Brien and Thomas A. Shannon, eds., *Catholic Social Thought: The Documentary Heritage* (Maryknoll, NY: Orbis Books, 1996).

Dorr, Donal. *Option for the Poor: One Hundred Years of Catholic Social Teaching.* Maryknoll, NY: Orbis Books, 1992.

Haughey, John C., ed. *The Faith That Does Justice: Examining the Christian Sources for Social Change.* Eugene, OR: Wipf and Stock Publishers, 1977.

Himes, Kenneth B., ed. *Modern Catholic Social Teaching: Commentaries and Interpretations.* Washington, DC: Georgetown University Press, 2005.

Pontifical Council for Justice and Peace, *Compendium of the Social Doctrine of the Church.* Dublin: Veritatis Publications, 2005.

12

Biomedical Ethics

Issues at the Beginning of Life

Learning Objectives

- Explain various types of artificial reproductive technologies.
- Explain and critically analyze the Catholic Church's arguments against the ethics of homologous and heterologous artificial reproductive technologies.
- Explain and critically analyze the inseparability principle that is the cornerstone of the Catholic Church's argument against both artificial reproductive technologies and artificial contraception.
- Explain and critically analyze the ethical difference between natural family planning that the Catholic Church permits as ethical, and artificial contraception that it condemns as unethical.

In the 1950s the marketing of effective oral contraceptives made it possible to have sexual intercourse without reproduction; in the 1980s the marketing of artificial reproductive technologies (ARTs) made it possible to have reproduction without sexual intercourse. The Congregation for the Doctrine of the Faith's 1987 *Instruction, Donum Vitae (Instruction on Respect for Human Life in Its Origin and on the Dignity of Procreation: Replies to Certain Questions of the Day)*, enunciates the controlling Catholic principle with respect to these two realities: "The Church's teaching on marriage and human procreation affirms the 'inseparable connection, willed by God and unable to be broken by man on his own initiative, between the two meanings of the conjugal act: the unitive

273

meaning and the procreative meaning'" (*Inst.* II,B,4,a).[1] Basing itself on the inseparability principle, the Catholic Church prohibits both contraception and "artificial procreation" or "artificial fertilization." In this chapter we deal directly with church teaching on the ethics of ARTs and contraception and indirectly with the ethics of abortion.

Artificial Reproductive Technologies

For the Catholic Church, artificial reproductive technologies, defined as "non-coital methods of conception that involve manipulation of both eggs and sperm,"[2] interfere with the inseparability principle by separating the unitive and procreative meanings of sexual intercourse. Progressive theologians tend to think that, although ARTs often do not rely on sexual intercourse for reproduction, they still may fulfill both the unitive and procreative ends of marriage considered as an intimate interpersonal whole. When the marital relationship is seen, as it is seen since Vatican II in contemporary Catholic theology, as an interpersonal, procreative whole, it seems reasonable to argue that at least some ARTs utilize modern science and technology to facilitate both the unitive and procreative meanings of the spousal relationship. *Gaudium et Spes* notes that "children really are the supreme gift of marriage" (*GS,* no. 50); if they are, and ARTs can help infertile couples realize this supreme gift, we may legitimately ask about the credibility of the church's inseparability principle in condemning all ARTs that separate the two meanings of the conjugal act. This, then, is the debate in this section. First, we define two types of ARTs; second, we explain and critique church teaching on ARTs, focusing primarily on the CDF's *Instruction;* third, we analyze and evaluate ARTs in light of our foundational principle for the morality of any sexual activity.

ARTs are used when at least one spouse in a marriage is believed to be infertile. One of the earliest ARTs to be used was artificial insemination. In this procedure male sperm is collected from either masturbation or a condom used in sexual intercourse and is inserted into the woman's cervical canal at or near the time of ovulation in order to fertilize the released ovum. The collected sperm may be used within a few hours of collection or frozen for later use. This procedure, in which fertilization takes place within the woman's body, is known as *in vivo* (in the body) artificial insemination.

---

[1] To bring *Donum Vitae* up to date, in 2007 the CDF issued a more recent statement, "Instruction *Dignitatis Personae* on Certain Bioethical Questions," which reaffirms the earlier teaching with regard to reproductive technologies.

[2] Linda J. Beckman and S. Marie Harvey, "Current Reproductive Technologies: Increased Access and Choice?" *Journal of Social Issues* 61 (2005): 2.

When the sperm is collected from the woman's husband, the entire procedure is known as homologous insemination; when it is collected from a donor who is not the woman's husband, it is heterologous insemination.

Another ART, one that differs from in vivo in terms of where fertilization takes place, is in vitro fertilization with embryo transfer (IVF-ET). In this procedure both sperm and ova are collected and fertilization takes place outside the woman's body in a laboratory. The simplest and most common way to collect ova is treatment of the woman with human menopausal gonadotropin, which causes ova to mature in the woman's body, and these ripe ova (oocytes) are then harvested by laparoscopic surgery. Once sperm and oocytes are collected, the sperm is capacitated or washed to enhance penetration and fertilization of several ova, creating several zygotes in a petri dish (in vitro). After fertilization and about forty hours of development, during which time the zygote is scientifically in the pre-embryo stage,[3] one to six healthy pre-embryos are selected and transferred through the woman's cervix to her uterus, anticipating implantation and development. Excess healthy pre-embryos can be frozen, a process known as cryopreservation, and used later if the embryo transfer is unsuccessful or if the couple desires another pregnancy. They may also be used for research. Unhealthy pre-embryos are typically destroyed. The processes of cryopreservation, research, and destruction of fertilized embryos raise their own ethical problems, and we must first address them before proceeding.

The Catholic principle is firm: "The human being must be respected—as a person—from the very first instant of his existence" (*Inst.* I,1). From the moment the ovum is fertilized, the CDF *Instruction* states, a new life is begun, the life of a new human being. "It would never be made human if it were not human already" (*Inst.* I,1). Pre-embryos are believed to be human beings with all the rights of human beings; therefore, the church condemns abortion as unethical because it is the direct killing of what it believes to be a human being, and it also condemns any act against the life of artificially reproduced pre-embryos (*inst.* I,5). For the very same reason, "respect for the dignity of the human being," it forbids as unethical all experimental manipulation or exploitation of the human embryo and the freezing or cryopreservation of embryos (*Inst.* I,4). This latter "constitutes an offence against the respect due to human beings by exposing them to grave risks of death or harm to their physical integrity and depriving them, at least temporarily, of maternal shelter and gestation" (*Inst.* I,6).

---

[3] The pre-embryo stage lasts from the completion of fertilization to the development of the primitive streak, which occurs "on about the fourteenth day of development." See Howard W. Jones and Susan L. Crockin, "On Assisted Reproduction, Religion, and Civil Law," *Fertility and Sterility* 73 (2000): 450.

The church's ethical stance could not be clearer. The human embryo is a human being from the moment of conception, has the same right to life as every other human being, and may not be deliberately destroyed or placed in a situation that may lead to its harm or destruction.

Assured the safety of every embryo, the question of the ethics of ARTs still remains for discussion. Theological ethicists who argue against the morality of ARTs do so on the basis that "fertilization is not directly the result of the marital act, since the semen used is not deposited by that act in the vagina, but by a technician's manipulation which substitutes for the marital act."[4] Since the integrity of marital intercourse and its direct relationship with reproduction is at the heart of the church's ethical analysis of ARTs, we next explore that analysis as it is articulated in the CDF's *Instruction.*

The CDF's *Instruction* and ARTs

The *Instruction* was issued by the CDF in 1987 in response to questions posed about the biomedical ability to intervene in the process of procreation (*Inst.,* Foreword). It draws some clear lines on the morality of fertility-related interventions. These interventions, the *Instruction* notes, "are not to be rejected on the grounds that they are artificial." As such, "they bear witness to the possibilities of the art of medicine." Rather, they "must be given a moral evaluation in reference to the dignity of the human person, who is called to realize his vocation from God to the gift of love and the gift of life" (*Inst.* Intro, 3). The *Instruction* addresses two main issues. The first is the fundamental respect due to human life and the longstanding Catholic principle that it "must be absolutely respected and protected from the moment of conception" (*Inst.* I,1) This principle rules out, as we have explained, any destruction of, experimentation with, or cryopreservation of embryos. The second issue is artificial insemination itself, which is to be assessed ethically on the basis of "the respect, defense and promotion of man, his dignity as a person who is endowed with a spiritual soul and with moral responsibility" (*Inst.* Intro, 1). We question the teaching of the *Instruction* largely because of its biological and physicalist approach to natural law.

The *Instruction* relies heavily on the personalist language of *Gaudium et Spes* to explain its perception of human dignity in relation to sexuality,

---

[4] Benedict Ashley and Kevin O'Rourke, *Health Care Ethics: A Theological Analysis,* 4th ed. (Washington, DC: Georgetown University Press, 1997), 247. See also Germain Grisez, *The Way of the Lord Jesus, Volume Three* (Quincy IL: Franciscan Press, 1997), 244–49.

marriage, and the conjugal act. "The moral criteria for medical intervention in procreation," it argues, "are deduced from the dignity of human persons, of their sexuality and of their origin. *Medicine which seeks to be ordered to the integral good of the person must respect the specifically human values of sexuality*" (*Inst.* II,B,7). These foundational values are grounded in "the integral dignity of the human person" (*Inst.* II,B,7) reflected in the "conjugal union" (*Inst.* Intro and II,B,5) of the spouses, which "must be actualized in marriage" through the conjugal act (*Inst.* Intro, 5). These laws, it is argued, establish the inseparable connection between the unitive and procreative meanings of every conjugal act. Any technological separation of these meanings, either artificial contraception or artificial reproduction, violates the intrinsic dignity of spousal intercourse and renders the separation a violation and unethical. Medicine, the *Instruction* notes, must respect "the integral dignity of the human person first of all in the act [of intercourse] and at the moment in which the spouses transmit life to a new person" (*Inst.* II,B,7). When the unitive and procreative meanings of the act of sexual intercourse are separated, the act loses its human dignity (*Inst.* II,B,5). There is, then, in the *Instruction* a clear "no" to ARTs, heavily based on the inseparability principle.

Heterologous Artificial Insemination and the Personalist Principle

While the *Instruction* utilizes personalist language to explain the meanings of marriage and human sexuality, there is a tension between personalist and biological arguments in its different treatment of heterologous and homologous artificial insemination. Recall that in heterologous artificial insemination, the sperm or ovum is provided by someone other than the spouse; in homologous artificial insemination, the sperm and ovum are provided by the spouses. The *Instruction* begins its consideration of heterologous artificial insemination by answering the question: "Why must human procreation take place in marriage?" Its answer is couched in personalist terms. Procreation "must be the fruit and the sign of the mutual self-giving of the spouses, of their love and of their fidelity." Notice that the emphasis is not on the biological act of intercourse, but on the interpersonal marital relationship, its mutual self-giving, love, and fidelity. Fidelity in the marital relationship implies a "reciprocal respect of their right to become a father and a mother only through each other." The *Instruction* grounds its moral assessment of heterologous artificial insemination in the personalist dimension of natural law. Procreation must take place within marriage and the personal and relational implications for the spouses with one another and with their child, who is "the living image of their love" and the "permanent sign of their conjugal union" (*Inst.* III,A,1). The clear focus of the *Instruction*'s treatment of heterologous artificial insemination is on the personal and relational dimensions of the spouses, their union, and their relationship with the child.

The *Instruction* formulates its rejection of heterologous artificial insemination by setting forth several ways in which it violates family relationships. First, heterologous artificial insemination violates the marital relationship. Heterologous artificial fertilization, the use of either sperm or ovum from a donor to achieve fertilization, "is contrary to the unity of marriage, to the dignity of the spouses, to the vocation proper to parents, and to the child's right to be conceived and brought into the world in marriage and from marriage." Respect "for the unity of marriage and for conjugal fidelity demands that the child be conceived in marriage; the bond existing between husband and wife accords the spouses, in an objective and inalienable manner, the exclusive right to become father and mother solely through each other." Second, the introduction of a third party into reproduction through the use of donor sperm or ova "constitutes a violation of the reciprocal commitment of the spouses and a grave lack in regard to that essential property of marriage which is its unity." Third, heterologous artificial insemination "violates the rights of the child; it deprives him of his filial relationship with his parental origins and can hinder the maturing of his personal identity." Fourth, "such damage to the personal relationships within the family has repercussions on civil society: what threatens the unity and stability of the family is a source of dissension, disorder and injustice in the whole of social life." The violation of all of these relationships leads "to a negative moral judgment concerning heterologous artificial fertilization" (*Inst.* II,A,2).

Homologous Artificial Insemination and the Inseparability Principle

When it addresses homologous artificial insemination, the *Instruction* shifts emphasis from personal relations to biological acts. The foundational principle for the *Instruction*'s ethical analysis of homologous artificial insemination is the inseparability principle:

> The Church's teaching on marriage and human procreation affirms the "inseparable connection, willed by God and unable to be broken by man on his own initiative, between the two meanings of the conjugal act: the unitive meaning and the procreative meaning. Indeed, by its intimate structure, the conjugal act, while most closely uniting

husband and wife, capacitates them for the generation of new lives, according to laws inscribed in the very being of man and of woman." (*Inst.* II,B,4,a)

Three questions emerge regarding the *Instruction*'s introduction of this inseparability principle. First, why does it make this methodological shift from a focus on relationships when ethically evaluating heterologous artificial insemination to a focus on the inseparability principle embedded in the act of spousal intercourse when ethically evaluating homologous artificial insemination? Second, what are the weaknesses of this inseparability principle with regard to homologous artificial insemination? Third, what would be the ethical implications for homologous artificial insemination if the *Instruction* were methodologically consistent?

First, while the arguments against heterologous artificial insemination seem reasonable to us given the relational complications of donor sperm or ova and their potential impact on family relationships, the relationship of the parents with the child, the donor's relationship with both the parents and the child, and the social implications with regard to the nature of the family, the same relational complications do not apply in homologous artificial insemination. When both sperm and ova belong to the parents, and a surrogate is not used to carry the embryo, no relational complication exists. All that can be claimed with certainty in the case of homologous artificial insemination is that the act of sexual intercourse is not immediately responsible for procreation. While this fact gives us insight into the procedure facilitating reproduction, it gives us no insight into the ethical meaning of that procedure. Ethical meaning is discerned not in a fact, in this case the fact of technological assistance in the process of reproduction, but in the meaning of that fact for family relationships. The application of the same personalist principle to both homologous artificial insemination and heterologous artificial insemination, we suggest, would lead to a different conclusion about the morality of homologous artificial insemination.

Second, by introducing the inseparability principle in its discussion of homologous artificial insemination, the *Instruction* clearly recognizes that there is a shift in the foundational principle in analyzing and ethically evaluating homologous artificial insemination and heterologous artificial insemination. The *Instruction*'s condemnation of homologous artificial insemination is "strictly dependent on the principles just mentioned" (*Inst.* II,B,5). In fact, there is a single principle, the inseparability principle. Richard McCormick notes that the *Instruction*'s claim of strict dependence is a "remarkable statement," since previous church documents indicated that the prohibition of homologous artificial insemination is "not strictly dependent on the analyses given or available to support it."[5] In addition, this principle is nowhere to be found in magisterial teaching prior to Pope Paul VI's encyclical *Humanae Vitae*, either on marriage or the prohibition of artificial reproduction (or contraception).[6] It follows from the *Instruction*'s strict dependence on a particular principle to justify its moral argument against homologous artificial insemination that the argument is only as strong as the principle; if the principle is weak, so too is any ethical conclusion drawn from the principle.

We believe the inseparability principle used to prohibit homologous artificial insemination (and also contraception) is a weak principle on several counts. First, there is no intrinsic procreative meaning to each and every sexual act. Sexual acts in an infertile or post-menopausal relationship, or sexual acts during periods in which the wife is known to be infertile, do not have and cannot have an intrinsic procreative meaning. In these cases, as well as in cases in which, following Pope Pius XII's ruling, the couple avoids procreation for grave reasons, there exists only a unitive meaning. Sexual intercourse may be said to be procreative only when actual reproduction is possible, and only then can the procreative meaning of the act be strictly distinguished from its unitive meaning. That is why many theologians choose to discuss the unitive and procreative meanings of not every sexual act but of the overall marital relationship.[7]

Second, the inseparability principle contains a "germ of truth" in what Richard McCormick calls an "aesthetic or ecological (bodily integrity) concern." He means that all artificial interventions into the sexual relationship, whether to prevent or procure reproduction, are a kind of "second best."[8] This is in line with the *Instruction*'s claim that conception realized through in vitro fertilization is "deprived of its proper function." To deprive a procedure of its proper function, however, does not make the procedure

---

[5] Richard A. McCormick, *The Critical Calling: Reflections on Moral Dilemmas Since Vatican II* (Washington, DC: Georgetown University Press, 1989), 347.

[6] Joseph A. Selling, "Overwriting Tradition: '*Humanae Vitae*' Replaced Real Church Teaching," *National Catholic Reporter* (May 29, 2018).

[7] See, for example, McCormick, *The Critical Calling*, 346–47; Joseph A. Selling, "The Development of Catholic Tradition and Sexual Morality," in *Embracing Sexuality: Authority and Experience in the Catholic Church*, ed. Joseph A. Selling (Burlington, VT: Ashgate, 2001), 149–62; Joseph A. Selling, "Magisterial Teaching on Marriage 1880–1986: Historical Constancy or Radical Development," in *Dialogue about Catholic Sexual Teaching: Readings in Moral Theology No. 8*, ed. Charles Curran and Richard McCormick (New York: Paulist Press, 1993), 93–97; Bernard Häring, "The Inseparability of the Unitive-Procreative Functions of the Marital Act," in Curran and McCormick, *Dialogue about Catholic Sexual Teaching*, 163–64; Lisa Sowle Cahill, "Sexuality: Personal, Communal, Responsible," in Selling, *Embracing Sexuality*, 165–72.

[8] McCormick, *The Critical Calling*, 348.

ipso facto ethically wrong in every situation. It does not do so, McCormick insists, unless we "elevate an aesthetic-ecological concern into an absolute moral imperative";[9] that is far from the experiential intentions of the vast majority of Catholic couples.

Third, the basis for the "aesthetic or ecological concern" is a product of the biologism and physicalism that has controlled the Catholic magisterial natural law tradition, grounded in both a flawed biology and an incomplete theology of marriage. In the Catholic tradition before the Second Vatican Council the primary end of marriage was always said to be procreation. This teaching reflected a history that goes back to the "wrong old days" when the male was considered the sole source of life,[10] and when procreation was recognized as the only legitimate meaning and end for sexual intercourse.[11] Our modern understanding of biology and human sexuality, however, teaches us that the male is not the sole source of life and that procreation is not even possible in the vast majority of sexual acts. A couple can ethically justify sexual intercourse when there is no possibility of procreation but, as we argued extensively in Chapter 8, they can never ethically justify their sexual intercourse when there is no unitive meaning. It is reasonable, therefore, to argue that not only are the unitive and procreative meanings of the sexual act separable, and on occasion in fact clearly separated, but also that the unitive meaning is now primary and the procreative meaning secondary.

Fourth, the tension between the personalist principle used to ethically evaluate heterologous artificial insemination and the inseparability principle used to ethically evaluate homologous artificial insemination is heightened when the *Instruction* claims that "homologous IVF and ET fertilization is not marked by all that ethical negativity found in extra-conjugal procreation; the family and marriage continue to constitute the setting for the birth and upbringing of the children" (*Inst.* II,B,5). By its own admission, then, the inseparability principle that the *Instruction* uses to condemn homologous artificial insemination does not carry the same ethical weight as the relational principle it uses to condemn heterologous artificial insemination. Relational considerations make homologous artificial insemination less ethically reprehensible than heterologous artificial insemination. Since there may be no conjugal act in homologous artificial

---

[9] Ibid.

[10] See Aristotle, *Generation of Animals* I, 21, 729b; Paige duBois, *Sowing the Body: Psychoanalysis and Ancient Representations of Women* (Chicago: University of Chicago Press, 1988), 39–85; Carol Delaney, *The Seed and The Soil: Gender and Cosmology in Turkish Village Society* (Berkeley and Los Angeles: University of California Press, 1991).

[11] See Michael G. Lawler, *Marriage in the Catholic Church: Disputed Questions* (Collegeville, MN: Liturgical Press, 2002), 27–42.

insemination, why would the *Instruction* base its moral condemnation of homologous artificial insemination on the conjugal act and the inseparability principle? It must do so because the relational considerations do not warrant an absolute prohibition of homologous artificial insemination. We do not, therefore, find the argument against homologous artificial insemination morally compelling.

Based on the foregoing analysis we draw what we believe is a reasonable conclusion about the ethics of homologous artificial insemination. Once again we assert that if the premise on which an argument is based is weak, then any conclusion drawn from it will also be weak. We believe the inseparability principle is weak and far from demonstrated and cannot bear the weight of the *Instruction*'s conclusion absolutely prohibiting homologous artificial insemination. Given the desperation of an infertile couple to have a child and their intention, grounded in the virtuous perspective of mutual justice, love, respect, and responsibility to have their marital relationship "crowned" (*GS,* no. 48) by their child, we believe the use of homologous artificial insemination can be ethical and facilitate both the unitive and procreative meanings of marriage.

We are in complete agreement here with Lisa Cahill. Many Catholics, she notes, "perceive a difference larger than the Vatican allows between therapies used in marriage, even if they do temporarily circumvent sexual intercourse, and methods which bring donors into the marital procreative venture." She believes, and we agree, that "donor methods are more morally objectionable because they do not appreciate the unity as relationships of sexual expression, committed partnership, and parenthood."[12] While procreation in homologous artificial insemination need not be the direct result of an act of sexual intercourse, it would be the fruit of an overall marital relational act that expresses and facilitates the just love, commitment, care, concern, and dignity of the couple shared with a new human being, their child. Our argument defending the moral acceptability of homologous artificial insemination is grounded not in the inseparability of the unitive and procreative meanings of a sexual act but in the meaning and nature of a marital relationship. It is in the overall marital relationship, not in each and every sexual act, that the unitive and procreative meanings may be legitimately inseparable.[13] With the *Instruction*, we affirm the connection

---

[12] Lisa Sowle Cahill, *Women and Sexuality* (New York: Paulist Press, 1992), 75. See also Thomas A. Shannon and Lisa Sowle Cahill, *Religion and Artificial Reproduction: An Inquiry into the Vatican Instruction on Respect for Life in Its Origin* (New York: Crossroad, 1987), 103–32; and Thomas A. Shannon, *Reproductive Technologies: A Reader* (New York: Sheed and Ward, 2004).

[13] The Ethics Committee of the American Fertility Society accuses the CDF of "barnyard physiology." "This means that the concept that intercourse is intended entirely for reproduc-

of marriage, sexual love, and parenthood. We judge, however, that its claim that genuine marital love is incompatible with the occasional use of artificial means to bring about a longed-for conception is unsupported and can be ethically ignored.

Contraception

In the preceding section we considered the ethics of conception without a marital sexual act. In this section we consider the ethics of a marital sexual act with the deliberate blocking of conception. We consider, in other words, contraception. The Catholic Church is concerned specifically with two ways to avoid conception. The first is abstinence from sexual intercourse during the wife's monthly fertile period, usually called natural family planning (NFP); the second is the use of an artificial barrier to prevent conception as a result of sexual intercourse, either a physical barrier like a condom or a diaphragm or a chemical barrier like an anovulant pill. The Catholic Church morally approves NFP (as long as the married couple practicing NFP does not have a contra-life will) since, it argues, NFP preserves the inseparability of the unitive and procreative meanings of the marital sexual act. It condemns all types of artificial contraception as unethical because they separate the unitive and procreative meanings of the marital sexual act. In what follows we consider only the ethics of artificial contraception.

In the Catholic tradition, which you will recall is a major source of Catholic ethical teaching, there is no doubt about the position of the church with regard to artificial contraception. No Catholic theologian has ever denied or legitimately could deny that, prior to the appearance of Pope Paul VI's encyclical *Humanae Vitae,* the Catholic Church's condemnation of artificial contraception was consistent and universal. In his masterful history of contraception John Noonan outlines the universal agreement. "Since the first clear mention of contraception by a Christian theologian . . . the teachers of the church have taught without hesitation or variation that certain acts preventing procreation are gravely sinful. No Catholic theologian has ever taught, 'contraception is a good act.'" That judgment was delivered in 1965, but even then Noonan hinted that a development may be forthcoming and that his study "may provide grounds for prophecy."[14] Noonan himself contributed to that development through

---

tion derives from observation of those animals who exhibit 'heat' and give an external sign of ovulation during which period the female will accept the male and at no other time." Cited in Jones and Crockin, "On Assisted Reproduction, Religion, and Civil Law," 449.

[14] John T. Noonan, *Contraception: A History of the Treatment by Catholic Theologians and Canonists* (Cambridge, MA: Harvard University Press, 1965), 6.

his positive participation in the Papal Birth Control Commission formed by Pope John XXIII to consider the question of the Catholic Church and contraception in the twentieth century.[15]

Pope John XXIII's Papal Birth Control Commission was confirmed and enlarged by his successor, Pope Paul VI, until it ultimately had seventy-one members. The final vote of the bishops on the commission answered two questions. For the question "Is contraception intrinsically evil?"—meaning its use to prevent conception could never be morally justified—nine bishops voted no, three voted yes, and three abstained. For the question "Is contraception, as defined by the majority report, in basic continuity with tradition and the declarations of the magisterium?," nine bishops voted yes, five voted no, and one abstained.[16] In response to the question "Is artificial contraception an intrinsically evil violation of the natural law? the theologian-advisers to the commission voted fifteen no and four yes.[17] Both a majority report and a minority report were submitted to Paul VI who, professing himself unconvinced by the arguments of the majority, approved the minority report in his encyclical *Humanae Vitae*.[18] The differential between the two reports is easily categorized.

The minority report, which became the controverted part of *Humanae Vitae,* argued that "each and every marital act must of necessity retain its intrinsic relationship to the procreation of human life" (*HV,* no. 11). Anyone who knows Catholic theological history also knows that this was the first time in theological history that the church's teaching was stated in this way. The prior tradition had always been that it is *marriage,* not each and every *marital act,* that is to be open to procreation, and that is what the majority report argued: "What had been condemned in the past and remains so today is the unjustified refusal of life . . . the rejection of procreation as a specific task of *marriage.*" It then asserted that "human intervention in the process of the marriage act for reasons drawn from the end of marriage itself should not always be excluded, provided that the criteria of morality are always safeguarded."[19] The differential in the two positions was the differential created by the two different models of marriage we discussed in Chapter 9, the minority report being based on the traditional procreative institution

---

[15] For a detailed account of the Papal Birth Control Commission, see Robert McClory, *Turning Point: The Inside Story of the Papal Birth Control Commission, and How Humanae Vitae Changed the Life of Patty Crowley and the Future of the Church* (New York: Crossroad, 1995).

[16] Ibid., 127.

[17] Ibid., 99.

[18] For detail on this, see Janet E. Smith, Humanae Vitae: *A Generation Later* (Washington, DC: Catholic University of America Press, 1991), 11–33.

[19] Cited in Robert Blair Kaiser, *The Politics of Sex and Religion* (Kansas City: Leaven Press, 1985), 260–61.

model, and the majority report being based on the emerging spousal union model that had been embraced by the Second Vatican Council. We believe that the majority report is the more satisfactory ethical formulation, which is today the judgment of the majority of Catholic theologians and the vast majority of Catholic couples, because they adhere to the same spousal union model on which the majority report was based. Margaret Farley summarizes the present position this way: "In much of Catholic moral theology and ethics, the procreative norm as the sole or primary justification of sexual intercourse is gone."[20] Fifty years after *Humanae Vitae,* despite a concerted minority effort to make adherence to it a test case of authentic Catholicity, the debate over the procreative institution and spousal union models continues in the church, causing what Julie Hanlon Rubio calls an "unnecessary and unhelpful" divide.[21]

When faced with such a divide, we believe church teaching makes the theologian's task clear. That task, in the words of the International Theological Commission, is one of "interpreting the documents of the past and present Magisterium, of putting them in the context of the whole of revealed truth, and of finding a better understanding of them by the use of hermeneutics."[22] *Humanae Vitae* left the debate about contraception open by choosing to ignore, rather than to refute, the arguments and recommendations of the majority of the Papal Birth Control Commission. We now examine the socio-historical contexts of the Catholic Church's teaching on the ethics of artificial contraception in the hope that the ethical principles involved in the debate will be illuminated to enable Catholic theologians to close the divide and Catholic spouses to choose in conscience the means for ensuring the "responsible parenthood"[23] to which they are called.

In the 1960s the Second Vatican Council sought to discern the "signs of the times" (*GS,* no. 4) with respect to every Catholic reality, including the reality of marriage and family. One outcome of the council, achieved by diocesan bishops and theologians over the insistent objections of Vatican functionaries,[24] was a reception of a renewed theology of marriage that altered the church's teaching on marriage as surely as the reception of

---

[20] Margaret A. Farley, *Just Love: A Framework for Christian Sexual Ethics* (New York: Continuum, 2006), 278.

[21] Julie Hanlon Rubio, "Beyond the Liberal/Conservative Divide on Contraception," *Horizons* 32 (2005): 271.

[22] International Theological Commission, *Theses on the Relationship between the Ecclesiastical Magisterium and Theology* (Washington, DC: USCCB, 1977), 6.

[23] The official title of the majority report of the Papal Birth Control Commission was "*Schema Documenti de Responsabili Paternitate,* Outline of a Document on Responsible Parenthood." See McClory, *Turning Point,* 171.

[24] See *History of Vatican II*, 3 vols., ed. Giuseppe Alberigo, English version ed. Joseph A. Komonchak (Maryknoll, NY: Orbis Books, 2000).

capitalist theories altered its teaching on usury, the reception of personalist theories altered its teaching on slavery, and its reception of theories of
freedom altered its teaching on religious freedom. An examination of the
socio-historical path to that reception will illuminate the issue of contraception. Before embarking on that examination we make a plea that the
search for relevant arguments be conducted with mutual Christian love,
respect, and justice, and not with the mutual sarcasm, anger, and dismissal
that has so often characterized it since the publication of *Humanae Vitae*.

The model of marriage as procreative institution was thrust on to center stage in the 1960s with the appearance of the female-cycle-regulating
anovulant pill. In 1962, Jesuit ethicist John Lynch wrote that "moralists
have never been less than unanimous in their assertion that natural law
cannot countenance the use of these progestational steroids for the purpose
of contraception."[25] In 1965, another distinguished Jesuit ethicist, Richard
McCormick, wrote: "Contraception continues to be . . . the major moral
issue troubling the Church," and also

> The effect of repeated authoritative Church pronouncements on a
> matter of this importance is a presumptive certitude of their cor-
> rectness. . . . Because there is a presumptive *certitude,* prudence
> demands the acceptance of the conclusion in defect of prevailing
> contrary evidence. But because this certitude is *only* presumptive,
> circumstances can arise which will create a duty for the theologian
> to test it in the light of changing fact, increasing understanding of
> ethical theory, etc.[26]

Two years later McCormick had been convinced to change his judgment of
presumptive certitude by the majority rebuttal from the Papal Birth Control Commission. "The documents of the Papal Commission," he wrote,
"represent a rather full summary of two points of view. . . . The majority
report, particularly the analysis in its 'rebuttal,' strikes this reader as much
the more satisfactory statement."[27] By 1967, McCormick's earlier suggestion of theological testing was well under way in the Catholic theological
community. In 1968, it was definitively focused with the publication of
Pope Paul VI's encyclical *Humanae Vitae,* which we have already stated
emerged from the traditional procreative model of marriage.

---

[25] John J. Lynch, "Current Theology: Notes on Moral Theology," *Theological Studies*
23 (1962): 239.
[26] Richard A. McCormick, *Notes on Moral Theology: 1965–1980* (Lanham, MD: University Press of America, 1981), 41–42.
[27] Ibid., 164.

The Personal Procreative-Union Model of Marriage

The unprecedented horrors of the First World War transformed the context of human affairs in Europe, where the horrors were localized. This period of "bereavement" and "national trauma"[28] gave birth to a philosophical movement that came to be known as personalism. This personalism gradually affected Catholic theology and made its first, tentative Catholic appearance in 1930, in Pope Pius XI's encyclical letter *Casti Connubii,* his response to the Anglican Church's approval of artificial contraception as ethical in certain circumstances. That encyclical initiated the expansion of the procreative institution model of marriage into a more personal spousal union model of conjugal love and intimacy. Procreation, Pius XI taught, is an important facet of marriage, but it does not encompass all that marriage is. Marriage has as its primary end procreation, but the spousal love and life of the spouses is also an important end.

This mutual love, expressed by loving acts, has, according to *Casti Connubii,* "as its primary purpose that man and wife help each other day by day in forming and perfecting themselves in the interior life . . . and above all that they may grow in true love toward God and their neighbor" (*CC,* no. 23). So important is the mutual love and life of the spouses, Pius XI argued, drawing on the *Catechism of the Council of Trent,* that it "can, in a very real sense . . . be said to be the chief reason and purpose of marriage provided matrimony be looked at not in the restricted sense as instituted for the proper conception and education of the child, but more widely as the blending of life as a whole and the mutual interchange and sharing thereof" (*CC,* no. 24). If we do not focus in a restrictive way on procreation, Pius taught, but broaden the model of marriage to embrace the spousal life and love of the couple, then that life and love is the primary reason for marriage. With this authoritative teaching Pius insinuated a new model of marriage that after thirty-five years of growing pains, blossomed into a new and previously unheard of Catholic model of marriage, a model of spousal union.

The Spousal Union Model of Marriage

In the spousal union model the primary end of sexual intercourse in marriage is the union of the couple, and this primary end is achieved in every act of intercourse through which the spouses enter into intimate communion. Even in childless marriages, which sociologists show to be

---

[28] The words are from Stephen Sloesser, *Jazz Age Catholicism: Mystic Modernism in Postwar Paris* (Toronto: University of Toronto Press, 2005). Sloesser's book provides an insightful look into this period.

increasingly common today, marriage and sexual intercourse achieve their primary end in the spousal union of the couple, their "two-in-oneness" in Heribert Doms's language: "The immediate purpose of marriage is the realization of its meaning, the conjugal two-in-oneness. . . . This two-in-oneness of husband and wife is a living reality, and the immediate object of the marriage ceremony and their legal union." The union and love of the spouses tends naturally to the creation of a new person, their child, who fulfills both parents individually and as a two-in-oneness. Society, however, "is more interested in the child than in the natural fulfillment of the parents, and it is this which gives the child primacy among the natural results of marriage."[29] Contemporary sociological data demonstrate the fallacy in assigning primacy to the child, for they demonstrate that the loving relationship of the parents is the key to the well-being of their child.[30]

The reaction of the institutional Catholic Church to these new ideas was, as so often in theological history, a blanket condemnation that made no effort to sift truth from error. In 1944, the Holy Office, now the Congregation for the Doctrine of the Faith, condemned "the opinion of some more recent authors, who either deny that the primary end of marriage is the generation and nurture of children, or teach that the secondary ends are not essentially subordinate to the primary end, but are equally primary and independent."[31] The Second Vatican Council attempted to resolve the divide between the two models of marriage and their followers by rejecting the model on which this CDF teaching was based. Though the council did not deal in detail with marriage in *Gaudium et Spes*, it provided material intimately related to our present discussion. Marriage, it taught, is a "communion of love . . . an intimate partnership of life and love." The council declared the mutual love of the spouses and their passionate desire to be best friends for life to be of the very essence of marriage. The spouses, it further taught, "mutually gift and accept one another" (*GS,* nos. 47–48); the focus on animal bodies and their acts is replaced by a focus on persons and their intimate intentions. In their marriages spouses create not a procreative institution but a spousal union of love that is to last as

---

[29] Heribert Doms, *The Meaning of Marriage* (London: Sheed and Ward, 1939), 94–95.

[30] See Michael Lamb and Abraham Sagi, *Fatherhood and Family Policy* (Hillsdale, NJ: Erlbaum, 1983); Ronald J. Angel and Jacqueline L. Angel, *Painful Inheritance: Health and the New Generation of Fatherless Families* (Madison: University of Wisconsin Press, 1993); Sara McLanahan and Gary Sandefur, *Growing Up with a Single Parent* (Cambridge, MA: Harvard University Press, 1994); David Blankenhorn, *Fatherlessness in America: Confronting Our Most Urgent Social Problem* (New York: Basic Books, 1995); Judith Wallerstein and Julia Lewis, *The Unexpected Legacy of Divorce: A Twenty-Five Year Landmark Study* (New York: Hyperion, 2000).

[31] *AAS* 36 (1944): 103.

long as life lasts and may or may not be procreative.[32] Marriage is, first, a social institution for the development of love and friendship between the spouses and, only then, as a result of this spousal love, an institution for the procreation of children.

The council devotes an entire section to the love that founds marriage, which in turn founds the Catholic sacrament of marriage. As is marriage, so also is the sacrament of marriage. Spousal love is "eminently human" and "involves the good of the whole person." It is expressed and perfected in sexual intercourse, which expresses and promotes "that mutual self-giving by which the spouses enrich one another" (*GS,* no. 49). Marriage and the marital love of the spouses are still said to be "ordained for the procreation of children" (*GS,* no. 48), but that "does not make the other ends of marriage of less account," and "marriage to be sure is not instituted solely for procreation" (*GS,* no. 50). The intense and well-documented debate that took place in the council sessions makes it impossible to claim, as some conservative ethicists still wish to claim,[33] that the refusal to sustain the received tradition of marriage was simply the avoidance of the traditional language. It was, rather, the result of deliberate and hotly deliberated choice, a choice replicated and given canonical formulation twenty years later in the church's revised *Code of Canon Law.*

Marriage, the *Code of Canon Law* prescribes, "is ordered to the well-being of the spouses and to the procreation and upbringing of children" (canon 1055, 1), with no suggestion that either end is superior to the other. Notice that, once again in the Catholic tradition, it is *marriage* and not *each and every marital act* that is ordered to procreation. Marriage is "brought into being by the lawfully manifested consent of persons who are legally capable" (canon 1057, 1), and that consent "is an act of the will by which a man and a woman by irrevocable covenant mutually give and accept one another for the purpose of establishing a marriage" (canon 1057, 2). The Catholic Church revised its laws about marriage in the twentieth century to bring them into line with a newly received and developing theology of marriage, moving beyond the model of marriage as procreative institution to embrace a model of marriage as spousal union in which the mutual life, love, and communion of the spouses are every bit as important as, perhaps even more important than, procreation.

The judgment of the majority on Pope John XXIII's Birth Control Commission continues to be the judgment of a large majority of Catholic

---

[32] For an extended analysis of covenant, see Michael G. Lawler, "Marriage as Covenant in the Catholic Tradition," in *Covenant Marriage in Comparative Perspective,* ed. John Witte, Jr., and Eliza Ellison, 70–91 (Grand Rapids, MI: Eerdmans, 2005).

[33] See Germain Grisez, *The Way of the Lord Jesus: Living a Christian Life* (Quincy, IL: Franciscan Herald Press, 1993), 565n.35.

couples and theological ethicists today. "Human intervention in the process of the marriage act [that is, artificial contraception]," they and we believe, "for reasons drawn from the end of marriage itself should not always be excluded, provided the criteria of morality are always safeguarded."[34] These couples and ethicists do not receive the *Humanae Vitae* tradition that every act of sexual intercourse must be open to new life, because they do not receive the procreative institution model of marriage on which that tradition is based. They accept and follow, rather, the spousal union model on which the majority report was based. Fifty years after the publication of *Humanae Vitae* and its underscoring of the inseparability of the unitive and procreative meanings of sexual intercourse, the divide between the procreative institution and spousal union models of marriage persists tenaciously in the church.[35] Church efforts to silence key voices in the theological debate, efforts that totally ignore the documented majority acceptance of the spousal union model, have not succeeded in silencing the debate. They have succeeded, however, as sociology again shows, in creating a loss of respect for church law about sexuality in general.[36] There is what might be called a silent schism[37] in the church over the question of contraception. Authority can dictate truth, but it cannot impose it. In the authentic Catholic tradition, which is a source of Catholic ethics, dictated truth becomes effective only when it is received by those under authority.

The scientifically documented lack of reception of *Humanae Vitae* and the nuanced reception of the spousal union model of marriage among both those expert in marriage and those expert in theological ethics suggest a contemporary example of development of doctrine in the church, in line with the developments that took place in the doctrines on usury, slavery, religious freedom, and membership in the body of Christ.[38] Sociological research suggests that development is now well under way. It shows that the assertion that the church believes that "each and every marital act must of necessity retain its intrinsic relationship to the procreation of human

---

[34] Cited in Clifford Longley, *The Worlock Archive* (London: Chapman, 2000), 233.

[35] For a statement in defense of *Humanae Vitae*, see "Affirmation of the Church's Teaching on the Gift of Sexuality" (Washington, DC: The Catholic University of America, nd), online at https://trs.cua.edu/humanae-vitae; for a statement contra, see "Catholic Scholars' Statement on the Ethics of Using Contraceptives," Wijngaards Institute for Catholic Research (October 2016, open to updates), online at www.wijngaardsinstitute.com/statement-on-contraceptives.

[36] See, for example, George Gallup, Jr., and Jim Castelli, *The American Catholic People: Their Beliefs, Practices, and Values* (New York: Doubleday, 1987).

[37] See Fergus Kerr, *Twentieth-Century Catholic Theologians* (Oxford: Blackwell, 2007), 219.

[38] See John T. Noonan, Jr., *A Church That Can and Cannot Change* (Notre Dame, IN: University of Notre Dame Press, 2005); Michael G. Lawler, *What Is and What Ought to Be: The Dialectic of Experience, Theology, and Church* (New York: Continuum, 2005), 119–42.

life" is not accepted as true today for the vast majority of Catholics who make up the people of God on whom the Second Vatican Council in *Lumen Gentium* placed such emphasis (*LG,* chap. 2). Theologians can never be comfortable with any statement of belief which can be shown to be experientially untrue. They have the "responsibility of reading the signs of the time and of interpreting them in the light of the gospel" (*GS,* no. 4). The majority lack of reception of *Humanae Vitae* is beyond any doubt a major sign of the Catholic time.

Amoris Laetitia *and the Organic Development of Doctrine*

What Christoff Cardinal Schönborn of Vienna refers to as an "organic development" of doctrine[39] is taking place with respect to the church's teaching on contraception and is most clearly reflected in Pope Francis's 2016 Apostolic Exhortation *Amoris Laetitia.* Although there is no explicit change in Catholic doctrine against the use of artificial contraception in *Amoris Laetitia,* there is no specific mention of the doctrine in relation to married couples, which is surprising given the focus of the exhortation on marriage and family. The only explicit condemnation of contraception is "the forced State intervention in favour of contraception, sterilization and even abortion" (*AL,* no. 42).[40] Instead of emphasizing the absolute norm prohibiting contraception, *Amoris Laetitia* emphasizes the principle of responsible parenthood.

Regarding this principle, it notes, citing *Humanae Vitae* (no. 10), that it "requires that husband and wife, keeping a right order of priorities, recognize their own duties towards God, themselves, their families and human society" (*AL,* no. 222). Guided by conscience, which we explained in detail in Chapter 6, it states, quoting *Gaudium et Spes* (no. 50), that "[the couple] will make decisions by common counsel and effort. Let them thoughtfully take into account both their own welfare and that of their children, those already born and those which the future may bring. . . . The parents themselves and no one else should ultimately make this judgment in the sight of God" (*AL,* no. 222). Furthermore, "the use of methods based on the 'laws of nature and the incidence of fertility' (*HV,* no. 11) are to be promoted, since 'these methods respect the bodies of the spouses, encourage tenderness between them and favour the education of an authentic freedom'" (*AL,* no. 222). Nowhere in *Amoris Laetitia* is *Humanae Vitae,* number 12, or *Familiaris Consortio,* number 32, which specifically condemn artificial contraception in the marital relationship, mentioned. Instead, the principle of responsible parenthood as

---

[39] See Gerard O'Connell, "'*Amoris Laetitia*' Represents an Organic Development of Doctrine, 'not a Rupture'," *America* (April 8, 2016).

[40] Citing *Relatio Finalis* (2015), 7.

interpreted and acted upon by the married couple's conscience is the basis for making responsible decisions to regulate fertility.

Historically, when the Catholic Church changes a doctrine, it does not explicitly publicize the change. Rather, organic development often means that the alteration of prior doctrine is not explicitly stated, but a revised doctrine is substituted in its place. This was certainly the case with church teaching on slavery, usury, and religious freedom. That seems to be what is taking place in Pope Francis's *Amoris Laetitia* on church teaching absolutely prohibiting artificial contraception. Such organic development reflects Vatican II's favored people-of-God ecclesiology, the lack of reception by the people of God of *Humanae Vitae*'s absolute prohibition of contraception, the authority and inviolability of an informed individual conscience, the theologically informed vision of the majority report, and the spousal union model of marriage on which it was based. This development is a call for careful discernment, by "the Bishops to the last of the faithful,"[41] so that all Catholics may be able to make an informed judgment of conscience as to whether it is or is not an authentic example of reception of the apostolic truth toward which the Spirit of truth is constantly leading the people of God.

Questions for Reflection

- What do you understand by the term *artificial reproductive technology*? What do you understand by the terms *homologous* and *heterologous* in this context?
- What are the Catholic Church's arguments against the ethics of homologous and heterologous artificial reproductive technologies? What do you think of those arguments?
- How do you understand the inseparability principle that is the cornerstone of the Catholic Church's argument against both artificial reproductive technologies and artificial contraception? Are you convinced by it?
- Do you see any ethical difference between natural family planning that the Catholic Church permits as ethical and artificial contraception that it condemns as unethical?
- What do you think of the church's argument against the ethics of artificial contraception? Is the judgment of the majority report from the Papal Birth Control Commission and of contemporary theological ethicists of any help to you in making your judgment?

---

[41] Augustine, *De Praed. Sanct.*, 14, 27, *PL* 44, 980. See also *LG*, no. 12.

Suggested Readings

Salzman, Todd A., and Michael G. Lawler. *The Sexual Person: Toward a Renewed Catholic Anthropology.* Moral Traditions Series. Washington, DC: Georgetown University Press, 2008. See especially Chapter 8.

Selling, Joseph, A., ed. *Embracing Sexuality: Authority and Experience in the Catholic Church.* Burlington, VT: Ashgate, 2001.

Shannon, Thomas A., ed. *Reproductive Technologies: A Reader.* New York: Sheed and Ward, 2004.

Shannon, Thomas A., and Lisa Sowle Cahill. *Religion and Artificial Reproduction: An Inquiry into the Vatican Instruction on Respect for Life in Its Origin.* New York: Crossroad, 1987.

13

Biomedical Ethics

Issues at the End of Life

Learning Objectives

- Distinguish between a persistent and permanent vegetative state.
- Distinguish between medical care and treatment.
- Explain Karl Rahner's theology of death and its anthropological and normative implications for permanent-vegetative-state (PVS) patients.
- Considering Rahner's theology of death, critically analyze the March 20, 2004, *Address of John Paul II to the Participants in the International Congress on "Life-Sustaining Treatments and Vegetative State: Scientific Advances and Ethical Dilemma"* and the Congregation for the Doctrine of the Faith's *Responses to Certain Questions of the United States Conference of Catholic Bishops concerning Artificial Nutrition and Hydration* and *Commentary* (responses to a letter from the president of the USCCB) and their normative implications for end-of-life decisions in general and PVS patients specifically.[1]

In the Introduction we noted that one of the slides we consider in our theological ethics course is a photo of Terri Schiavo in a permanent vegetative state (PVS), and we discuss whether the decision to remove her from artificial nutrition and hydration (ANH), which was followed by her death, was morally right or wrong. Students debate the morality of this decision. Some students argue that removing Terri from ANH was tantamount to

---

[1] Hereafter, these three documents will be referred to as *Address, Responses,* and *Commentary.*

murder; other students argue that it was morally acceptable because Terri was already "brain dead." What divides the two perspectives is not relativism but different virtuous perspectives and definitions of human dignity and norms that facilitate attaining human dignity, even in the dying process.

Missing from all the responses, and indeed from most discussions of ANH and PVS patients, is something we regard as central to every Catholic end-of-life issue, namely, a theology of dying and death. In this chapter we consider our students' different perspectives, what science tells us about PVS patients, and experience, in order to analyze and evaluate the Schiavo case specifically and end-of-life issues in general. We also examine Karl Rahner's theology of dying and death, explain John Paul II's March 2004 *Address*, and address two questions about that *Address* that we deem most important: first, its continuity and discontinuity with the Catholic ethical tradition with respect to ANH and PVS patients[2] and, second, the medical and normative implications for treating PVS patients that flow from the *Address* and the theology of dying and death we have developed. We do so from the virtuous perspective of patience, courage, perseverance, and hope and a personal readiness for death and the theological virtues of faith, hope, and love of the God revealed in Jesus.

Permanent Vegetative State

Before proceeding, we must define PVS and address recent literature on its misdiagnosis. First, there is general agreement in the scientific literature on the definition of the vegetative state as "a clinical condition of complete unawareness of the self and the environment." That complete unawareness of self, by definition, prevents PVS patients not only from experiencing pain but also from exercising his/her freedom and relationality in history.[3] In the scientific, medical, and bioethical literature, it is not always clear what the *P* in PVS designates. It may mean either "persistent" or "permanent." Scientific and medical literature often distinguishes between *persistent,* a *diagnosis* that "refers only to a condition of past and continuing disability with an uncertain future," and *permanent,* a *prognosis* that "implies irreversibility." A person

---

[2] The classical study of that tradition is Daniel A. Cronin, "The Moral Law in Regard to the Ordinary and Extraordinary Means of Conserving Life," Part I, in *Conserving Human Life*, ed. Russell E. Smith (Braintree, MA: Pope John Center, 1988). See also Donald E. Henke, "A History of Ordinary and Extraordinary Means," in *Artificial Nutrition and Hydration and the Permanently Unconscious Patient: The Catholic Debate*, ed. Ronald P. Hamel and James J. Walter (Washington, DC: Georgetown University Press, 2007), 53–78.

[3] See Multi-Society Task Force on PVS, "Medical Aspects of the Persistent Vegetative State (2)," *New England Journal of Medicine* 330, no. 22 (1994): 1572–79.

moves from a persistent to a permanent vegetative state "when the diagnosis of irreversibility can be established with a high degree of clinical certainty."[4] Since all clinical diagnoses and prognoses are based on clinical *probabilities*, not certainties, that "high degree of clinical certainty" must be understood as a high degree of clinical probability. In this chapter the *P* in PVS will always mean *permanent,* and PVS will always mean *permanent vegetative state.*

Second, recent studies have confirmed a high number of misdiagnoses of the vegetative state by relying solely upon clinical consensus.[5] This gives credence to John Paul II's concern, voiced in the March 2004 *Address* that "medical science, up until now, is still unable to *predict with certainty* who among patients in [the vegetative state] . . . will recover and who will not" (no. 2). While the scientific studies and John Paul's warnings are important to the discussion of ANH and PVS patients, they do not directly affect our discussion here of freedom, action in history, and relationality and their roles and functions in a theology of dying and death. We submit two reasons for that judgment.

The first reason is that these concerns are not based on an inaccurate definition of the vegetative state; rather, they are based on whether PVS can be properly diagnosed in a particular patient. A study examined fifty-four patients in England and Belgium with disorders of consciousness (vegetative or minimally conscious state) to evaluate whether these patients could willfully modulate their brain activity, thus indicating some cognition and awareness. Only five out of the fifty-four demonstrated this capacity. The study concludes that "careful clinical examination will result in *reclassification* of the state of consciousness in some of these patients."[6] We acknowledge the concerns surrounding the diagnosis of PVS, the need to consult the medical sciences as research on the accuracy of diagnosis

---

[4] Ibid., 1501.

[5] Caroline Schnakers et al., "Diagnostic Accuracy of the Vegetative State and Minimally Conscious State: Clinical Consensus Versus Standardized Neurobehavioral Assessment," *BMC Neurology* 9, no. 35 (2009): 1. This article cites studies that indicate up to 43 percent of patients with consciousness disorders are erroneously diagnosed to be in a vegetative state. See Nancy L. Childs et al., "Accuracy of Diagnosis of Persistent Vegetative State," *Neurology* 43, no. 8 (1993): 1465–67; Keith Andrews et al., "Misdiagnosis of the Vegetative State: Retrospective Study in a Rehabilitation Unit," *British Medical Journal* 313 (1996): 13–16; and Helen Gill-Thwaites, "Lotteries, Loopholes, and Luck: Misdiagnosis in the Vegetative State Patient," *Brain Injury* 20, nos. 13–14 (2006): 1321–28.

[6] Martin M. Monti et al., "Willful Modulation of Brain Activity in Disorders of Consciousness," *New England Journal of Medicine* 362, no. 7 (February 18, 2010): 579, emphasis added. See also, "Correspondence: Willful Modulation of Brain Activity in Disorders of Consciousness," *New England Journal of Medicine* 362, no. 20 (May 20, 2010): 1936–37; Neil Messer, *Theological Neuroethics: Christian Ethics Meets the Science of the Human Brain* (London: Bloomsbury, 2017), 105–42.

continues, and the need to expand and improve the criteria and methods for making such a diagnosis. These concerns, however, do not touch our argument in this chapter, for the argument becomes relevant only *if* and *when* a patient is accurately diagnosed to be in a PVS.

The second reason that concerns us about John Paul's March 2004 *Address* for PVS is that, it seems to us, John Paul's warning raises the bar too high for moral decision making. It has never before been the case in the Catholic tradition that a moral agent must "predict with certainty" a contingent state of affairs before making a moral judgment. The scientific literature speaks of probabilities, even high probabilities ("a high degree of clinical certainty"), not absolute certainty; so does the ethical literature. Misdiagnoses of PVS patients are certainly grounds for concern, and medical science is working to reduce this number through neurological studies and improved neuro-behavioral rating scales. As this data becomes available, it will be integrated into ethical reflections. However, the lack of this data does not prohibit us from making moral judgments now based on the data, particularities, and probabilities available. If it did, the pope would have used a stronger phrase than "in principle" to describe the obligation to provide ANH for PVS patients. Besides, the scientific studies suggest that the majority of clinically diagnosed PVS cases, even those relying solely on clinical consensus, are accurate diagnoses.

Karl Rahner's Theology of Dying and Death

The *Catechism of the Catholic Church* explains a virtuous perspective guided by Christian hope and faith in the face of death. "Because of Christ, Christian death has a positive meaning." Christians were buried with Christ sacramentally "by baptism into death, so that as Christ was raised from the dead by the glory of the Father, we too might walk in newness of life" (Rom 6:4). "Physical death," the *Catechism of the Catholic Church* continues, "completes this 'dying with Christ' and so completes our incorporation into him in his redeeming act" (*CCC*, no. 10). This theology is reinforced by other Catholic doctrines: the value of freely and consciously suffering with Christ, purgatory, the universal resurrection of the dead, and eternal life. As the Preface of the Mass of Christian Burial makes plain, for Christ's faithful "life is changed not ended. When the body of our earthly dwelling lies in death we gain an everlasting dwelling place in heaven." John Paul's *Address* hints at this long-established theology but gives it no substantive place in statements concerning ANH and PVS patients. This absence makes possible the definition of human dignity with a focus on biological life as, at least, a quasi-absolute good, rather than as human dignity with a focus on relational life, where biological life is an aspect of relational life but not a quasi-absolute good.

In the universal Catholic tradition, death is described as the separation of the soul from the body (*CCC,* no. 1005). The German theologian Karl Rahner, generally accepted among the leading Catholic theologians of the twentieth century, demonstrated an ongoing interest in the theology of death throughout his distinguished career,[7] at a time when Catholic theology gave little attention to death. The theology of death he developed, a theology that is, of course, not official Catholic teaching but widespread in the contemporary Catholic *theological* tradition,[8] offers a fruitful Catholic theological perspective on dying and death and the situation of PVS patients. While affirming the traditional *description* of physical death, which coincides with the *Catechism*'s description, he finds it inadequate as a theological *definition* of the death of a specifically personal being. The traditional description focuses on the physical, biological death of a human person, "but it fails completely to indicate the specifically human element in the death of a man."[9] To correct this failure, to underscore that "it is *man* who dies,"[10] Rahner proposes a nuanced definition of death specific to the human being. This definition has theological implications not only for our understanding of the dying and death of a human person but also for the implications of this understanding for issues surrounding ANH and PVS patients.

Three critical dimensions of Rahner's theological anthropology or definition of human nature and dignity are relevant to our purposes in this chapter: the human person is *essentially* free, historical, and relational.[11] We emphasize the word *essentially* to accentuate that freedom, historicity, and relationality are not three accidental characteristics of the person in the

---

[7] For a comprehensive view of Karl Rahner's theology of death, see Karl Rahner, *On the Theology of Death* (Freiburg: Herder and Herder, 1961); idem, "On Christian Dying," *Theological Investigations,* vol. 7, *Further Theology of the Spiritual Life* (London: Darton, Longman and Todd, 1971), 285–93; idem, "Ideas for a Theology of Death," *Theological Investigations*, vol. 13, *Theology Anthropology, Christology* (New York: Seabury Press, 1975), 169–88; idem, "Christian Dying," *Theological Investigations,* vol. 18, *God and Revelation* (New York: Crossroad, 1983), 226–56.

[8] See, for instance, Joseph Ratzinger, *Death and Eternal Life* (Washington, DC: Catholic University of America Press, 2007); Shannon Nichole Craigo-Snell, *Silence, Love and Death: Saying "Yes" to God in the Theology of Karl Rahner* (Milwaukee: Marquette University Press, 2008); Terence Nichols, *Death and Afterlife: A Theological Introduction* (Grand Rapids, MI: Brazos, 2010).

[9] Rahner, *On the Theology of Death*, 25.

[10] Ibid., 26.

[11] See Karl Rahner, "The Dignity and Freedom of Man," *Theological Investigations,* vol. 2, *Man in the Church* (Baltimore: Helicon Press, 1963) 239–40.

abstract but three essential, *ontological* properties that define the person in the concrete. If one, two, or all three are lacking in the concrete, the human person integrally and adequately considered is seriously ontologically damaged. The human person integrally and adequately considered "is the criterion for discovering whether an act is morally right."[12] Freedom, historicity, and relationality are *existentials* of every human being, elements in the ontological constitution of the human being precisely as human, elements constitutive of concrete human nature prior to any exercise of freedom.[13] These existentials are central to the ontological definition of the human person and, therefore, central also to the definition of the person's dying and death and to norms guiding end-of-life decisions. We consider each in turn. We introduce here something that will be important later: the damage done to a person by the loss of one or other of the existentials under discussion does not result in the total loss of the person's human dignity. That dignity may be somewhat damaged in the concrete but it remains in the abstract, and that fact will be important later when we consider decisions about maintaining PVS patients on ANH or withdrawing it from them.

Rahner accepts Kant's turn to the subject and the implications this turn has on the shift from a physical, biological definition of dying and death as a merely biological event to a person-centered definition of dying and death as also a personal, free, historical, and relation-ending event. With this shift comes the need to know the person-subject in his or her freedom, for "man *is* personal freedom."[14] This freedom is both categorical and transcendental or foundational. Categorical freedom is the freedom to choose particular actions: to go fishing, to read a book, to continue or discontinue ANH. Categorical freedom is the more obvious of the two freedoms in a human life. Transcendental freedom, which is distinct from but related to categorical freedom as root is to shoot, is the subject's being responsible for self. "In real [foundational] freedom the subject always intends himself, understands and posits himself. Ultimately, he does not do *something*, but does *himself*."[15] My personal foundational freedom is the ontological ground for my categorically affirming the fullness of self, neighbor, and God.[16] This affirming and drawing ever closer to God in freedom and love

---

[12] Richard M. Gula, *Reason Informed by Faith: Foundations of Catholic Morality* (New York: Paulist Press, 1989), 64, 66–73. See also *Schema Constitutionis pastoralis de ecclesia in mundo huius temporis: Expensio modorum partis secundae* (Rome: Vatican Library, 1965), 37–38; and *Gaudium et Spes*, no. 51.

[13] Karl Rahner, *Foundations of Christian Faith: An Introduction to the Idea of Christianity* (New York: Crossroad, 1978), 16.

[14] Rahner, "On Christian Dying," 287.

[15] Rahner, *Foundations of Christian Faith*, 94.

[16] See Karl Rahner, "Theology of Freedom," in *Theological Investigations*, vol. 6, *Concerning Vatican Council II* (Baltimore: Helicon Press, 1961), 178–96.

is expressed in Catholic theology in the metaphor of the pilgrimage (*CCC*, no. 1013).[17]

Historicity is easy to characterize: "In terms of his nature a man exists in space and time."[18] An existential characteristic of the person is that of being a person-in-the-world, an embodied person who is realized in his or her ultimate core only in bodily existence and relationality within a community. The human is a being whose origin, life, and death lie within the world, a being who has roots in empirical realities, a being by nature an inescapably historical creature. An external world of other persons and other things is an *essential* part of a person's nature, and it is only in interaction in and with this external world that humans continuously actualize themselves and continue on their personal pilgrimage. The irretrievable loss of the ability to exercise one's foundational and categorical freedom and relationality in history, as in the case with PVS patients, is contrary to and damaging to not only human personality psychologically but also human personhood ontologically. This is the ultimate problematic of the PVS patient.

One of the things persons do to essentially realize themselves in history is to enter freely into mutually realizing relationships with other persons. The human person, Rahner argues, is an essentially "community-building person"; as a person the human "is intended for community with other persons."[19] We prefer to say that, as a person the human is intended for mutual and mutually realizing relationship with other persons, and that such relationality is an existential of the human person. Friendship, or in contemporary language relationality, Aquinas suggests, has three characteristics: benevolence, reciprocity, and mutual indwelling.[20] In friendship, I seek the other's well-being (Aquinas's definition of love is now well-known, *amare est velle bonum*[21]), the other responds in kind, and the result is mutual indwelling, intimacy, and self-realization. Friendship is among the most personally creative of human relationships.

Human freedom, which "actualizes one thing, the single subject in the unique totality of his history,"[22] historicity, which actualizes that subject in the world, and friendship, which actualizes the subject in relationship with others, together existentially ground full human being, human nature

---

[17] See also Rahner, *On the Theology of Death*, 35–39; Ladislas Boros, *The Mystery of Death* (New York: Herder, 1965), 86–99.

[18] Karl Rahner, *Hearers of the Word* (New York: Herder, 1969), 132.

[19] Rahner, "The Dignity and Freedom of Man," 239.

[20] Thomas Aquinas, *Summa Theologiae Sancti Thomae de Aquino* II-II 23. 1, resp (hereinafter, *ST*). Paul J. Wadell has incisively developed these three characteristics in *Friendship and the Moral Life* (Notre Dame, IN: University of Notre Dame Press, 1989), 130–41.

[21] *ST* I-II 28, 1c.

[22] Rahner, *Foundations of Christian Faith*, 95.

and person, and human values. Since freedom, history, and relationship are of the ontological essence of the human, the permanent incapacity to exercise freedom, living history, and relationship, as is the case of the PVS patient, has normative implications for defining dying and death as a natural, personal, and theological event.

For Rahner, since the human person is "both spirit and matter," the person's death must exhibit this ontological dialectic, so intrinsic and essential to him.[23] The death of a human person, an embodied spirit in the world, that is, must have both a physical and a spiritual or personal aspect. The description of death as the separation of body and soul focuses on death as a biological event defined by medical criteria. This description, however, "fails completely to indicate the specifically human element in the death of [a] man."[24] As a personal consummation of the self, dying and death cannot be experiences that are suffered only passively, though on occasion, a sudden accident for instance or while under sedation to control pain, dying and death are suffered passively. But death "must also be understood as a human act, as a deed of man, originating within."[25]

If humans *are* personal freedom, then it follows that all persons, as individuals, can and do use the resources of their own innermost nature and self to form themselves by their own free act. By the exercise of this freedom each can "definitively determine the shape of his life as a whole and decide what his ultimate end is to be."[26] All persons can, that is, make a fundamental disposition of their life and of themselves, sometimes as an act of foundational freedom, but more often in acts of categorical freedom, which manifest this fundamental self-disposition in history. In historical reality men and women are dying at every moment of their lives, and every moment of life is a moment that points to and is overshadowed by death. Catholic tradition refers to this "always dying" as *prolixitas mortis* and teaches that it is never to be forgotten. There are undoubtedly the occasions mentioned above, fatal accidents or while under sedation to control pain, when death comes suddenly or unconsciously and apparently passively to a person without any exercise of personal freedom. Such a judgment of complete passivity, however, ignores the prior and ongoing free choices that a person, dying daily, might have made and remade on the journey to death, resurrection, and the eternal presence and unimaginable hospitality of God (cf. 1 Cor 2:9).

The Catholic tradition urges *prolixitas mortis* on all its believers, inviting them to be not only aware but also actively accepting of their mortality,

---

[23] Rahner, *On the Theology of Death*, 38.

[24] Ibid., 25.

[25] Ibid., 38.

[26] Rahner, "On Christian Dying," 287.

not out of any morbid fear of death but as a way to escape that fear and achieve maturity. "Keep death daily before your eyes," commands the rule of St. Benedict. "Remember man that thou art dust and unto dust thou shalt return," commands the traditional Ash Wednesday prayer. These injunctions are intended to highlight *prolixitas mortis* and instill a positive and mature attitude toward dying, death, and especially life. Humans can, and frequently do, run away from their mortality, looking upon it, in Heidegger's words, as a "social inconvenience" or "downright tactlessness."[27] Or they can freely embrace their mortality and the finitude and limitation it imposes, and thus realize and dispose of themselves in both foundational and categorical freedom. Such an ongoing attitude leads, first, to the acceptance of their life of relative freedom (historicity precludes absolute freedom), and then to the virtue of courage in the face of every threat to life, including PVS. In a Catholic *theological* context *sub prolixitate mortis*, death is never merely a passive event; it is always, at least in its daily preparation, a free and active event.[28]

As Christ's human reality reaches its full perfection only in his freely embraced death, so also all persons definitively posit themselves only in death as the final and ultimately fulfilling act of freedom. The *Catechism of the Catholic Church* insinuates this final act of foundational freedom in more traditional theological language, teaching that the human "can transform his own death into an act of obedience and love toward the Father, after the example of Christ" (*CCC*, no. 1011). That human death contains "this characteristic element of final decision is not at all indicated by the expression, 'the separation of body and soul.'"[29] Such a free, personal, and final self-disposition *can,* and when physical death occurs when the exercise of an unconscious patient's personal freedom is no longer an option *must,* take place earlier than death in the physical sense. "Dying in the physical sense, and dying as an act of freedom need not coincide chronologically."[30] The implications for PVS patients of the distinction between personal and physical death are obvious.

As a human act, therefore, the act of dying *sub prolixitate mortis* is a process that is free, historical, and personal. For the PVS patient, who has irretrievably lost the ability to exercise any freedom, living history, or

---

[27] Martin Heidegger, *Being and Time* (San Francisco: Harper, 1962), 298.

[28] Nobody has described life *sub prolixitate mortis* better than Jesuit Anthony de Mello. See his *Sadhana: A Way to God: Christian Exercises in Eastern Form* (Garden City, NY: Image Press, 1984), esp. 89–96.

[29] Rahner, *On the Theology of Death*, 26. See also *Enchiridion Symbolorum Devinitionum et Declarationum de Rebus Fidei et Morum*, ed. H. Denzinger and A. Schoenmetzer (Fribourg: Herder, 1965), nos. 1000 and 1304–6 (hereafter *DS*).

[30] Rahner, "The Liberty of the Sick," 107. See also "Christian Dying," 229.

relationality, any free self-disposition must precede the onset of the PVS, which marks the personal death that is the end of the patient's personal pilgrimage. When there is no potential to exercise personal freedom and relationship in history, neither is there any potential to further pursue one's personal pilgrimage to selfhood, personhood, and God; and when one's personal pilgrimage is over, one's personal life is over. One element of Catholic teaching about death is that death brings a person "a kind of finality and consummation which renders his decision for or against God, reached during the time of his bodily life, final and unalterable."[31] The person's biological life, over which PVS patients have no moral control and in respect of which they are therefore passive, may continue; the personal, specifically human life, over which the person has active control, has come to an end. With death, both physical death and, for the PVS patient, personal death in the sense we have explained, a person disposes of himself or herself in relation to God.

The suggestion by some commentators that the withholding or withdrawing of ANH at this point of personal death is, in fact, euthanasia is rejected by the Congregation for the Doctrine of the Faith (CDF) in its May 5, 1980, "Declaration on Euthanasia."

> One cannot impose on anyone the obligation to have recourse to a technique which is already in use but which carries a risk or is burdensome. Such a refusal is not the equivalent of suicide; on the contrary, it should be considered as an acceptance of the human condition, or a wish to avoid the application of a *medical procedure* disproportionate to the results that can be expected, or a desire not to impose excessive expense on the family or the community." (IV)

That declaration remains in force, unabrogated by John Paul II's non-infallible papal *Address*. The personal condition the CDF's declaration refers to is this: the normal human process of dying has reached the point of personal death as we have explained it. There remains only for that process to reach biological death, the final end of the human condition. The withdrawal of ANH at the point of personal death is not "euthanasia by omission," as John Paul suggests (*Address*, no. 4). It is no more, the CDF teaches, than a final acceptance of the natural human condition, religiously strengthened by the Catholic belief that, in death, life is changed not ended.

Nigel Biggar puts this situation concisely: for the PVS patient, "biological" life continues, but "biographical" life ceases.[32] An amendment of

---

[31] Rahner, *On the Theology of Death*, 35.

[32] Nigel Biggar, *Aiming to Kill: The Ethics of Suicide and Euthanasia* (London: Darton, Longman, and Todd, 2004), 31–47.

Biggar's "biographical" to "autobiographical" perfectly summarizes our argument. For Christians who believe that "life is changed not ended," and that "the doctrine of purgatory, of the coming resurrection of the body, and the future consummation of the whole universe already indicates a further development of man towards his ultimate perfection,"[33] that ought not to be cause for inconsolable sadness or the desperate determination to maintain biological life at all costs. In Catholic teaching a fundamental self-disposition *for* God in life and in death, personal and biological, results in a dying with Christ and a raising to a new, eternal life in which one enjoys the eternal presence and unimaginable hospitality of God; a fundamental self-disposition *against* God results in a rejection of God and eternal death.[34] It is, at least in part, this Catholic teaching on death that sustains the universal Catholic ethical tradition that biological life is not an absolute value and need not, therefore, be maintained by extraordinary or disproportionate means.[35]

While the basic human dignity of PVS patients undoubtedly perdures, as we noted earlier, a critical point in their daily dying has been reached, namely, the irretrievable loss of the ability to exercise human freedom, living history, and relationship, which define a person *qua* human person. Terri's Schiavo's ability to exercise her freedom, history, and relationality, and therefore to continue her autobiographical pilgrimage in relation to herself, her loved ones, and God, ended, though she remained a biologically alive person. We submit that it is in the dimensions of personal freedom, living history, and relationality that Rahner's anthropology of dying and death provides a theological foundation for assessing John Paul II's *Address* and the CDF's September 16, 2007, *Responses to Certain Questions of the United States Conference of Catholic Bishops Concerning Artificial Nutrition and Hydration,* and its *Commentary.*

Traditional Principle Guiding Administration of ANH

The Catholic tradition with respect to ANH and PVS patients prior to John Paul's March 2004 *Address* is easily stated. First, there should be "a presumption in favor of providing nutrition and hydration to all patients, including patients who require medically assisted nutrition and hydration,

---

[33] Rahner, *On the Theology of Death*, 35.

[34] See *DS,* nos. 838–39, 856–58, 925–26, 1000–1002, 1304–6, 1488.

[35] See CDF, "Declaration on Euthanasia," IV; USCCB, *Ethical and Religious Directives* (2009), Directive 57; Texas Bishops and the Texas Conference of Catholic Health Facilities, "On Withdrawing Artificial Nutrition and Hydration," in Hamel and Walter, *Artificial Nutrition and Hydration and the Permanently Unconscious Patient*, 110.

as long as this is of sufficient benefit to outweigh the burdens involved to the patient."[36] Second, that presumption is not unconditional and absolute. It can "yield in cases where such procedures have no medically reasonable hope of sustaining [physical] life or pose excessive risks or burdens"[37] to either the patient or the patient's loved ones. In disproportionate or burdensome cases, ANH can ethically be withheld or withdrawn, though it cannot be withheld or withdrawn when its omission is "intended to cause a patient's death."[38] The direct intention to cause death would be euthanasia which, in the Catholic moral tradition, is always immoral.

This universal Catholic ethical tradition, which permits the ethical "refusal of overzealous treatment" (*CCC*, no. 2278), has a long, magisterial history and was carefully explained by Pope Pius XII in his "Address to Doctors and Medical Students" in 1957. "Normally one is held to use only ordinary means—according to circumstances of persons, places, times, and culture—that is to say, means that do not involve any grave burden for oneself or another. A more strict obligation would be too burdensome for most people and would render the attainment *of the higher, more important good* too difficult" (emphasis added). The tradition was reiterated by the CDF in its May 5, 1980, "Declaration on Euthanasia": "Everyone has the duty to care for his or her own health. . . . However, is it necessary in all circumstances to have recourse to all possible remedies? In the past moralists replied that one is never obliged to use 'extraordinary' means" (IV). The CDF goes on to suggest how one might distinguish between "ordinary" and "extraordinary" means. One considers "the type of treatment to be used, its degree of complexity or risk, its cost and the possibilities of using it, and comparing these elements with the results that can be expected, taking into account the state of the sick person and his or her physical and *moral* resources" (emphasis added). The refusal of extraordinary care is not the equivalent of suicide but "should be considered as an acceptance of the human condition, or a wish to avoid the application of a medical procedure disproportionate to the results that can be expected, or a desire not to impose excessive expense on the family of the community."[39] This very

---

[36] USCCB, *Ethical and Religious Directives for Catholic Health Care Services*, 4th ed. (Washington, DC: USCCB, 2001).

[37] Hamel and Walter, *Artificial Nutrition and Hydration and the Permanently Unconscious Patient*, 130.

[38] Ibid.

[39] The CDF did not explain what these "moral resources" might be, but Padraig Corkery, suggests that moral resources would include the virtues of patience, courage, perseverance, and hope and a personal readiness for death. See Padraig Corkery, *Bioethics and the Catholic Moral Tradition* (Dublin: Veritas Publications, 2010), 85. We agree and add the theological virtues of faith in and love of the God revealed in Jesus.

same doctrine and judgment was repeated in 1995 by Pope John Paul II in *Evangelium Vitae* (no. 65).

In November 2004, six months after the March *Address* that ignited the present debate, John Paul taught in his "Address to the Participants in the 19th International Conference of the Pontifical Council for Health Pastoral Care" that "the possible decision either not to start or to halt a treatment will be deemed ethically correct if the treatment is ineffective or obviously disproportionate to the aims of sustaining life or recovering health. Consequently, the decision to forego aggressive treatment *is an expression of respect that is due to the patient at every moment*" (no. 4, emphasis added). The *Catechism of the Catholic Church* neatly sums up this universal Catholic ethical tradition. "Discontinuing medical procedures that are burdensome, dangerous, extraordinary, or disproportionate to the expected outcome can be legitimate; it is the refusal of 'over-zealous treatment.' Here one does not will to cause death; one's inability to impede it is merely accepted" (*CCC*, no. 2278).

Thomas Shannon and James Walter protest that the articulation of the Catholic end-of-life tradition as a "*presumption* in favor of providing medically assisted nutrition and hydration" is a modern revisionist approach to that tradition. The tradition "from at least the 16th century through Pius XII, the Congregation for the Doctrine of the Faith in 1980, and the vast majority of moral theologians has determined this obligation by having the patient consider the benefits and burdens of the intervention to determine if they were proportionate or disproportionate."[40] Only *after* the intervention has been judged proportionate or disproportionate can the judgment be made that it is either ordinary and obligatory or extraordinary and non-obligatory.[41] We agree with that judgment but retain the language of presumption to focus on the language of the John Paul's March *Address,* and the CDF's *Responses* and *Commentary,* which appear to abandon the five-hundred-year-old traditional benefit-burden assessment and to suggest that ANH is ordinary care in the abstract, and therefore morally obligatory, prior to any benefit/burden analysis of the particular case. Once the judgment of ANH as ordinary care is made, it then is said to be ethically obligatory. We ask, however, if such a medical and moral judgment can be made in the abstract, or must the particular, concrete situation be taken into account, as the Catholic ethical tradition insists it must be to make a moral judgment?

---

[40] Thomas A. Shannon and James J. Walter, "Assisted Nutrition and Hydration and the Catholic Tradition," *Theological Studies* 66 (2005), 660.

[41] For a clear explanation of the technical terms *ordinary* and *extraordinary*, see Daniel P. Sulmasy, "The Last Word: The Catholic Case for Advance Directives," *America* (November 29, 2010), 13–16.

Address, Responses, and *Commentary:*
Continuity and Discontinuity with Tradition

In his *Address* John Paul II writes:

> I should like particularly to underline how the administration of food and water, even when provided by artificial means, always represents a *natural means* of preserving life, not a *medical act.* Its use, furthermore, should be considered, in principle, *ordinary and proportionate*, and as such morally obligatory, insofar as and until it is seen to have attained its proper finality, which in the present case consists in providing nourishment to the patient and alleviation of his suffering" (no. 4).

We wish to show here, in partial disagreement with those who conjecture otherwise,[42] both the continuity *and* discontinuity of this text with the Catholic moral tradition with respect to ANH and PVS patients.

John Paul's judgment that nutrition and hydration are "in principle" ordinary and proportionate means of preserving life "insofar as and until it is seen to have attained its proper finality," implies, as the Catholic tradition has always held, that the moral obligation to provide food and water is not absolute and unconditional. "In principle" suggests, first, an abstract principle, akin to "thou shalt not kill." It suggests, second, therefore, with the universal Catholic moral tradition, that the principle might have exceptions in concrete circumstances, as does "thou shalt not kill" in circumstances of just war and proportionate self-defense. The moral obligation to provide food and water to PVS patients exists in principle and in the abstract; it might have exceptions for a particular patient in the concrete. John Paul specifies only one exception, when, for whatever reason, it does not achieve its "proper finality," which he specifies as "providing nourishment to the patient and alleviation of his suffering." But his careful "in principle" suggests that there may be other circumstances for discontinuing ANH, and we may include the traditional disproportionate burdens to the patient or to the patient's loved ones. These include biological, relational, emotional, social, spiritual, economic, and the CDF's "moral" burdens emphasized earlier.

---

[42] See, for example, Thomas A. Shannon and James J. Walter, "Implications of the Papal *Address* on Feeding Tubes," *Hastings Center Report* 34 (2004): 18–20; R. Hamel and M. Panicola, "Must We Preserve Life?," *America* (April 2004), 6–13; Edward R. Sunshine, "Truncating Catholic Tradition," *National Catholic Reporter* (April 8, 2005).

In his November 2004 "Address to the Participants in the 19th International Conference of the Pontifical Council for Health Pastoral Care," already cited, an address that is as authoritative as his March 2004 *Address*, John Paul II asserted that "the possible decision either not to start or to halt a treatment will be deemed ethically correct if the treatment is ineffective or obviously disproportionate to the aims of sustaining life or recovering health." This address, largely ignored in the current debate over ANH and PVS patients, at the very least attenuates the judgment expressed in the March *Address*. When unpacked and allied with the *Address's* "in principle," it clearly suggests the traditional view that in some concrete circumstances medical treatment might be judged extraordinary and disproportionate, and therefore either withheld or discontinued.

The CDF's *Responses* and *Commentary* suggest the same conclusion, namely, that in certain circumstances it is ethical to withhold or withdraw ANH from a PVS patient. "Finally," the *Commentary* notes, "the possibility is not *absolutely* excluded that, in some rare cases, artificial nourishment and hydration may be excessively burdensome for the patient" (emphasis added). It does not specify the criteria that would justify withholding or withdrawing ANH in "excessively burdensome" circumstances, but the fact that the *Responses* and *Commentary* use the phrase "in principle" and that the *Commentary* has recourse to the traditional language of "excessively burdensome" suggests that extraordinary cases should be guided by a benefit/burden analysis. The general benefit/burden principle represented in these documents is in continuity with the long Catholic tradition. It is in the judgment that ANH "always represents a natural means of preserving life, not a medical act" (*Address*, no. 4) in the *criteria* of the benefit/burden principle, in *who* determines whether or not the criteria have been fulfilled, and in the definition of life, dying, and death when applied to the PVS patient, where there is discontinuity with, and a substantial revision of, the tradition in these documents.

ANH: Medical Procedure or Care?

As already noted, the CDF's "Declaration on Euthanasia" distinguishes between euthanasia and suicide, which is always morally prohibited, and "a wish to avoid the application of a *medical procedure* disproportionate to the results that can be expected," which is ethically acceptable (IV, emphasis added). In the present debate about ANH and PVS patients, ethical considerations hinge on whether ANH is a medical procedure, and therefore subject to a benefit/burden analysis, or care, and therefore required "in principle." In his March *Address*, John Paul states that ANH is "a *natural means* of preserving life, not a *medical act*" and that the withdrawal of

ANH, "if done knowingly and willingly," is "euthanasia by omission" (no. 4). Classifying ANH as care marks a significant change from the "Declaration on Euthanasia" and from the universal Catholic tradition in which it is embedded.[43] This shift is evident in an earlier statement by the Pontifical Academy of Sciences in 1985 that notes: "If the patient is in a permanent irreversible coma, as far as can be foreseen, treatment is not required, but all *care* should be lavished on him, *including feeding*."[44] We agree with James Walter, who write, "Such a shift to the requirement that assisted nutrition and hydration *must be used* essentially takes the decision about this intervention out of the patient-centered approach that has so characterized the historical tradition of the past."[45]

While the *Address*, *Responses*, and *Commentary* all consider ANH care, the *Commentary* is conceptually confused and confusing, since it employs the traditional criterion of *burden* and makes allowance for exceptions that go beyond both the *Address* and the *Responses*. It states that ANH "always represents a *natural means* for preserving life and is not a *therapeutic treatment*," but then it equivocates on this assertion by noting that such means, "in some rare cases . . . may be *excessively burdensome* for the patient." By labeling ANH care but allowing exceptions on the basis of whether or not the care is excessively burdensome, the *Commentary* uses the *language* of a medical procedure subject to benefit/burden analysis. In addition, all three documents consider ANH to be, by definition, *ordinary* and *proportionate*.

The American Academy of Neurology lists ANH as a medical treatment and indicates that the decision to discontinue ANH should be made, as is every medical decision, on the basis of "a careful evaluation of the patient's diagnosis and prognosis, the prospective benefits and burdens of the treatment, and the stated preferences of the patient and family." Regarding the PVS patient, it emphatically states that medical treatment, including ANH, "provides no benefit" to the patient since it "merely prolongs or suspends the dying process without providing any possible cure."[46] Many Catholic

---

[43] For an insightful historical study that explores cases where food was considered medicine, see Julia Fleming, "When 'Meats Are Like Medicines': Vitoria and Lessius on the Role of Food in the Duty to Preserve Live," *Theological Studies* 69 (2008): 99–115.

[44] The Pontifical Academy of Sciences, "The Artificial Prolongation of Life," *Origins* 15 (December 5, 1985): 415, emphasis added.

[45] Thomas A. Shannon and James J. Walter, "Assisted Nutrition and Hydration and the Catholic Tradition: The Case of Terry Schiavo," *Theological Studies* 66 (2005): 660.

[46] American Academy of Neurology, "Position of the American Academy of Neurology on Certain Aspects of the Care and Management of the Persistent Vegetative State Patient," in Hamel and Walter, *Artificial Nutrition and Hydration and the Permanently Unconscious Patient*, 10, 11.

theologians concur. Medical procedures are used "with the intent and hope for substantive recovery" of the patient.[47] In the case of the PVS patient, by definition, substantive recovery is not possible; ANH merely maintains the PVS patient in biological life without any hope of ever regaining free, historical, and relational capabilities. "When life support is removed because it does not offer hope of benefit [substantive recovery] or imposes an excessive burden [to the patient or family], the cause of death is the pathology which is no longer abated or circumvented."[48] The universal Christian teaching of *prolixitas mortis* accepts that death is a natural part of life; humans are by nature inescapably mortal beings. That, to some terrifying, teaching is softened and strengthened by the virtue of hope and the universal Christian doctrine of resurrection.[49]

The criteria of the traditional benefit/burden analysis, which is entirely person and patient centered, include biological, relational, spiritual, psychological, ethical, and economic considerations, determined by the patient, the patient's loved ones, and/or the patient's designated power of attorney for healthcare, and recognize a Catholic holistic definition of life, dying, and death. The criteria of the revised benefit/burden analysis, which take any decision about either withholding or withdrawing ANH out of the patient's hands, rely solely on biological considerations, implicitly posit the physician as sole decision maker, and focus only on biological life, dying, and death. The discontinuity between the traditional and revised principles may be demonstrated by considering the normative implications of Rahner's theology of dying and death for ANH and the PVS patient.

Rahner's Theology of Dying and Death: Normative Implications

What are the implications of Rahner's distinction between death as a loss of personal freedom, historicity, and relationality and death as a loss of biological life for assessing the *Address*, *Responses*, and *Commentary*? Comparing the statements in these documents with earlier patient-and-person-centered magisterial statements on maintaining or withdrawing

---

[47] John J. Hardt and Kevin D. O'Rourke, "Nutrition and Hydration: The CDF Response in Perspective," *Health Progress* 88, no. 1 (November-December 2007): 46.

[48] Ibid.

[49] For more on end-of-life issues, see Corkery, *Bioethics and the Catholic Moral Tradition*, 79–107.

ANH, it appears that what is morally permissible in the former is dictated by an exclusive focus on death in the biological sense and in the latter by a focus on death as an act of personal, foundational, and categorical freedom. We explore this inconsistency.

In the *Address*, *Responses*, and *Commentary*, dying and death for the PVS patient are considered only as biological events in which the freedom to determine the imminence of death is assigned to a physician's clinical judgment based on purely biological criteria. The first question of the *Responses* asks if the administration of food and water to the PVS patient is ethically obligatory. The affirmative answer recognizes two exceptions to this obligation. First, when ANH "cannot be assimilated by the patient's *body*," and second, when they "cannot be administered to the patient without causing significant *physical discomfort*" (emphasis added). It is significant that these two exceptions to the ordinary and proportionate principles requiring the administration of ANH to the PVS patient "in principle," allowing a physician to withhold ANH, are granted on the basis of *physical* criteria. We repeat again that such an approach, depending on the treatment decisions of the PVS patient as expressed in a living will or by a designated power of attorney for healthcare, may disregard the PVS patient's freedom and, in doing so, violate the patient's dignity as an embodied spiritual person. We have already seen John Paul II's judgment expressed in his March *Address* that "if treatment is ineffective or obviously disproportionate to the aims of sustaining life or recovering health . . . the decision to forego aggressive treatment *is an expression of respect that is due to the patient at every moment*" (no. 4, emphasis added).

We suggest that the determination to maintain or withdraw ANH should be made only as a result of a case-by-case analysis that recognizes that, for a human being, especially one *sub prolixitate mortis*, dying and death are acts of foundational, categorical, and theological freedom as much as they are passive, biological acts, and that for Catholic believers they are the doorway to what Pius XII called "the higher, more important good," namely, entrance into the eternal presence and unimaginable hospitality of God. We further suggest that any determination about the administration or withdrawal of ANH should be made by the patient through wishes expressed in a living will, or by the patient's freely designated power of attorney for healthcare in dialogue with a physician. That dialogue should be guided by the benefit/burden analysis, which includes a consideration of the patient's total relational, biological, and economic situation. No decision should be permitted to be made only by a physician and only on the basis of physical, biological criteria.

The Revised Directive 58 of the USCCB's *Ethical and Religious Directives* (2009) argues that ANH "may become excessively burdensome and therefore not obligatory in light of their very limited ability to prolong [biological] life or provide comfort." However, since the PVS patient "can reasonably be expected to live [physically] indefinitely if given such care," ANH is an obligation. David Jones argues to the "very strong presumption" that ANH should not be withdrawn because "the unconscious patient cannot experience any discomfort from the presence of the tubes."[50] Any argument, however, based on the comfort or discomfort of the PVS patient misunderstands the medical reality of PVS articulated by The Multi-Society Task Force on PVS. "Patients in a persistent vegetative state," the task force correctly states, "are unaware and insensate and therefore lack the cerebral cortical capacity to be conscious of pain."[51] If PVS patients cannot experience any discomfort from the presence of tubes, neither can they experience any discomfort from the absence of tubes and the nutrition and hydration they deliver.

The exclusive prioritization of physical considerations that trump all other considerations, including relational, psychological, spiritual, ethical, and economic ones, indicates the methodological reductionism of the revised benefit/burden principle that emphasizes dying and death primarily as biological and medical events. In the *Address*, *Responses*, and *Commentary*, the ethical justification for withholding or withdrawing ANH from PVS patients is based exclusively on physical criteria, though the *Commentary* does mention that "in principle" that does not exclude the physical impossibility of administering ANH, as in the cases of "very remote places" or "extreme poverty." This reductionism is in stark contrast to the original tradition that allowed for a benefit/burden analysis that included physical, emotional, relational, spiritual, ethical, and economic considerations and resulted in a free decision by the patient and/or the patient's designated healthcare proxy.

The reductionist prioritization, not the *absolutization*, of the biological over the personal is further reflected in the *Responses'* judgment on the "proper finality" of ANH, described as "the hydration and nourishment of the patient." Sustaining biological life is certainly *a* finality of ANH for the PVS patient, but it cannot equally be argued that ANH alone sustains *personal* life. We respectfully disagree with all those who claim, including

---

[50] David Jones, *Approaching the End: A Theological Exploration of Death and Dying* (New York: Oxford University Press, 2007), 218.

[51] The Multi-Society Task Force on PVS, "Medical Aspects of the Persistent Vegetative State (2)," 1572–79.

John Paul II in his *Address*, that the PVS patient "remains a person in the *full* sense of the term."[52] We do not disagree in the abstract that PVS patients remain persons and retain all the dignity due to persons, but, we submit, in their concrete circumstances of unfreedom, inaction in history, and unrelationality, they are far from fully human persons. In terms of the philosophy of death and dying we have articulated, ontologically, in terms of what *essentially* constitutes the specificity of the *fully* human person, PVS patients have suffered the irretrievable loss of the capacity to exercise their freedom, living history, and relationality, all existentials of person-hood integral to its fullness.

Foregoing or withdrawing ANH from Terri Schiavo, then, who was di-agnosed to be in a PVS, was not tantamount to euthanasia. It was, rather, simply accepting the fact that she had come to the end of her specifically personal life and should not be impeded from proceeding to her natural, biological death.[53] She had permanently lost essential components of the full human person, namely, the rational, affective, relational, spiritual, and moral capabilities that distinguish specifically human animals from lower animals. We respectfully disagree with those who, despite their protesta-tions to the contrary, argue, on the basis of a philosophy that prioritizes biological over personal life, against the position we have just articulated.[54] For Terri and all PVS patients, personal death has already taken place, though biological death has not. We propose that the "proper finality" of ANH must be assessed in terms of the personal as much as the physical, and we further propose that when it is assessed in terms of the personal it does not attain any personal finality in the PVS patient and can be with-held or discontinued.

Conclusion

In this chapter we have done essentially three things. First, we have articu-lated a Catholic theology of dying and death; second, we have analyzed

---

[52] See Kevin O'Rourke, "Reflections on the Papal *Address* concerning Care for Persistent Vegetative State Patients," in Hamel and Walter, *Artificial Nutrition and Hydration and the Permanently Unconscious Patient*, 237, emphasis added.

[53] See the Texas Bishops and the Texas Conference of Catholic Health Facilities, "On Withdrawing Artificial Nutrition and Hydration," 112.

[54] See, for instance, William E. May, "Caring for Persons in the Persistent Vegetative State," *Our Sunday Visitor* (September 1, 2000); Mark S. Latkovic, "The Morality of Tube Feeding PVS Patients: A Critique of the View of Kevin O'Rourke, O.P.," in *Artificial Nu-trition and Hydration: The New Catholic Debate*, ed. Christopher Tollefson (Dordrecht: Springer, 2008), 196–200.

the 2004 *Address of John Paul II to the Participants in the International Congress on 'Life-Sustaining Treatments and Vegetative State: Scientific Advances and Ethical Dilemmas'"* and the CDF's *Responses* and *Commentary* explicating that *Address;* third, we have debated the normative implications of this theological theory and these documents for the issue of ANH and PVS patients. We have argued that John Paul II's *Address* and the CDF's *Responses* and *Commentary* give priority to dying and death as biological events, disregard the patient's freedom to determine dying and death as acts of personal freedom, transfer that freedom implicitly to the clinical judgment of a physician, and suggest only reductionist, physical criteria to determine how that freedom will be exercised. We have also argued that to assess any body-soul being, which the universal Catholic tradition holds the human being to be, on only bodily, physical grounds, is to treat the person with indignity and is objectively unreasonable and, therefore, objectively unethical.

Earlier magisterial statements, which had long become traditional, give priority to dying and death as a free, personal choice, recognize that foundational and categorical freedom are to be exercised by the patient or the patient's designated power of attorney for healthcare and the patient's physician in dialogue, and consider the ethical determination to maintain or withdraw ANH to be the outcome of a benefit/burden analysis in light of relational, emotional, spiritual, ethical, medical, and economic considerations. The shift in focus from active dying and death as acts of personal freedom *sub prolixitate mortis* to dying and death as passive, biological events, and the prioritizing of biological life over personal life, is a distortion of a genuinely Catholic theology of dying and death and a distorted application of traditional Catholic principles guiding the administration of ANH for PVS patients. That the shift has been prescribed in response to a papal pronouncement founded, as the *Code of Canon Law* states, on "contingent and conjectural elements," and therefore owed due respect (canon 218; see 752–53) but not absolute, theological faith, suggests that the proposed shift has been hasty and is open to reconsideration.

Questions for Reflection

- What is the difference between a persistent and a permanent vegetative state? Why is this distinction ethically significant when making end-of-life decisions?
- Do you believe that ANH is medical care or medical treatment? What are the normative implications of your belief for PVS patients?

- Explain how Pope John Paul II's *Address* and the CDF's *Responses* and *Commentary* were different from past official statements on end-of-life issues. What are the strengths and weaknesses of the different perspectives?
- Explain Karl Rahner's theology of death. What are the anthropological and normative implications of his theology of death for PVS patients?
- Would you have removed Terri Schiavo from ANH? Explain.

Suggested Readings

Cronin, Daniel A. "The Moral Law in regard to the Ordinary and Extraordinary Means of Conserving Life." In Russell E. Smith, ed., *Conserving Human Life.* Braintree, MA: Pope John Center, 1988.

Hamel, Ronald P., and James J. Walter. *Artificial Nutrition and Hydration and the Permanently Unconscious Patient: The Catholic Debate.* Washington, DC: Georgetown University Press, 2007.

Rahner, Karl. *On the Theology of Death.* Freiburg: Herder and Herder, 1961.

Possible Future Directions
for Christian Ethics

Pope Francis
and *Amoris Laetitia*

Anthropological and Methodological Developments in Catholic Theological Ethics

---

Learning Objectives

- Explain methodological developments in Catholic theological ethics in *Amoris Laetitia*.
- Explain anthropological developments in Catholic theological ethics in *Amoris Laetitia*.
- Understand and explain the interrelationship between Catholic sexual teaching and Catholic social teaching.
- Articulate the ethical implications of these methodological and anthropological developments for doing theological ethics in the twenty-first century.

We began this book with the fundamental metaethical question of whether or not there is ethical truth. We have argued throughout that there is ethical truth, that "the good" can be defined as human dignity and what facilitates its attainment, and that this definition is justified from a virtuous perspective by the selection, interpretation, prioritization, and integration of the sources of ethical knowledge: scripture, tradition, science/reason, and human experience. Furthermore, the selection, interpretation, prioritization, and integration of these ethical sources, guided by an informed conscience, serve to formulate and justify norms to facilitate attaining human dignity and avoid frustrating it. The metaethical theory that we proposed and defended, perspectivism, allows for plural definitions of human dignity and plural formulations and justifications of the norms that facilitate attaining human dignity. This pluralism, however, is a form of objectivism, not a cultural or individual relativism. There are parameters in a virtuous perspective, established in dialogue with a community historically, culturally, and contextually, for what can and cannot be an authentic definition of human dignity and norms that flow from that definition. Slavery, by definition, falls outside those parameters; just and loving same-sex relationships fall within those parameters. Historical consciousness recognizes the ongoing individual and communal discernment of the definition of human dignity and the norms that facilitate its attainment.

We then proposed a methodological and anthropological virtuous perspective to guide the formation of conscience, drawing from the best of the Catholic tradition to define both human dignity and norms to facilitate its attainment, and applied this perspective and those norms to different sexual, social, and biomedical ethical issues. We conclude this book by exploring recent ethical, anthropological, and methodological contributions in Pope Francis's Apostolic Exhortation *Amoris Laetitia* and discuss the implications of those developments for the future of Catholic theological ethics. We do so in six cumulative sections. First, we highlight the tension in Catholic theological ethics between Catholic social teaching and Catholic sexual teaching; second, we explore *Amoris Laetitia*'s anthropological integration of Catholic social teaching and Catholic sexual teaching; third, we explore the new pastoral methods advanced by *Amoris Laetitia* and their implications; fourth, we explore its methodological integration of Catholic social teaching and Catholic sexual teaching; fifth, we demonstrate how the anthropological and methodological insights of *Amoris Laetitia* might provide a more integrated and credible response to a contemporary ethical issue; and sixth, we indicate the theological ethical implications of these developments for the future of Catholic theological ethics.

The Tension between
Catholic Sexual Teaching and Catholic Social Teaching

On the return flight from his 2015 visit to Africa, Pope Francis reflected on the complex relationship between reality and church teaching. When asked if the church should consider a change in its absolute prohibition of the use of condoms to prevent the spread of HIV/AIDS, the pope responded that the question seemed too small. "I think the morality of the Church on this point finds itself in a dilemma: is it the fifth or the sixth commandment? To defend life, or is the sexual relation open to life? But this is not the problem." The first problem in Africa, and indeed worldwide, is much bigger and more complex than the use of condoms. The first problem is the reality of "denutrition, the exploitation of people, slave labor, lack of drinking water. . . . These are the problems."[1] Condom use may or may not address a small part of the human problem, but the greater problem to be addressed is systemic social injustice and violations of human dignity throughout the world. A second problem is the relationship between church law and human dignity. Francis recalled a specious question put to Jesus by those seeking to accuse him: "Is it lawful to cure on the sabbath?" (Matt 12:10). Jesus answered that any one of them would rescue his sheep on the sabbath and "how much more valuable is a human being than a sheep" (Matt 12:12). "Do justice," is Francis's answer, "but do not think whether it is allowed or not to heal on the sabbath. And when all these are cured, when there are no injustices in this world, then we can talk about the Sabbath."[2] Jesus's response is prophetic, and so is the pope's. It foreshadows a shift in focus in how the magisterium and Catholic theological ethicists should prioritize questions relating to social justice and sexual ethics, and how, therefore, they should approach those questions anthropologically and methodologically.

Pope Francis's reflection on the relationship between the prevention of HIV/AIDS and the social injustice of systemic poverty highlights some of the ethical methodological inconsistencies that Catholic ethicists have long noted between Catholic social teaching found in documents such as *Populorum Progressio* and Catholic sexual teaching found in documents such as *Humanae Vitae*. Since the Second Vatican Council,[3] Catholic social ethics has been largely principle oriented, relation focused, dynamic, developmental, and inductive, while Catholic sexual ethics continues to be largely law oriented, legalistic, act focused, static, and deductive. In this chapter we argue that this methodological divide between Catholic social ethics and Catholic sexual ethics is bridged in Pope Francis's *Amoris Laetitia*.

Anthropology and *Amoris Laetitia*

Amoris Laetitia is in continuity with anthropological developments in both Catholic social and sexual teaching and builds on those developments. It affirms the dimensions of the human person integrally and adequately

---

[1] Gerard O'Connell, "Pope Francis on Paris Climate Change Summit: 'It's Either Now or Never,'" *America* (November 30, 2015).

[2] Ibid.

[3] See Charles E. Curran, *Catholic Social Teaching: A Historical, Theological, and Ethical Analysis* (Washington, DC: Georgetown University Press, 2002).

considered we developed in Chapter 5; it is in continuity with anthropological developments in both Catholic social teaching and Catholic sexual teaching and builds on those developments. It also more thoroughly integrates the method of Catholic social teaching into Catholic sexual teaching and creates an opening for the development of specific sexual norms. *Amoris Laetitia* reflects the anthropology developed in *Populorum Progressio* and in much of Catholic social teaching. The human person is a free subject (not an object) (*AL*, nos. 33, 153); in corporeality, but physical and spiritual are integrated (*AL*, no. 151); in relationship to the material world (*AL*, no. 277), to others (*AL*, nos. 187–98), to social groups (*AL*, no. 222), and to self (*AL*, no. 32); created in the image and likeness of God (*AL*, no. 10); a historical being (*AL*, no. 193); and fundamentally unique but equal to all other persons (*AL*, no. 54). There are, however, fundamental sexual anthropological developments in *Amoris Laetitia*. In its absolute proscriptive norms traditional Catholic sexual anthropology prioritizes the biological function of the sexual act over its relational and spiritual meanings; Francis emphasizes the relational and spiritual in moral decision making. This is especially evident in his emphasis on personal conscience, discernment, and virtue, to which we now turn.

Pope Francis on Conscience

Sociological surveys repeatedly affirm the disconnect between the magisterium's absolute sexual norms that prohibit artificial contraception, homosexual acts, and communion for the divorced and remarried without annulment, for example, and the perspectives of the Catholic faithful. According to these surveys the majority of adult, educated Catholics judge that these norms are detached from reality; these Catholics are following their adult and informed consciences to make practical judgments on these and other ethical matters.[4] In both *Evangelii Gaudium* and *Amoris Laetitia* Francis brings to the fore the Catholic doctrine on the authority and inviolability of personal conscience, especially as it relates to "irregular situations" in marital and sexual relationships, such as cohabitation, divorce and remarriage, and same-sex relationships. "We also must learn to listen more to our conscience," which "is the interior space in which we can listen to and hear the truth, the good, the voice of God. It is the inner place of our relationship with Him, who speaks to our heart and helps us to discern, to understand the path we ought to take, and once the decision

---

[4] For a worldwide sociological survey of Catholic beliefs on a variety of sexual ethical issues, see Univision Communications, *Global Survey of Roman Catholics*, Executive Summary (New York, February 2014).

is made to move forward, to remain faithful."[5] This statement reflects a model of conscience very different from Francis's two predecessors, John Paul II and Benedict XVI, and is more faithful to the long-established Catholic tradition on the inviolability of conscience. Indeed, his teaching on conscience is one of the central teachings in *Amoris Laetitia*.[6] He judges that "individual conscience needs to be better incorporated into the Church's praxis in certain situations which do not objectively embody our understanding of marriage," or indeed of any complex ethical issue. He quotes Aquinas frequently—especially significant is Aquinas's teaching that the more we descend into the details of situations the more will general principles be found to fail. Francis concurs with Paul VI's earlier statements in *Octogesima Adveniens* on Catholic social teaching (nos. 4, 49, 50) that there is such an "immense variety of concrete situations" that *Amoris Laetitia* cannot "provide a new set of rules, canonical in nature and applicable to all cases" (*AL*, no. 300). The pathway to the ethical solution of any and every situation is the pathway not of uninformed obedience to some law or rule but of an internal forum or conscience decision, a process of discernment, perhaps guided by a spiritual advisor, and a final practical judgment of conscience that commands a free subject to do this or not to do that. Only such an informed conscience can make a moral judgment about the details of any and every particular situation. Such a judgment is reached only after a serious and conscientious process of discernment.

Discernment

Discernment in moral decision making complements the role and authority of conscience and seeks to inform and form it. The emphasis on discernment in *Amoris Laetitia* is a distinct anthropological contribution to both Catholic social and sexual teaching. Although it is hardly surprising to find discernment used frequently by a son of Ignatius of Loyola, it is surprising to find it used so centrally as a basis for guiding responsible decisions in the realm of sexual ethics. In the Jesuit tradition, discernment is the art of prayerful decision making that relies upon spiritual practices,[7] including the practices of seeing, judging, and acting from a perspective informed

---

[5] Pope Francis, "Jesus Always Invites Us: He Does Not Impose," *Angelus* (June 30, 2013).

[6] See James F. Keenan, "Receiving *Amoris Laetitia*," *Theological Studies* 78 (2017): 193–212; Conor M. Kelly, "The Role of the Moral Theologian in the Church: A Proposal in Light of *Amoris Laetitia*," *Theological Studies* 77 (2016): 922–48; James T. Bretzke, "In Good Conscience," *America* (April 8, 2016).

[7] James Martin, "Understanding Discernment Is Key to Understanding *Amoris Laetitia*," *America* (April 8, 2016).

by scripture, tradition, science/reason, and human experience. This approach is clearly reflected in Catholic social teaching. In his commentary on *Amoris Laetitia*, Parisian Cardinal Vingt-Trois writes that it invites all pastoral workers—and, we add, all Christians—to return to "meditating on the message of Christ and the Christian tradition of the family and to seek to understand how this message could help to accompany families in the challenges that face them today."[8] Discernment, Francis writes, requires "humility, discretion, and love for the Church and her teaching, in a sincere search for God's will and a desire to make a more perfect response to it" (*AL*, no. 300).

Virtue

Discernment is much more than simply following rules and absolute norms and moves us from a deontological-type ethic to a virtue-type ethic grounded in the virtues of faith, hope, charity, patience, mercy, justice, and prudence. That perspective helps us to see and to judge from a uniquely Christian perspective and to act in a uniquely Christian way. Seeing and judging may lead to acts that follow rules and guidelines presented by the church, or they may lead to the act of challenging those rules and guidelines. Authentic discernment and an informed conscience allow for, and sometimes may even demand, dissent from magisterial teaching. The voice of conscience, Chicago's Cardinal Cupich asserts, "could very well affirm the necessity of living at some distance from the Church's understanding of the ideal," while nevertheless calling a person to "new stages of growth."[9] That theological assertion is a remarkable echo of Thomas Aquinas's thirteenth-century assertion that "anyone upon whom the ecclesiastical authorities, in ignorance of the true facts, impose a demand that offends against his clear conscience should perish in excommunication rather than violate his conscience."[10] Since conscience is a practical judgment that comes at the end of a deliberative process, it necessarily involves the virtue of prudence, by which "right reason is applied to action."[11]

The shift from a focus on rules and acts to a focus on virtue is a third fundamental anthropological and methodological shift in *Amoris Laetitia*. As we have discussed extensively throughout this book, virtue focuses

---

[8] See Anne-Bénédicte Hoffner, "*Amoris Laetitia* Requires an Effort of Formation of Discernment," *LaCroix International* (October 19, 2016).

[9] Claire Chretien, "Cardinal Cupich Lays Out Why *Amoris Laetitia* Is 'Revolutionary' for Catholic Teaching," *LifeSiteNews* website (February 9, 2018).

[10] Thomas Aquinas, *In IV Sent.*, distinctio 28, q. 2, art. 4.

[11] Thomas Aquinas, *Summa Theologiae Sancti Thomae de Aquino* (hereafter *ST)* II–II, 47, 2.

first on the character of a person rather than on the person's acts, on being rather than doing, but there is still an ongoing dialectic between virtue and acts. Acts are important, because they both reflect and, when repeated, shape virtuous character; virtue both manifests and creates itself in acts. The focus in *Amoris Laetitia* is not on acts and rules but on ways of being in the world, where the person is invited to strive to live a life like Christ in the service of God, spouse, family, neighbor, and society, all the while understanding that God's mercy is infinite for those who fall short. Chapter four of *Amoris Laetitia*, "Love in Marriage," is a beautiful reflection on St. Paul's poetic passage in First Corinthians on the nature of true love and the virtues associated with it. Love is patient, directed toward service, generous, forgiving; love is not jealous, boastful, or rude. It is noteworthy that the virtue of chastity, so central in the traditional Catholic approach to love, sexuality, and marriage, and so often deductively applied as a legalistic submission to the church's absolute proscriptive laws on sexuality, is mentioned only once in *Amoris Laetitia*, and this in the context of proving "invaluable for the genuine growth of love between persons" (*AL*, no. 206). Rather than a focus on chastity, there is greater focus on the virtues of love, patience, mercy, compassion, reconciliation, forgiveness, and prudence, the cardinal virtue that guides all other virtues and is a prerequisite virtue for both conscience and discernment. Prudence discerns the first principles of ethics, applies them to particular situations, and enables conscience to make practical judgments that this is the right thing to do on this occasion and with this good intention.[12]

Method and *Amoris Laetitia*

Cardinal Schönborn of Vienna judges that *Amoris Laetitia* "is the great text of theological ethics we have been waiting for since the days of the [Second Vatican] Council."[13] Cardinal Cupich calls it "revolutionary,"[14] and Cardinal Parolin notes that it indicates a "paradigm shift" that calls for a "new spirit, a new [method]" to help "incarnate the Gospel in the family."[15] *Amoris Laetitia* notes that the dialogue during the 2014 and 2015 synods on marriage and the family raised the suggestion of new pastoral

---

[12] Aquinas, *ST* II–II, 47, 6.

[13] Cindy Wooden, "*Amoris Laetitia*' at Three Months: Communion Question Still Debated," *National Catholic Reporter* (July 7, 2016).

[14] Chretien, "Cardinal Cupich Lays Out Why *Amoris Laetitia* Is 'Revolutionary' for Catholic Teaching."

[15] Edward Pentin, "Cardinal Parolin: *Amoris Laetitia* Represents New Paradigm, Spirit, and Approach," *National Catholic Register* (January 11, 2018).

methods tailored to different communities and the marital, familial, and relational realities of those communities. It incorporates Catholic social teaching's methodological developments philosophically, focusing on inductive reasoning, historical consciousness, and an appreciation of culture, experience, and the sciences. It focuses theologically on scripture and an ecclesiology, not of an unequal society but of an equal communion, and bridges the traditional disconnect between theological ethics and pastoral counseling.[16] We consider each in turn.

Philosophical Method

A major methodological shift in Catholic sexual teaching in *Amoris Laetitia* is from a deductive to an inductive ethical method. Deductive reasoning begins with a universally accepted formal definition of human dignity and universal principles or norms that facilitate or frustrate its attainment. Inductive reasoning begins with material, particular, cultural, and contextual definitions of human dignity and formulates and justifies norms that facilitate or frustrate its attainment. "It is *reductive*," *Amoris Laetitia* notes, "simply to consider whether or not an individual's actions correspond to a general law or rule, because that is not enough to discern and ensure full fidelity to God in the concrete life of a human being" (*AL*, no. 304, emphasis added). We must begin with the particular, contextual reality of the human person to discern what rule applies or what new rule needs to be formulated to address the reality.

Amoris Laetitia cites with approval, for the first time ever in Catholic sexual teaching, Aquinas's warning that, although there is necessity in the general principles, the more we descend to matters of detail, the more frequently we encounter defects. "In matters of action, truth or practical rectitude is not the same for all, as to matters of detail, but only as to the general principles; and where there is the same rectitude in matters of detail, it is not equally known to all. . . . The principle will be found to fail, according as we descend further into detail'" (*AL*, no. 304; *ST* I–II, 94, 4). Aquinas's principle has often been cited by Catholic theological ethicists to refute claims to absolute sexual norms. By aligning with Aquinas, at the very least *Amoris Laetitia* is cautioning against a deductive, one-rule-fits-all approach to moral decision making and is emphasizing the importance of particular contexts and circumstances and an inductive approach.

---

[16] Norbert Rigali, "The Unity of Ethical and Pastoral Truth," *Chicago Studies* 25 (1986): 225.

Second, *Amoris Laetitia* recognizes historical consciousness in its law of gradualness, borrowed from John Paul II in *Familiaris Consortio*, which acknowledges that the human being "knows, loves, and accomplishes moral good by different stages of growth" (*FC*, no. 34; *AL*, no. 295). This is illustrated best in Francis's discussion of the ethics of cohabitation. Nowhere in *Amoris Laetitia* does he condemn cohabitation in blanket fashion, as he surely would have to do if he were following Catholic marital and sexual norms. Contrary to the "Final Report" from the synods, which condemns all cohabitation, he makes a distinction between "cohabitation which totally excludes any intention to marry" (*AL*, no. 53) and cohabitation dictated by "cultural or contingent situations," like poverty, that can lead to marriage when circumstances permit it. Acknowledging the law of gradualness, an overt expression of historical consciousness, Francis recognizes that some types of cohabitation may be genuinely loving relationships that will grow into marriages. The same law of gradualness may be conscientiously discerned to apply to other sexual ethical issues.

We note a third shift in philosophical method. *Gaudium et Spes* opened the church to a new method that starts with the human person and the human situation and works upward to specific ethical rules and general ethical principles. It emphasized: "Thanks to the *experience* of past ages, the progress of the *sciences*, and the treasures hidden in the various forms of *human culture*, the nature of man himself is revealed and *new roads to truth are opened*" (*GS*, no. 44, emphasis added). This trilogy—human experience, culture, and science—is paradigmatic for an inductive, historically conscious approach to theological ethics and is widely reflected in *Amoris Laetitia*.

First, *Amoris Laetitia* is based on "the joy of love experienced by families [that] is also the joy of the Church" (*AL*, no. 1). It is grounded in experience and bases its reflections on the experience of actual married life, of the human sexuality complexly reflected in it, and of socioeconomic factors like poverty and hunger that so affect it worldwide (*AL*, no. 25). We agree with Margaret Farley's assertion that is apposite here: "It is inconceivable that moral norms can be formulated without consulting the experience of those whose lives are at stake."[17] Second, *Amoris Laetitia* recognizes and embraces the import of particular cultural contexts, noting that "each country or region . . . can seek solutions [to ethical and/or pastoral issues] better suited to its *culture* and sensitive to its traditions and *local needs*" (*AL*, no. 3, emphasis added). The sciences, finally, can be helpful for the education and development of children in families (*AL*, nos. 273, 280).

---

[17] Margaret A. Farley, "Moral Discourse in the Public Arena," in *Vatican Authority and American Catholic Dissent*, ed. William W. May (New York: Crossroad, 1987), 29.

Theological Method

Amoris Laetitia demonstrates some theological development in its use
of scripture and a unique ecclesiological perspective when approaching
marital, familial, and sexual ethical issues. First, there is a shift to virtue,
highlighted best in chapter four's beautiful reflection on St. Paul's First
Corinthians. There is a fundamental shift from proscriptive rules to virtues
and to scripture as a pedagogical source for the development of virtues
in a marital and moral life. *Amoris Laetitia*'s use of scripture on issues
like marriage and divorce, however, is at times selective and incomplete.
It presents Matthew's teaching on the indissolubility of marriage, for example, but fails to note his permission for divorce in the case of *porneia*
(unlawful sex). It also fails to acknowledge the reality that the church has
granted and continues to grant divorces through the Pauline Privilege and
has also historically granted them through the misnamed Petrine Privilege,
based on marital situations caused by slavery.[18] It does not cite any scriptural text to condemn homosexual relationships and avoids much of the
proof-texting of scripture that earlier magisterial documents utilize, when
addressing specific ethical issues.

Second, much like Catholic social teaching that empowers local bishops'
conferences to formulate and apply Catholic social teaching on the basis
of their particular cultural and socioeconomic contexts, *Amoris Laetitia*
refers extensively to bishops' conferences and how they have responded
to particular ethical questions with respect to married and family life. Pope
Francis has made a concerted effort toward decentralization of power from
the Vatican to local bishops' conferences, and his consultation of the laity
before and during both synods shows his commitment also to the *sensus
fidelium* and ecclesial synodality. Some theological explanation is needed
here.

Sensus fidelium is a theological concept that denotes "the instinctive
capacity of the whole church to recognize the infallibility of the Spirit's
truth."[19] It is a charism of discernment, possessed by the whole church,
laity and clergy alike, which receives a church teaching as apostolic and
therefore to be held in both faith and *praxis*. Vatican II bishops argued
that, although the magisterium spoke *for* the church, it was also obliged
to speak *from* the church, and that when it ignored a clear *sensus fidelium*
in the whole church, it was being unfaithful to the church's rule of faith.
Lumen Gentium is clear: "The body of the faithful *as a whole*, anointed

---

[18] See Michael G. Lawler and Todd A. Salzman, "Catholic Doctrine on Divorce and
Remarriage: A Practical Theology Analysis," *Theological Studies* 78 (2017): 326–47.

[19] John E. Thiel, *Senses of Tradition: Continuity and Development in Catholic Faith*
(Oxford: Oxford University Press, 2000), 47.

as they are by the Holy One . . . cannot err in matters of belief. Thanks to a supernatural sense of the faith *(sensus fidelium)* which characterizes the people *as a whole*, it manifests this unerring quality when, 'from the bishops to the last of the faithful,'[20] it manifests universal agreement in matters of faith and morals" (*LG,* no. 12, emphasis added). In the church now reemerging from the Second Vatican Council, which is believed to be not an unequal, hierarchical society but an equal ecclesial communion, any effort to evaluate a magisterial teaching will automatically include open dialogue, uncoerced judgment, and free consensus. That is the way universal *sensus fidelium* is formed. Surveys of laity leading up to the synods and *Amoris Laetitia*, which attempts to include the voices from those surveys, reflect a useful process for discerning the *sensus fidelium*.

This discernment is a complex process, which takes time, patience, and a commitment to the kind of honest and charitable dialogue that Pope Francis so appreciated at the 2014 Synod on Marriage and the Family and characterized in his speech at the synod's conclusion on October 18, 2014, as "a spirit of collegiality and synodality." Some see a defining characteristic of his papacy as seeking to realize synodality, the ecclesiology of Vatican II that focuses on seriously journeying together and listening to the input from all quarters of the church, laity and clergy alike, to engage in charitable, honest, and constructive dialogue to discern God's will and the path the church must follow to live according to that will.[21] The two synods that laid the foundation for *Amoris Laetitia* modeled this dialogue in a way that synods in the past had not done.

Amoris Laetitia and New Pastoral Methods

Pope Francis notes that the two synods preceding *Amoris Laetitia* "raised the need for new pastoral methods . . . that respect both the Church's teaching and local problems and needs" (*AL*, no. 199). The concept of new pastoral methods in *Amoris Laetitia* draws from both philosophical and theological methods and, for those who interpret *Amoris Laetitia*, highlights a fundamental methodological distinction between moral and pastoral theology, and between the objective and subjective realms of morality. Norbert Rigali addressed this issue thirty years ago, and his observations are especially relevant today in the post–*Amoris Laetitia* era. Rigali argued there has been and, we add, continues to be, a "chasm" for some Catholic

---

[20] Augustine, *De praed. sanct.* 14, 27, *PL* 44, 980.

[21] The English word *synod* is linguistically significant. It derives from the Greek *sun*, meaning "together," and *hodos*, meaning "traveling" or "journeying." It literally means, therefore, "journeying together."

ethicists between theological ethics, with its focus on the objective realm of ethics, and pastoral theology, with its focus on the subjective realm of ethics.[22] The former emphasizes objective norms, natural law, and magisterial teaching; the latter emphasizes pastoral guidance and subjective conscience. The result is a "two-moral truths theory,"[23] one objective and the other subjective. The distinction between the objective and subjective realms of ethics thinking reflects an ongoing debate on the role and function of conscience in relationship to objective norms. To clarify the ethical implications of this debate, we return to our discussion on conscience.

It is common in contemporary theological ethics to distinguish between what is called the object orientation and the subject orientation of conscience. The former highlights the external law or moral norm; the latter highlights conscience's internal discernment, selection, interpretation, and application of the law or norm in light of a complex lived reality, all the contextual and relational circumstances of a given situation. Theological ethicists highlight different orientations, which leads to competing models on the interrelationship between magisterial teaching and conscience. Both models of conscience are evident in Catholic tradition. Those who highlight an object orientation argue that moral norms *must* be followed and, therefore, control the subjective conscience. Those who highlight a subject orientation argue to the contrary that the subjective conscience is free and that, when it makes a moral decision, it *must* take into consideration not only moral norms but also immediate, concrete circumstances that can affect the selection, interpretation, and application of norms. The two models are clearly evident in efforts to interpret *Amoris Laetitia*.

In *Pastoral Guidelines for Implementing* Amoris Laetitia (July 1, 2016), Archbishop Chaput of Philadelphia writes that "Catholic teaching makes clear that the subjective conscience of the individual can never be set against objective moral truth as if conscience and truth were two competing principles for moral decision making." In one sense, Chaput is correct. There is only one moral truth; conscience and moral truth are not two competing truths but two complementary ways of arriving at that one truth. In another sense, by prioritizing the external, object orientation of a norm, objective moral truth *in itself*,[24] over against the subject orientation of conscience, he is incorrect. An assertion of an object orientation of conscience that obligates the subjective conscience simply to obey magisterial teaching without any personal discernment is contrary to Catholic teaching. Any conscience decision must discern moral truth in the subject in light of

---

[22] Rigali, "The Unity of Ethical and Pastoral Truth," 224–25.

[23] Ibid., 225.

[24] Josef Fuchs, *Christian Morality: The Word Becomes Flesh*, trans. Brian McNeil (Dublin: Gill and MacMillan, 1987), 125.

any and every relevant circumstance. We agree with Rigali. Moral truth is not something that objectively exists *in itself* over against the moral subject but rather something to be discerned by the moral subject as existing *in myself*, that is within the moral subject. Moral truth is knowledge within the knowing subject of the interrelationship between the moral object and the moral subject; moral truth exists only in the moral subject.[25] Pope Francis seems to defend this kind of prioritization of the moral subject and the subject's conscience. This is evident in several different ways in *Amoris Laetitia*.

Speaking of those in the "irregular situation" of being divorced and remarried without annulment, he acknowledges that they "can find themselves in a variety of situations, which should not be pigeonholed or fit into overly rigid classifications leaving no room for personal and pastoral discernment" (*AL*, no. 298). In a footnote that became instantly famous, he cites the Second Vatican Council's judgment that if they take the option the church offers them of living as brother and sister, "it often happens that faithfulness is endangered and the good of the children suffers" (*AL*, no. 298n329; see *GS*, no. 51). For these reasons, the pope continues, "a pastor cannot feel that it is enough simply to apply moral laws to those living in 'irregular' situations, as if they were stones to throw at people's lives. This would bespeak the closed heart of one used to hiding behind the Church's [objective] teachings, 'sitting on the chair of Moses and judging at times with superiority and superficiality difficult cases and wounded families'" (*AL*, no. 305). Acknowledging the influence on a conscience judgment of the various concrete factors and circumstances he has enumerated, the pope advises that subjective "individual conscience needs to be better incorporated into the Church's praxis in certain situations which do not *objectively* embody our understanding of marriage" (*AL*, no. 303, emphasis added). His argument applies to every concrete personal moral situation.

It is clear that Francis holds and teaches what the Catholic Church he pastors holds and teaches but has been reticent to speak about in recent centuries, namely, a subject orientation rather than an object orientation of conscience. In the case of irregular situations, it is not the case that the norm has exceptions, which would be the case in an object-orientation focus. Rather, it is that the norm has nothing to say in such situations without subjective understanding and application, which is the case in a subject-orientation focus of conscience.[26] In other words, an object orientation gives priority to a moral norm like no premarital sex and evaluates subjective conscience on whether or not it conforms to the norm. A subject orientation discerns the contextual situation, which norm applies

---

[25] Rigali, "The Unity of Ethical and Pastoral Truth," 225–27.
[26] Ibid., 229.

in it, and makes a conscience decision illumined by both the norm and all the morally relevant circumstances. In the case where a norm does not apply—for example, the norm prohibiting communion for a divorced and remarried couple where living as brother and sister would damage marital and familial relationships—another norm that allows for participating in the sacraments may apply. In addition, when irregular situations become regularized in terms of human experience, such as the lived reality of just and loving same-sex relationships, the objective norm must be revised to reflect that lived experience, just as the objective norm allowing slavery was revised to prohibit slavery and the norm to prohibit usury was revised to allow usury.

Methodologically, Francis's call in *Amoris Laetitia* for the "need for new pastoral methods" that "respect both the Church's teaching and local problems and needs" (*AL*, no. 199) places him firmly within tradition by prioritizing a subject orientation rather than an object orientation of conscience, overcomes the chasm between theological ethics and pastoral counseling, and places a single moral truth where it belongs, in the moral subject's conscience. In other words, "there is not moral law *and* conscience; there is only moral law *of* conscience, the moral law constituting conscience itself."[27]

The established tradition in Catholic social teaching, expressed in the *Catechism of the Catholic Church,* that the church "proposes *principles for reflection; it provides criteria for judgment. . .* [and] it gives *guidelines for action*" (*CCC,* no. 2423, emphasis added) is more reflective of the prioritization of subject orientation, whereas Catholic sexual teaching and the magisterium's absolute proscriptive sexual norms are more reflective of the prioritization of object orientation. Pope Francis's suggestion of new pastoral methods lights a pathway to greater anthropological and methodological consistency between Catholic social teaching and Catholic sexual teaching by consistently prioritizing the moral subject orientation of a discerning conscience over the moral object orientation of norms external to the subject.

The Integration of Catholic Social and Sexual Teaching: An Example

An essential methodological consideration in *Amoris Laetitia* that explicitly brings together Catholic social teaching and Catholic sexual teaching is the recognition of the impact the experience of poverty has on relational

---

[27] Ibid., 226.

decisions. Francis offers the example of a couple who cohabit "primarily because celebrating a marriage is considered too expensive in the social circumstances. As a result, material poverty drives people into *de facto* unions" (*AL,* no. 294). Socioeconomic realities profoundly influence human relationships and human decisions; their impact is often overlooked in magisterial teaching that proposes one-size-fits-all norms in Catholic sexual teaching, as illustrated by an incident on Pope Francis's visit to the Philippines in January 2015.

On this visit a former homeless girl, Glyzelle Palomar, gave a heart-wrenching address to the pope and some thirty thousand young people gathered for Filipino Youth Sunday. In that address she burst into tears recounting her experience of homelessness. "There are many children neglected by their own parents. There are also many who became victims and many terrible things happened to them like drugs or prostitution. Why is God allowing such things to happen, even if it is not the fault of the children? And why are there only very few people helping us?"[28] Pope Francis responded to her with the profound compassion that characterizes his papacy, imploring Christians to learn how to weep in solidarity with those who suffer, especially the most vulnerable in society.

What was left unaddressed in both the pope's and the Philippine bishops' responses to Glyzelle's plight, and that of countless others like her, is the correlation between poverty and homelessness, especially among children, and the rigid stance of the Philippine bishops, who stridently resist the legalization of birth control in the country. A Guttmacher Institute study indicates that 50 percent of all pregnancies in the Philippines are unintended, and 90 percent of these unintended pregnancies are due to a lack of access to birth control.[29] Only in 2012 did Filipino lawmakers pass a bill for free family planning and access to contraceptives, legislation that the bishops of the Philippines fiercely resisted and continue to resist.[30] On the flight home from the Philippines, Francis reiterated the church's stance against artificial birth control and promoted natural family planning. He also recounted an encounter he had with a young Filipino woman who had seven children and was currently pregnant. He called this irresponsible and commented, "Some think . . . that in order to be good Catholics we have

---

[28] Catholic News Agency, "What Pope Francis Learned from Homeless Girl: 'Cry with the Suffering!'" (January 17, 2015).

[29] Lawrence B. Finer and Rubina Hussain, "Unintended Pregnancy and Unsafe Abortion in the Philippines: Context and Consequences," *Guttmacher Institute* (August 2013).

[30] Stephen Vincent, "Filipino Church Vows Continued Opposition to 'Reproductive Health' Bill," *National Catholic Register* (December 20, 2012).

to be like rabbits—but no."[31] Though we commend the pope for advocating responsible parenthood, we respectfully disagree with his position that natural family planning is the *only* moral method for realizing responsible parenthood.

There seems to be a surprising unawareness on the part of the pope and bishops worldwide of how patriarchal cultures, gender norms, familial relations, socioeconomic factors, and political factors affect reproductive decisions in marriages. This unawareness is a reflection of the fundamental methodological distinction between Catholic social teaching and Catholic sexual teaching. The former prioritizes subject orientation by offering moral principles and criteria for careful discernment and personal judgment of an informed conscience; the latter prioritizes object orientation by offering absolute moral proscriptive norms for submissive obedience. An integrated methodological approach that prioritizes moral subject orientation would offer a general, formal principle—responsible parenthood, for example—and allow a married couple to discern and judge in conscience a particular, material norm to realize this principle in the contextual, relational, social, and gender circumstances. We agree fully with Pope Francis's earlier statement on the prioritization of first meeting basic needs, social issues relating to the fifth commandment, before we talk about "the sabbath," in this case sexual issues relating to the sixth commandment. *Amoris Laetitia* makes some progress in integrating the two methodological perspectives of Catholic social teaching and Catholic sexual teaching, especially in its reflection on economic-driven cohabitation, but more integration is needed.

This integration of the methodologies and anthropologies of Catholic social teaching and Catholic sexual teaching has profound implications for how we consider our ongoing understanding of ethical truth and how we formulate and justify norms to guide an informed conscience. First, it is the role, function, and inviolable authority of personal conscience to determine whether or not a norm has anything to say about a particular life situation. Highlighting irregular situations, Pope Francis seems to indicate that not only is the situation irregular but the norm guiding the situation is also irregular, and conscience must discern which norm to select and how to interpret and apply it in a given situation. In the case of the divorced and remarried without an annulment, for example, it is not the case that a couple may be permitted to take communion as an exception to the general norm; it is that the norm itself does not apply universally to all the different situations of divorced couples. Second, as irregular situations gradually become regular, as is now the case with cohabiting couples

---

[31] Sonia Narang, "Catholic Leaders Battle against Free Birth Control in the Philippines," *Public Radio International* (January 22, 2015).

already committed to marry each other, those we have called nuptial cohabitors, and couples practicing artificial contraception in their marital relationship, there may need to be an "organic development of doctrine,"[32] perhaps similar to the development of the doctrines on slavery, usury, and religious freedom, that fundamentally changes the doctrine. Even though at this point *Amoris Laetitia* changes no specific Catholic doctrines,[33] its anthropological and methodological developments lay the foundation for an organic development of doctrine that can effect doctrinal change, in much the same way as Pope John XXIII's encyclical *Pacem in Terris* laid a sure foundation for the Second Vatican Council's *Dignitatis Humanae* and its entirely reformulated doctrine on religious freedom.

Ethical Implications for the Future of Catholic Theological Ethics

On the basis of *Amoris Laetitia*'s anthropological focus on conscience, discernment, and a virtue-based subjective approach to decision making, we can anticipate some normative development on ethical, including sexual, issues. We can anticipate also, perhaps, a revision of some absolute proscriptive sexual norms that many of the faithful, through discerning consciences, have already subjectively revised and are at peace with their revision. These developments will be supported by Francis's methodological focus on inductive reason, historical consciousness, appreciation of culture, integration of the sciences, explicit concern for the effect of socioeconomic conditions on relationships, critical use of scripture, a communion ecclesiology, and the introduction of new pastoral methods that acknowledge the reality and legitimacy of subject-oriented ethical truth.

There remains much theological-ethical work to be done to draw out the full anthropological, methodological, and normative implications of *Amoris Laetitia* for Catholic sexual ethics, but it is clear that it will stimulate, indeed has already stimulated, debate around the ethical issues involved in irregular sexual situations that appeared magisterially settled with the publication of Pope John Paul II's *Veritatis Splendor* in 1993. The items we have focused on in the grand plan of *Amoris Laetitia* will, we believe, be in the forefront of that theological debate and reflection: first, the reinstatement of the authority and inviolability of an informed conscience in making decisions leading to action judged to be ethical

---

[32] See Gerard O'Connell, "'*Amoris Laetitia*' Represents an Organic Development of Doctrine, 'Not a Rupture,'" *America* (April 8, 2016).

[33] See Michael G. Lawler and Todd A. Salzman, "*Amoris Laetitia*: Has Anything Changed?," *Asian Horizons* 11 (2017): 62–74.

and virtuous and guided by new pastoral methods; second, the law of gradualness, of progressively growing into Christian and marital life, which it takes for granted; third, the emphasis on the virtues of love, compassion, mercy, justice, and the prudential nonjudgment of other people and their situations; and fourth, Francis's articulated vision of the church as essentially synodal.

The *Catechism of the Catholic Church* teaches that "the Church's social teaching proposes principles for reflection; it provides criteria for judgment; it gives guidelines for action" (*CCC*, no. 2423). This trinity—principles for reflection, criteria for judgment, and guidelines for action—was implicit in Paul VI's 1967 encyclical *Populorum Progressio*, was introduced into Catholic social teaching in his 1971 *Octogesima Adveniens,* and was repeated in both the Congregation for the Doctrine of the Faith's *Instruction on Christian Freedom and Liberation* in 1986 and in John Paul II's *Sollicitudo Rei Socialis* in 1987. It is now an established part of Catholic socio-ethical teaching that increasingly underscores individual responsibility, which John Paul II accentuates when he teaches that the church seeks "to *guide* people to *respond*, with the support of rational reflection and of the human sciences, to their vocation as *responsible* builders of earthly society" (*SRS,* nos. 1, 41, emphasis added). In social ethics the church guides; responsible persons, drawing on the church's guidance, their own practical judgment of conscience that prioritizes the subject orientation over the object orientation, and the findings of the human sciences, respond responsibly. Unfortunately, this model of relationship-responsibility still appears to apply for the magisterium only in social ethics and, to a certain extent, in biomedical ethics.

In sexual ethics the place where one would expect to be "more than any other the place where all is referred to the informed conscience,"[34] a model antithetical to personal freedom and responsibility still applies. In sexual ethics, the hierarchical magisterium provides no principles and guidelines for reflection, judgment, and action, only absolute norms to be obeyed. Since both social and sexual ethics are exercised by the same persons, it appears to us illogical that there should be this double methodological standard. It also appears to us, however, that Pope Francis's *Amoris Laetitia* lights a pathway for the transformation of this double standard to a single standard in both Catholic social teaching and Catholic sexual teaching. We have no doubt that in *Amoris Laetitia* Pope Francis has pointed the way, not to any abrogation of Catholic ethical doctrine, but to its organic development, a renewed gospel, and therefore Catholic,

---

[34] Jean-Yves Calvez, "Ethicale sociale et ethicale sexuelle," *Etudes* 378 (1993): 648.

way to approach it. As new ethical issues arise, such as issues related to technology and biotechnology, or existing issues evolve and develop, such as the complexity of ethical issues that climate change poses, we can, from a virtuous perspective, draw from and expand the anthropological and methodological contributions Pope Francis has made in *Amoris Laetitia* to address these issues. Francis appears to be aware of and submissive to *Dignitatis Humanae*'s teaching that "truth cannot impose itself except by virtue of its own truth, as it makes its entrance into the mind at once quietly and with power" (*DH,* no. 1). If ethical truth resides anywhere, it resides in the discerning conscience of the moral knower.

We conclude with one final comment. In this book we have proposed an ethical method and anthropology guided by a virtuous perspective and, we believe, by the best of the Catholic theological ethical tradition. We also realize that people will agree or disagree, in whole or in part, with our proposal. For both those who agree and those who disagree, we propose a traditional theological principle (expressed by John XXIII in 1959 in *Ad Petri Cathedram*), guided by the virtue of charity, for the ongoing communal search for and discernment of ethical truth: "In essentials, unity; in doubtful matters, liberty; in all things, charity" (no. 72).

Questions for Reflection

- Discuss methodological differences between Catholic sexual teaching and Catholic social teaching. What are the ethical implications for Catholic sexual teaching if one integrates Catholic social and sexual ethical methods?
- Discuss anthropological differences between Catholic sexual teaching and Catholic social teaching. What are the ethical implications for Catholic sexual teaching if one integrates Catholic social and sexual anthropologies?
- Discuss how *Amoris Laetitia* integrates Catholic social and sexual teaching. What are the implications of this integration for sexual ethical issues such as same-sex relationships, transgender ethical issues, and cohabitation?
- Discuss the ethical implications of the methodological and anthropological developments in *Amoris Laetitia* for Catholic theological ethics on issues related to ecology, technology, biomedical ethics, and sexual ethics. How do these developments provide ethical tools to address new ethical issues?

Suggested Readings

Curran, Charles E. *Catholic Social Teaching: A Historical, Theological, and Ethical Analysis.* Washington, DC: Georgetown University Press, 2002.

Lawler, Michael G., and Todd A. Salzman. "*Amoris Laetitia*: Has Anything Changed?" *Asian Horizons* 11 (2017): 62–74.

Rausch, Thomas, and Roberto Dell'Oro. *Amoris Laetitia.* New York: Paulist Press: 2018.

Salzman, Todd A., and Michael G. Lawler, "*Amoris Laetitia*: Towards a Methodological and Anthropological Integration of Catholic Social and Sexual Ethics," *Theological Studies* 79, no. 3 (2018): 634–52.

Index

Index